AMERICA'S DIVERSE POPULATION

A COMPARISON OF RACE, ETHNICITY, AND SOCIAL CLASS IN GRAPHIC DETAIL

MICHAEL D. DULBERGER

Published in the United States of America
by Bernan Press, a wholly owned subsidiary of
The Rowman & Littlefield Publishing Group, Inc.
4501 Forbes Boulevard, Suite 200
Lanham, Maryland 20706

Bernan Press
800-865-3457
www.rowman.com

ISBN-13: 978-1-59888-914-7
eISBN-13: 978-1-59888-915-4

Contents

Hispanic or Latino Origin

White

Black or African American

Asian

American Indian and Alaska Native

Native Hawaiian and Pacific Islander

Native Hawaiian and Pacific Islander (continued)

Two or more races

Some Other Race

Chapter 2: Immigration

Chapter 2: Immigration (continued)

Chapter 3: Life and Death

Chapter 4: Health

Chapter 5: Society

Chapter 5: Society (continued)

Households

Chapter 6: Crime

Crime Victims and Offenders by Race and Ethnicity

Chapter 7: Correctional System

Chapter 8: Employment

Employment by Race and Ethnicity

Chapter 9: Income, Poverty, and Wealth

Income

Earnings by Education

Earnings by Occupation

Mean Money Income

Wealth and Debt

Chapter 10: Education

Chapter 10: Education (continued)

College Education

Educational Test Scores

Index

~

Introduction

Most adults living in the United States over the past several decades leading up to 2017 have become aware of the rapid demographic shifts occurring in some regions of the country. For many, these shifts were not experienced by first-hand observations, rather through media reports and political dialogue. The growth of the once burgeoning non-Hispanic White population in the United States has slowed to 130,000 per year, while minority racial and ethnic groups, collectively, are increasing by almost two million each year. Grade school enrollment is a reliable predictor of the future adult population and in 2013 enrollment in grades K–8 for non-Hispanic White children fell below 50 percent, nationally, for the first time.

Diversity, as used in this book, refers to the collective union of persons of different races, ethnicities, genders, and religions that comprise the population of the United States. The measurement of expanding diversity has two major components: changes to aggregate numbers and geographic dispersion. National statistics are indicative of averages, however the most dramatic demographic shifts are occurring locally. Minority groups tend to be concentrated geographically and there remain many regions in the country where the non-Hispanic White population continues to be a very dominant majority. In 2015, over one-third of all counties consisted of 90 to 98 percent non-Hispanic White residents, quite isolated from the changes occurring in other regions of the country.

If you ever try to research what is meant by a person's race you will soon realize that this question has been debated by the experts and anthropologists for centuries—with some even disputing the existence of any anatomical differences among the members of the homo sapiens species. Merriam-Webster defines race as "a family, tribe, people, or nation belonging to the same stock and a class or kind of people unified by shared interests, habits, or characteristics". Equally ambiguous is the term ethnicity, defined by Merriam-Webster as "relating to large groups of people classed according to common racial, national, tribal, religious, linguistic, or cultural origin or background". Notice how the definition of ethnicity includes race! To understand the difference between a person's race and ethnicity is purely a function of which organization or agency is asking the question and for what purpose.

The U.S. Census Bureau included questions on race during the first census in 1790, and continues to do so, arguing that race is key to implementing any number of federal programs and is critical for the basic research behind numerous policy decisions. Also, the states require race data to meet legislative redistricting requirements and are needed to monitor compliance with the Voting Rights Act by local jurisdictions. Federal programs rely on race data to assess racial disparities in housing, income, education, employment, health, and environmental risks.

In order to be more precise and inclusive of more races and ethnicities on the census forms the categories for self-identification of race and ethnicity have been greatly expanded and continue to evolve at each decennial census. The alleged role played by the U.S. Census Bureau in identifying Japanese-Americans for internment during World War II may have created an enduring distrust by some minorities with the consequence that minorities may actually be under-reported since most data are based on self-reporting of race and ethnicity.

This fear may have been rekindled by bold statements made during the 2016 campaign by President Donald Trump when he was a candidate, questioning the patriotism of some foreign-born and ethnic minority groups, and promising to deport undocumented aliens. Other unsubstantiated statements during the campaign claimed levels of crime, unemployment, and poverty among some minority groups that were exaggerations or distortions of statistically correct interpretations of data. These concerns may lead to less-than-truthful responses to the census questionnaire however despite these short-comings the official census data are the only source of comprehensive demographic data of the American population.

This book has been created to bypass the news media filters and hyperbole of the political machinery, and to provide information seekers with direct unvarnished data on diversity in the United States in 2017. U.S. government agencies provided the resources for the majority of data presented in the charts of this book, and each chart includes its data sources and corresponding website addresses to enable the reader to delve into the subject matter in greater depth.

The graphic format of this book delivers maximum information to the reader with minimum effort. While many charts raise questions about cause and effect it is incumbent on intelligent people to recognize that complex subjects are inter-related with many issues, and generally quick-sound-bite explanations are often misleading or patently wrong!

~

Chapter 1: Demographics

The U.S. Constitution requires that the federal government conduct a census of the population every ten years to enable apportionment of congressional representatives. The U.S. Census Bureau has become the official source for data defining the size, race, ethnicity, and geographic distribution of the U.S. population.

Populations change in three ways: people may be born (births), they may die (deaths), or they may move (domestic and international migration). The U.S. Census Bureau's Population Estimates program measures this change and adds it to the last decennial census to produce updated population estimates every year.

Each year, the United States Census Bureau produces and publishes estimates of the population for the nation, states, counties, state/county equivalents, and Puerto Rico. They estimate the resident population for each year between formal census counts, by using measures of population change. The resident population includes all people currently residing in the United States.

The estimates are derived from the demographic balancing equation:

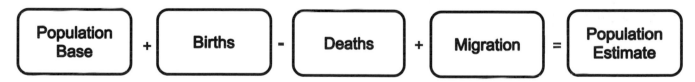

The population estimate at any given time point starts with a population base, as with the 2010 decennial census, adds births, subtracts deaths, and adds net migration (both international and domestic).

Starting with the 1960 census people could choose their own race whereas census-takers commonly determined the race of the people they counted before 1960. Prior to 2000 people could only select a single racial category however starting in 2000 they could include themselves in more than one. The 2010 census changed the questionnaire again allowing for responses that included one or more of the race groups defined by the Office of Management and Budget in 1997: White, Black or African American, American Indian and Alaska Native, Asian, and Native Hawaiian and Other Pacific Islander. The 2010 census also allowed responses that included "Some Other Race."

The questions regarding race and ethnicity one answers on the census questionnaire has been a source of some confusion, especially Hispanic origin, which is an ethnicity and not a race. Persons of Hispanic origin can be of any race and almost nine-of-ten Hispanic people identify their race as White. In the 2010 census, many reports published by the Census Bureau provided two data sets, with and without Hispanic origin listed separately. Other reports show Hispanic and non-Hispanic White as separate categories while the ethnicities and other races are left unspecified. To reduce confusion in the future, the Census Bureau is considering completely revamping the race and ethnicity categories for the 2020 census.

Another characteristic recorded by the Census Bureau is country of birth, i.e. nativity. The 1850 decennial census was the first census in which data were collected on the nativity of the population. Between 1850 and 1950, the highest percentage foreign born was 14.8 percent, in 1890. By 1950, the foreign-born population of the United States had declined to 6.9 percent of the total population, reflecting the extremely low level of immigration during the 1930s and 1940s. The foreign-born population then dropped slowly to a record low of 4.7 percent in 1970. Since then, the foreign-born population of the United States has increased rapidly due to large-scale immigration, primarily from Latin America and Asia, and by 2015 had reached 13.5 percent—more than one-in-eight persons.

Despite inaccuracies inherent in the detailed computation of race and ethnicity there is little doubt that significant changes have occurred, and continue to occur, to the composition of the residents of the United States. This is most apparent by comparing the population in 1920, when 89.7 percent were White compared with 2015, with 61.6 percent non-Hispanic White. Based on current trends the Census Bureau projects that in 2043 the percentage of non-Hispanic White persons will fall below 50 percent, and there will no longer be any majority group in the United States. In 2015, there were already four states where non-Hispanic White persons were less than the majority, as were 370 counties out of 3,142 total (11.8 percent).

The demographic shift is occurring due to the combined effect of two significant trends. First, the non-Hispanic White population has become the oldest group, and their birth rates are at historic low levels, declining faster than other race or ethnic groups. In the period 2010–2015, non-Hispanic White deaths exceeded births by approximately 200,000 and the only growth in this population group was due to immigration. During this same period, births exceeded deaths for all other groups by a combined 8.4 million persons.

Second, the immigrant population has shifted from primarily non-Hispanic White Europeans to Latin Americans and Asians, as evidenced by only sixteen percent of the 5.5 million immigrants between 2010–2015 being non-Hispanic White.

As of the 2010 census, the U.S. Census Bureau defined races and ethnicities as follows:

- Native Hawaiian or Other Pacific Islander is a person having origins in any of the original peoples of Hawaii, Guam, Samoa, or other Pacific Islands.

- American Indian or Alaska Native is a person having origins in any of the original peoples of North and South America (including Central America) who maintains cultural identification through tribal affiliation or community attachment.

- Asian is a person having origins in any of the original peoples of the Far East, Southeast Asia, or the Indian Subcontinent, including, for example, Cambodia, China, India, Japan, Korea, Malaysia, Pakistan, the Philippine Islands, Thailand, and Vietnam.

- Black or African American is a person having origins in any of the Black racial groups of Africa.

- White is a person having origins in any of the original peoples of Europe, the Middle East, or North Africa.

- Hispanic or Latino is a person of Cuban, Mexican, Puerto Rican, South or Central American, or other Spanish culture or origin, regardless of race.

~

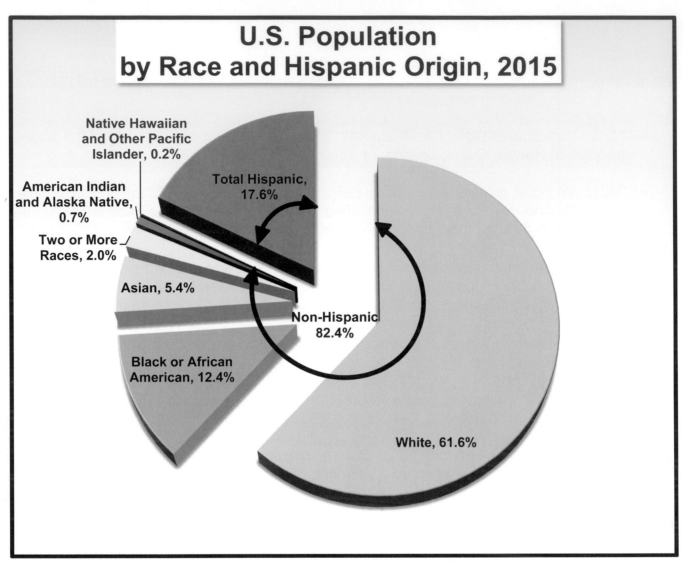

U.S. Population by Race and Hispanic Origin, 2015

Native Hawaiian and Other Pacific Islander, 0.2%

American Indian and Alaska Native, 0.7%

Two or More Races, 2.0%

Asian, 5.4%

Black or African American, 12.4%

Total Hispanic, 17.6%

Non-Hispanic 82.4%

White, 61.6%

In 2015, three-of-five residents in the United States were non-Hispanic White persons.

The graph shows the percent of total population who are Hispanic compared with percent of persons who are non-Hispanic in race categories.

Hispanic origin is considered an ethnicity, not a race. Hispanics may be of any race.

Source: U.S. Census Bureau, Population Division, Annual Estimates of the Resident Population by Sex, Race, and Hispanic Origin for the United States, States, and Counties: April 1, 2010 to July 1, 2015, Release Date: June 2016, http://www.census.gov/popest/data/counties/asrh/2015/CC-EST2015-ALLDATA.html

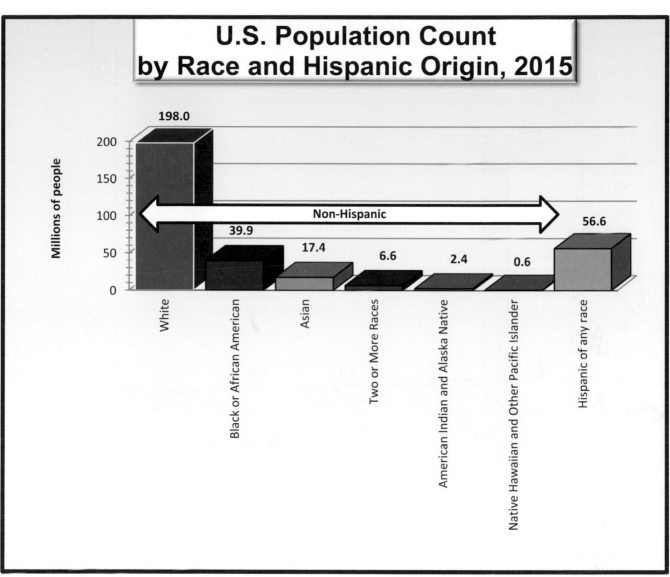

In 2015, nearly 200 million non-Hispanic White persons resided in the United States.

The total U.S. population increased from 321.4 million persons as of July 1, 2015, to 323.1 million as of July 1, 2016—a one year increase of 1.7 million persons.

Hispanic or Latino is a person of Cuban, Mexican, Puerto Rican, South or Central American, or other Spanish culture or origin, regardless of race.

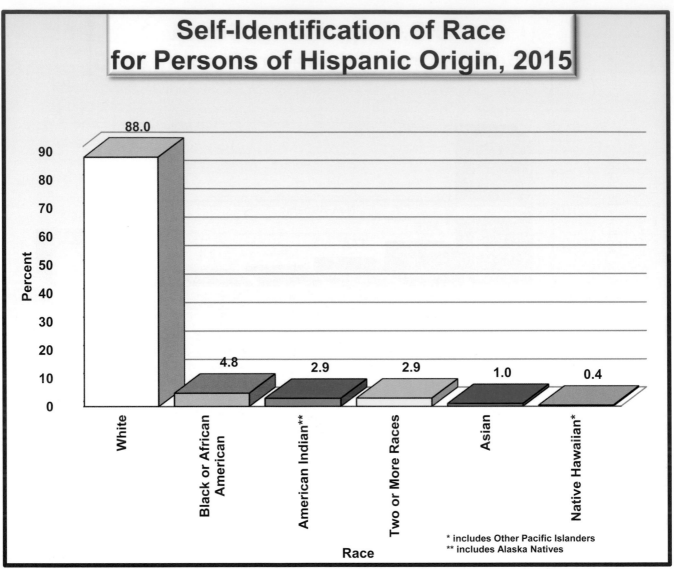

Self-Identification of Race for Persons of Hispanic Origin, 2015

* includes Other Pacific Islanders
** includes Alaska Natives

Race

In 2015, approximately nine-of-ten persons of Hispanic or Latino origin self-identified as being of the "White" race.

Hispanic origin is considered an ethnicity, not a race. Hispanics may be of any race.

Source: U.S. Census Bureau, Population Division, Annual Estimates of the Resident Population by Sex, Race, and Hispanic Origin for the United States, States, and Counties: April 1, 2010 to July 1, 2015, Release Date: June 2016, http://factfinder.census.gov/faces/tableservices/jsf/pages/productview.xhtml?src=bkmk

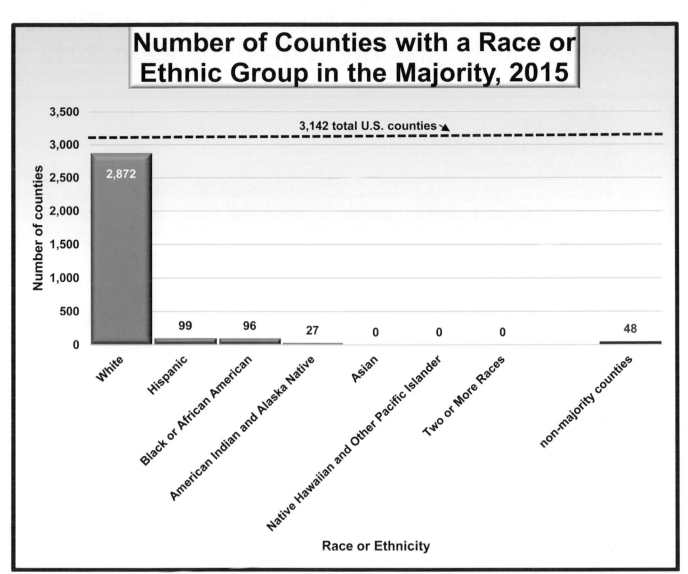

Number of Counties with a Race or Ethnic Group in the Majority, 2015

3,142 total U.S. counties

Number of counties

- White: 2,872
- Hispanic: 99
- Black or African American: 96
- American Indian and Alaska Native: 27
- Asian: 0
- Native Hawaiian and Other Pacific Islander: 0
- Two or More Races: 0
- non-majority counties: 48

Race or Ethnicity

In 2015, there were 48 counties where the population did not have any race or ethnic group in the majority (50 percent or more of the county's population). Only White, Black or African American, American Indian and Alaska Native, and Hispanic groups are in the majority in one or more of the 3,142 counties. Asian, Native Hawaiian and Other Pacific Islanders are not a majority in any county.

Source: U.S. Census Bureau, 2015 American Community Survey 1-Year Estimates,
http://www.census.gov/popest/data/counties/asrh/2015/CC-EST2015-ALLDATA.html

Distribution of Counties Where No Race or Ethnic Group is in the Majority of the Population, 2015

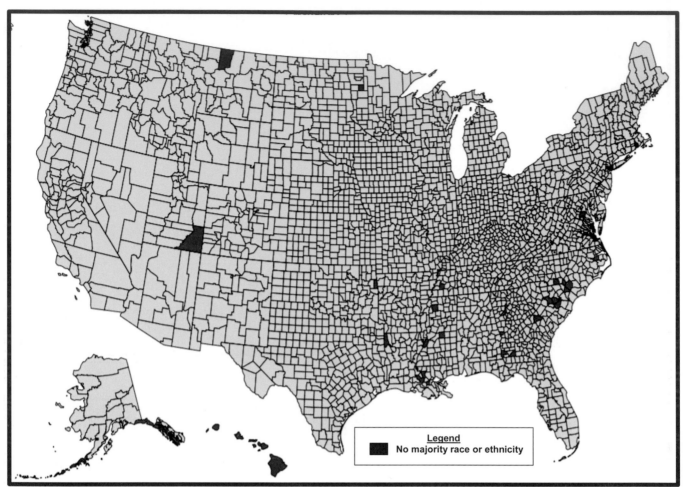

Legend
No majority race or ethnicity

In 2015, 48 out of 3,142 counties, distributed in 18 different states, had no race or ethnic group in the majority of population.

Of the 3,142 counties that comprise the United States only 48 did not have a majority race or ethnic group in 2015. There were 2,872 counties with White persons in the majority, 99 Hispanic, 96 Black or African American and 27 American Indian or Alaska Native.

Source: U.S. Census Bureau, 2015 American Community Survey, http://www.census.gov/popest/data/counties/asrh/2015/CC-EST2015-ALLDATA.html

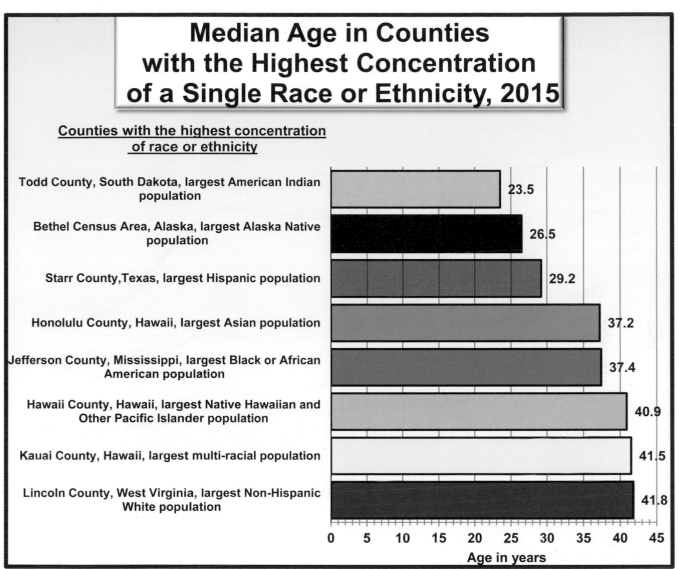

Median Age in Counties with the Highest Concentration of a Single Race or Ethnicity, 2015

Counties with the highest concentration of race or ethnicity

County	Age in years
Todd County, South Dakota, largest American Indian population	23.5
Bethel Census Area, Alaska, largest Alaska Native population	26.5
Starr County, Texas, largest Hispanic population	29.2
Honolulu County, Hawaii, largest Asian population	37.2
Jefferson County, Mississippi, largest Black or African American population	37.4
Hawaii County, Hawaii, largest Native Hawaiian and Other Pacific Islander population	40.9
Kauai County, Hawaii, largest multi-racial population	41.5
Lincoln County, West Virginia, largest Non-Hispanic White population	41.8

Age in years

The median age of residents in Todd County, South Dakota—where one-of-four residents identify as American Indian—was 23.5 years old in 2015, compared with 41.8 years old in Lincoln County, West Virginia—the county with highest percent of non-Hispanic White persons.

A county is a political and geographic subdivision of a state. The Census Bureau considers the parishes of Louisiana and the boroughs of Alaska and the District of Columbia to be equivalent to counties for statistical purposes.

Hispanic origin is considered an ethnicity, not a race. Hispanics may be of any race.

Source: U.S. Census Bureau, American Fact Finder, Community Facts, 2015 Population Estimates Program, accessed 10/17/16, http://factfinder.census.gov/faces/nav/jsf/pages/community_facts.xhtml#

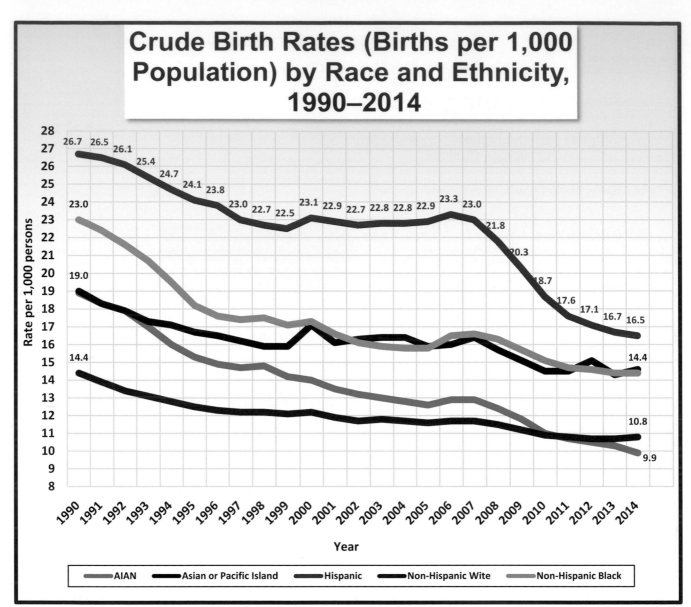

Crude Birth Rates (Births per 1,000 Population) by Race and Ethnicity, 1990–2014

Between 1990 and 2014 the crude birth rate for all races and ethnicities decreased. American Indian and Alaska Natives experienced the greatest decline at 48 percent.

The average annual number of births during a year per 1,000 population at midyear is called the crude birth rate.

American Indian and Alaska Native (AIAN). Data are based on birth certificates. Race and ethnicity are based on the mother.

Source: CDC/NCHS, National Vital Statistics System, public-use Birth File. Hamilton BE, Martin JA, Osterman MJK, et al. Births: Final data for 2014. National vital statistics reports; volume 64 no 12. Hyattsville, MD: NCHS. 2015;
Available from: http://www.cdc.gov/nchs/data/nvsr/nvsr64/nvsr64_12.pdf, http://www.cdc.gov/nchs/hus/contents2015.htm#059

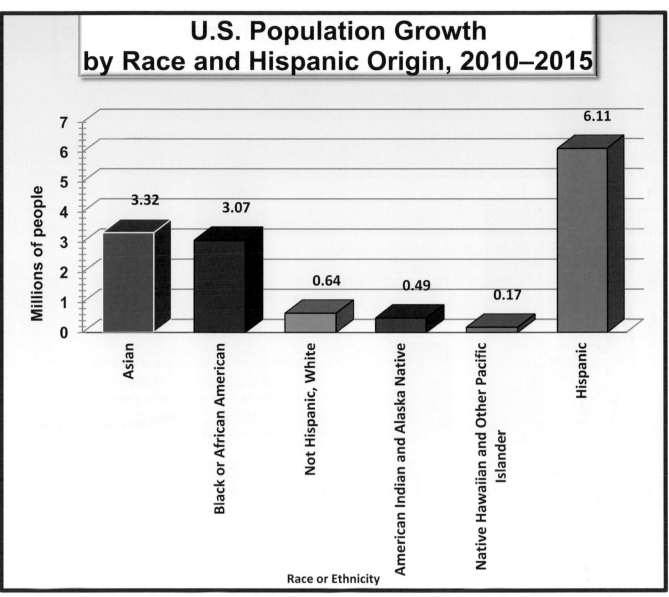

U.S. Population Growth by Race and Hispanic Origin, 2010–2015

In the period 2010–2015, the Hispanic population grew by over six million, the Asian, Black and African American populations both rose by over three million while the non-Hispanic White population increased by approximately two-thirds million.

Population growth is measured as the net increase due to natural growth (births minus deaths) plus net immigration. Between 2010–2015, the population grew by more than 12.6 million persons, but non-Hispanic Whites accounted for only 5 percent.

Hispanic or Latino is a person of Cuban, Mexican, Puerto Rican, South or Central American, or other Spanish culture or origin, regardless of race.

Source: U.S. Census Bureau, Population Division, Annual Estimates of the Resident Population by Sex, Race, and Hispanic Origin for the United States, States, and Counties: April 1, 2010 to July 1, 2015, Release Date: June 2016
http://factfinder.census.gov/faces/tableservices/jsf/pages/productview.xhtml?pid=PEP_2015_PEPCCOMPN&prodType=table

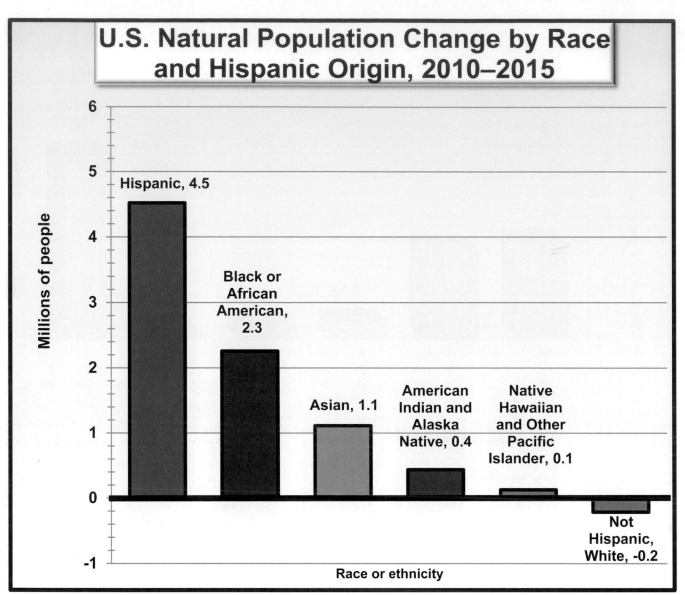

U.S. Natural Population Change by Race and Hispanic Origin, 2010–2015

Millions of people

Hispanic, 4.5

Black or African American, 2.3

Asian, 1.1

American Indian and Alaska Native, 0.4

Native Hawaiian and Other Pacific Islander, 0.1

Not Hispanic, White, -0.2

Race or ethnicity

Between 2010–2015, 55 percent of the natural population increase in the United States were persons of Hispanic origin.

Hispanic or Latino is a person of Cuban, Mexican, Puerto Rican, South or Central American, or other Spanish culture or origin, regardless of race. Natural population change is the net sum of births minus deaths.

Source: U.S. Census Bureau, Population Division, Annual Estimates of the Resident Population by Sex, Race, and Hispanic Origin for the United States, States, and Counties: April 1, 2010 to July 1, 2015, Release Date: June 2016
http://factfinder.census.gov/faces/tableservices/jsf/pages/productview.xhtml?pid=PEP_2015_PEPCCOMPN&prodType=table

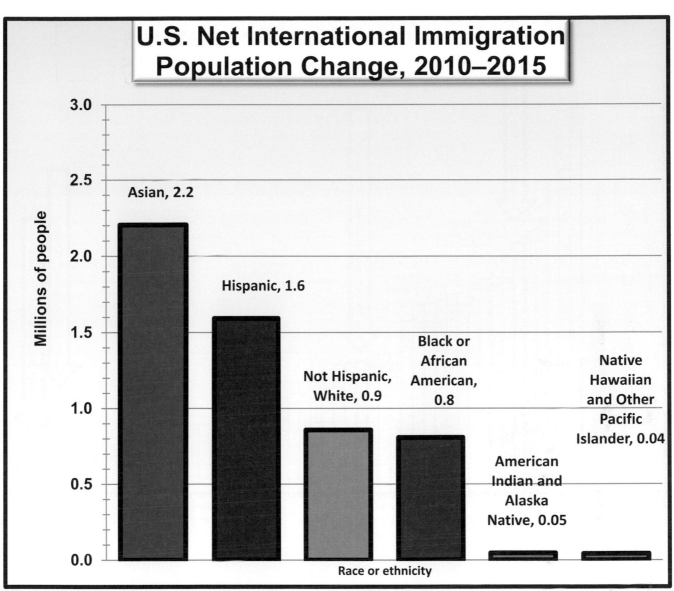

U.S. Net International Immigration Population Change, 2010–2015

Between 2010–2015, approximately 40 percent of the net immigration increase in the United States were Asian persons—the highest of any group.

Between 2010–2015, the net immigration surplus into the United States was 5.5 million people. Net immigration is the quantity of persons entering minus leaving.

Net international migration for the United States includes the international migration of both native and foreign-born populations. Specifically, it includes: (a) the net international migration of the foreign born, (b) the net migration between the United States and Puerto Rico, (c) the net migration of natives to and from the United States, and (d) the net movement of the Armed Forces population between the United States and overseas. Net international migration for Puerto Rico includes the migration of native and foreign-born populations between the United States and Puerto Rico.

Source: U.S. Census Bureau, Population Division, Annual Estimates of the Resident Population by Sex, Race, and Hispanic Origin for the United States, States, and Counties: April 1, 2010 to July 1, 2015, Release Date: June 2016
http://factfinder.census.gov/faces/tableservices/jsf/pages/productview.xhtml?pid=PEP_2015_PEPCCOMPN&prodType=table

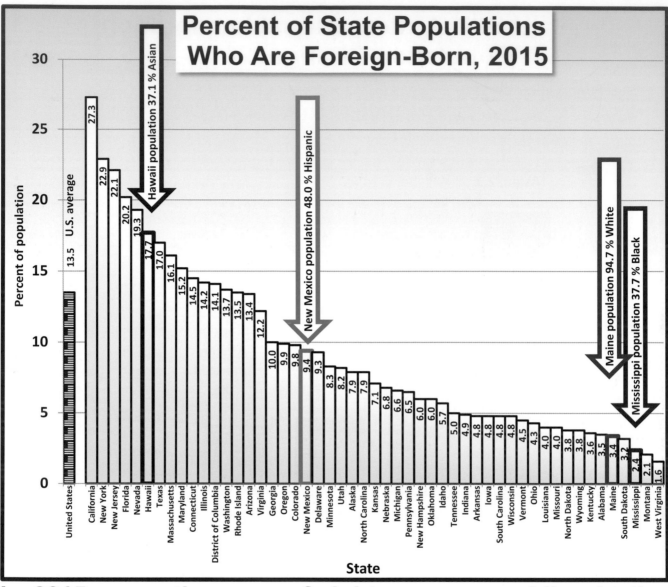

Percent of State Populations Who Are Foreign-Born, 2015

In 2015, more than one-of-eight persons residing in the United States was born elsewhere, as were more than one-in-four residents of California. States with the highest percent of Whites or Blacks had less than four percent of foreign-born individuals.

The U.S. Census Bureau uses the term foreign born to refer to anyone who is not a U.S. Citizen at birth. This includes naturalized citizens, lawful permanent residents, temporary migrants (such as foreign students), humanitarian migrants (such as refugees), and undocumented migrants. The term native born refers to anyone born in the United States, Puerto Rico, or a U.S. Island Area, or those born abroad of at least one U.S. citizen parent.

Source: U.S. Census Bureau, 2015 American Community Survey 1-Year Estimates Table 501, http://www.census.gov/programs-surveys/acs/data/summary-file.html

Distribution of States with the Highest Percent Foreign-Born Population, 2015

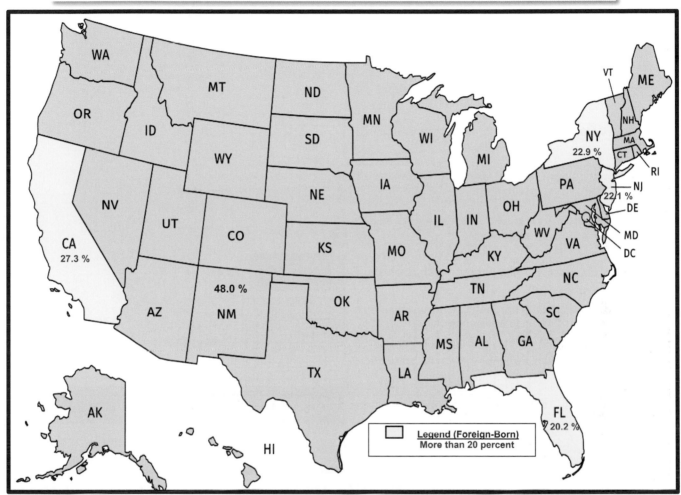

In 2015, more than one-in-four residents of California were born outside the United States as were one-of-five residents in New York, New Jersey, and Florida.

The U.S. Census Bureau uses the term foreign born to refer to anyone who is not a U.S. Citizen at birth. This includes naturalized citizens, lawful permanent residents, temporary migrants (such as foreign students), humanitarian migrants (such as refugees), and undocumented migrants. The term native born refers to anyone born in the United States, Puerto Rico, or a U.S. Island Area, or those born abroad of at least one U.S. citizen parent.

Although the American Community Survey (ACS) produces population, demographic, and housing unit estimates, it is the Census Bureau's Population Estimates Program that produces and disseminates the official estimates of the population for the nation, states, counties, cities, and towns and estimates of housing units for states and counties.

Source: U.S. Census Bureau, 2015 American Community Survey 1-Year Estimates Table 501, http://www.census.gov/programs-surveys/acs/data/summary-file.html

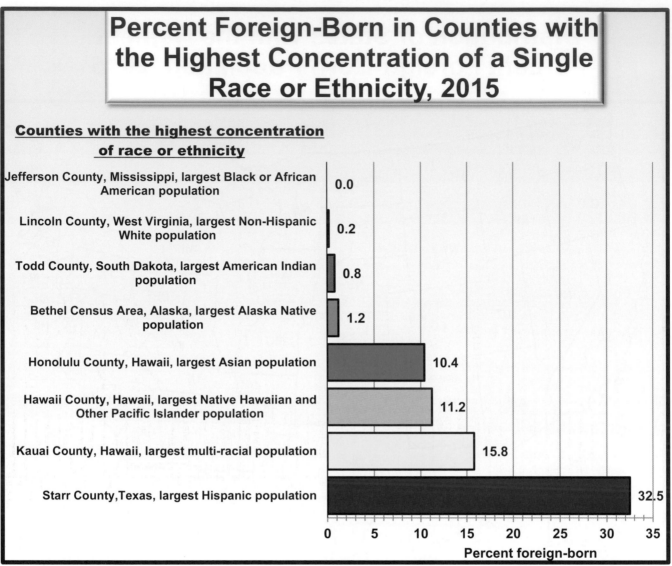

Percent Foreign-Born in Counties with the Highest Concentration of a Single Race or Ethnicity, 2015

Counties with the highest concentration of race or ethnicity

County	Percent foreign-born
Jefferson County, Mississippi, largest Black or African American population	0.0
Lincoln County, West Virginia, largest Non-Hispanic White population	0.2
Todd County, South Dakota, largest American Indian population	0.8
Bethel Census Area, Alaska, largest Alaska Native population	1.2
Honolulu County, Hawaii, largest Asian population	10.4
Hawaii County, Hawaii, largest Native Hawaiian and Other Pacific Islander population	11.2
Kauai County, Hawaii, largest multi-racial population	15.8
Starr County, Texas, largest Hispanic population	32.5

Percent foreign-born

In 2015, 32.5 percent of the population in Starr county, Texas was foreign-born. Starr county has the highest concentration (95.8 percent) of Hispanic or Latino residents in the United States.

The United States is comprised of 3,142 counties. A county is a political and geographic subdivision of a state. The Census Bureau considers the parishes of Louisiana and the boroughs of Alaska and the District of Columbia to be equivalent to counties for statistical purposes.

Hispanic origin is considered an ethnicity, not a race. Hispanics may be of any race.

Source: U.S. Census Bureau, American Fact Finder, Community Facts, 2015 Population Estimates Program, accessed 10/17/16, http://factfinder.census.gov/faces/nav/jsf/pages/community_facts.xhtml#

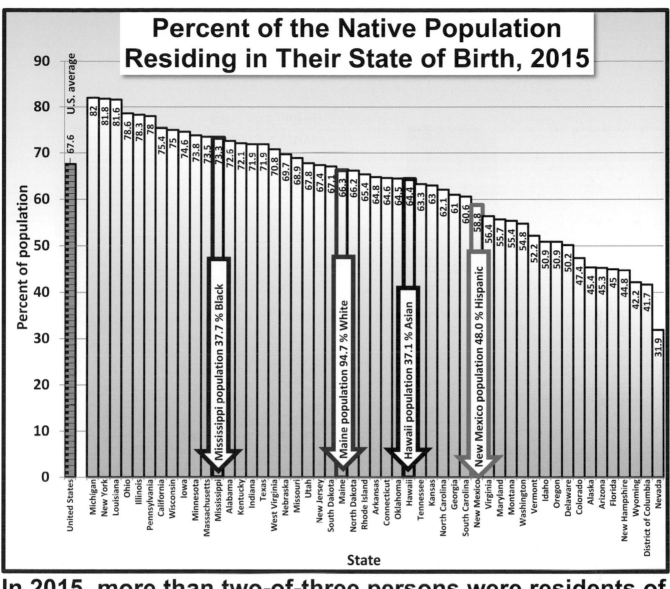

Percent of the Native Population Residing in Their State of Birth, 2015

In 2015, more than two-of-three persons were residents of their state of birth.

Although the American Community Survey (ACS) produces population, demographic, and housing unit estimates, it is the Census Bureau's Population Estimates Program that produces and disseminates the official estimates of the population for the nation, states, counties, cities, and towns as well as estimates of housing units for states and counties.

Source: U.S. Census Bureau, 2015 American Community Survey 1-Year Estimates Table RO601, http://www.census.gov/programs-surveys/acs/data/summary-file.html

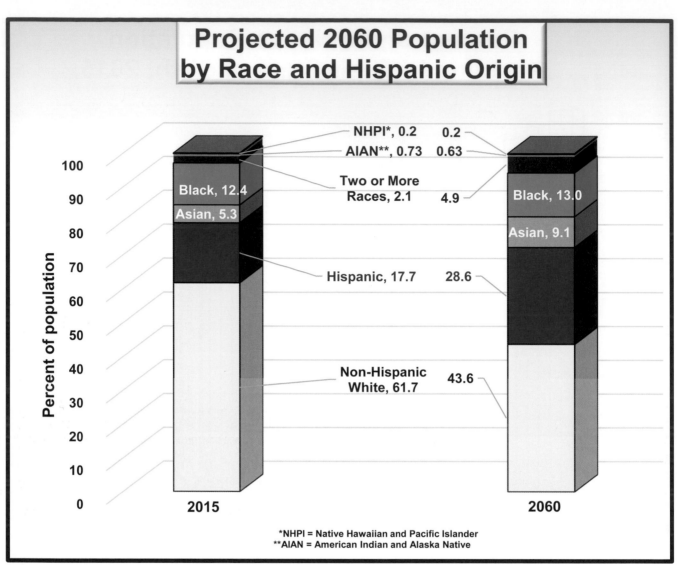

Projected 2060 Population by Race and Hispanic Origin

*NHPI = Native Hawaiian and Pacific Islander
**AIAN = American Indian and Alaska Native

The U.S. Census Bureau projects that by the year 2060 the sum of multi-racial, Asian, and Hispanic persons will equal the number of non-Hispanic White persons.

*NHPI = Native Hawaiian or Other Pacific Islander is a person having origins in any of the original peoples of Hawaii, Guam, Samoa, or other Pacific Islands;

**AIAN = American Indian or Alaska Native is a person having origins in any of the original peoples of North and South America (including Central America) who maintains cultural identification through tribal affiliation or community attachment.

Hispanic or Latino is a person of Cuban, Mexican, Puerto Rican, South or Central American, or other Spanish culture or origin, regardless of race.

Source: U.S. Census Bureau, Population Division, Table 13. Projections of the Population by Nativity, Hispanic Origin, and Race for the United States: 2015 to 2060 (NP2014-T13) http://www.census.gov/population/projections/data/national/2014/summarytables.html

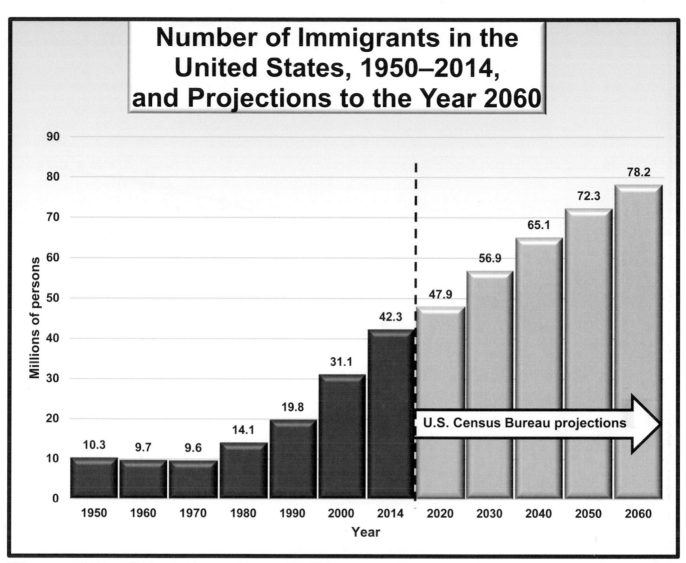

Number of Immigrants in the United States, 1950–2014, and Projections to the Year 2060

U.S. Census Bureau projections

Millions of persons / Year

1950: 10.3
1960: 9.7
1970: 9.6
1980: 14.1
1990: 19.8
2000: 31.1
2014: 42.3
2020: 47.9
2030: 56.9
2040: 65.1
2050: 72.3
2060: 78.2

The immigrant population grew an average of approximately three-quarters million persons per year, between 2000 and 2014, and the U.S. Census Bureau projects that rate to continue.

Source: Center for Immigration Studies ✤ analysis of U.S. Census Bureau data, accessed October 26 2016, http://cis.org/sites/cis.org/files/imm-pop-record-sept_2.pdf

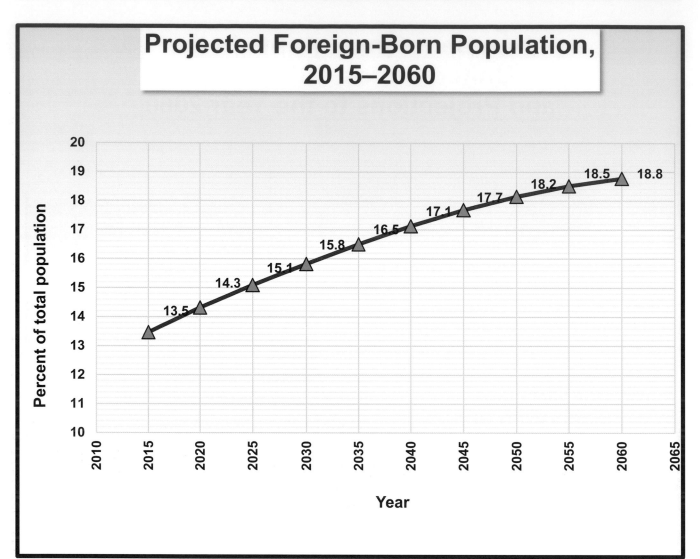

Projected Foreign-Born Population, 2015–2060

The U.S. Census Bureau projects that nearly one-of-five persons residing in the United States will be foreign-born by 2060.

Nativity is determined based on country of birth. Those born in the United States or in U.S. territories are considered native born while those born elsewhere are considered foreign born.

Source: U.S. Census Bureau, Population Division, Table 13. Projections of the Population by Nativity, Hispanic Origin, and Race for the United States: 2015 to 2060 (NP2014-T13), http://www.census.gov/population/projections/data/national/2014/summarytables.html

Chapter 1: Demographics

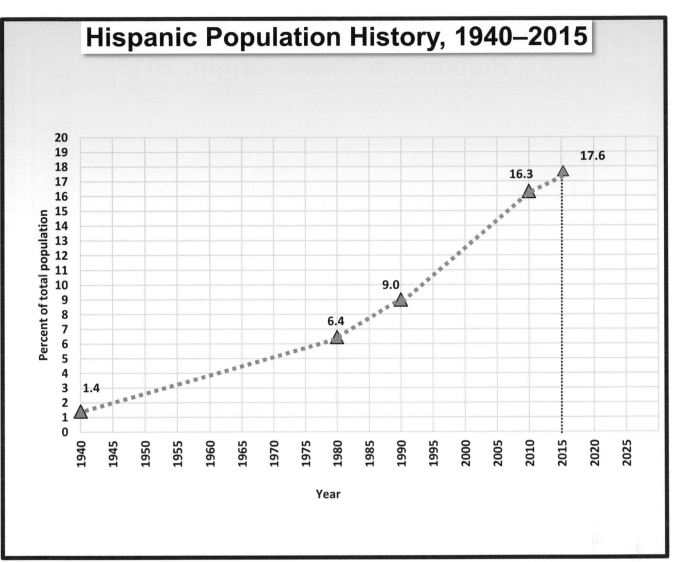

Hispanic Population History, 1940–2015

Percent of total population

Year

Data points: 1.4, 6.4, 9.0, 16.3, 17.6

Approximately one-of-six persons residing in the United States in 2015 was of Hispanic origin. This share has approximately doubled since 1990.

The U.S. Census Bureau began reporting Hispanic origin in the 1940 census, based on the White population of Spanish mother tongue. Hispanic origin is considered an ethnicity, not a race. Hispanic or Latino is a person of Cuban, Mexican, Puerto Rican, South or Central American, or other Spanish culture or origin, regardless of race.

Source: U.S. Census Bureau, https://www.census.gov/population/www/documentation/twps0076/twps0076.html, Table A-1. Race and Hispanic Origin for the United States, 2010-15 Data: https://www.census.gov/quickfacts/table/RHI125215/00

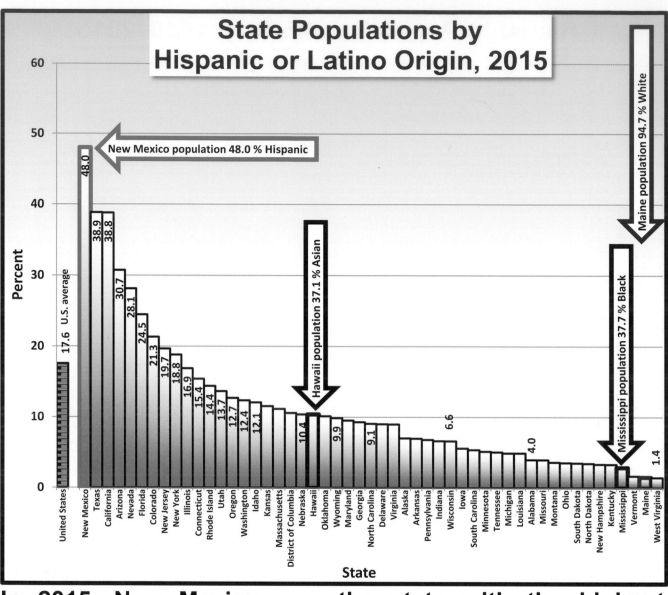

State Populations by Hispanic or Latino Origin, 2015

New Mexico population 48.0 % Hispanic

Hawaii population 37.1 % Asian

Mississippi population 37.7 % Black

Maine population 94.7 % White

In 2015, New Mexico was the state with the highest percentage of Hispanic or Latino persons at 48 percent, followed by Texas and California both with 39 percent.

Hispanic or Latino is not a race. Persons of Hispanic or Latino ethnicity can be of any race.

Source: U.S. Census Bureau, 2015 American Community Survey 1-Year Estimates, Table B03002, http://www.citylab.com/politics/2015/09/americas-leading-immigrant-cities/406438/

Distribution of States with the Highest Percent Hispanic or Latino Population, 2015

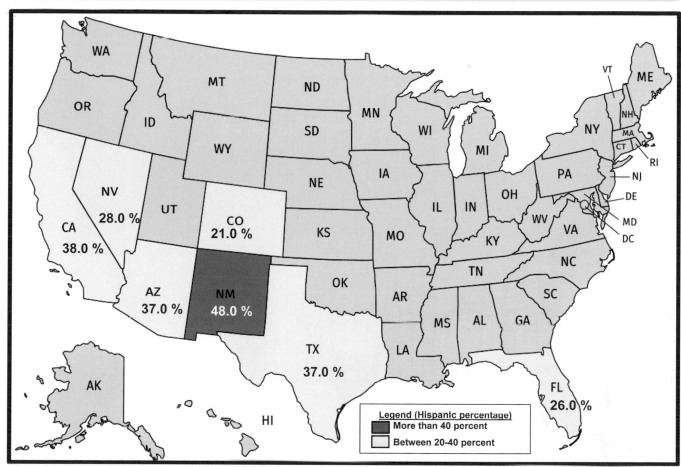

In 2015, nearly one-half of all residents in New Mexico were Hispanic or Latino persons.

Hispanic or Latino is not a race. Persons of Hispanic or Latino ethnicity can be of any race.

Source: U.S. Census Bureau, 2015 American Community Survey 1-Year Estimates, Table B03002, http://www.citylab.com/politics/2015/09/americas-leading-immigrant-cities/406438/

Distribution of Counties Where Persons of Hispanic Origin Are the Majority Population, 2015

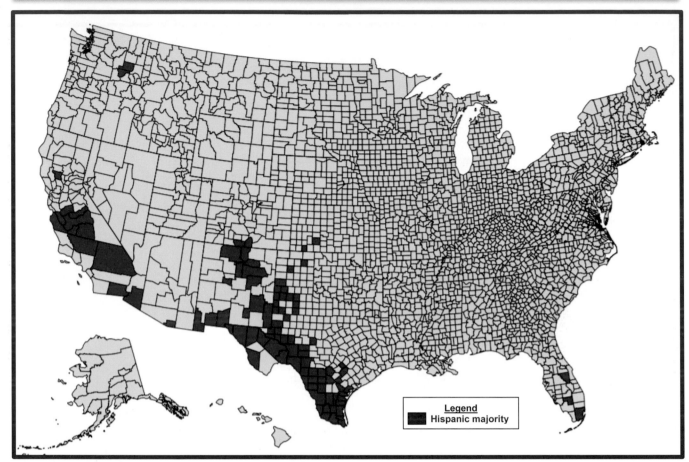

Legend
Hispanic majority

In 2015, 99 out of 3,142 counties had a population of Hispanic or Latino persons greater than 50 percent.

All counties with majority Hispanic or Latino populations were located in the southwestern region, except for one county in New York (Bronx County); three counties in Florida (Hendry County, Miami-Dade, Osceola County); and two counties in Washington (Adams County and Franklin County).

Source: U.S. Census Bureau, 2015 American Community Survey, http://www.census.gov/popest/data/counties/asrh/2015/CC-EST2015-ALLDATA.html

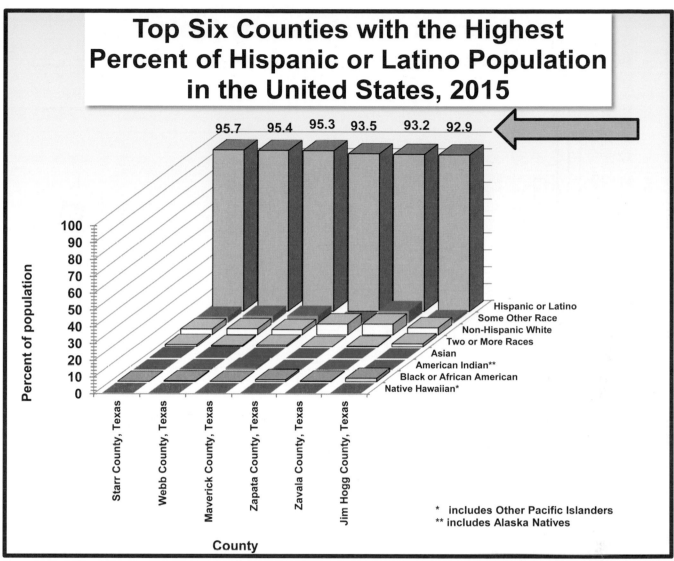

Top Six Counties with the Highest Percent of Hispanic or Latino Population in the United States, 2015

95.7 95.4 95.3 93.5 93.2 92.9

Percent of population

100
90
80
70
60
50
40
30
20
10
0

Hispanic or Latino
Some Other Race
Non-Hispanic White
Two or More Races
Asian
American Indian**
Black or African American
Native Hawaiian*

Starr County, Texas
Webb County, Texas
Maverick County, Texas
Zapata County, Texas
Zavala County, Texas
Jim Hogg County, Texas

County

*   includes Other Pacific Islanders
** includes Alaska Natives

In 2015, there were six counties in the United States with Hispanic or Latino populations that exceeded 90 percent, and all are located in Texas.

Hispanic or Latino are persons who identify with the terms "Hispanic," "Latino," or "Spanish" and who classify themselves in one of the specific Hispanic, Latino, or Spanish categories listed on the Census Bureau questionnaire as well as those who indicate that they are "another Hispanic, Latino, or Spanish origin." Up to two write-in responses to the "another Hispanic, Latino, or Spanish origin" category were coded. Origin can be viewed as the heritage, nationality group, lineage, or country of birth of the person or the person's parents or ancestors before their arrival in the United States or Island Area. People who identify their origin as Hispanic, Latino, or Spanish may be of any race.

Source: U.S. Census Bureau, American Fact Finder, Community Facts, 2015 Population Estimates Program, accessed 10/17/16, http://factfinder.census.gov/faces/nav/jsf/pages/community_facts.xhtml#

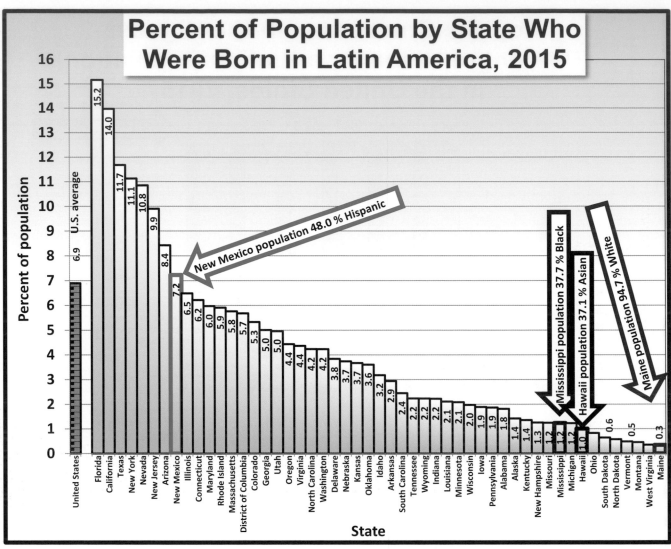

Percent of Population by State Who Were Born in Latin America, 2015

Percent of population vs *State*

- United States: 6.9 (U.S. average)
- Florida: 15.2
- California: 14.0
- Texas: 11.7
- New York: 11.1
- Nevada: 10.8
- New Jersey: 9.9
- Arizona: 8.4
- New Mexico: 7.2 (New Mexico population 48.0 % Hispanic)
- Illinois: 6.5
- Connecticut: 6.2
- Maryland: 6.0
- Rhode Island: 5.9
- Massachusetts: 5.8
- District of Columbia: 5.7
- Colorado: 5.3
- Georgia: 5.0
- Utah: 5.0
- Oregon: 4.4
- Virginia: 4.4
- North Carolina: 4.2
- Washington: 4.2
- Delaware: 3.8
- Nebraska: 3.7
- Kansas: 3.7
- Oklahoma: 3.6
- Idaho: 3.2
- Arkansas: 2.9
- South Carolina: 2.4
- Tennessee: 2.2
- Wyoming: 2.2
- Indiana: 2.2
- Louisiana: 2.1
- Minnesota: 2.1
- Wisconsin: 2.0
- Iowa: 1.9
- Pennsylvania: 1.9
- Alabama: 1.8
- Alaska: 1.4
- Kentucky: 1.4
- New Hampshire: 1.3
- Missouri: 1.2
- Mississippi: 1.2 (Mississippi population 37.7 % Black)
- Michigan: 1.2
- Hawaii: 1.0 (Hawaii population 37.1 % Asian)
- Ohio: 0.6
- South Dakota: 0.6
- North Dakota: 0.5
- Vermont: 0.5
- Montana: (Maine population 94.7 % White)
- West Virginia: 0.3
- Maine: 0.3

In 2015, more than one-of-seven people residing in Florida were born in Latin America—more than double the national average.

Although the American Community Survey (ACS) produces population, demographic, and housing unit estimates, it is the Census Bureau's Population Estimates Program that produces and disseminates the official estimates of the population for the nation, states, counties, cities, and towns as well as estimates of housing units for states and counties.

Source: U.S. Census Bureau, 2015 American Community Survey 1-Year Estimates Table 504, http://www.census.gov/programs-surveys/acs/data/summary-file.html

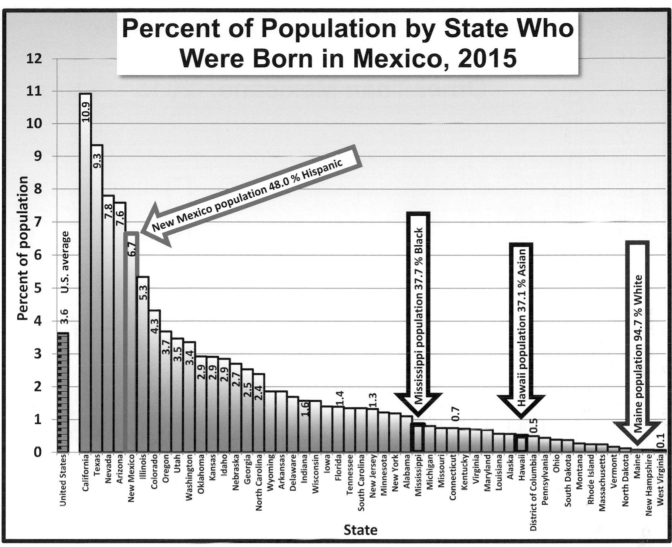

Percent of Population by State Who Were Born in Mexico, 2015

In 2015, almost one-of-nine persons residing in California was born in Mexico as was almost one-of-ten persons residing in Texas.

Although the American Community Survey (ACS) produces population, demographic and housing unit estimates, it is the Census Bureau's Population Estimates Program that produces and disseminates the official estimates of the population for the nation, states, counties, cities, and towns and estimates of housing units for states and counties.

Source: U.S. Census Bureau, 2015 American Community Survey 1-Year Estimates Table 505, http://www.census.gov/programs-surveys/acs/data/summary-file.html

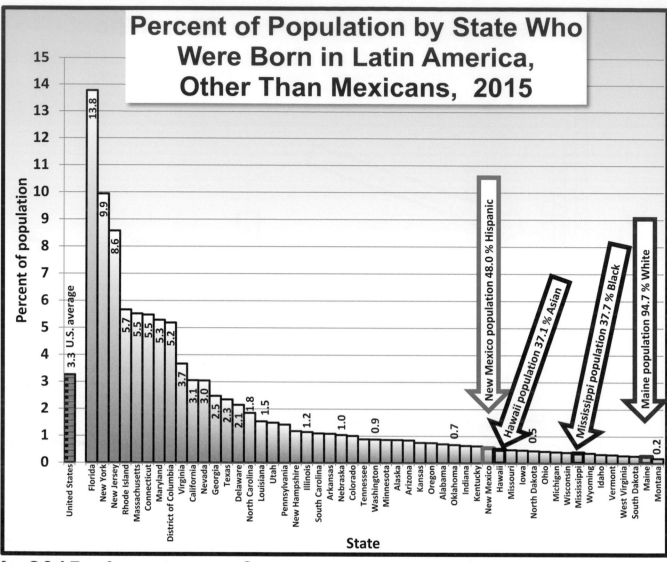

Percent of Population by State Who Were Born in Latin America, Other Than Mexicans, 2015

In 2015, almost one-of-seven persons in Florida was a non-Mexican, Latino person.

Although the American Community Survey (ACS) produces population, demographic, and housing unit estimates, it is the Census Bureau's Population Estimates Program that produces and disseminates the official estimates of the population for the nation, states, counties, cities, and towns as well as estimates of housing units for states and counties.

Source: U.S. Census Bureau, 2015 American Community Survey 1-Year Estimates Table 506, http://www.census.gov/programs-surveys/acs/data/summary-file.html

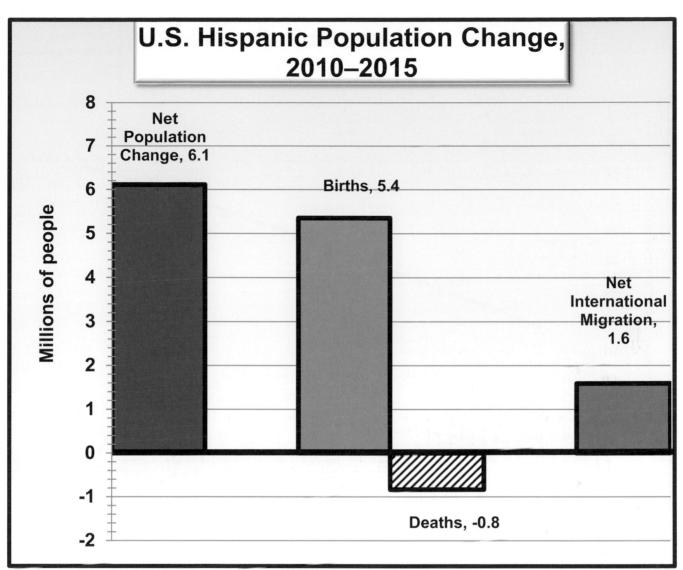

U.S. Hispanic Population Change, 2010–2015

Millions of people

Net Population Change, 6.1

Births, 5.4

Net International Migration, 1.6

Deaths, -0.8

Natural increases of Hispanic persons averaged 920,000 annually, between 2010–2015, compared with their annual increase of 320,000 due to net immigration.

Hispanic or Latino is a person of Cuban, Mexican, Puerto Rican, South or Central American, or other Spanish culture or origin, regardless of race.

Net international migration for the United States includes the international migration of both native and foreign-born populations. Specifically, it includes: (a) the net international migration of the foreign born, (b) the net migration between the United States and Puerto Rico, (c) the net migration of natives to and from the United States, and (d) the net movement of the Armed Forces population between the United States and overseas. Net international migration for Puerto Rico includes the migration of native and foreign-born populations between the United States and Puerto Rico.

Source: U.S. Census Bureau, Population Division, Annual Estimates of the Resident Population by Sex, Race, and Hispanic Origin for the United States, States, and Counties: April 1, 2010 to July 1, 2015, Release Date: June 2016
http://factfinder.census.gov/faces/tableservices/jsf/pages/productview.xhtml?pid=PEP_2015_PEPCCOMPN&prodType=table

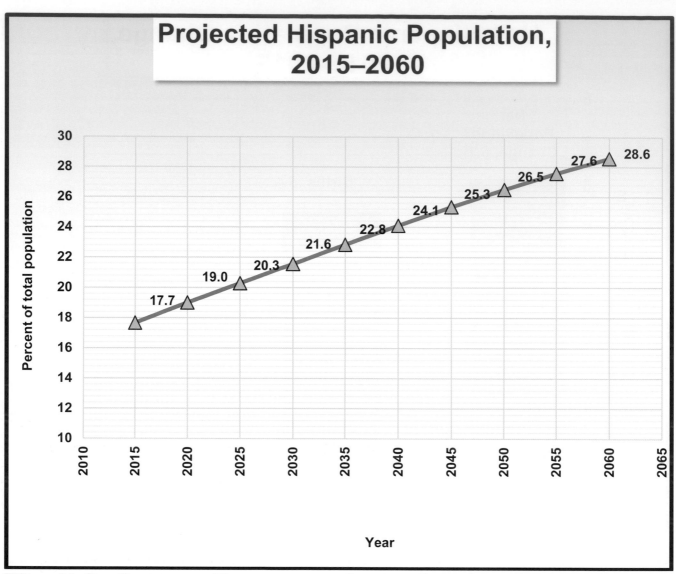

Projected Hispanic Population, 2015–2060

Percent of total population

Year	Value
2015	17.7
2020	19.0
2025	20.3
2030	21.6
2035	22.8
2040	24.1
2045	25.3
2050	26.5
2055	27.6
2060	28.6

Year

The U.S. Census Bureau projects that by the year 2060 nearly three-of-ten persons will be of Hispanic origin.

Hispanic or Latino is a person of Cuban, Mexican, Puerto Rican, South or Central American, or other Spanish culture or origin, regardless of race.

Source: U.S. Census Bureau, Population Division, Table 13. Projections of the Population by Nativity, Hispanic Origin, and Race for the United States: 2015 to 2060 (NP2014-T13) http://www.census.gov/population/projections/data/national/2014/summarytables.html

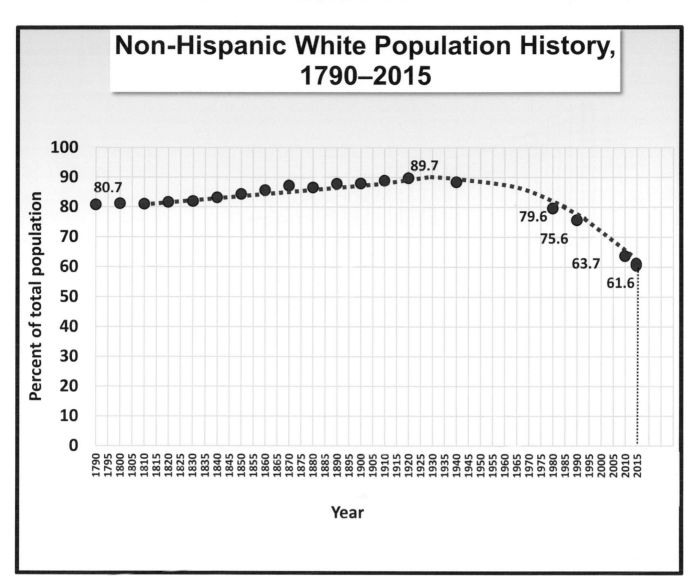

Non-Hispanic White Population History, 1790–2015

The non-Hispanic White population as a percent of the total population of the United States peaked in 1920 at approximately 90 percent.

The White population, as a percent of total U.S. population, peaked around 1920, at almost ninety percent. The U.S. Census Bureau didn't begin to record Hispanic origin until the 1940 census and at which time the Hispanic origin population was based on having Spanish as your mother tongue. Therefore, the non-Hispanic White population on the graph doesn't start until 1940. In the 1940 census the Hispanic origin White was 1.41 percent of the population.

The non-Hispanic White portion of U.S. population declined by almost one-third between 1920 and 2015. Hispanic origin is considered an ethnicity, not a race. Hispanic or Latino is a person of Cuban, Mexican, Puerto Rican, South or Central American, or other Spanish culture or origin, regardless of race. White is a person having origins in any of the original peoples of Europe, the Middle East, or North Africa.

Source: U.S. Census Bureau, https://www.census.gov/population/www/documentation/twps0076/twps0076.html, Table A-1. Race and Hispanic Origin for the United States, 2010-15 Data: https://www.census.gov/quickfacts/table/RHI125215/00

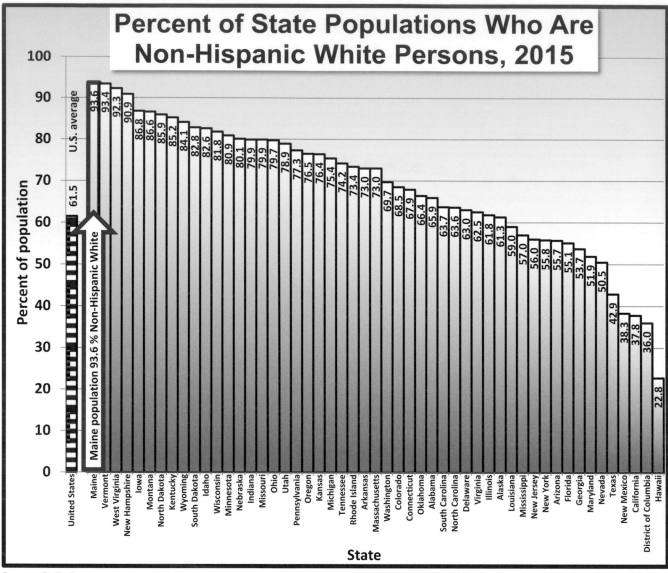

Percent of State Populations Who Are Non-Hispanic White Persons, 2015

In 2015, non-Hispanic White persons were not in the majority in four states: Hawaii, California, New Mexico, and Texas. However, they comprised over 90 percent of the population in four other states: Maine, Vermont, West Virginia, and New Hampshire.

Although the American Community Survey (ACS) produces population, demographic, and housing unit estimates, it is the Census Bureau's Population Estimates Program that produces and disseminates the official estimates of the population for the nation, states, counties, cities, and towns as well as estimates of housing units for states and counties.

Source: U.S. Census Bureau, 2015 American Community Survey 1-Year Estimates Table 209, http://www.census.gov/programs-surveys/acs/data/summary-file.html

Distribution of States with the Highest Percent Non-Hispanic White Population, 2015

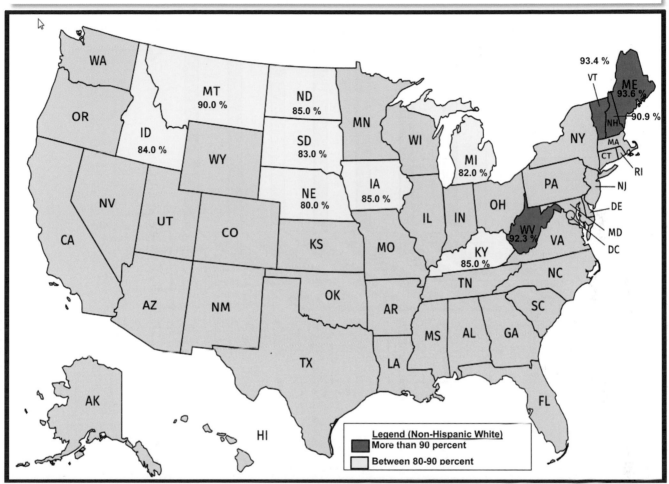

In 2015, non-Hispanic White persons exceeded 90 percent of the population in four states: Maine, Vermont, West Virginia, and New Hampshire. In nine other states the non-Hispanic White population was between 80 to 90 percent.

Although the American Community Survey (ACS) produces population, demographic, and housing unit estimates, it is the Census Bureau's Population Estimates Program that produces and disseminates the official estimates of the population for the nation, states, counties, cities, and towns as well as estimates of housing units for states and counties.

Source: U.S. Census Bureau, 2015 American Community Survey 1-Year Estimates Table 209, http://www.census.gov/programs-surveys/acs/data/summary-file.html

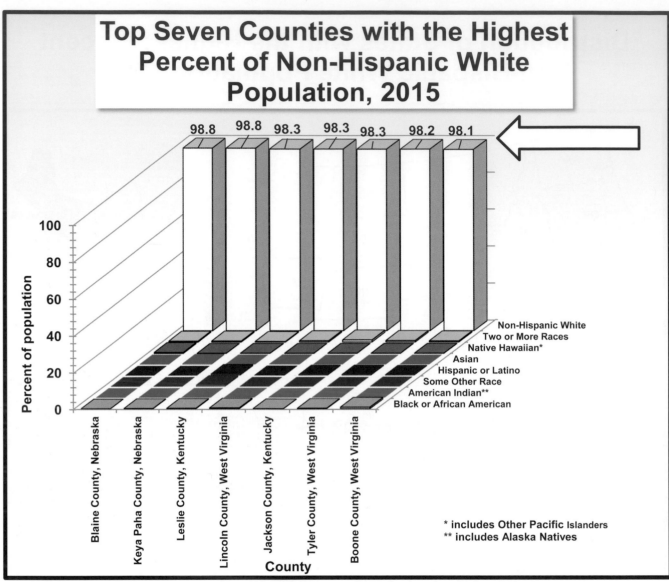

Top Seven Counties with the Highest Percent of Non-Hispanic White Population, 2015

98.8 98.8 98.3 98.3 98.3 98.2 98.1

Percent of population

100
80
60
40
20
0

Non-Hispanic White
Two or More Races
Native Hawaiian*
Asian
Hispanic or Latino
Some Other Race
American Indian**
Black or African American

Blaine County, Nebraska
Keya Paha County, Nebraska
Leslie County, Kentucky
Lincoln County, West Virginia
Jackson County, Kentucky
Tyler County, West Virginia
Boone County, West Virginia

County

* includes Other Pacific Islanders
** includes Alaska Natives

In 2015, there were seven counties with non-Hispanic White populations in excess of 98 percent. These counties were located in three states: Nebraska, Kentucky, and West Virginia.

A person having origins in any of the original peoples of Europe, the Middle East, or North Africa. It includes people who indicate their race as "White" or report entries such as Irish, German, Italian, Lebanese, Arab, Moroccan, or Caucasian.

The United States is comprised of 3,142 counties. A county is a political and geographic subdivision of a state. The Census Bureau considers the parishes of Louisiana and the boroughs of Alaska and the District of Columbia to be equivalent to counties for statistical purposes. Hispanic origin is considered an ethnicity, not a race. Hispanics may be of any race.

Source: U.S. Census Bureau, American Fact Finder, Community Facts, 2015 Population Estimates Program, accessed 10/17/16, http://factfinder.census.gov/faces/nav/jsf/pages/community_facts.xhtml#

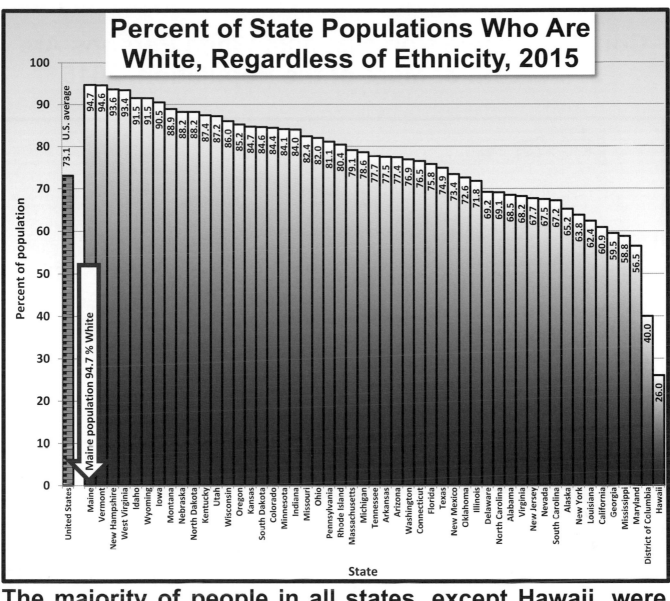

Percent of State Populations Who Are White, Regardless of Ethnicity, 2015

The majority of people in all states, except Hawaii, were White in 2015. In Hawaii, approximately one-of-four persons were White.

The data shown for White race regardless of ethnicity. Hispanic origin can be any race.

White is a person having origins in any of the original peoples of Europe, the Middle East, or North Africa.

Although the American Community Survey (ACS) produces population, demographic, and housing unit estimates, it is the Census Bureau's Population Estimates Program that produces and disseminates the official estimates of the population for the nation, states, counties, cities, and towns and estimates of housing units for states and counties.

Source: U.S. Census Bureau, 2015 American Community Survey 1-Year Estimates Table 201, http://www.census.gov/programs-surveys/acs/data/summary-file.html

Counties Where Non-Hispanic White Persons Are 97 Percent or More of the Population, 2015

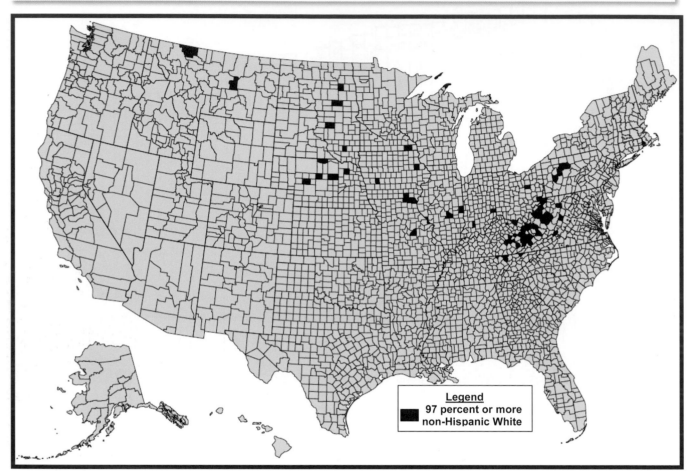

Legend
97 percent or more
non-Hispanic White

In 2015, 70 out of 3,142 counties had non-Hispanic White populations greater than 97 percent and in 1,112 counties (35.4 percent) they exceeded 90 percent.

All counties with 97 percent or more non-Hispanic White persons were located in the northern region.

Source: U.S. Census Bureau, 2015 American Community Survey, http://www.census.gov/popest/data/counties/asrh/2015/CC-EST2015-ALLDATA.html

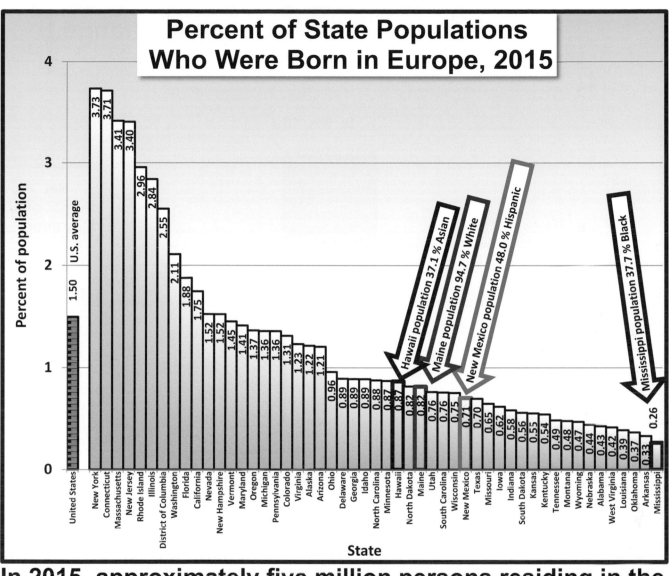

Percent of State Populations Who Were Born in Europe, 2015

Percent of population

State	Percent
United States (U.S. average)	1.50
New York	3.73
Connecticut	3.71
Massachusetts	3.41
New Jersey	3.40
Rhode Island	2.96
Illinois	2.84
District of Columbia	2.55
Washington	2.11
Florida	1.88
California	1.75
Nevada	1.52
New Hampshire	1.52
Vermont	1.45
Maryland	1.41
Oregon	1.37
Michigan	1.36
Pennsylvania	1.36
Colorado	1.31
Virginia	1.23
Alaska	1.22
Arizona	1.21
Ohio	0.96
Delaware	0.89
Georgia	0.89
Idaho	0.89
North Carolina	0.88
Minnesota	0.87
Hawaii	0.87
North Dakota	0.82
Maine	0.82
Utah	0.76
South Carolina	0.76
Wisconsin	0.75
New Mexico	0.71
Texas	0.70
Missouri	0.65
Iowa	0.62
Indiana	0.58
South Dakota	0.56
Kansas	0.55
Kentucky	0.54
Tennessee	0.49
Montana	0.48
Wyoming	0.47
Nebraska	0.44
Alabama	0.43
West Virginia	0.42
Louisiana	0.39
Oklahoma	0.37
Arkansas	0.33
Mississippi	0.26

Hawaii population 37.1 % Asian

Maine population 94.7 % White

New Mexico population 48.0 % Hispanic

Mississippi population 37.7 % Black

In 2015, approximately five million persons residing in the United States were born in Europe.

Although the American Community Survey (ACS) produces population, demographic, and housing unit estimates, it is the Census Bureau's Population Estimates Program that produces and disseminates the official estimates of the population for the nation, states, counties, cities, and towns as well as estimates of housing units for states and counties.

Source: U.S. Census Bureau, 2015 American Community Survey 1-Year Estimates Table 502, http://www.census.gov/programs-surveys/acs/data/summary-file.html

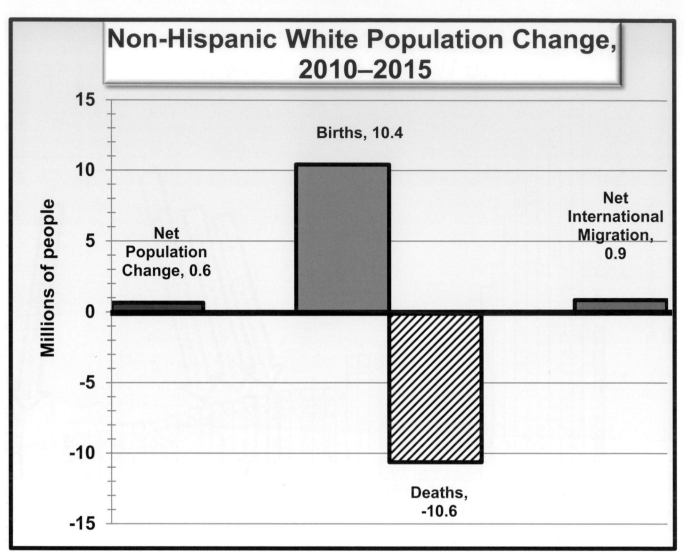

Non-Hispanic White Population Change, 2010–2015

Births, 10.4

Net International Migration, 0.9

Net Population Change, 0.6

Deaths, -10.6

Millions of people

Between 2010–2015, the birth rate of non-Hispanic White persons was lower than their death rate by approximately 40,000 persons per year.

White is a person having origins in any of the original peoples of Europe, the Middle East, or North Africa; Hispanic or Latino is a person of Cuban, Mexican, Puerto Rican, South or Central American, or other Spanish culture or origin, regardless of race.

Source: U.S. Census Bureau, Population Division, Annual Estimates of the Resident Population by Sex, Race, and Hispanic Origin for the United States, States, and Counties: April 1, 2010 to July 1, 2015, Release Date: June 2016
http://factfinder.census.gov/faces/tableservices/jsf/pages/productview.xhtml?pid=PEP_2015_PEPCCOMPN&prodType=table

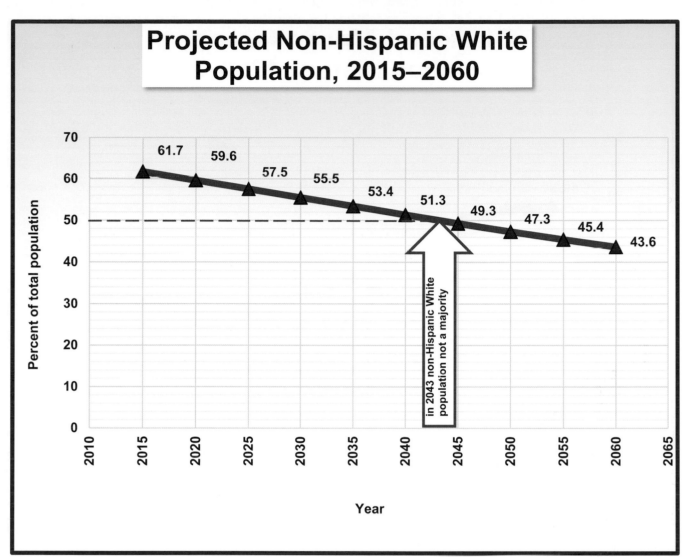

Projected Non-Hispanic White Population, 2015–2060

Percent of total population

Year

61.7 59.6 57.5 55.5 53.4 51.3 49.3 47.3 45.4 43.6

in 2043 non-Hispanic White population not a majority

The U.S. Census Bureau projects that in the year 2043 the non-Hispanic White population will no longer be a majority.

White is a person having origins in any of the original peoples of Europe, the Middle East, or North Africa; Hispanic origin is considered an ethnicity, not a race. Hispanics may be of any race.

Source: U.S. Census Bureau, Population Division, Table 13. Projections of the Population by Nativity, Hispanic Origin, and Race for the United States: 2015 to 2060 (NP2014-T13) http://www.census.gov/population/projections/data/national/2014/summarytables.html

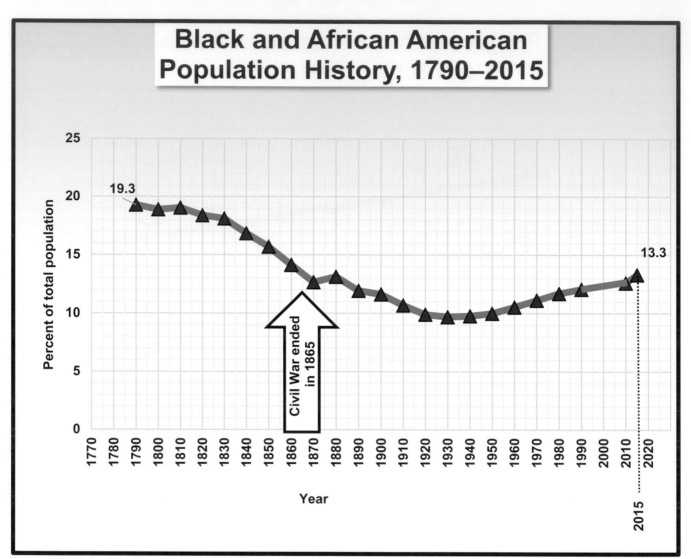

Black and African American Population History, 1790–2015

The Black or African American population, as a percent of the total population of the United States, declined after the Civil War and has been slowly increasing since 1940.

Black or African American is a person having origins in any of the Black racial groups of Africa.

Source: U.S. Census Bureau, https://www.census.gov/population/www/documentation/twps0076/twps0076.html, Table A-1. Race and Hispanic Origin for the United States, 2010-15 Data: https://www.census.gov/quickfacts/table/RHI125215/00

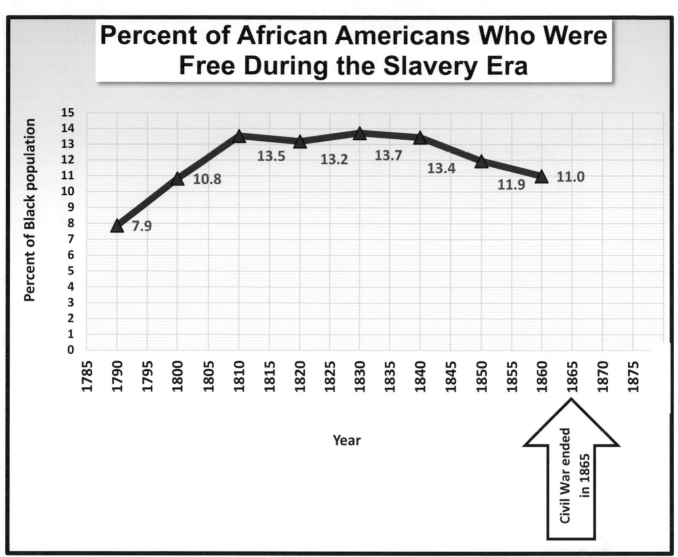

Percent of African Americans Who Were Free During the Slavery Era

Percent of Black population

7.9
10.8
13.5
13.2
13.7
13.4
11.9
11.0

Year

Civil War ended in 1865

At the time of the Civil War, approximately one-of-nine African Americans were free.

Black or African American is a person having origins in any of the Black racial groups of Africa.

Source: U.S. Census Bureau, https://www.census.gov/population/www/documentation/twps0076/twps0076.html, Table A-1. Race and Hispanic Origin for the United States, 2010-15 Data: https://www.census.gov/quickfacts/table/RHI125215/00

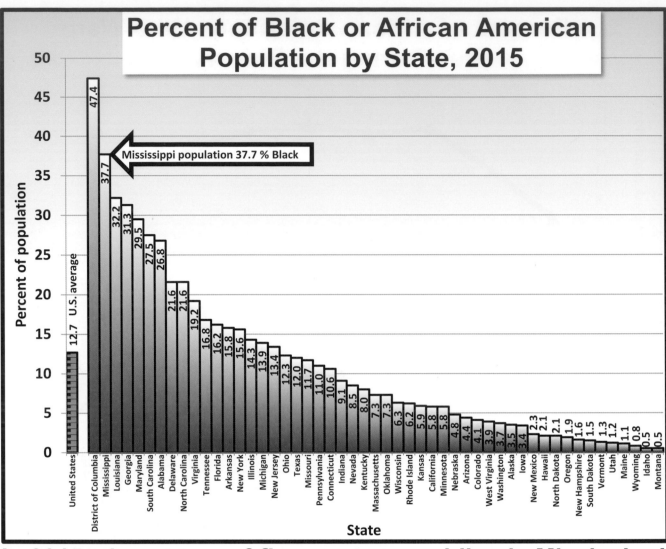

Percent of Black or African American Population by State, 2015

In 2015, almost two-of-five persons residing in Mississippi were Black or African American.

Black or African American is a person having origins in any of the Black racial groups of Africa.

Although the American Community Survey (ACS) produces population, demographic, and housing unit estimates, it is the Census Bureau's Population Estimates Program that produces and disseminates the official estimates of the population for the nation, states, counties, cities, and towns as well as estimates of housing units for states and counties.

Source: U.S. Census Bureau, 2015 American Community Survey 1-Year Estimates Table 202, http://www.census.gov/programs-surveys/acs/data/summary-file.html

Distribution of States
Where Black or African Americans
Are More Than 20 Percent of the Population, 2015

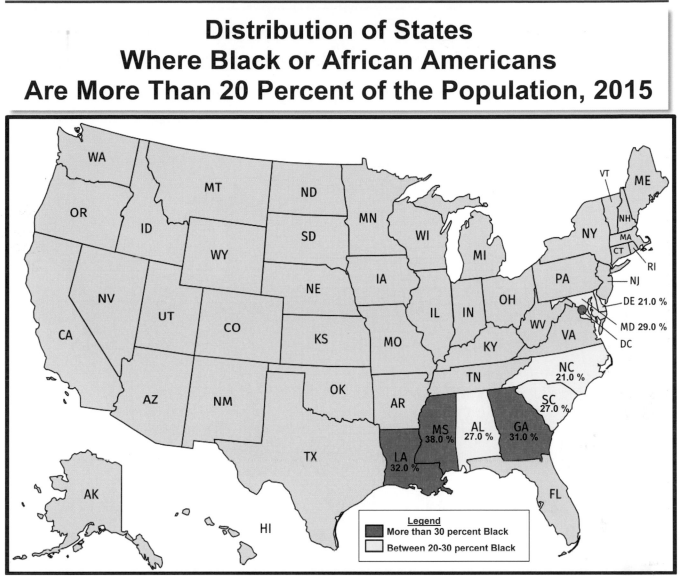

In 2015, three states had populations that were more than 30 percent Black or African American—Mississippi, Louisiana, and Georgia.

Black or African American is a person having origins in any of the Black racial groups of Africa.

Although the American Community Survey (ACS) produces population, demographic, and housing unit estimates, it is the Census Bureau's Population Estimates Program that produces and disseminates the official estimates of the population for the nation, states, counties, cities, and towns as well as estimates of housing units for states and counties.

Source: U.S. Census Bureau, 2015 American Community Survey 1-Year Estimates Table 202, http://www.census.gov/programs-surveys/acs/data/summary-file.html

Distribution of Counties Where Black or African Americans Are the Majority Population, 2015

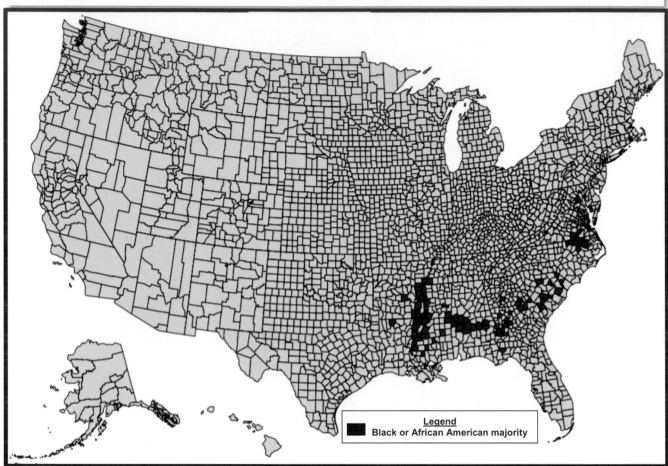

In 2015, 96 out of 3,142 counties, had a Black or African American population that was greater than 50 percent, and they were all concentrated in the southeastern part of the country.

All counties with majority Black or African American populations were located in the southeastern region except for two counties in Maryland: Baltimore City County and Prince George's County.

Source: U.S. Census Bureau, 2015 American Community Survey, http://www.census.gov/popest/data/counties/asrh/2015/CC-EST2015-ALLDATA.html

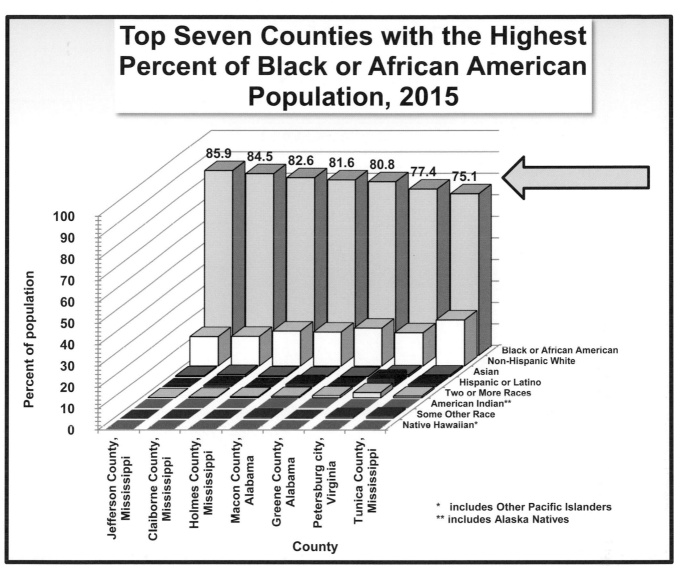

Top Seven Counties with the Highest Percent of Black or African American Population, 2015

85.9   84.5   82.6   81.6   80.8   77.4   75.1

Percent of population

100
90
80
70
60
50
40
30
20
10
0

Black or African American
Non-Hispanic White
Asian
Hispanic or Latino
Two or More Races
American Indian**
Some Other Race
Native Hawaiian*

Jefferson County, Mississippi
Claiborne County, Mississippi
Holmes County, Mississippi
Macon County, Alabama
Greene County, Alabama
Petersburg city, Virginia
Tunica County, Mississippi

County

*   includes Other Pacific Islanders
** includes Alaska Natives

In 2015, seven counties had a Black or African American population which exceeded 75 percent. Four of the seven counties are in Mississippi.

Black or African American is a person having origins in any of the Black racial groups of Africa. It includes people who indicate their race as "Black, African American, or Negro" or report entries such as African American, Kenyan, Nigerian, or Haitian.

The United States is comprised of 3,142 counties. A county is a political and geographic subdivision of a state. The Census Bureau considers the parishes of Louisiana and the boroughs of Alaska and the District of Columbia to be equivalent to counties for statistical purposes. Hispanic origin is considered an ethnicity, not a race. Hispanics may be of any race.

Source: U.S. Census Bureau, American Fact Finder, Community Facts, 2015 Population Estimates Program, accessed 10/17/16, http://factfinder.census.gov/faces/nav/jsf/pages/community_facts.xhtml#

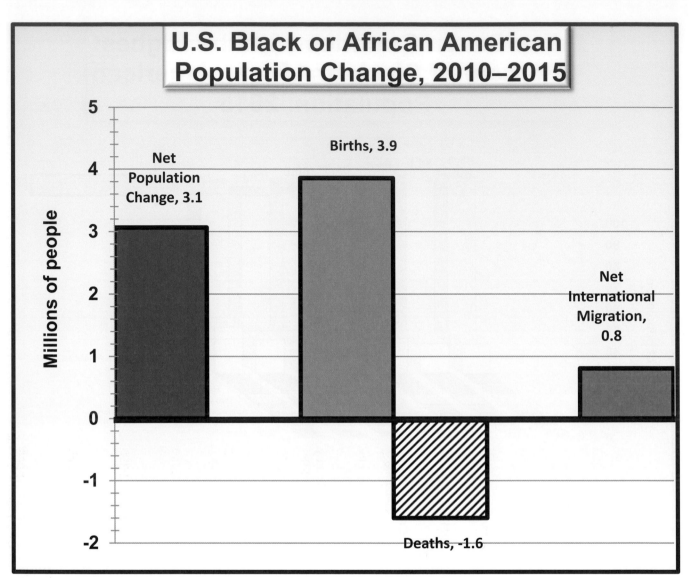

U.S. Black or African American Population Change, 2010–2015

Births, 3.9

Net Population Change, 3.1

Net International Migration, 0.8

Deaths, -1.6

Millions of people

Between 2010–2015, natural growth of the Black or African American population was three times greater than their net immigration.

Net international migration for the United States includes the international migration of both native and foreign-born populations. Specifically, it includes: (a) the net international migration of the foreign born, (b) the net migration between the United States and Puerto Rico, (c) the net migration of natives to and from the United States, and (d) the net movement of the Armed Forces population between the United States and overseas. Net international migration for Puerto Rico includes the migration of native and foreign-born populations between the United States and Puerto Rico.

Hispanic origin is considered an ethnicity, not a race. Hispanics may be of any race.

Source: U.S. Census Bureau, Population Division, Annual Estimates of the Resident Population by Sex, Race, and Hispanic Origin for the United States, States, and Counties: April 1, 2010 to July 1, 2015, Release Date: June 2016
http://factfinder.census.gov/faces/tableservices/jsf/pages/productview.xhtml?pid=PEP_2015_PEPCCOMPN&prodType=table

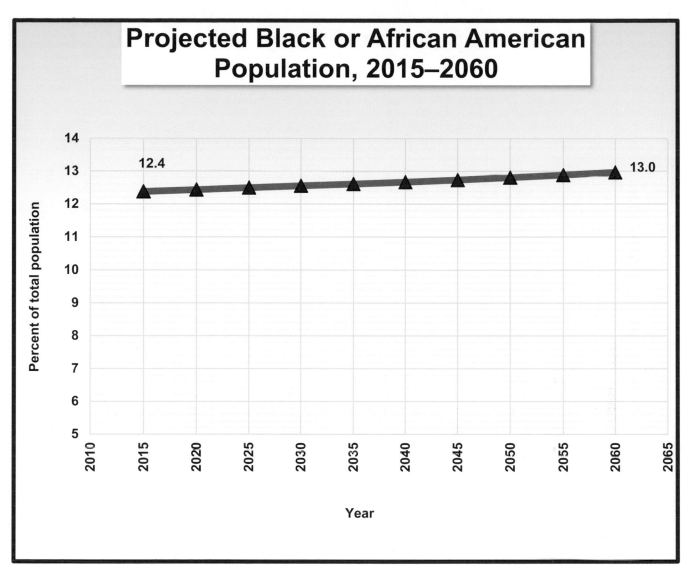

Projected Black or African American Population, 2015–2060

The proportion of the United States population that is Black or African American is projected by the U.S. Census Bureau to remain relatively unchanged between 2015–2060.

Black or African American is a person having origins in any of the Black racial groups of Africa.

Source: U.S. Census Bureau, Population Division, Table 13. Projections of the Population by Nativity, Hispanic Origin, and Race for the United States: 2015 to 2060 (NP2014-T13) http://www.census.gov/population/projections/data/national/2014/summarytables.html

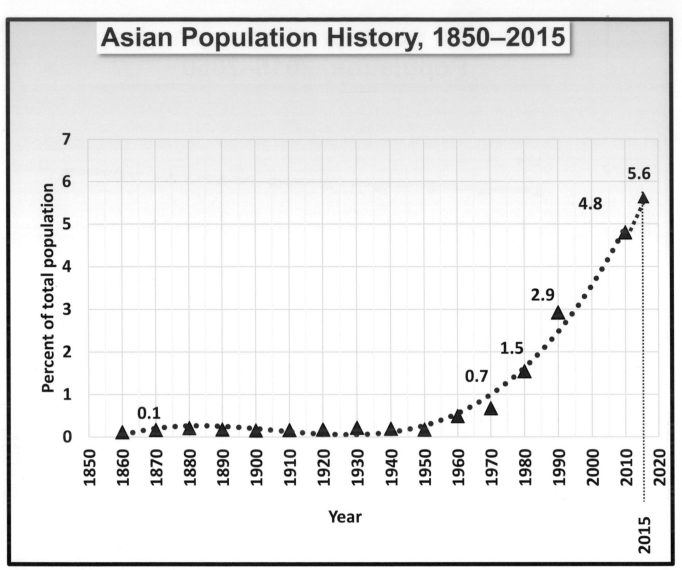

Asian Population History, 1850–2015

Between 1983–2015, the Asian portion of the population of the United States tripled.

Asian is a person having origins in any of the original peoples of the Far East, Southeast Asia, or the Indian Subcontinent, including, for example, Cambodia, China, India, Japan, Korea, Malaysia, Pakistan, the Philippine Islands, Thailand, and Vietnam.

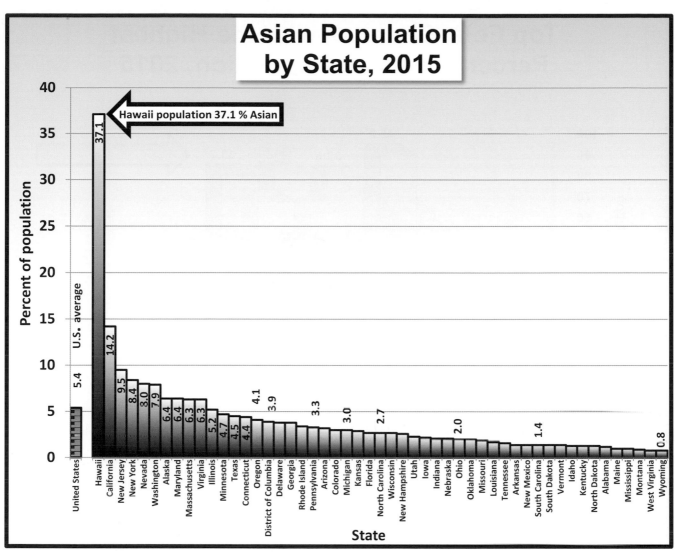

Asian Population by State, 2015

Hawaii population 37.1 % Asian

Percent of population vs **State**

(United States U.S. average 5.4; Hawaii 37.1; California 14.2; New Jersey 9.5; New York 8.4; Nevada 8.0; Washington 7.9; Alaska 6.4; Maryland 6.4; Massachusetts 6.3; Virginia 6.3; Illinois 5.2; Minnesota 4.7; Texas 4.5; Connecticut 4.4; Oregon 4.1; District of Columbia 3.9; Delaware; Georgia; Rhode Island 3.3; Pennsylvania; Arizona; Colorado 3.0; Michigan; Kansas; Florida 2.7; North Carolina; Wisconsin; New Hampshire; Utah; Iowa; Indiana; Nebraska 2.0; Ohio; Oklahoma; Missouri; Louisiana; Tennessee; Arkansas; New Mexico 1.4; South Carolina; South Dakota; Vermont; Idaho; Kentucky; North Dakota; Alabama; Maine; Mississippi; Montana; West Virginia; Wyoming 0.8)

In 2015, almost two-of-five persons who resided in Hawaii were Asian.

An Asian person can have origins in any of the original peoples of the Far East, Southeast Asia, or the Indian subcontinent including, for example, Cambodia, China, India, Japan, Korea, Malaysia, Pakistan, the Philippine Islands, Thailand, and Vietnam.

Although the American Community Survey (ACS) produces population, demographic, and housing unit estimates, it is the Census Bureau's Population Estimates Program that produces and disseminates the official estimates of the population for the nation, states, counties, cities, and towns as well as estimates of housing units for states and counties.

Source: U.S. Census Bureau, 2015 American Community Survey 1-Year Estimates Table 204, http://www.census.gov/programs-surveys/acs/data/summary-file.html

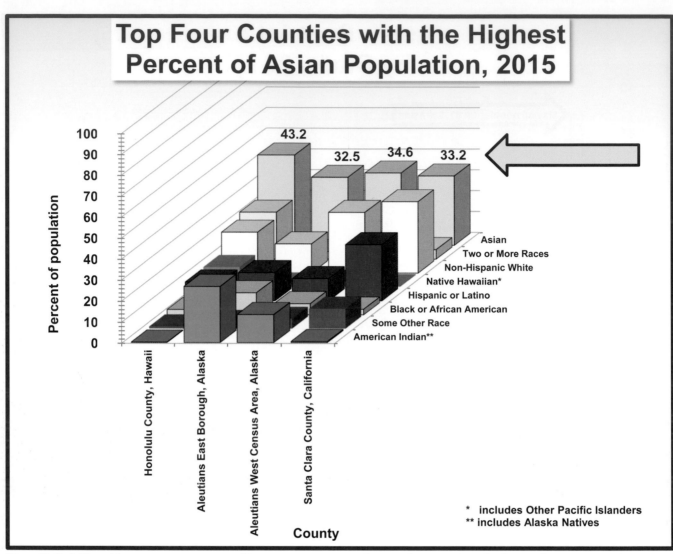

Top Four Counties with the Highest Percent of Asian Population, 2015

In 2015, there were four counties located in three states with Asian populations approximately one-third or more of the total county's population.

Asian is a person having origins in any of the original peoples of the Far East, Southeast Asia, or the Indian subcontinent, including, for example, Cambodia, China, India, Japan, Korea, Malaysia, Pakistan, the Philippine Islands, Thailand, and Vietnam. It includes people who indicate their race as "Asian Indian," "Chinese," "Filipino," "Korean," "Japanese," "Vietnamese," and "Other Asian" or provide other detailed Asian responses.

Hispanic origin is considered an ethnicity, not a race. Hispanics may be of any race.

Source: U.S. Census Bureau, American Fact Finder, Community Facts, 2015 Population Estimates Program, accessed 10/17/16, http://factfinder.census.gov/faces/nav/jsf/pages/community_facts.xhtml#

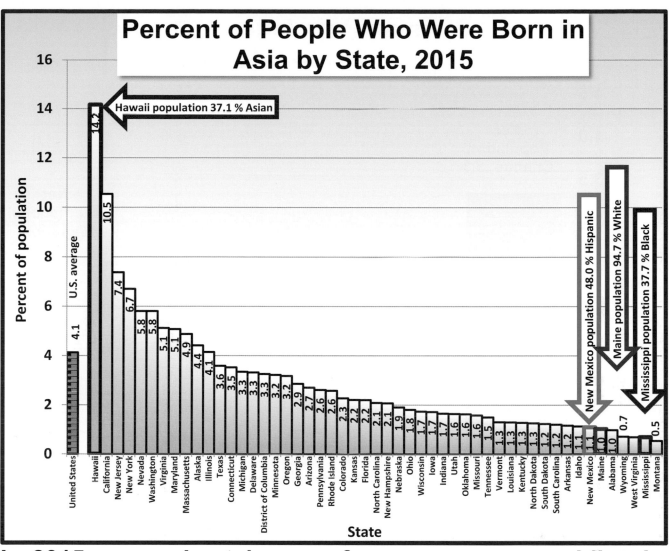

Percent of People Who Were Born in Asia by State, 2015

Hawaii population 37.1 % Asian

New Mexico population 48.0 % Hispanic

Maine population 94.7 % White

Mississippi population 37.7 % Black

Percent of population

U.S. average

Y-axis: 0, 2, 4, 6, 8, 10, 12, 14, 16

Values: United States 4.1, Hawaii 14.2, California 10.5, New Jersey 7.4, New York 6.7, Nevada 5.8, Washington 5.8, Virginia 5.1, Maryland 5.1, Massachusetts 4.9, Alaska 4.4, Illinois 4.1, Texas 3.6, Connecticut 3.5, Michigan 3.3, Delaware 3.3, District of Columbia 3.3, Minnesota 3.2, Oregon 3.2, Georgia 2.9, Arizona 2.7, Pennsylvania 2.6, Rhode Island 2.6, Colorado 2.3, Kansas 2.2, Florida 2.2, North Carolina 2.1, New Hampshire 2.1, Nebraska 1.9, Ohio 1.8, Wisconsin 1.7, Iowa 1.7, Indiana 1.6, Utah 1.6, Oklahoma 1.6, Missouri 1.5, Tennessee 1.3, Vermont 1.3, Louisiana 1.3, Kentucky 1.3, North Dakota 1.2, South Dakota 1.2, South Carolina 1.2, Arkansas 1.1, Idaho 1.1, New Mexico 1.0, Maine 1.0, Alabama 0.7, Wyoming, West Virginia, Mississippi 0.5, Montana

State

In 2015, approximately one-of-seven persons residing in Hawaii was born outside the United States.

Although the American Community Survey (ACS) produces population, demographic, and housing unit estimates, it is the Census Bureau's Population Estimates Program that produces and disseminates the official estimates of the population for the nation, states, counties, cities, and towns as well as estimates of housing units for states and counties.

Source: U.S. Census Bureau, 2015 American Community Survey 1-Year Estimates Table 503, http://www.census.gov/programs-surveys/acs/data/summary-file.html

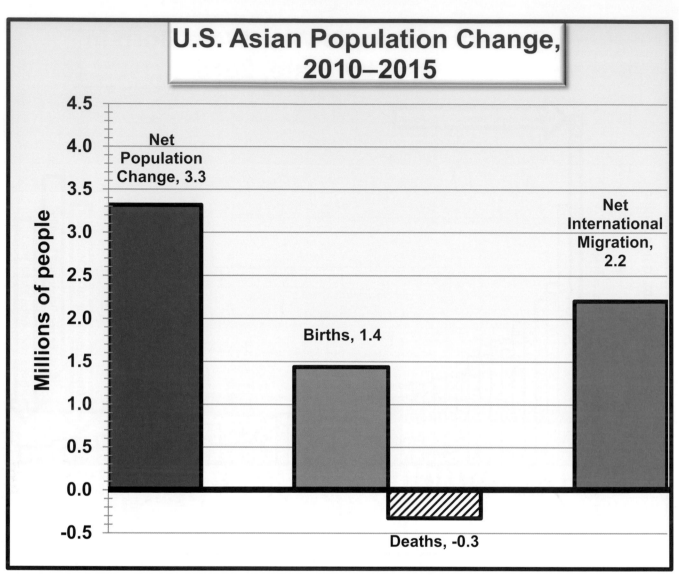

U.S. Asian Population Change, 2010–2015

Millions of people

- Net Population Change, 3.3
- Births, 1.4
- Deaths, -0.3
- Net International Migration, 2.2

The Asian population grew annually by approximately 680,000 persons, between 2010–2015.

Asian is a person having origins in any of the original peoples of the Far East, Southeast Asia, or the Indian Subcontinent, including, for example, Cambodia, China, India, Japan, Korea, Malaysia, Pakistan, the Philippine Islands, Thailand, and Vietnam.

Net international migration for the United States includes the international migration of both native and foreign-born populations. Specifically, it includes: (a) the net international migration of the foreign born, (b) the net migration between the United States and Puerto Rico, (c) the net migration of natives to and from the United States, and (d) the net movement of the Armed Forces population between the United States and overseas. Net international migration for Puerto Rico includes the migration of native and foreign-born populations between the United States and Puerto Rico.

Source: U.S. Census Bureau, Population Division, Annual Estimates of the Resident Population by Sex, Race, and Hispanic Origin for the United States, States, and Counties: April 1, 2010 to July 1, 2015, Release Date: June 2016
http://factfinder.census.gov/faces/tableservices/jsf/pages/productview.xhtml?pid=PEP_2015_PEPCCOMPN&prodType=table

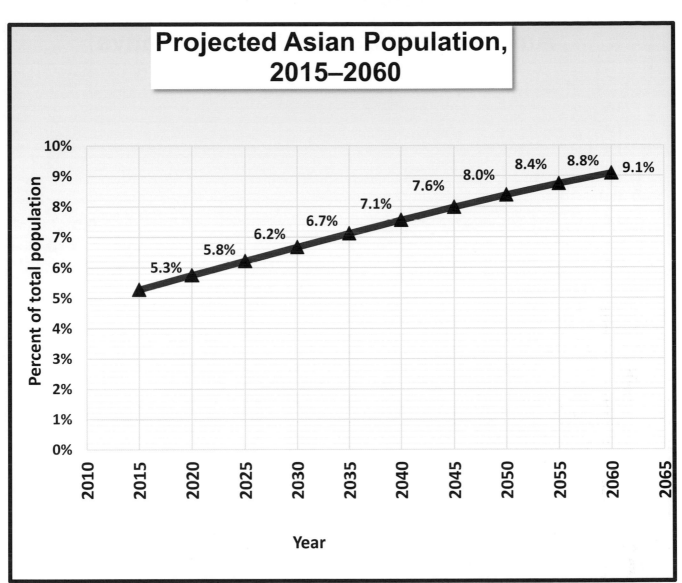

Projected Asian Population, 2015–2060

Percent of total population

5.3% · 5.8% · 6.2% · 6.7% · 7.1% · 7.6% · 8.0% · 8.4% · 8.8% · 9.1%

Year

The proportion of the population of the United States that is Asian is projected by the U.S. Census Bureau to grow from approximately one-of-twenty to one-of-eleven between 2015–2060.

Asian is a person having origins in any of the original peoples of the Far East, Southeast Asia, or the Indian Subcontinent, including, for example, Cambodia, China, India, Japan, Korea, Malaysia, Pakistan, the Philippine Islands, Thailand, and Vietnam.

Source: U.S. Census Bureau, Population Division, Table 13. Projections of the Population by Nativity, Hispanic Origin, and Race for the United States: 2015 to 2060 (NP2014-T13) http://www.census.gov/population/projections/data/national/2014/summarytables.html

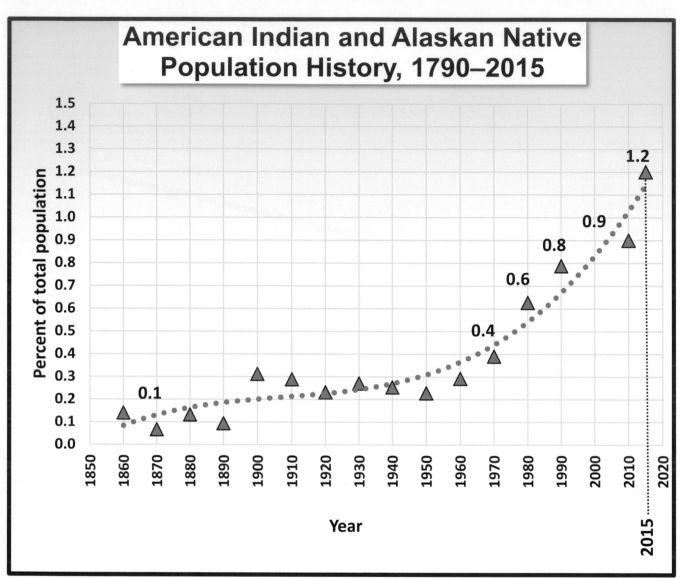

American Indian and Alaskan Native Population History, 1790–2015

Percent of total population (y-axis: 0.0 to 1.5)

Year (x-axis: 1850 to 2020)

Data point labels: 0.1, 0.4, 0.6, 0.8, 0.9, 1.2

Between 1980–2015, the American Indian and Alaskan Native portion of the population of the United States doubled.

American Indian or Alaska Native (AIAN) is a person having origins in any of the original peoples of North and South America (including Central America) who maintains cultural identification through tribal affiliation or community attachment.

Source: U.S. Census Bureau, https://www.census.gov/population/www/documentation/twps0076/twps0076.html, Table A-1. Race and Hispanic Origin for the United States, 2010-15 Data: https://www.census.gov/quickfacts/table/RHI125215/00

Chapter 1: Demographics

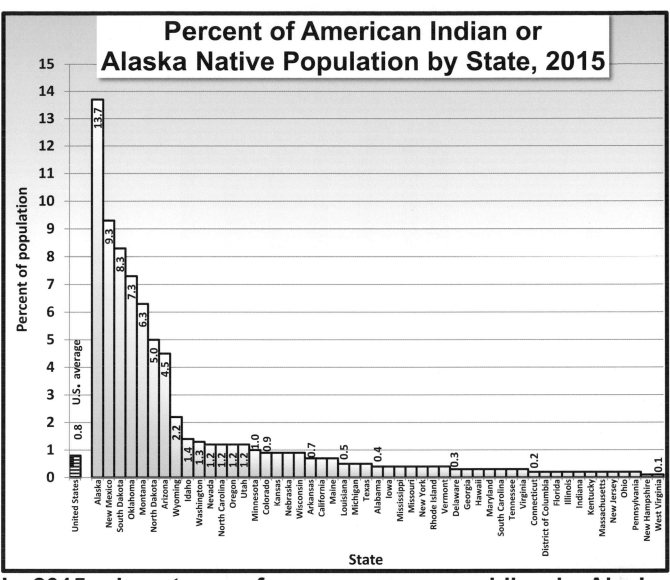

Percent of American Indian or Alaska Native Population by State, 2015

In 2015, almost one-of-seven persons residing in Alaska was an Alaska Native and almost one-of-ten residing in New Mexico was American Indian.

American Indian or Alaska Native is a person having origins in any of the original peoples of North and South America (including Central America) and who maintains tribal affiliation or community attachment.

Although the American Community Survey (ACS) produces population, demographic, and housing unit estimates, it is the Census Bureau's Population Estimates Program that produces and disseminates the official estimates of the population for the nation, states, counties, cities, and towns as well as estimates of housing units for states and counties.

Source: U.S. Census Bureau, 2015 American Community Survey 1-Year Estimates Table 203, http://www.census.gov/programs-surveys/acs/data/summary-file.html

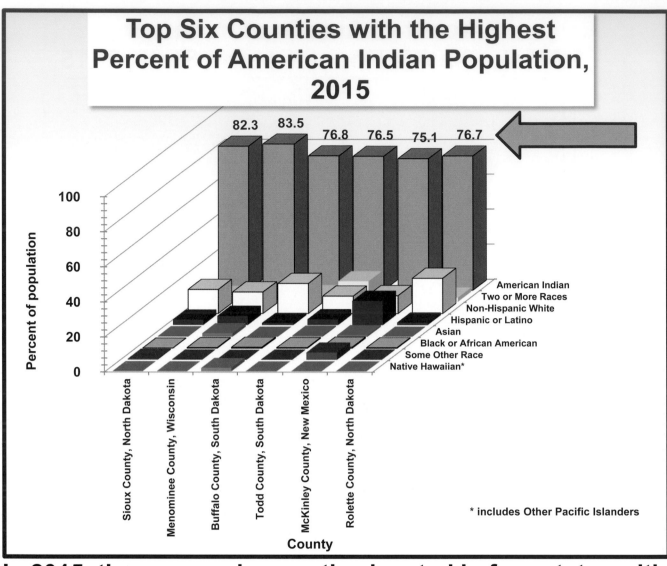

Top Six Counties with the Highest Percent of American Indian Population, 2015

82.3   83.5   76.8   76.5   75.1   76.7

Percent of population

100
80
60
40
20
0

American Indian
Two or More Races
Non-Hispanic White
Hispanic or Latino
Asian
Black or African American
Some Other Race
Native Hawaiian*

Sioux County, North Dakota
Menominee County, Wisconsin
Buffalo County, South Dakota
Todd County, South Dakota
McKinley County, New Mexico
Rolette County, North Dakota

* includes Other Pacific Islanders

County

In 2015, there were six counties located in four states with American Indian populations that exceeded three-quarters of the total county's population.

Only six counties had American Indian populations that exceeded seventy-five percent of the total county population in 2015, and are shown on the chart.

American Indian is a person having origins in any of the original peoples of North and South America (including Central America) and who maintains tribal affiliation or community attachment. This category includes people who indicate their race as "American Indian or Alaska Native" or report entries such as Navajo, Blackfeet, Inupiat, Yup'ik, Central American Indian groups, or South American Indian groups.

Hispanic origin is considered an ethnicity, not a race. Hispanics may be of any race.

Source: U.S. Census Bureau, American Fact Finder, Community Facts, 2015 Population Estimates Program, accessed 10/17/16, http://factfinder.census.gov/faces/nav/jsf/pages/community_facts.xhtml#

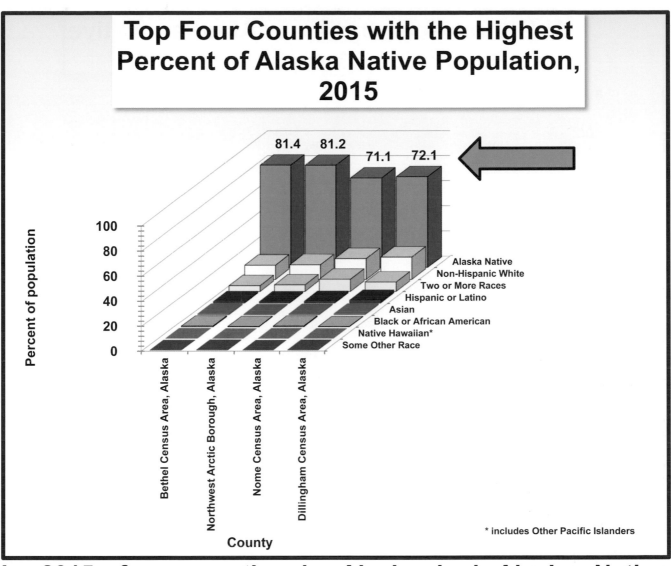

Top Four Counties with the Highest Percent of Alaska Native Population, 2015

In 2015, four counties in Alaska had Alaska Native populations that exceeded 70 percent of the county's population.

Alaska native people are self-identified as people of Alaska Native descent. Only four counties (boroughs) had Alaska Native populations that exceeded seventy percent of the total county population in 2015, and are shown on the chart.

The United States is comprised of 3,142 counties. A county is a political and geographic subdivision of a state. The Census Bureau considers the parishes of Louisiana and the boroughs of Alaska and the District of Columbia to be equivalent to counties for statistical purposes.

Hispanic origin is considered an ethnicity, not a race. Hispanics may be of any race.

Source: U.S. Census Bureau, American Fact Finder, Community Facts, 2015 Population Estimates Program, accessed 10/17/16, http://factfinder.census.gov/faces/nav/jsf/pages/community_facts.xhtml#

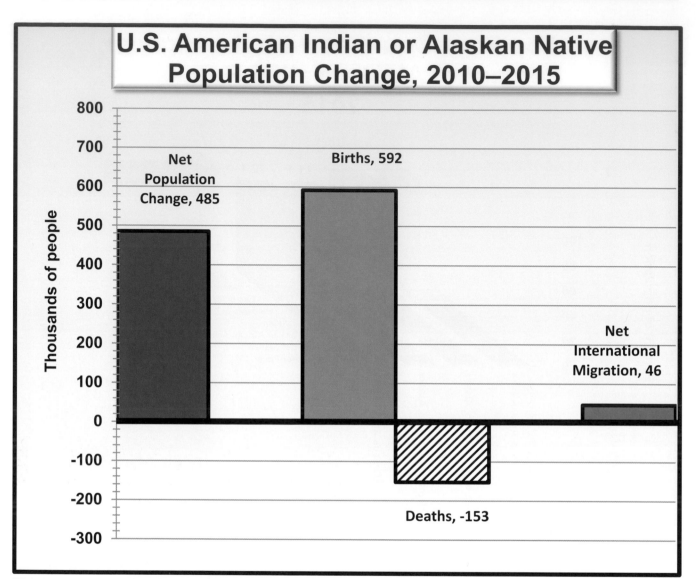

U.S. American Indian or Alaskan Native Population Change, 2010–2015

Net Population Change, 485

Births, 592

Net International Migration, 46

Deaths, -153

Thousands of people

Between 2010–2015, less than 10 percent of American Indian or Alaska Native population growth was due to immigration.

American Indian or Alaska Native (AIAN) are persons having origins in any of the original peoples of North and South America (including Central America) who maintains cultural identification through tribal affiliation or community attachment.

Net international migration for the United States includes the international migration of both native and foreign-born populations. Specifically, it includes: (a) the net international migration of the foreign born, (b) the net migration between the United States and Puerto Rico, (c) the net migration of natives to and from the United States, and (d) the net movement of the Armed Forces population between the United States and overseas. Net international migration for Puerto Rico includes the migration of native and foreign-born populations between the United States and Puerto Rico.

Source: U.S. Census Bureau, Population Division, Annual Estimates of the Resident Population by Sex, Race, and Hispanic Origin for the United States, States, and Counties: April 1, 2010 to July 1, 2015, Release Date: June 2016
http://factfinder.census.gov/faces/tableservices/jsf/pages/productview.xhtml?pid=PEP_2015_PEPCCOMPN&prodType=table

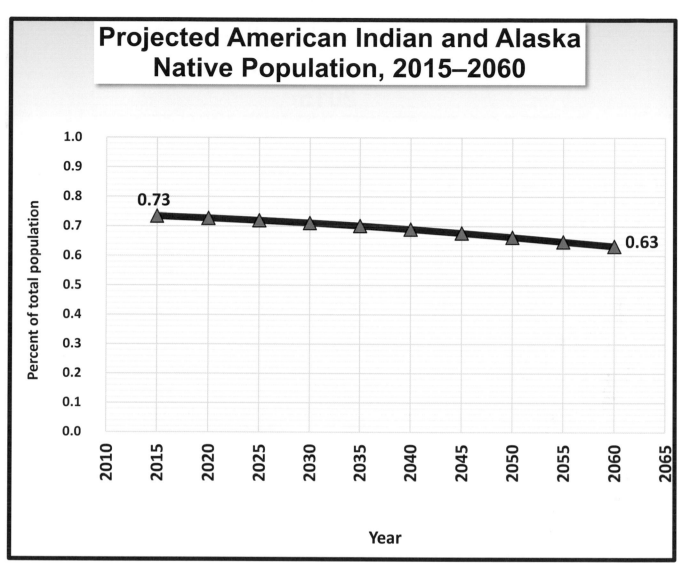

Projected American Indian and Alaska Native Population, 2015–2060

Percent of total population

0.73

0.63

Year

The proportion of the population of the United States that is American Indian or Alaska Native is projected by the U.S. Census Bureau to remain relatively unchanged between 2015–2060.

American Indian or Alaska Native (AIAN) is a person having origins in any of the original peoples of North and South America (including Central America) who maintains cultural identification through tribal affiliation or community attachment.

Source: U.S. Census Bureau, Population Division, Table 13. Projections of the Population by Nativity, Hispanic Origin, and Race for the United States: 2015 to 2060 (NP2014-T13) http://www.census.gov/population/projections/data/national/2014/summarytables.html

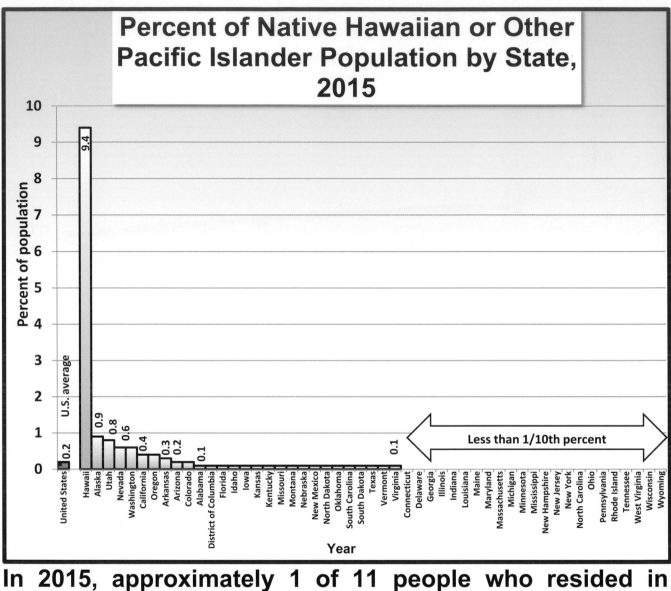

Percent of Native Hawaiian or Other Pacific Islander Population by State, 2015

In 2015, approximately 1 of 11 people who resided in Hawaii were Native Hawaiian.

Native Hawaiian or Other Pacific Islander is a person having origins in any of the original peoples of Hawaii, Guam, Samoa, or other Pacific Islands.

Although the American Community Survey (ACS) produces population, demographic, and housing unit estimates, it is the Census Bureau's Population Estimates Program that produces and disseminates the official estimates of the population for the nation, states, counties, cities, and towns as well as estimates of housing units for states and counties.

Source: U.S. Census Bureau, 2015 American Community Survey 1-Year Estimates Table 205, http://www.census.gov/programs-surveys/acs/data/summary-file.html

Counties Where American Indian or Alaska Natives Are the Majority Population, 2015

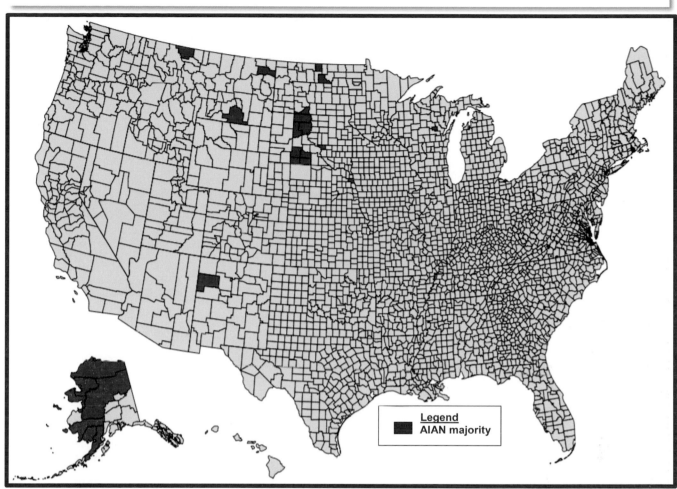

In 2015, 27 out of 3,142 counties had an American Indian or Alaska Natives (AIAN) population greater than 50 percent.

All counties with majority American Indian or Alaska Native populations were located in the either the north-central region or in Alaska, except for one county in Arizona (Apache County). There were no states where American Indian or Alaska Natives were in the majority.

Source: U.S. Census Bureau, 2015 American Community Survey, http://www.census.gov/popest/data/counties/asrh/2015/CC-EST2015-ALLDATA.html

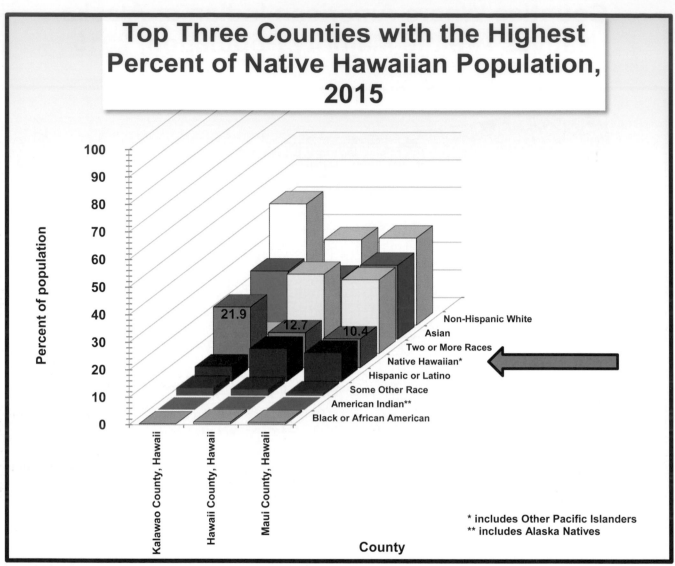

Top Three Counties with the Highest Percent of Native Hawaiian Population, 2015

Percent of population

100
90
80
70
60
50
40
30
20
10
0

21.9   12.7   10.4

Non-Hispanic White
Asian
Two or More Races
Native Hawaiian*
Hispanic or Latino
Some Other Race
American Indian**
Black or African American

Kalawao County, Hawaii
Hawaii County, Hawaii
Maui County, Hawaii

County

* includes Other Pacific Islanders
** includes Alaska Natives

In 2015, Kalawao county, Hawaii, was the only county with more than 20 percent of residents of Native Hawaiian heritage.

Native Hawaiian includes Other Pacific Islanders. These are persons having origins in any of the original peoples of Hawaii, Guam, Samoa, or other Pacific Islands. It includes people who indicate their race as "Native Hawaiian," "Guamanian or Chamorro," "Samoan," and "Other Pacific Islander" or provide other detailed Pacific Islander responses.

Only three counties had Native Hawaiian and Pacific Islander populations that exceeded ten percent of the total county population in 2015, and are shown on the chart.

Hispanic origin is considered an ethnicity, not a race. Hispanics may be of any race.

Source: U.S. Census Bureau, American Fact Finder, Community Facts, 2015 Population Estimates Program, accessed 10/17/16, http://factfinder.census.gov/faces/nav/jsf/pages/community_facts.xhtml#

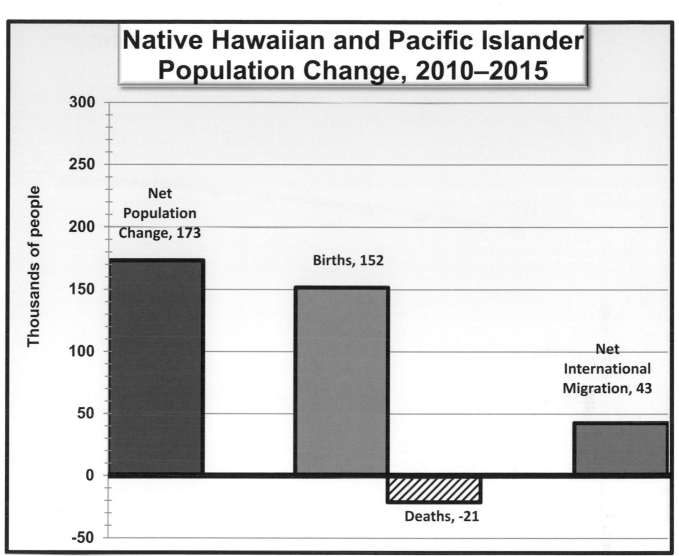

Native Hawaiian and Pacific Islander Population Change, 2010–2015

Between 2010–2015, births of Hawaiian or Pacific Island persons exceeded deaths by approximately seven-to-one.

Native Hawaiian or Other Pacific Islander (NHPI) is a person having origins in any of the original peoples of Hawaii, Guam, Samoa, or other Pacific Islands

Net international migration for the United States includes the international migration of both native and foreign-born populations. Specifically, it includes: (a) the net international migration of the foreign born, (b) the net migration between the United States and Puerto Rico, (c) the net migration of natives to and from the United States, and (d) the net movement of the Armed Forces population between the United States and overseas. Net international migration for Puerto Rico includes the migration of native and foreign-born populations between the United States and Puerto Rico.

Source: U.S. Census Bureau, Population Division, Annual Estimates of the Resident Population by Sex, Race, and Hispanic Origin for the United States, States, and Counties: April 1, 2010 to July 1, 2015, Release Date: June 2016
http://factfinder.census.gov/faces/tableservices/jsf/pages/productview.xhtml?pid=PEP_2015_PEPCCOMPN&prodType=table

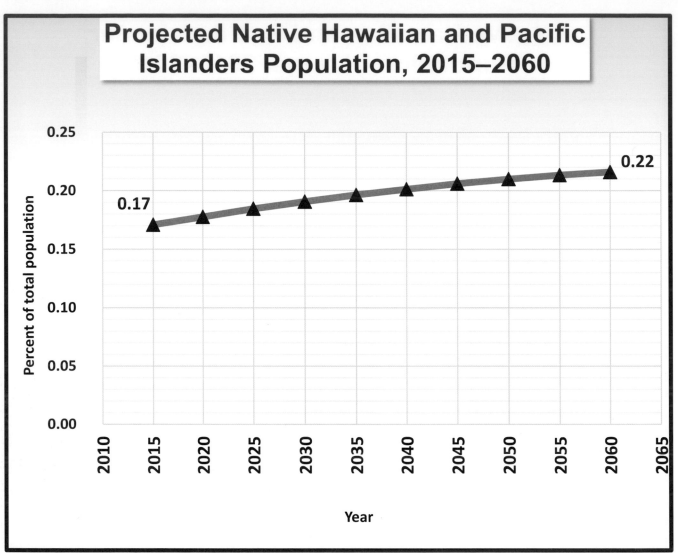

Projected Native Hawaiian and Pacific Islanders Population, 2015–2060

The proportion of the United States population that is Native Hawaiian or Pacific Islander is projected by the U.S. Census Bureau to increase by approximately one-third, between 2015–2060.

NHPI = Native Hawaiian or Other Pacific Islander is a person having origins in any of the original peoples of Hawaii, Guam, Samoa, or other Pacific Islands

Source: U.S. Census Bureau, Population Division, Table 13. Projections of the Population by Nativity, Hispanic Origin, and Race for the United States: 2015 to 2060 (NP2014-T13) http://www.census.gov/population/projections/data/national/2014/summarytables.html

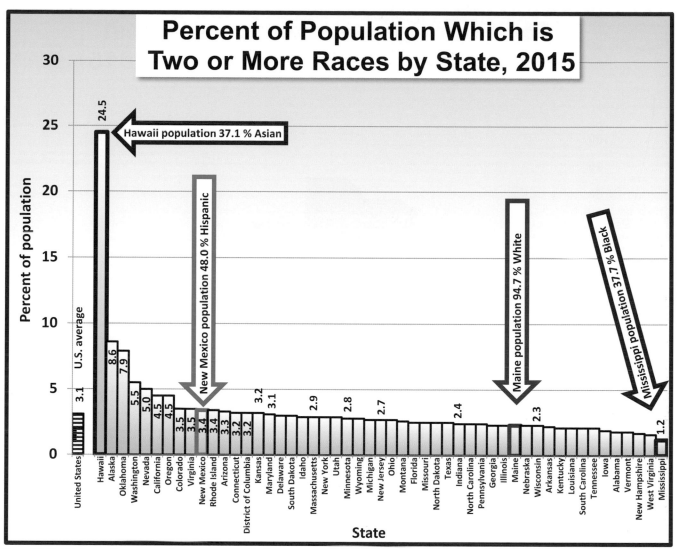

Percent of Population Which is Two or More Races by State, 2015

Hawaii population 37.1 % Asian

New Mexico population 48.0 % Hispanic

Maine population 94.7 % White

Mississippi population 37.7 % Black

In 2015, almost one-of-four persons residing in Hawaii was of more than one race.

Although the American Community Survey (ACS) produces population, demographic, and housing unit estimates, it is the Census Bureau's Population Estimates Program that produces and disseminates the official estimates of the population for the nation, states, counties, cities, and towns as well as estimates of housing units for states and counties.

Source: U.S. Census Bureau, 2015 American Community Survey 1-Year Estimates Table 207, http://www.census.gov/programs-surveys/acs/data/summary-file.html

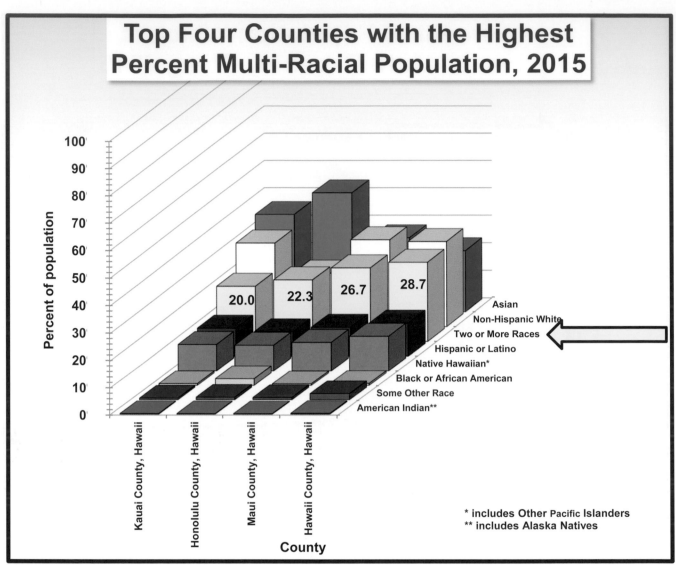

Top Four Counties with the Highest Percent Multi-Racial Population, 2015

Percent of population

County

Kauai County, Hawaii — 20.0
Honolulu County, Hawaii — 22.3
Maui County, Hawaii — 26.7
Hawaii County, Hawaii — 28.7

Asian
Non-Hispanic White
Two or More Races
Hispanic or Latino
Native Hawaiian*
Black or African American
Some Other Race
American Indian**

* includes Other Pacific Islanders
** includes Alaska Natives

In 2015, there were four counties in Hawaii with more than 20 percent of the population self-identified as being of "Two or More Races".

"Two or More Races" refers to combinations of two or more of the following race categories: White, Black or African American, American Indian or Alaska Native, Asian, Native Hawaiian or Other Pacific Islander, or Some Other Race. Hispanic origin is considered an ethnicity, not a race. Hispanics may be of any race. Only four counties had multi-racial (two or more races) populations that exceeded twenty percent of the total county population in 2015, and are shown on the chart.

The United States is comprised of 3,142 counties. A county is a political and geographic subdivision of a state. The Census Bureau considers the parishes of Louisiana and the boroughs of Alaska and the District of Columbia to be equivalent to counties for statistical purposes.

Source: U.S. Census Bureau, American Fact Finder, Community Facts, 2015 Population Estimates Program, accessed 10/17/16, http://factfinder.census.gov/faces/nav/jsf/pages/community_facts.xhtml#

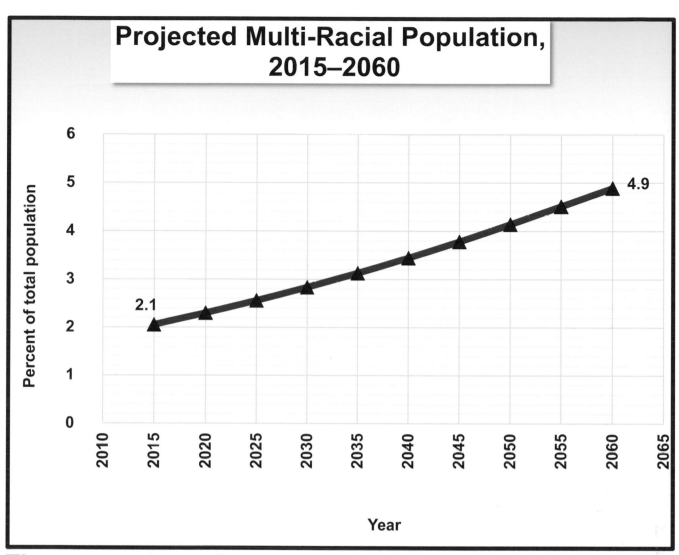

Projected Multi-Racial Population, 2015–2060

The proportion of the United States population that is multi-racial is projected by the U.S. Census Bureau to more than double between 2015–2060. By the year 2060, it is projected that almost 1 of 20 persons will be multi-racial.

Source: U.S. Census Bureau, Population Division, Table 13. Projections of the Population by Nativity, Hispanic Origin, and Race for the United States: 2015 to 2060 (NP2014-T13) http://www.census.gov/population/projections/data/national/2014/summarytables.html

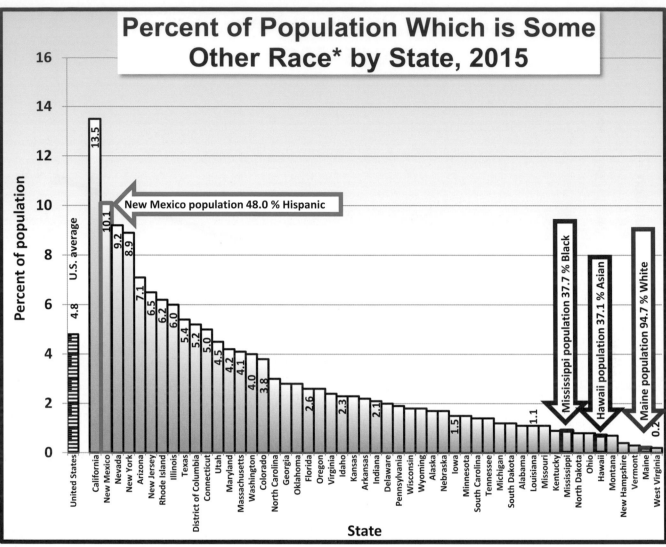

Percent of Population Which is Some Other Race* by State, 2015

New Mexico population 48.0 % Hispanic

Mississippi population 37.7 % Black

Hawaii population 37.1 % Asian

Maine population 94.7 % White

U.S. average

Percent of population

State

Approximately five percent of persons residing in the United States are of a race other than the most common five racial groups: White, Black or African American, Asian, Native Hawaiian/Pacific Islander, and American Indian/Alaska Native. More than one-of-eight persons residing in California self-identified as "Some Other Race" in 2015.

*Some Other Race means not White, Black, Asian, Native Hawaiian/Pacific Islander, or American Indian/Alaska Native. Note that Hispanic is not a race.

In 2015, there were 15.5 million U.S. residents who identified as being of "Some Other Race".

Source: U.S. Census Bureau, 2015 American Community Survey 1-Year Estimates Table 206, http://www.census.gov/programs-surveys/acs/data/summary-file.html

Chapter 2: Immigration

Since the passage of the Homeland Security Act of 2002, the Department of Homeland Security's Office of Immigration Statistics has had responsibility to carry out two statutory requirements: 1.) to collect and disseminate to Congress and the public data and information useful in evaluating the social, economic, environmental, and demographic impact of immigration laws; and 2.) to establish standards of reliability and validity for immigration statistics collected by the department's operational components.

There are three broad categories of non-citizens in the United States:

Lawful Permanent Residents (LPRs), also known as "green card" holders, are non-citizens who are lawfully authorized to live permanently within the United States. After a waiting period, generally five years, the majority of LPRs are eligible for naturalization. Naturalization confers U.S. citizenship upon foreign nationals who have fulfilled the requirements congress established in the Immigration and Nationality Act. LPRs include refugees and asylees. A refugee is a person outside his or her country of nationality who is unable or unwilling to return to his or her country of nationality because of persecution or a well-founded fear of persecution. An asylee is a person who meets the definition of refugee and is already present in the United States or is seeking admission at a port of entry.

In 2014, approximately one million LPRs were admitted, including 5,600 adopted orphans, one-third of which were born in the People's Republic of China (Red China). Admissions are based on formulae under the Immigration and Naturalization Act, the body of law governing current immigration policy. The formulae favor persons who are related to U.S. citizens. In 2013, there were 13.1 million LPRs in the U.S. of which one-quarter were from Mexico. The waiting list to become a LPR is typically over four million persons.

In addition to the formulae, each year the president and Congress set Refugee admissions levels. In 2016, 85,000 persons were granted refugee or asylee status, of which the Democratic Republic of Congo, Syria, Burma, and Iraq comprised 60 percent.

Nonimmigrants are foreign nationals granted temporary admission into the United States. The largest category, approximately 59 million persons in 2014, were visitors for pleasure, of which approximately one-third entered under the visa waiver program, in place between 38 countries. Other nonimmigrants categories include students and temporary workers. In 2014, 3.4 million temporary workers entered, of which approximately one-third were from Canada.

Unauthorized aliens are also referred to as unlawful immigrants, undocumented immigrants, undocumented foreign nationals or illegal aliens. In 2011, the Department of Homeland Security estimated there were 11.5 million unauthorized aliens in the United States. Subsequently, The PEW Research Center estimated in 2014 that the number had declined by 1.1 million from a peak in 2007 of 12.2 million.

In 2011, one-half of unauthorized aliens were born in Mexico. Approximately 3 million resided in California, 1.5 million in Texas, and 1.5 million between New York and Florida. Approximately 80 percent had been in the U.S. for over five years and nearly one-half did not speak English well. Their unemployment rate of 9.8 percent, in 2011, was near the national average of 9.0 percent. One-third earned income below the poverty level compared with one-seventh of the general population.

In 2015, 98 percent of all apprehensions of unauthorized aliens by U.S. border patrols occurred at the border with Mexico, and 55 percent of those apprehended were Mexicans. The total number of apprehensions had declined from 1.6 million in 2012 to 300,000 in 2015.

An estimated 145,000 unauthorized aliens were imprisoned in state or federal prisons in 2009, of which two-thirds were arrested for immigration law violations. The percent of arrests for offenses other than immigration violations was approximately the same as for the general population.

~

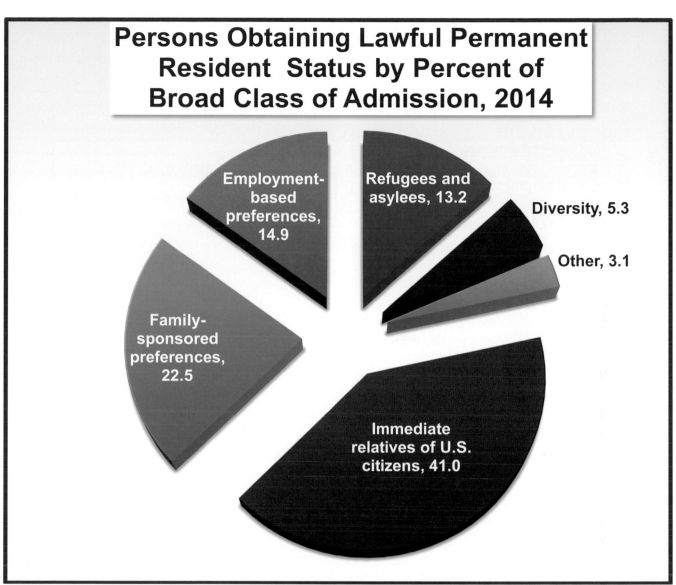

Persons Obtaining Lawful Permanent Resident Status by Percent of Broad Class of Admission, 2014

Employment-based preferences, 14.9

Refugees and asylees, 13.2

Diversity, 5.3

Other, 3.1

Family-sponsored preferences, 22.5

Immediate relatives of U.S. citizens, 41.0

In 2014, almost one-of-seven immigrants were refugees or asylees.

Of 1,016,518 persons obtaining lawful permanent resident status in fiscal year 2014, 13.2 percent were refugees or asylees. Fiscal year 2014 is defined as October 1, 2013 to September 30, 2014.

An asylee is an alien in the United States or at a port of entry whereas a refugee is outside his or her country of nationality but not within the U.S. or port of entry. Both asylees and refugees are eligible to adjust to lawful permanent resident status after one year of continuous presence in the United States. A refugee or asylee is a person who is found to be unable or unwilling to return to his or her country of nationality, or to seek the protection of that country because of persecution or a well-founded fear of persecution. Persecution or the fear thereof must be based on the alien's race, religion, nationality, membership in a particular social group, or political opinion.

Source: U.S. Department of Homeland Security, Table 9, https://www.dhs.gov/yearbook-immigration-statistics-2014-lawful-permanent-residents

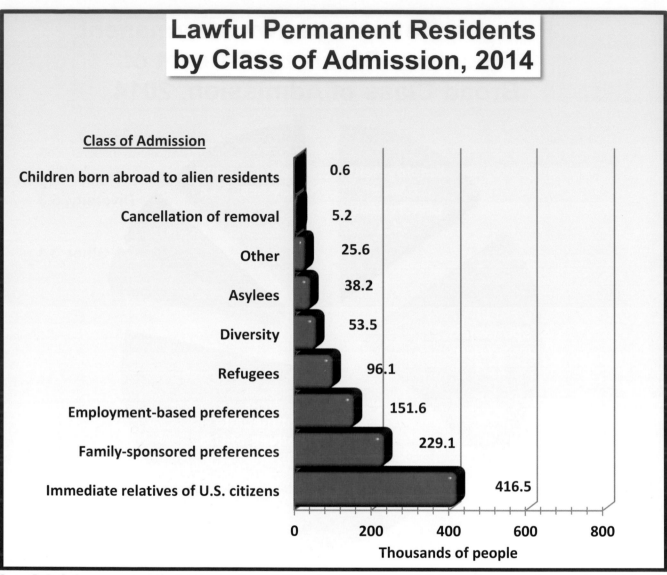

Lawful Permanent Residents by Class of Admission, 2014

Class of Admission

Class	Thousands of people
Children born abroad to alien residents	0.6
Cancellation of removal	5.2
Other	25.6
Asylees	38.2
Diversity	53.5
Refugees	96.1
Employment-based preferences	151.6
Family-sponsored preferences	229.1
Immediate relatives of U.S. citizens	416.5

Thousands of people

In 2014, approximately 40 percent of immigrants admitted were immediate relatives of United States citizens.

Lawful Permanent Residents (LPRs) are classified into nine major categories of admission. Of the 1,016,518 LPRs admitted in fiscal year 2014, 40 percent are immediate relatives of United States citizens, of which spouses comprise 57 percent. Fiscal year 2014 is defined as October 1, 2013 to September 30, 2014.

Immediate relatives of U.S. citizens are comprised of spouse, children, orphans and parents. The classification: Family-sponsored preferences is comprised of Priority 1: unmarried sons/daughters of U.S. citizens and their children; Priority 2: spouses, children, and unmarried sons/daughters of alien residents; Priority 3: married sons/daughters of U.S. citizens and their spouses and children; Priority 4: brothers/sisters of U.S. citizens (at least 21 years of age) and their spouses and children.

Source: U.S. Department of Homeland Security, Table 6, https://www.dhs.gov/yearbook-immigration-statistics-2014-lawful-permanent-residents

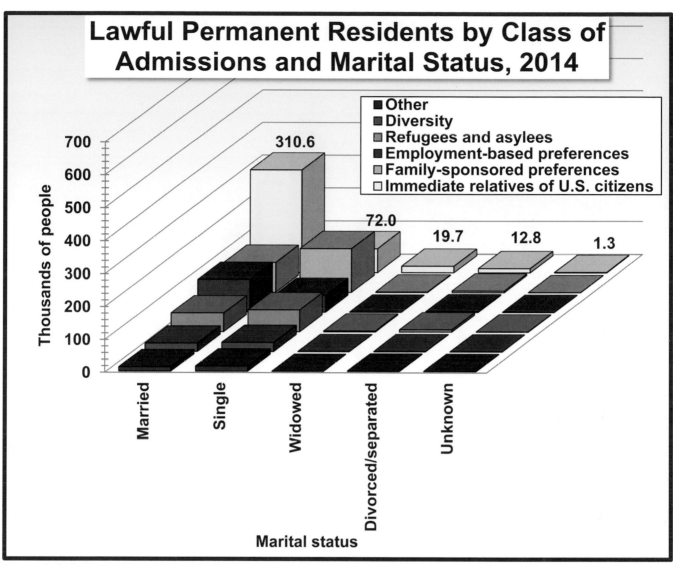

Lawful Permanent Residents by Class of Admissions and Marital Status, 2014

Legend:
- Other
- Diversity
- Refugees and asylees
- Employment-based preferences
- Family-sponsored preferences
- Immediate relatives of U.S. citizens

Values shown: 310.6, 72.0, 19.7, 12.8, 1.3

Y-axis: Thousands of people (0–700)

X-axis: Marital status — Married, Single, Widowed, Divorced/separated, Unknown

In 2014, three-of-four immigrants who were immediate relatives of United States citizens were also married.

In fiscal year 2014 nearly three-of-four (74.6 percent) of the legal permanent resident classification group "immediate relative of a United States citizen" were married. Fiscal year 2014 is defined as October 1, 2013 to September 30, 2014.

Source: U.S. Department of Homeland Security, Table 9, https://www.dhs.gov/yearbook-immigration-statistics-2014-lawful-permanent-residents

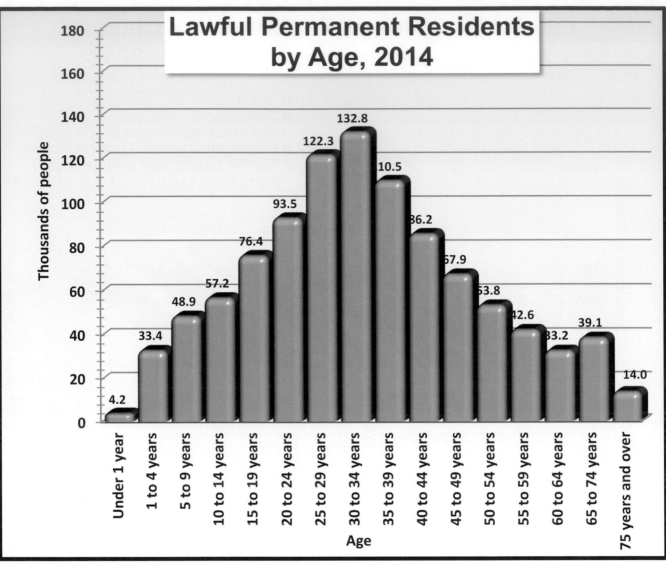

Lawful Permanent Residents by Age, 2014

In 2014, almost one-half of all immigrants admitted were between the ages of 20–39.

Forty-five percent of the 1,016,518 lawful immigrant residents admitted in fiscal year 2014 were between the ages 20-39. Fifty-eight percent were married and fourteen percent were under age 14. Fiscal year 2014 is defined as October 1, 2013 to September 30, 2014. Fiscal year 2014 is defined as October 1, 2013 to September 30, 2014.

Source: U.S. Department of Homeland Security, Table 8, https://www.dhs.gov/yearbook-immigration-statistics-2014-lawful-permanent-residents

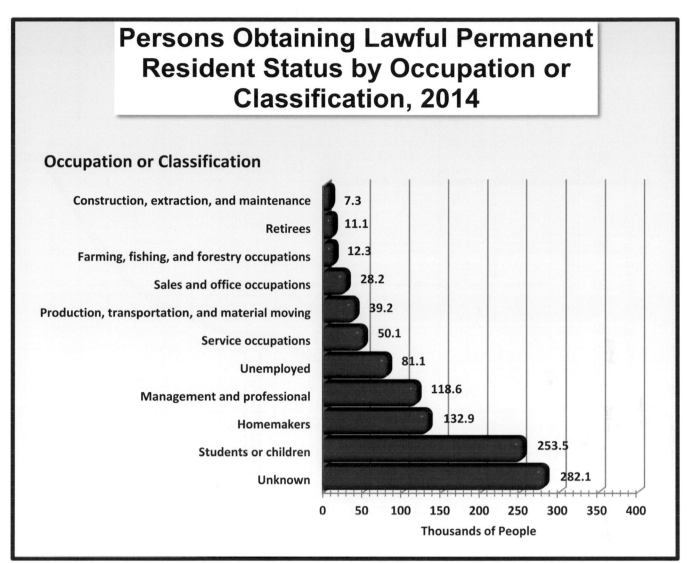

Persons Obtaining Lawful Permanent Resident Status by Occupation or Classification, 2014

Occupation or Classification

Occupation or Classification	Thousands of People
Construction, extraction, and maintenance	7.3
Retirees	11.1
Farming, fishing, and forestry occupations	12.3
Sales and office occupations	28.2
Production, transportation, and material moving	39.2
Service occupations	50.1
Unemployed	81.1
Management and professional	118.6
Homemakers	132.9
Students or children	253.5
Unknown	282.1

In 2014, approximately one-of-four Lawful Permanent Residents admitted were either students or children.

Of the 1,016,518 persons obtaining lawful permanent resident status in fiscal year 2014 persons, 24.9 percent are students or children. Fiscal year 2014 is defined as October 1, 2013 to September 30, 2014.

Lawful permanent residents are also commonly referred to as immigrants; however, the Immigration and Nationality Act (INA) broadly defines an immigrant as any alien in the United States, except one legally admitted under specific nonimmigrant categories, INA section 101(a)(15). An illegal alien who entered the United States without inspection, for example, would be strictly defined as an immigrant under the INA but is not a permanent resident alien. Lawful permanent residents are legally accorded the privilege of residing permanently in the United States. They may be issued immigrant visas by the Department of State overseas or adjusted to permanent resident status by the Department of Homeland Security in the United States.

Source: U.S. Department of Homeland Security, Table 8, https://www.dhs.gov/yearbook-immigration-statistics-2014-lawful-permanent-residents

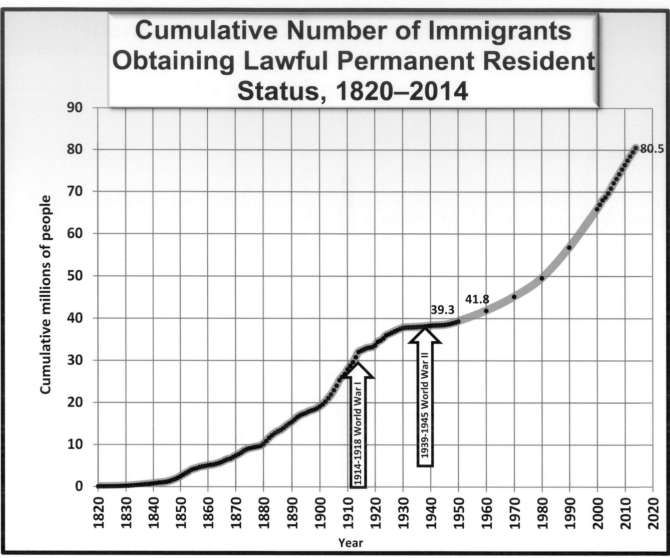

Cumulative Number of Immigrants Obtaining Lawful Permanent Resident Status, 1820–2014

Over 40 million people have immigrated to the United States between 1950 and 2014 and 80 million since 1820.

By 2014, 80,500,089 people had obtained lawful permanency residency status in the United States.

Official recording of immigration to the United States began in 1820 after the passage of the Act of March 2, 1819.

Lawful permanent residents are also commonly referred to as immigrants; however, the Immigration and Nationality Act (INA) broadly defines an immigrant as any alien in the United States, except one legally admitted under specific nonimmigrant categories, INA section 101(a)(15). An illegal alien who entered the United States without inspection, for example, would be strictly defined as an immigrant under the INA but is not a permanent resident alien.

Source: U.S. Department of Homeland Security, Table 1, https://www.dhs.gov/yearbook-immigration-statistics-2014-lawful-permanent-residents

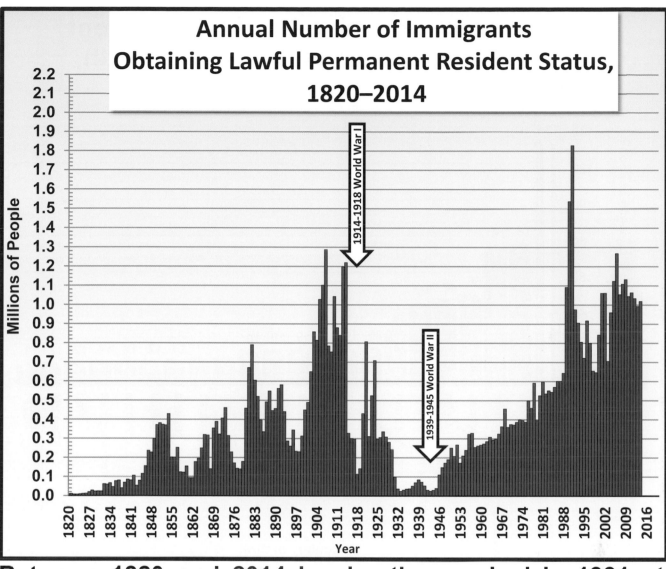

Annual Number of Immigrants Obtaining Lawful Permanent Resident Status, 1820–2014

Between 1820 and 2014 immigration peaked in 1991 at 1,827,000 persons.

United States lawful permanent residency is the immigration status of a person authorized to live and work in the U.S. permanently.

In 1991, the year the Soviet Union dissolved, the number of new U.S. lawful permanent residents peaked at 1,826,595 people.

Most of these lawful permanent residents, also commonly referred to as "green card holders", were eligible for and were granted naturalized citizenship after a five-year waiting period.

Source: U.S. Department of Homeland Security, Table 1, https://www.dhs.gov/yearbook-immigration-statistics-2014-lawful-permanent-residents

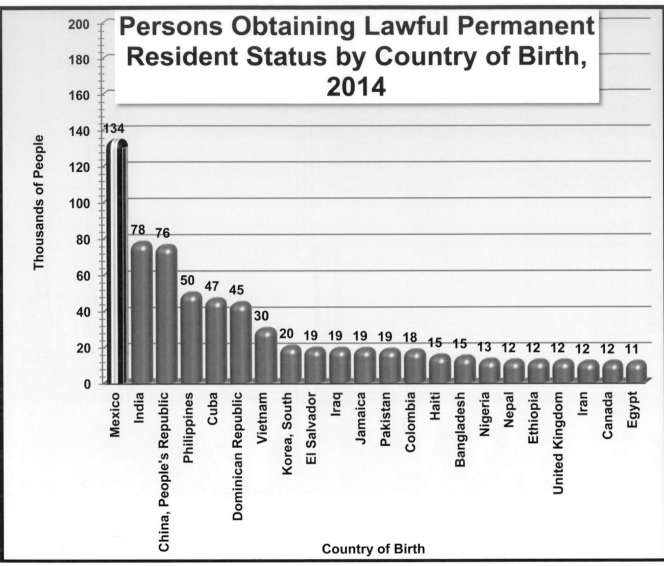

Persons Obtaining Lawful Permanent Resident Status by Country of Birth, 2014

Thousands of People

- Mexico: 134
- India: 78
- China, People's Republic: 76
- Philippines: 50
- Cuba: 47
- Dominican Republic: 45
- Vietnam: 30
- Korea, South: 20
- El Salvador: 19
- Iraq: 19
- Jamaica: 19
- Pakistan: 19
- Colombia: 18
- Haiti: 15
- Bangladesh: 15
- Nigeria: 13
- Nepal: 12
- Ethiopia: 12
- United Kingdom: 12
- Iran: 12
- Canada: 12
- Egypt: 11

Country of Birth

Approximately eight percent of the Lawful Permanent Residents (LPRs) admitted in 2014 were born in the People's Republic of China (Red China), about the same as born in India. Those born in Mexico made up the largest group of LPRs at 13 percent.

Lawful, or legal, permanent residents (LPRs) are foreign nationals who have been granted the right to reside permanently in the United States. LPRs are also known as "permanent resident aliens" and "green card holders."

Almost all people receiving lawful permanent resident status in the U.S. in 2014 reported that their country of birth was the same as their country of last residence. Fiscal year 2014 is defined as October 1, 2013 to September 30, 2014.

Source: U.S. Department of Homeland Security, Table 3d, https://www.dhs.gov/yearbook-immigration-statistics-2014-lawful-permanent-residents

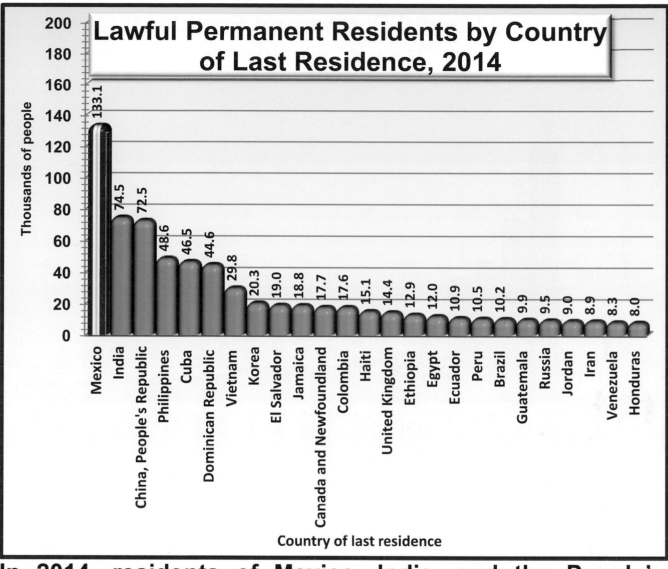

Lawful Permanent Residents by Country of Last Residence, 2014

Thousands of people / Country of last residence

Mexico 133.1
India 74.5
China, People's Republic 72.5
Philippines 48.6
Cuba 46.5
Dominican Republic 44.6
Vietnam 29.8
Korea 20.3
El Salvador 19.0
Jamaica 18.8
Canada and Newfoundland 17.7
Colombia 17.6
Haiti 15.1
United Kingdom 14.4
Ethiopia 12.9
Egypt 12.0
Ecuador 10.9
Peru 10.5
Brazil 10.2
Guatemala 9.9
Russia 9.5
Jordan 9.0
Iran 8.9
Venezuela 8.3
Honduras 8.0

In 2014, residents of Mexico, India, and the People's Republic of China (Red China) were the leading countries of residency for immigrants into the United States, accounting for approximately 28 percent of the total.

In fiscal year 2014, 1,016,518 people were granted lawful permanent resident status in the U.S. Fiscal year 2014 is defined as October 1, 2013 to September 30, 2014. Residents from Mexico were the leading donor country with 133,107 people, accounting for 13.1 percent of the total. The twenty-one countries listed above comprise 67.1 percent of the total.

Lawful permanent residents are legally accorded the privilege of residing permanently in the United States. They may be issued immigrant visas by the Department of State overseas or adjusted to permanent resident status by the Department of Homeland Security in the United States.

Source: U.S. Department of Homeland Security, Table 2, https://www.dhs.gov/yearbook-immigration-statistics-2014-lawful-permanent-residents

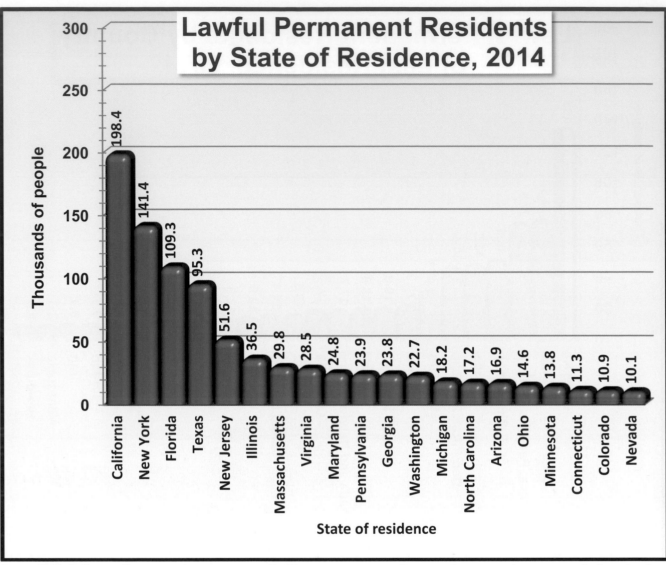

Lawful Permanent Residents by State of Residence, 2014

In 2014, almost one-of-five new immigrants resided in California.

California became home state to 198,379 new lawful permanent residents (LPR) in fiscal year 2014, representing 19.5 percent of the 1,016,518 new LPRs in the United States that year. In combination, California, New York, Florida, and Texas became the states of residency for 52.6 percent of the total LPRs whereas the combined total population of these four states represents only 32.8 percent of the total U.S. Population. Fiscal year 2014 is defined as October 1, 2013 to September 30, 2014.

The 20 states shown represent 88.4 percent of 1,016,518 total new LPRs for fiscal year 2014.

Source: U.S. Department of Homeland Security, Table 4, https://www.dhs.gov/yearbook-immigration-statistics-2014-lawful-permanent-residents

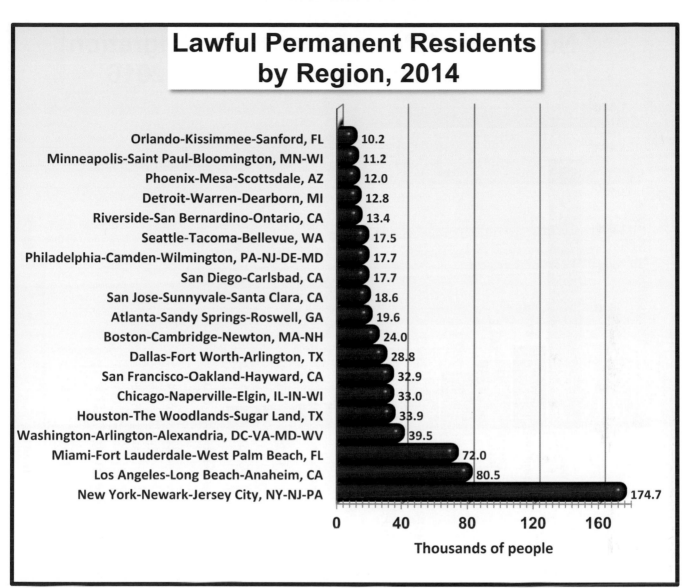

Lawful Permanent Residents by Region, 2014

Region	Thousands of people
Orlando-Kissimmee-Sanford, FL	10.2
Minneapolis-Saint Paul-Bloomington, MN-WI	11.2
Phoenix-Mesa-Scottsdale, AZ	12.0
Detroit-Warren-Dearborn, MI	12.8
Riverside-San Bernardino-Ontario, CA	13.4
Seattle-Tacoma-Bellevue, WA	17.5
Philadelphia-Camden-Wilmington, PA-NJ-DE-MD	17.7
San Diego-Carlsbad, CA	17.7
San Jose-Sunnyvale-Santa Clara, CA	18.6
Atlanta-Sandy Springs-Roswell, GA	19.6
Boston-Cambridge-Newton, MA-NH	24.0
Dallas-Fort Worth-Arlington, TX	28.8
San Francisco-Oakland-Hayward, CA	32.9
Chicago-Naperville-Elgin, IL-IN-WI	33.0
Houston-The Woodlands-Sugar Land, TX	33.9
Washington-Arlington-Alexandria, DC-VA-MD-WV	39.5
Miami-Fort Lauderdale-West Palm Beach, FL	72.0
Los Angeles-Long Beach-Anaheim, CA	80.5
New York-Newark-Jersey City, NY-NJ-PA	174.7

Thousands of people

In 2014, one-of-six new immigrants resided in or near New York City.

Of the 1,016,518 persons who became lawful permanent residents in fiscal year 2014, 174,714, or 17.2 percent resided in the New York City/Newark/Jersey City region, designated a Core Based Statistical Area (CBSA). Fiscal year 2014 is defined as October 1, 2013 to September 30, 2014.

Core Based Statistical Areas (CBSAs) are geographic areas defined by the U.S. Office of Management and Budget. CBSAs are comprised of Metropolitan and Micropolitan Statistical Areas which are defined in terms of whole counties. Metropolitan Statistical Areas have at least one urbanized area of 50,000 or more population and Micropolitan Statistical Areas have at least one urban cluster of at least 10,000 but less than 50,000 population. Both areas include adjacent territory that has a high degree of economic and social integration with the core as measured by commuting ties.

Source: U.S. Department of Homeland Security, Table 5, https://www.dhs.gov/yearbook-immigration-statistics-2014-lawful-permanent-residents

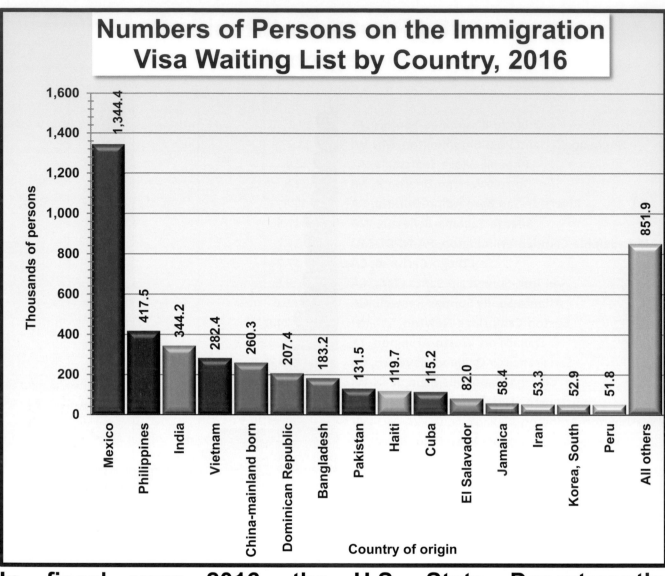

Numbers of Persons on the Immigration Visa Waiting List by Country, 2016

Thousands of persons

- Mexico — 1,344.4
- Philippines — 417.5
- India — 344.2
- Vietnam — 282.4
- China-mainland born — 260.3
- Dominican Republic — 207.4
- Bangladesh — 183.2
- Pakistan — 131.5
- Haiti — 119.7
- Cuba — 115.2
- El Salvador — 82.0
- Jamaica — 58.4
- Iran — 53.3
- Korea, South — 52.9
- Peru — 51.8
- All others — 851.9

Country of origin

In fiscal year 2016, the U.S. State Department's immigration waiting list was 4,556,021 persons worldwide, of which almost one-third were Mexicans.

Immigrant visa issuances during fiscal year 2016 was limited to no more than 226,000 in the family-sponsored preferences and approximately 140,000 in the employment-based preferences. Visas for "Immediate Relatives" (i.e., spouses, unmarried children under the age of 21 years, and parents of U.S. citizens) are not subject to numerical limitation.

The 15 countries with the highest number of waiting list registrants in fiscal year 2016 are shown on the chart and represent 81 percent of the total. This list includes all countries with at least 50,000 persons on the waiting list. There is a seven percent per-country limit, which visa issuances to any single country may not exceed. This limit serves to avoid the potential monopolization of virtually all the annual limitation by applicants from only a few countries. That limitation is not a quota to which any particular country is entitled, however for FY 2016 the per-country limit was approximately 25,620.

Source: https://travel.state.gov/content/dam/visas/Statistics/Immigrant-Statistics/WaitingListItem.pdf

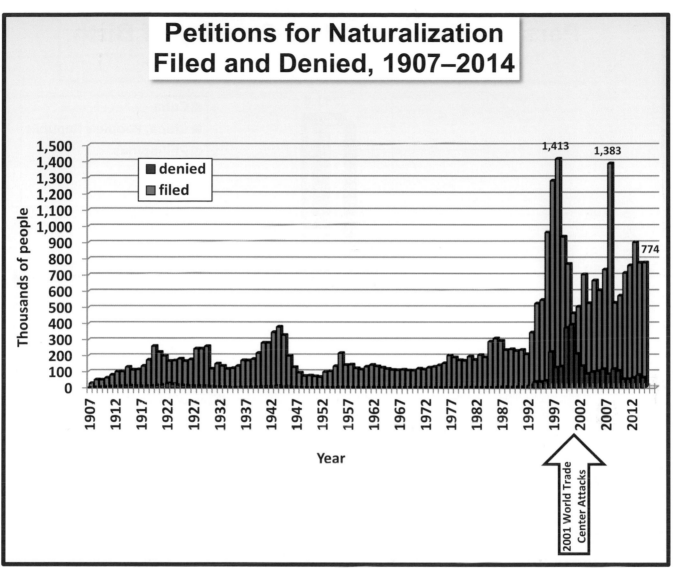

Petitions for Naturalization Filed and Denied, 1907–2014

Between 1970 and 2014, the number of filings for naturalization to become a United States citizen hit peaks in 1996 and 2007, at approximately 1.4 million persons.

Naturalization is the conferring, by any means, citizenship upon a person after birth.

Source: U.S. Department of Homeland Security, Table 20, https://www.dhs.gov/yearbook-immigration-statistics-2014-lawful-permanent-residents

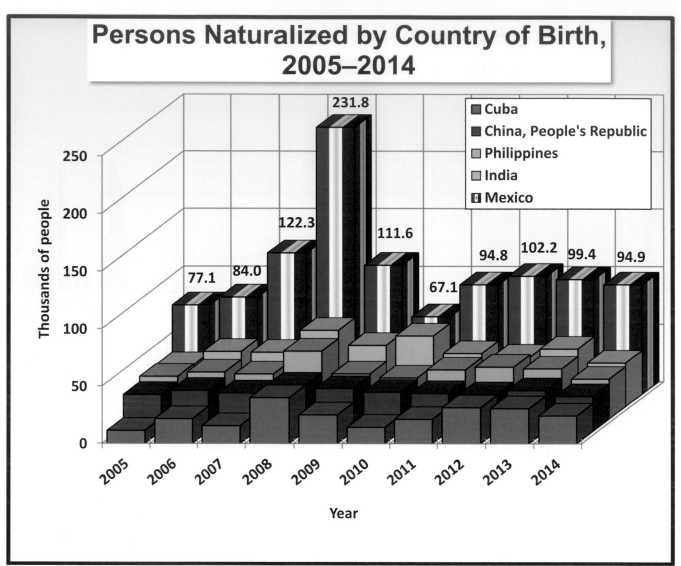

Persons Naturalized by Country of Birth, 2005–2014

Approximately one-of-seven persons naturalized in 2014 was born in Mexico, a reduction from the peak in 2008 when almost one-of-four persons naturalized was born in Mexico.

In fiscal year 2008, naturalizations peaked at 1,046,539 persons of which 22.1 percent were born in Mexico. By fiscal year 2014, this declined to 653,416 naturalizations.

The five countries shown were the leading countries of birth for naturalized persons and accounted for 42 percent of all naturalizations in 2008 and 34 percent in 2014.

Source: U.S. Department of Homeland Security, Table 21, https://www.dhs.gov/yearbook-immigration-statistics-2014-lawful-permanent-residents

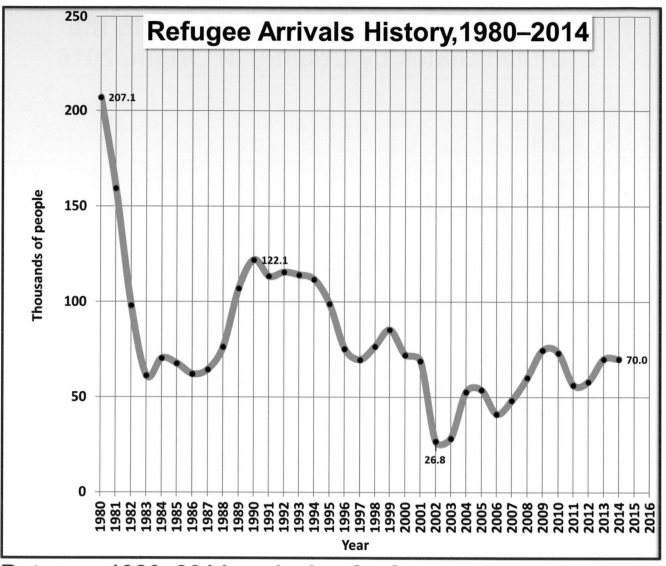

Refugee Arrivals History,1980–2014

Between 1980–2014, arrivals of refugees declined by two-thirds.

In fiscal year 1980, there were 207,000 refugee arrivals in the United States compared with only 70,000 in fiscal year 2014. Fiscal year 2014 is defined as October 1, 2013 to September 30, 2014.

Source: U.S. Department of State, Bureau of Population, Refugees, and Migration (PRM), Worldwide Refugee Admissions Processing System (WRAPS), Fiscal Years 1980 to 2014, Table 13, https://www.dhs.gov/yearbook-immigration-statistics-2014-lawful-permanent-residents

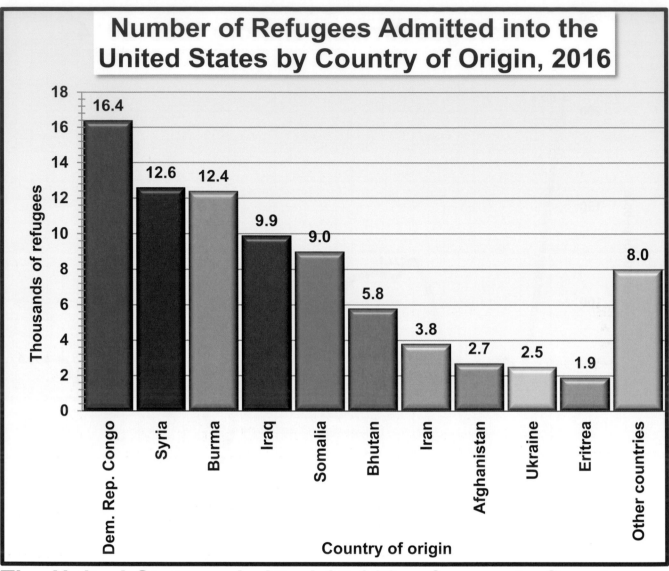

Number of Refugees Admitted into the United States by Country of Origin, 2016

Thousands of refugees

- Dem. Rep. Congo: 16.4
- Syria: 12.6
- Burma: 12.4
- Iraq: 9.9
- Somalia: 9.0
- Bhutan: 5.8
- Iran: 3.8
- Afghanistan: 2.7
- Ukraine: 2.5
- Eritrea: 1.9
- Other countries: 8.0

Country of origin

The United States admitted 85,000 refugees in fiscal year 2016, with the highest number originating from the Democratic Republic of the Congo.

A refugee is a person outside his or her country of nationality but not within the United States. or port of entry.

According to the PEW Research Center 99 percent of the Syrians admitted are Muslim.

Source: PEW Research Center, http://www.pewresearch.org/fact-tank/2016/10/05/u-s-admits-record-number-of-muslim-refugees-in-2016//

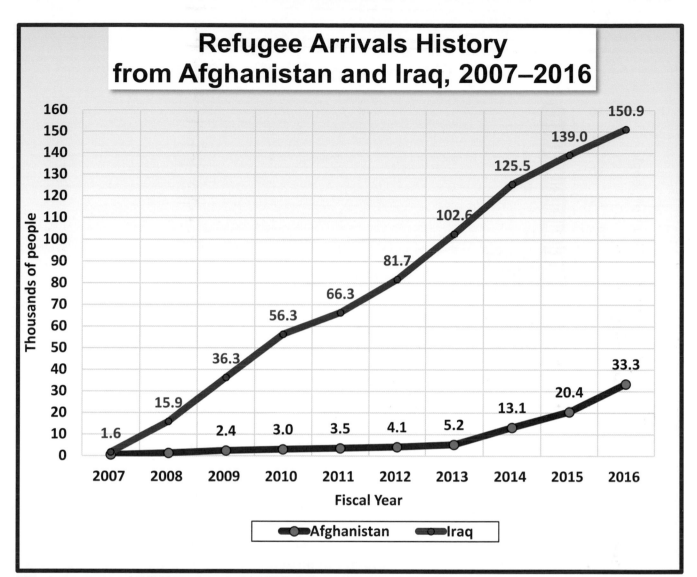

**Refugee Arrivals History
from Afghanistan and Iraq, 2007–2016**

Between 2007 and 2016, the United States admitted approximately 17,000 refugees annually from Iraq, compared with approximately 3,000 from Afghanistan.

A refugee is a person outside his or her country of nationality but not within the United States or port of entry.

Data include Refugee and Special Immigrant Visa (SIV) Arrivals. Only includes those SIV arrivals who have elected and received U.S. Refugee Admissions Program (USRAP) Reception and Placement (R&P) benefits.

Source: Department of State, Bureau of Population, Refugees, and Migration, Office of Admissions - Refugee Processing Center, http://www.acf.hhs.gov/orr/resource/refugee-arrival-data, http://www.wrapsnet.org/Reports/AdmissionsArrivals/tabid/211/Default.aspx

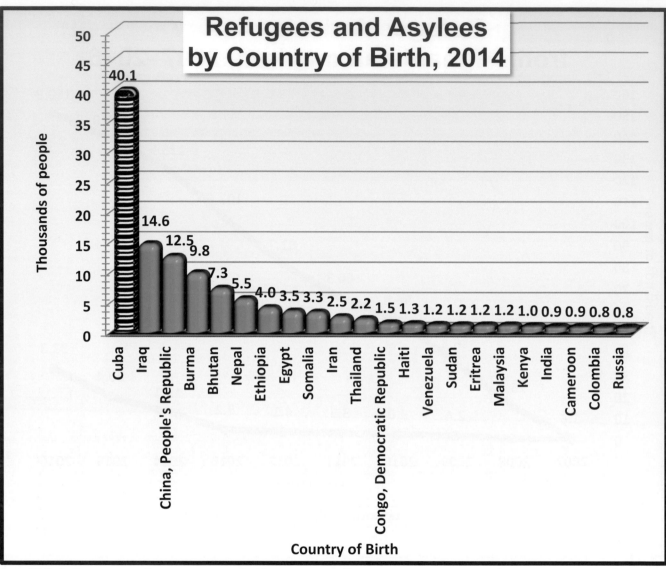

Refugees and Asylees by Country of Birth, 2014

In 2014, nearly one-of-three refugees or asylees were born in Cuba.

In fiscal year 2014, 29.8 percent of all refugees/asylees obtaining lawful permanent resident status were from Cuba. Fiscal year 2014 is defined as October 1, 2013 to September 30, 2014.

A refugee or asylee is a person who is found to be unable or unwilling to return to his or her country of nationality, or to seek the protection of that country because of persecution or a well-founded fear of persecution. Persecution or the fear thereof must be based on the alien's race, religion, nationality, membership in a particular social group, or political opinion. An asylee is an alien in the United States or at a port of entry whereas a refugee is outside his or her country of nationality but not within the U.S. or port of entry. Both asylees and refugees are eligible to adjust to lawful permanent resident status after one year of continuous presence in the United States.

Source: U.S. Department of Homeland Security, Table 10, https://www.dhs.gov/yearbook-immigration-statistics-2014-lawful-permanent-residents

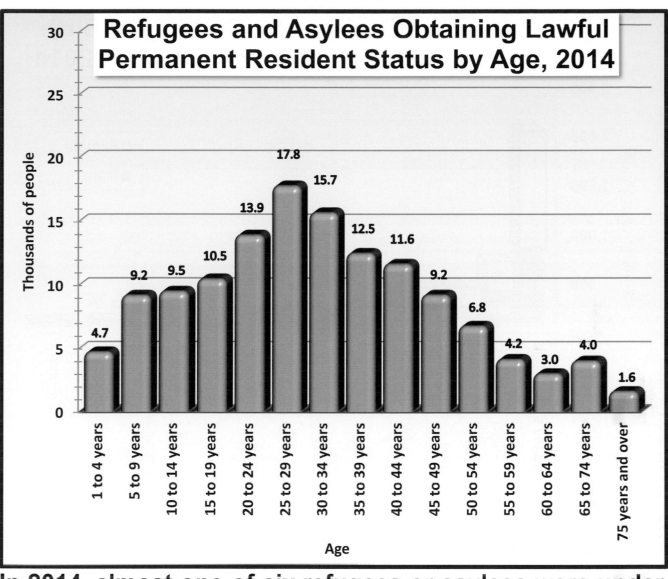

Refugees and Asylees Obtaining Lawful Permanent Resident Status by Age, 2014

Thousands of people (y-axis)

Age (x-axis)

- 1 to 4 years: 4.7
- 5 to 9 years: 9.2
- 10 to 14 years: 9.5
- 15 to 19 years: 10.5
- 20 to 24 years: 13.9
- 25 to 29 years: 17.8
- 30 to 34 years: 15.7
- 35 to 39 years: 12.5
- 40 to 44 years: 11.6
- 45 to 49 years: 9.2
- 50 to 54 years: 6.8
- 55 to 59 years: 4.2
- 60 to 64 years: 3.0
- 65 to 74 years: 4.0
- 75 years and over: 1.6

In 2014, almost one-of-six refugees or asylees were under the age of 15.

In fiscal year 2014, 134,232 persons were granted refugee or asylee status in the United States, including 23,441 children under age 15. Fiscal year 2014 is defined as October 1, 2013 to September 30, 2014.

A refugee or asylee is a person who is found to be unable or unwilling to return to his or her country of nationality, or to seek the protection of that country because of persecution or a well-founded fear of persecution. Persecution or the fear thereof must be based on the alien's race, religion, nationality, membership in a particular social group, or political opinion. An asylee is an alien in the United States or at a port of entry whereas a refugee is outside his or her country of nationality but not within the U.S. or port of entry. Both asylees and refugees are eligible to adjust to lawful permanent resident status after one year of continuous presence in the United States.

Source: U.S. Department of Homeland Security, Table 9, https://www.dhs.gov/yearbook-immigration-statistics-2014-lawful-permanent-residents

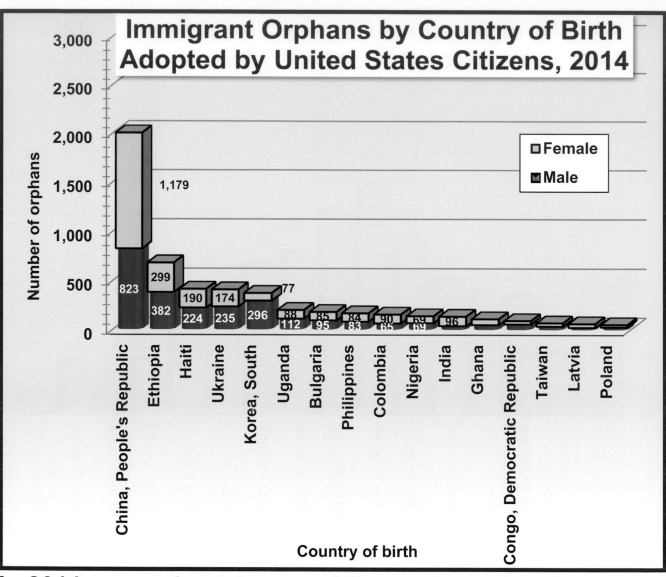

Immigrant Orphans by Country of Birth Adopted by United States Citizens, 2014

Number of orphans

Female
Male

China, People's Republic: 1,179 / 823
Ethiopia: 299 / 382
Haiti: 190 / 224
Ukraine: 174 / 235
Korea, South: 296
Uganda: 77 / 88 / 112
Bulgaria: 85 / 95
Philippines: 84 / 83
Colombia: 90 / 65
Nigeria: 69 / 69
India: 96

Country of birth

In 2014, approximately one-of-three adopted orphans was born in the People's Republic of China (Red China).

Orphans born in the People's Republic of China (Red China) accounted for 33.4 percent of all orphans adopted by U.S. citizens in fiscal year 2014 of which 59 percent were girls. There was a total of 5,594 orphans adopted and the 16 countries shown represent 87 percent.
Fiscal year 2014 is defined as October 1, 2013 to September 30, 2014.

Source: U.S. Department of Homeland Security, Table 12, https://www.dhs.gov/yearbook-immigration-statistics-2014-lawful-permanent-residents

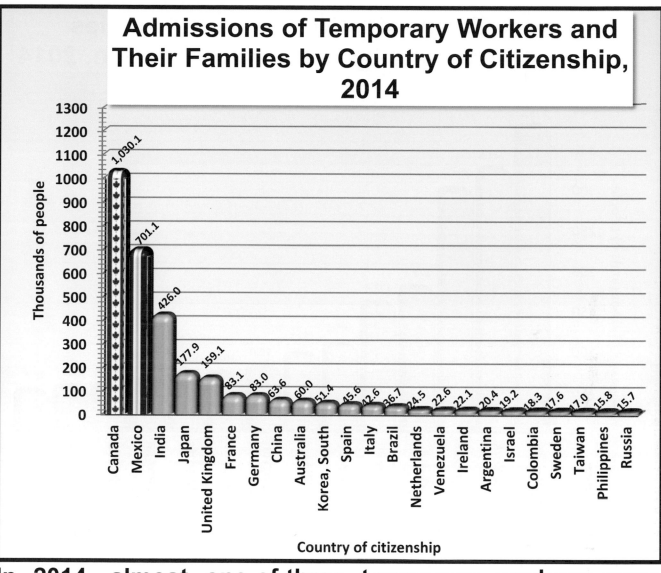

Admissions of Temporary Workers and Their Families by Country of Citizenship, 2014

Thousands of people

Country of citizenship

Canada: 1,030.1
Mexico: 701.1
India: 426.0
Japan: 177.9
United Kingdom: 159.1
France: 83.1
Germany: 83.0
China: 63.6
Australia: 60.0
Korea, South: 51.4
Spain: 45.6
Italy: 42.6
Brazil: 36.7
Netherlands: 24.5
Venezuela: 22.6
Ireland: 22.1
Argentina: 20.4
Israel: 19.2
Colombia: 18.3
Sweden: 17.6
Taiwan: 17.0
Philippines: 15.8
Russia: 15.7

In 2014, almost one-of-three temporary workers were Canadian citizens.

In fiscal year 2014, 3.4 million temporary workers were granted admission to the United States of which one million were Canadian citizens. Mexican citizens were the second largest group with 700,000. Citizens of Canada and Mexico comprised 51 percent of all temporary workers in fiscal year 2014. The countries listed in the chart represent 93 percent.

Note that China refers to the People's Republic (Red China) plus Hong Kong and Macau.

Fiscal year 2014 is defined as October 1, 2013 to September 30, 2014.

Source: U.S. Department of Homeland Security, Table 28, https://www.dhs.gov/yearbook-immigration-statistics-2014-lawful-permanent-residents

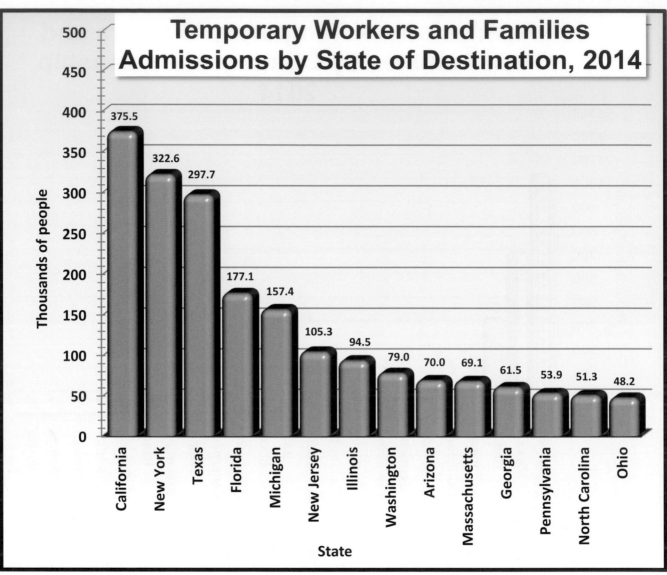

Temporary Workers and Families Admissions by State of Destination, 2014

In 2014, over three million temporary workers were admitted and 11 percent worked in California.

In fiscal year 2014, there were 3,398,961 temporary workers and families admitted into the United States. Thirty-five percent identified the states of California, New York, Texas, or Florida as their destination. Citizens from the countries identified on the chart represent 57.8 percent of the total.

Fiscal year 2014 is defined as October 1, 2013 to September 30, 2014.

Source: U.S. Department of Homeland Security, Table 30, https://www.dhs.gov/yearbook-immigration-statistics-2014-lawful-permanent-residents

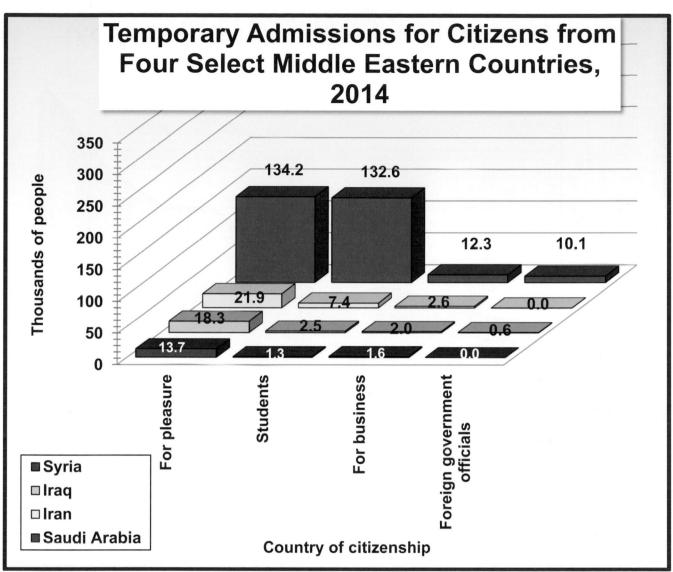

Temporary Admissions for Citizens from Four Select Middle Eastern Countries, 2014

Legend:
- ■ Syria
- □ Iraq
- □ Iran
- ■ Saudi Arabia

Country of citizenship

In 2014, almost 14,000 Syrians visited the United States as tourists.

There were 360,961 nonimmigrant admissions for citizens of the four select middle-eastern countries shown in the chart, for fiscal year 2014, including 21,860 tourists from Iran and 13,737 tourists from Syria.

Fiscal year 2014 is defined as October 1, 2013 to September 30, 2014.

Source: U.S. Department of Homeland Security, https://www.dhs.gov/yearbook-immigration-statistics-2014-lawful-permanent-residents, NI Supplement table 1

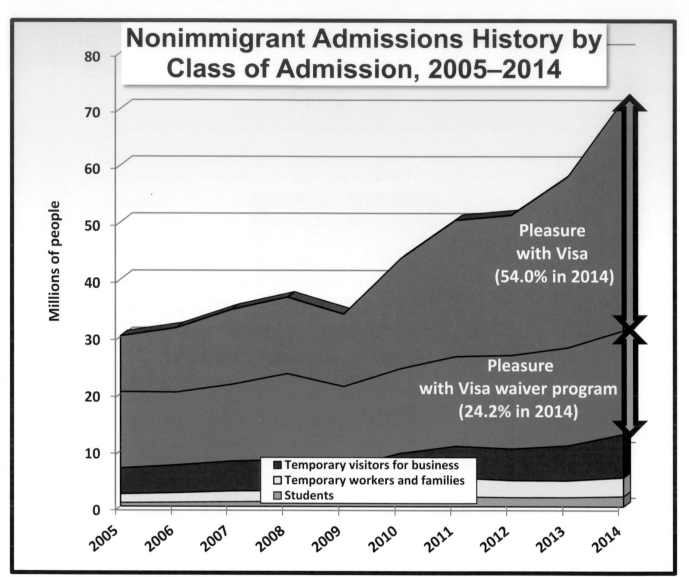

Nonimmigrant Admissions History by Class of Admission, 2005–2014

Millions of people

Pleasure
with Visa
(54.0% in 2014)

Pleasure
with Visa waiver program
(24.2% in 2014)

■ Temporary visitors for business
□ Temporary workers and families
■ Students

2005 2006 2007 2008 2009 2010 2011 2012 2013 2014

Between 2009 and 2014, the number of temporary visitors doubled to over 70 million persons, and approximately three-quarters were pleasure-visitors.

In 2014, a total of 74,930,606 non-immigrant visitors entered the United States. Temporary visitors for pleasure comprised 76.2 percent of all visitors and approximately one-third of those were admitted under the visa waiver program. Only 4.5 percent of temporary visitors were workers or their families.

The Visa Waiver Program allows citizens of certain selected countries, traveling temporarily to the United States under the nonimmigrant admission classes of visitors for pleasure and visitors for business, to enter the United States without obtaining nonimmigrant visas. Admission is for no more than 90 days. The Visa Waiver Program was made permanent in 2000.

Source: U.S. Department of Homeland Security, Table 25, https://www.dhs.gov/yearbook-immigration-statistics-2014-lawful-permanent-residents

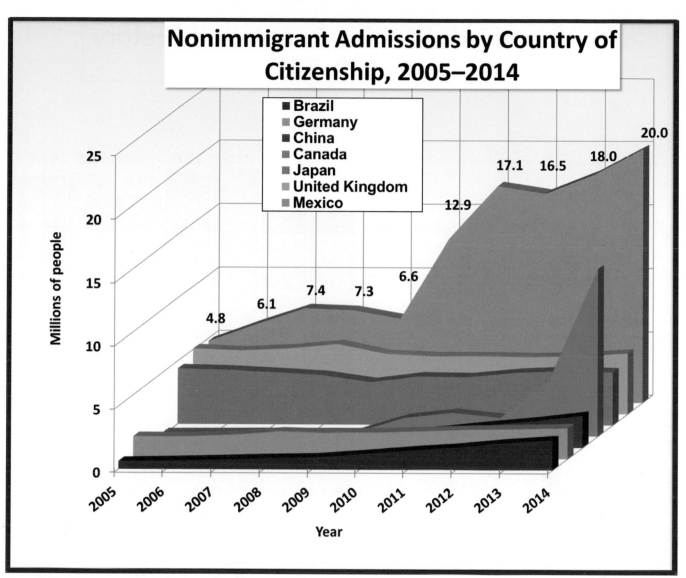

Nonimmigrant Admissions by Country of Citizenship, 2005–2014

Legend:
- Brazil
- Germany
- China
- Canada
- Japan
- United Kingdom
- Mexico

Y-axis: Millions of people
X-axis: Year

Data labels: 4.8, 6.1, 7.4, 7.3, 6.6, 12.9, 17.1, 16.5, 18.0, 20.0

In 2014, citizens of Mexico were the leading visitors to the United States.

The total number of nonimmigrant admissions to the U.S. has increased from 32.0 million in 2005 to 74.9 million in 2014. Citizens from the countries shown on the chart accounted for 66.3 percent of those admissions in 2014 and Mexico, alone, accounted for 26.7 percent.

Admissions by citizens of Canada have surged from 1.4 million in 2012 to 13.3 million in 2014 However, this may be due to a more complete count of Canadian air and sea admissions.

Source: U.S. Department of Homeland Security, Table 26, https://www.dhs.gov/yearbook-immigration-statistics-2014-lawful-permanent-residents

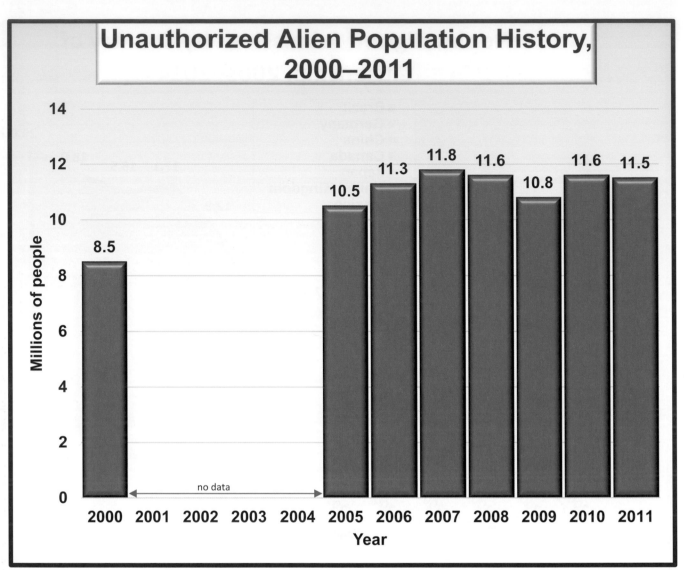

Unauthorized Alien Population History, 2000–2011

Millions of people / *Year*

- 2000: 8.5
- 2001–2004: no data
- 2005: 10.5
- 2006: 11.3
- 2007: 11.8
- 2008: 11.6
- 2009: 10.8
- 2010: 11.6
- 2011: 11.5

In 2011, the Department of Homeland Security estimated there were 11.5 million unauthorized aliens in the United States.

The legally resident immigrant population as defined for these estimates includes all persons who were granted lawful permanent residence, granted asylum, admitted as refugees, or admitted as nonimmigrants for a temporary stay in the United States and not required to leave by January 1, 2011. Nonimmigrant residents refer to certain aliens who were legally admitted temporarily to the United States such as students and temporary workers.

An alien is any person not a citizen or national of the United States.

Source: Department of Homeland Security (DHS)," Estimates of unauthorized immigrant population residing in the United States, January 2011", https://www.dhs.gov/sites/default/files/publications/ois_ill_pe_2011_0.pdf

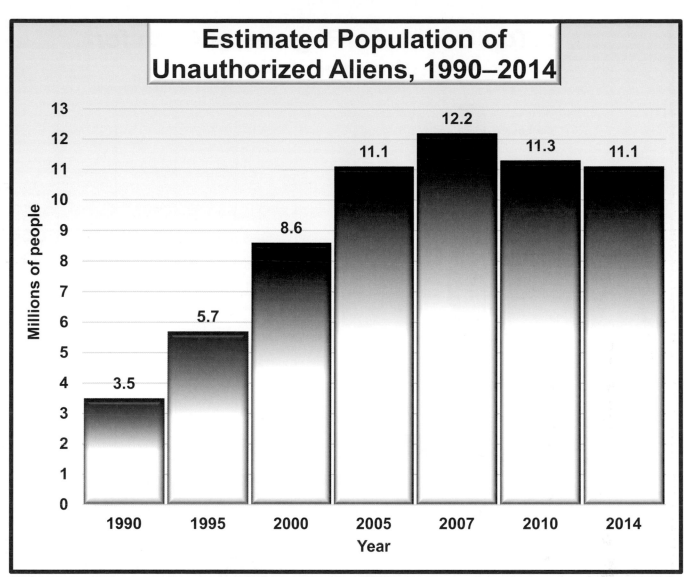

Estimated Population of Unauthorized Aliens, 1990–2014

Millions of people

- 1990: 3.5
- 1995: 5.7
- 2000: 8.6
- 2005: 11.1
- 2007: 12.2
- 2010: 11.3
- 2014: 11.1

Year

The number of unauthorized aliens was estimated by the PEW Research Center to have declined by 1.1 million between 2007 and 2014.

According to estimates by PEW Research the undocumented immigrant population peaked in 2012 at 12.2 million.

Source: PEW Research Center, Five Facts About Illegal Immigration, September 16, 2016, accessed October 28, 2016, http://www.pewresearch.org/fact-tank/2016/09/20/5-facts-about-illegal-immigration-in-the-u-s/

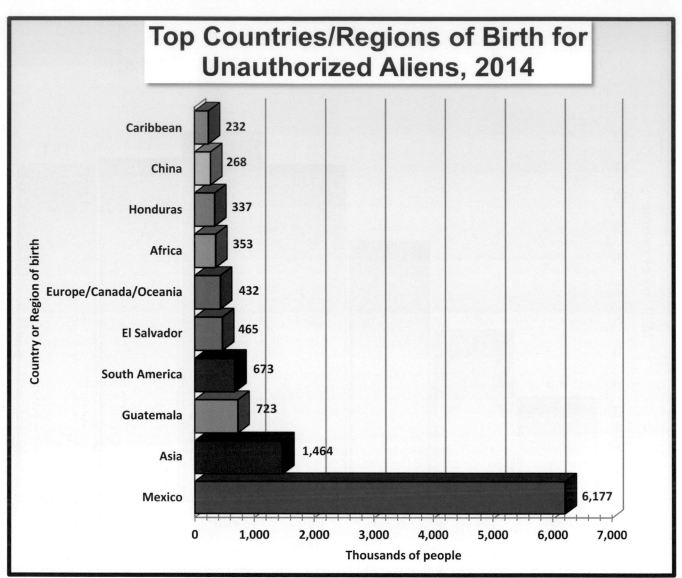

Top Countries/Regions of Birth for Unauthorized Aliens, 2014

Country or Region of birth

- Caribbean 232
- China 268
- Honduras 337
- Africa 353
- Europe/Canada/Oceania 432
- El Salvador 465
- South America 673
- Guatemala 723
- Asia 1,464
- Mexico 6,177

0   1,000   2,000   3,000   4,000   5,000   6,000   7,000

Thousands of people

In 2014, an estimated 56 percent of unauthorized aliens were born in Mexico.

The Migration Policy Institute's estimates use commonly accepted benchmarks from other research studies to determine the size of the unauthorized population. These estimates have the same sampling and coverage errors as any other survey-based estimates that rely on American Community Survey (ACS) and other Census Bureau data.

An alien is any person not a citizen or national of the United States.

Source: Source: Migration Policy Institute (MPI) Data Hub, "Unauthorized Immigrant Population Profiles", accessed October 15, 2016, http://www.migrationpolicy.org/programs/us-immigration-policyprogram-data-hub/unauthorized-immigrant-population-profiles

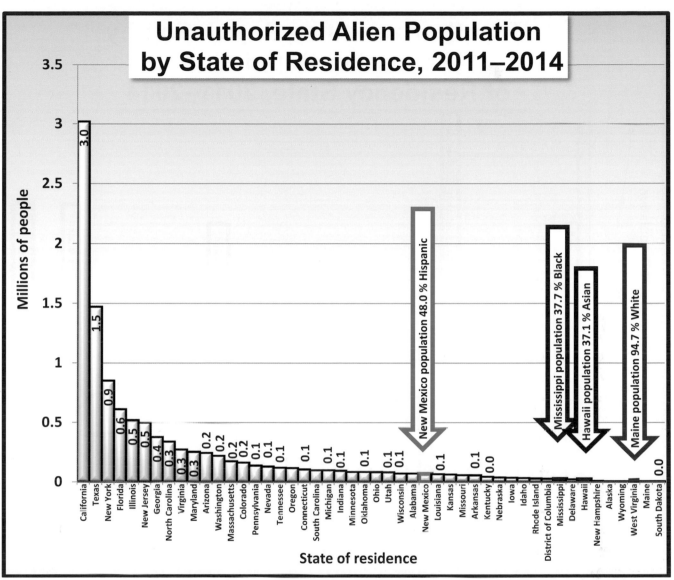

Unauthorized Alien Population by State of Residence, 2011–2014

In 2014, California led the nation with an estimated three million unauthorized aliens.

The Migration Policy Institute's estimates use commonly accepted benchmarks from other research studies to determine the size of the unauthorized population. These estimates have the same sampling and coverage errors as any other survey-based estimates that rely on American Community Survey (ACS) and other Census Bureau data.

Data for Vermont, Montana, and North Dakota are not available.

An alien is any person not a citizen or national of the United States.

Source: Migration Policy Institute (MPI) Data Hub, "Unauthorized Immigrant Population Profiles", accessed October 15, 2016, http://www.migrationpolicy.org/programs/us-immigration-policyprogram-data-hub/unauthorized-immigrant-population-profiles

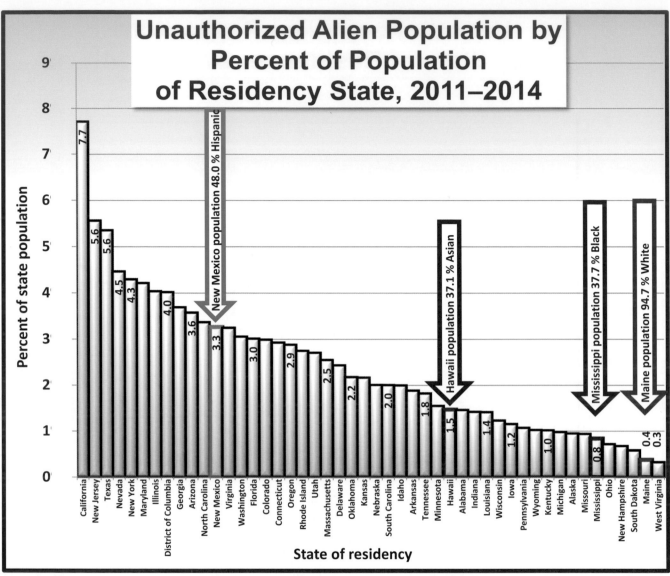

Unauthorized Alien Population by Percent of Population of Residency State, 2011–2014

Percent of state population / State of residency

California 7.7, New Jersey 5.6, Texas 5.6, Nevada 4.5, New York 4.3, Maryland, Illinois 4.0, District of Columbia, Georgia 3.6, Arizona, North Carolina, New Mexico 3.3 (New Mexico population 48.0 % Hispanic), Virginia, Washington, Florida 3.0, Colorado, Connecticut, Oregon 2.9, Rhode Island, Utah, Massachusetts 2.5, Delaware, Oklahoma 2.2, Kansas, Nebraska, South Carolina 2.0, Idaho, Arkansas, Tennessee 1.8, Minnesota, Hawaii 1.5 (Hawaii population 37.1 % Asian), Alabama, Indiana, Louisiana 1.4, Wisconsin, Iowa 1.2, Pennsylvania, Wyoming, Kentucky 1.0, Michigan, Alaska, Missouri, Mississippi 0.8 (Mississippi population 37.7 % Black), Ohio, New Hampshire, South Dakota, Maine 0.4 (Maine population 94.7 % White), West Virginia 0.3

In 2014, almost eight percent of California's population was estimated to be unauthorized aliens—the highest in the nation.

In 2011, there were an estimated 11,009,000 unauthorized immigrants in the United States. Percentages shown on graph utilized 2015 population survey by U.S. Census Bureau. The Migration Policy Institute's estimates use commonly accepted benchmarks from other research studies to determine the size of the unauthorized population. These estimates have the same sampling and coverage errors as any other survey-based estimates that rely on American Community Survey (ACS) and other Census Bureau data.

Data for Vermont, Montana, and North Dakota are not available. An alien is any person not a citizen or national of the United States.

Source: Migration Policy Institute (MPI) Data Hub, "Unauthorized Immigrant Population Profiles", accessed October 15, 2016, http://www.migrationpolicy.org/programs/us-immigration-policyprogram-data-hub/unauthorized-immigrant-population-profiles, 2015 population estimates from U.S. Census Bureau, 2015 American Community Survey 1-Year Estimates, http://www.census.gov/programs-surveys/acs/data/summary-file.html

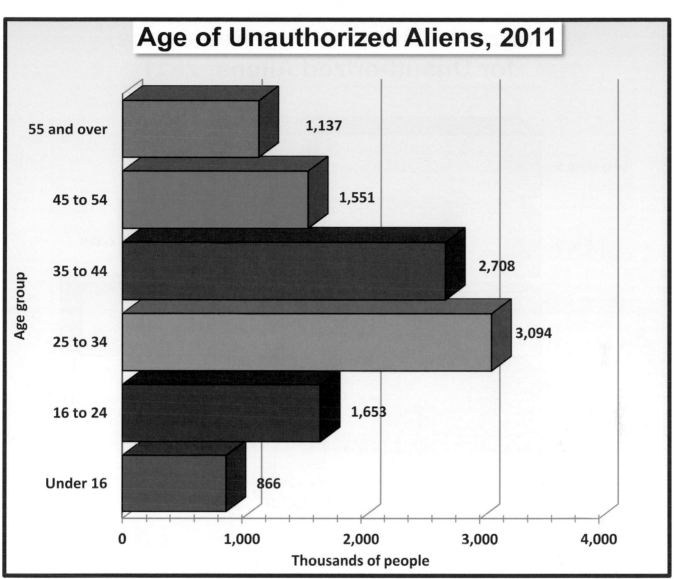

Age of Unauthorized Aliens, 2011

Age group	Thousands of people
55 and over	1,137
45 to 54	1,551
35 to 44	2,708
25 to 34	3,094
16 to 24	1,653
Under 16	866

In 2011, an estimated eight percent of unauthorized aliens were under the age of 16.

The Migration Policy Institute's estimates use commonly accepted benchmarks from other research studies to determine the size of the unauthorized population. These estimates have the same sampling and coverage errors as any other survey-based estimates that rely on American Community Survey (ACS) and other Census Bureau data.

An alien is any person not a citizen or national of the United States.

Source: Migration Policy Institute (MPI) Data Hub, "Unauthorized Immigrant Population Profiles", accessed October 15, 2016, http://www.migrationpolicy.org/programs/us-immigration-policyprogram-data-hub/unauthorized-immigrant-population-profiles, Department of Homeland Security (DHS)," Estimates of unauthorized immigrant population residing in the United States, January 2011", https://www.dhs.gov/sites/default/files/publications/ois_ill_pe_2011_0.pdf

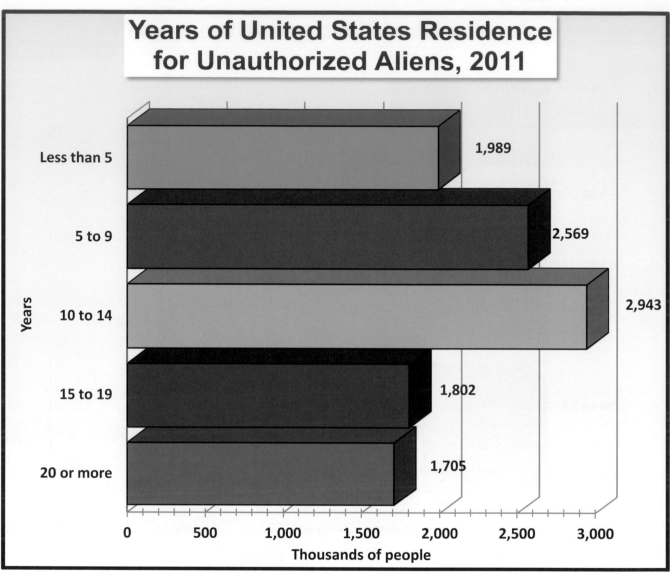

Years of United States Residence for Unauthorized Aliens, 2011

Less than 5 — 1,989
5 to 9 — 2,569
10 to 14 — 2,943
15 to 19 — 1,802
20 or more — 1,705

Years

Thousands of people

In 2011, an estimated 15 percent of unauthorized aliens lived in the United States for 20 years or more.

In 2011, there were an estimated 11,009,000 unauthorized immigrants in the United States. An estimated 15 percent, based on the 2015 population survey by U.S. Census Bureau, have lived in the United States for more than 20 years.

The Migration Policy Institute's estimates use commonly accepted benchmarks from other research studies to determine the size of the unauthorized population. These estimates have the same sampling and coverage errors as any other survey-based estimates that rely on American Community Survey (ACS) and other Census Bureau data.

An alien is any person not a citizen or national of the United States.

Source: Migration Policy Institute (MPI) Data Hub, "Unauthorized Immigrant Population Profiles", accessed October 15, 2016, http://www.migrationpolicy.org/programs/us-immigration-policyprogram-data-hub/unauthorized-immigrant-population-profiles

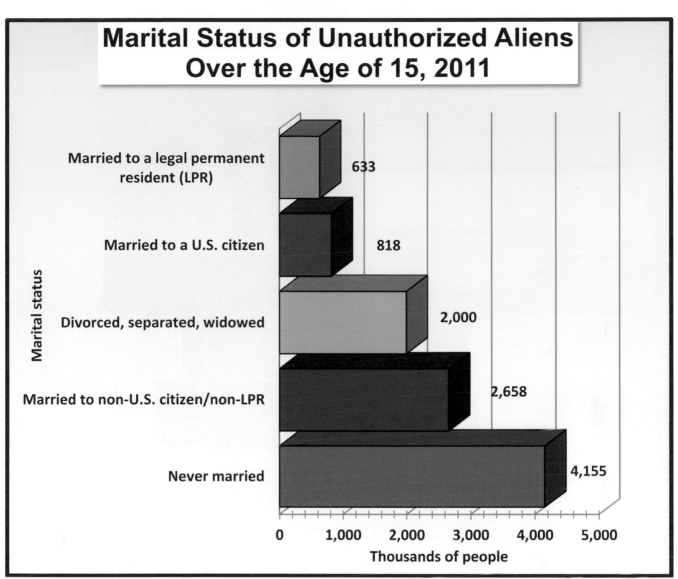

Marital Status of Unauthorized Aliens Over the Age of 15, 2011

Married to a legal permanent resident (LPR) — 633

Married to a U.S. citizen — 818

Divorced, separated, widowed — 2,000

Married to non-U.S. citizen/non-LPR — 2,658

Never married — 4,155

Marital status

Thousands of people

In 2011, eight percent of unauthorized aliens over the age of 15 were estimated to be married to a United States citizen.

The Migration Policy Institute's estimates use commonly accepted benchmarks from other research studies to determine the size of the unauthorized population. These estimates have the same sampling and coverage errors as any other survey-based estimates that rely on American Community Survey (ACS) and other Census Bureau data.

An alien is any person not a citizen or national of the United States.

Source: Migration Policy Institute (MPI) Data Hub, "Unauthorized Immigrant Population Profiles", accessed October 15, 2016, http://www.migrationpolicy.org/programs/us-immigration-policyprogram-data-hub/unauthorized-immigrant-population-profiles

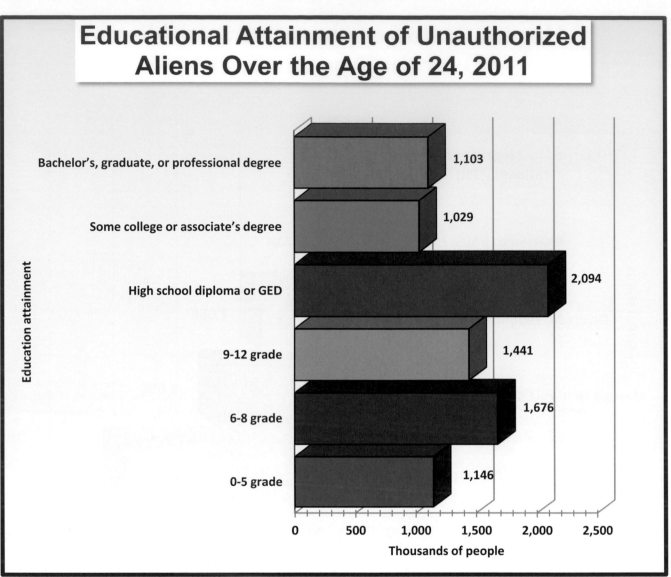

Educational Attainment of Unauthorized Aliens Over the Age of 24, 2011

Bachelor's, graduate, or professional degree — 1,103

Some college or associate's degree — 1,029

High school diploma or GED — 2,094

9-12 grade — 1,441

6-8 grade — 1,676

0-5 grade — 1,146

Education attainment

Thousands of people

In 2011, an estimated one-of-four unauthorized aliens over the age of 24 had an associate's degree or higher.

The Migration Policy Institute's estimates use commonly accepted benchmarks from other research studies to determine the size of the unauthorized population. These estimates have the same sampling and coverage errors as any other survey-based estimates that rely on American Community Survey (ACS) and other Census Bureau data.

An alien is any person not a citizen or national of the United States.

Source: Migration Policy Institute (MPI) Data Hub, "Unauthorized Immigrant Population Profiles", accessed October 15, 2016, http://www.migrationpolicy.org/programs/us-immigration-policyprogram-data-hub/unauthorized-immigrant-population-profiles

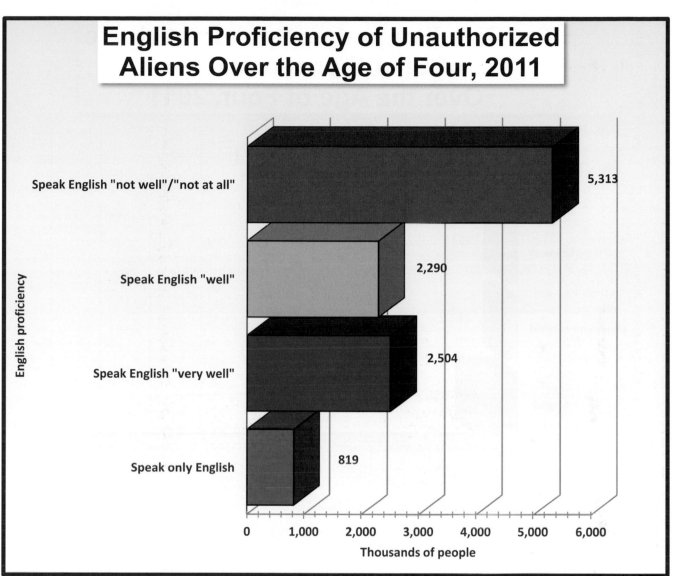

English Proficiency of Unauthorized Aliens Over the Age of Four, 2011

English proficiency

Speak English "not well"/"not at all" — 5,313

Speak English "well" — 2,290

Speak English "very well" — 2,504

Speak only English — 819

0   1,000   2,000   3,000   4,000   5,000   6,000

Thousands of people

In 2011, an estimated one-half of unauthorized aliens over the age of four did not speak English well, or not at all.

The Migration Policy Institute's estimates use commonly accepted benchmarks from other research studies to determine the size of the unauthorized population. These estimates have the same sampling and coverage errors as any other survey-based estimates that rely on American Community Survey (ACS) and other Census Bureau data.

An alien is any person not a citizen or national of the United States.

Source: Migration Policy Institute (MPI) Data Hub, "Unauthorized Immigrant Population Profiles", accessed October 15, 2016, http://www.migrationpolicy.org/programs/us-immigration-policyprogram-data-hub/unauthorized-immigrant-population-profiles

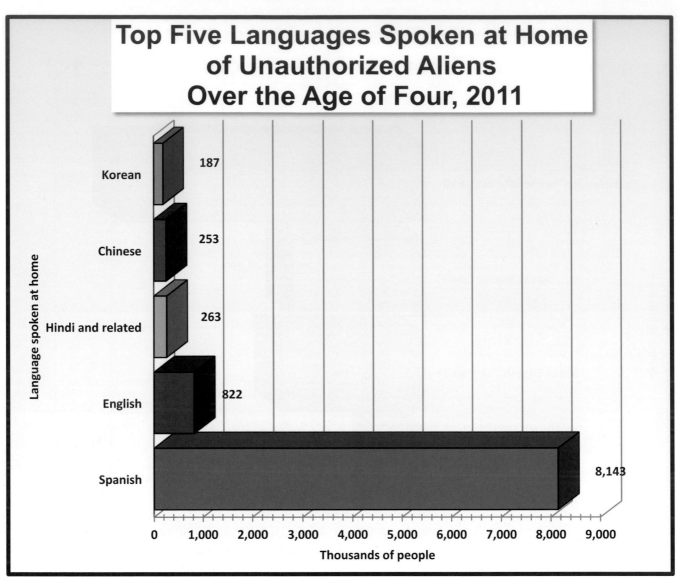

Top Five Languages Spoken at Home of Unauthorized Aliens Over the Age of Four, 2011

Language spoken at home

Korean — 187

Chinese — 253

Hindi and related — 263

English — 822

Spanish — 8,143

Thousands of people

In 2011, an estimated 84 percent of unauthorized aliens over the age of four spoke Spanish at home compared with seven percent who spoke English at home.

"Chinese" includes Mandarin, Cantonese, and other Chinese languages; "English" includes English, Jamaican Creole, Krio, and Pidgin Krio; "Hindi and related" includes Hindi, Urdu, Bengali, Punjabi, Marathi, Gujarati, Sindhi, Sinhalese, and Kannada

An alien is any person not a citizen or national of the United States.

Source: Migration Policy Institute (MPI) Data Hub, "Unauthorized Immigrant Population Profiles", accessed October 15, 2016, http://www.migrationpolicy.org/programs/us-immigration-policyprogram-data-hub/unauthorized-immigrant-population-profiles

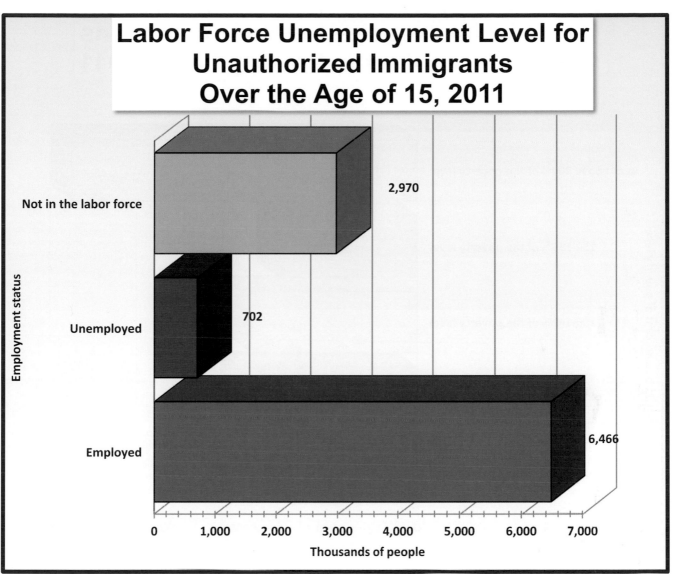

Labor Force Unemployment Level for Unauthorized Immigrants Over the Age of 15, 2011

In 2011, an estimated 9.7 percent of unauthorized aliens over the age of 15 were unemployed similar to 9.0 percent of the general United States population.

In 2011, the Migration Policy Institute estimated that .70 million were unemployed and 2.97 million were employed (9.8 percent unemployed), which was below the national average of 9.0 percent, published by the U.S. Bureau of Labor Statistics. In 2011, there were an estimated 11,009,000 unauthorized immigrants in the United States. Percentages shown on graph utilized 2015 population survey by U.S. Census Bureau. The Migration Policy Institute's estimates use commonly accepted benchmarks from other research studies to determine the size of the unauthorized population. These estimates have the same sampling and coverage errors as any other survey-based estimates that rely on American Community Survey (ACS) and other Census Bureau data.

An alien is any person not a citizen or national of the United States.

Source: Migration Policy Institute (MPI) Data Hub, "Unauthorized Immigrant Population Profiles", accessed October 15, 2016, http://www.migrationpolicy.org/programs/us-immigration-policyprogram-data-hub/unauthorized-immigrant-population-profiles

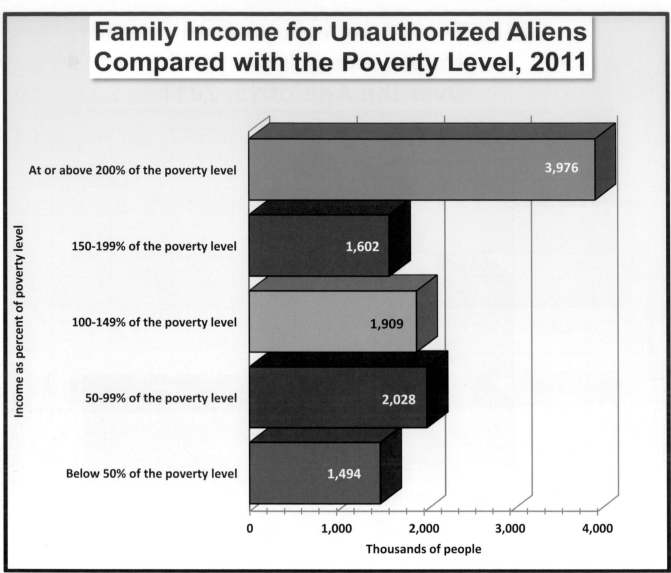

Family Income for Unauthorized Aliens Compared with the Poverty Level, 2011

Income as percent of poverty level

- At or above 200% of the poverty level — 3,976
- 150-199% of the poverty level — 1,602
- 100-149% of the poverty level — 1,909
- 50-99% of the poverty level — 2,028
- Below 50% of the poverty level — 1,494

0   1,000   2,000   3,000   4,000

Thousands of people

In 2011, an estimated one-third of unauthorized alien families earned income at or below the poverty level.

The Migration Policy Institute's estimates use commonly accepted benchmarks from other research studies to determine the size of the unauthorized population. These estimates have the same sampling and coverage errors as any other survey-based estimates that rely on American Community Survey (ACS) and other Census Bureau data.

An alien is any person not a citizen or national of the United States.

Source: Migration Policy Institute (MPI) Data Hub, "Unauthorized Immigrant Population Profiles", accessed October 15, 2016, http://www.migrationpolicy.org/programs/us-immigration-policyprogram-data-hub/unauthorized-immigrant-population-profiles

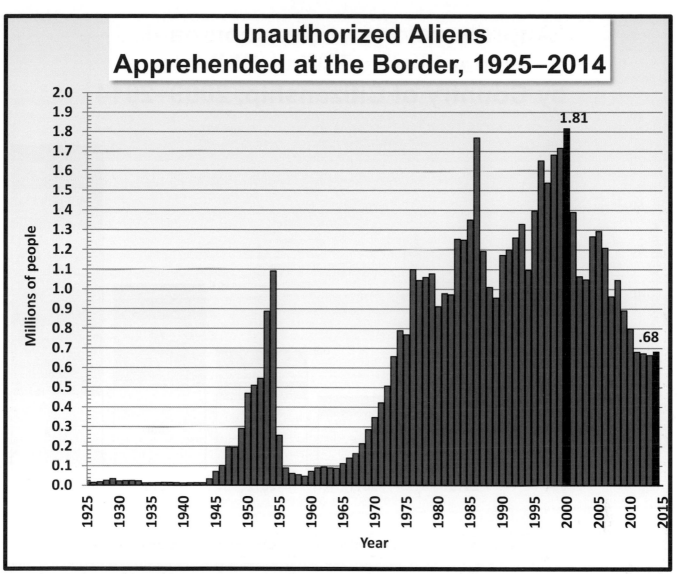

Unauthorized Aliens Apprehended at the Border, 1925–2014

Border apprehensions of unauthorized aliens dropped by 62 percent, between 2000–2014.

Data refer to total apprehensions by patrol and Immigration and Customs Enforcement (ICE) arrests. Prior to 1952, data refer to only border patrol apprehensions.

An alien is any person not a citizen or national of the United States.

Source: U.S. Department of Homeland Security, https://www.dhs.gov/yearbook-immigration-statistics-2014-lawful-permanent-residents, Table 33

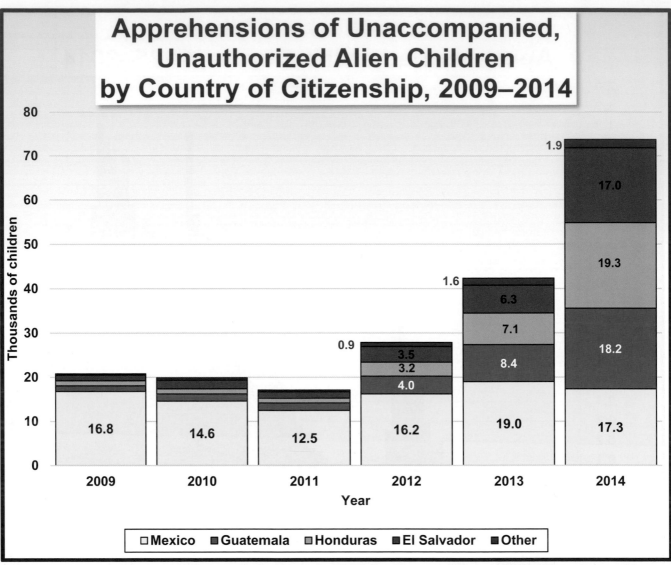

Apprehensions of Unaccompanied, Unauthorized Alien Children by Country of Citizenship, 2009–2014

The number of unaccompanied, unauthorized alien children apprehended from Central American countries increased ten-fold, between 2012 and 2014, reaching 55,000, a level more than three times greater than those from Mexico.

Data are for fiscal years 2009–2014.

An alien is any person not a citizen or national of the United States.

Source: United States Government Accountability Office. GAO analysis of Department of Homeland Security data. Accessible text file for GAO report number GAO-16-163T, accessed October 28, 2016 http://www.gao.gov/assets/680/673414.pdf

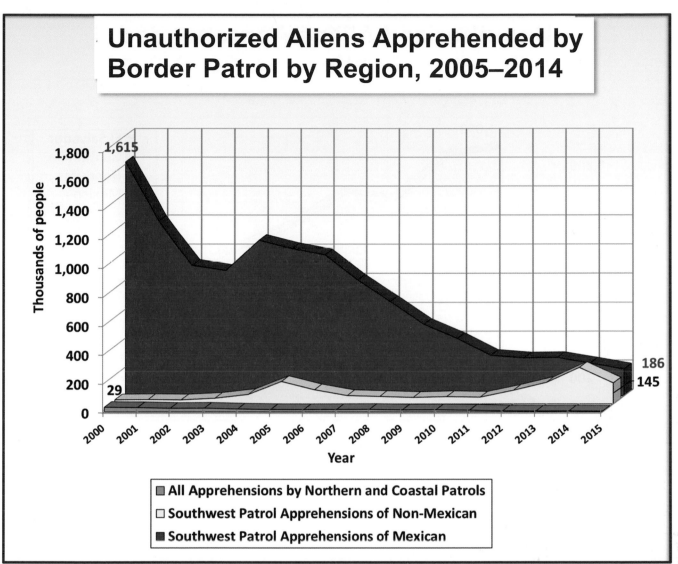

Unauthorized Aliens Apprehended by Border Patrol by Region, 2005–2014

Legend:
- ■ All Apprehensions by Northern and Coastal Patrols
- □ Southwest Patrol Apprehensions of Non-Mexican
- ■ Southwest Patrol Apprehensions of Mexican

X-axis: Year (2000–2015); Y-axis: Thousands of people. Values shown: 1,615; 29; 186; 145

Between 2005–2014, over 98 percent of border patrol apprehensions of unauthorized aliens occurred at the Southwest border.

In fiscal year 2015, there were 331,333 undocumented immigrants apprehended by the Southwest (SW) Border Patrol of which 186,017 (55.2 percent) were Mexican. In the same period, only 5,784 people from all other countries, were apprehended by the Northern and Coastal Border Patrols. Fiscal year 2015 is defined as October 1, 2014 to September 30, 2015. The U.S. Border Patrol is specifically responsible for patrolling nearly 6,000 miles of Mexican and Canadian international land borders and over 2,000 miles of coastal waters surrounding the Florida Peninsula and the island of Puerto Rico.

An alien is any person not a citizen or national of the United States.

Source: U.S. Border Patrol, "Total Illegal Alien Apprehensions by Fiscal Year", https://www.cbp.gov/sites/default/files/documents/BP%20Total%20Apps%2C%20Mexico%2C%20OTM%20FY2000-FY2015.pdf

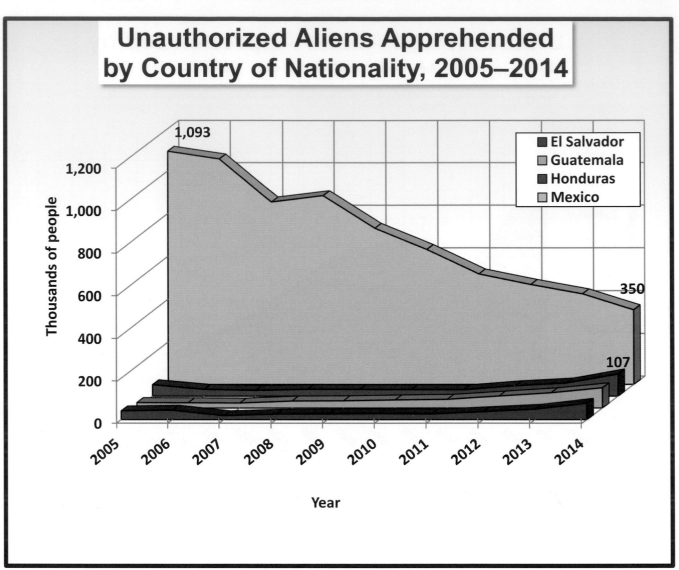

Unauthorized Aliens Apprehended by Country of Nationality, 2005–2014

Legend:
- El Salvador
- Guatemala
- Honduras
- Mexico

(y-axis: Thousands of people; x-axis: Year)

Data labels: 1,093; 350; 107

Between 2005 and 2014, the number of apprehended unauthorized aliens from Mexico declined by two-thirds.

Unauthorized aliens who entered the United States without inspection, for example, are defined as an immigrant but not a permanent resident alien. Lawful permanent residents are legally accorded the privilege of residing permanently in the United States. They may be issued immigrant visas by the Department of State overseas or adjusted to permanent resident status by the Department of Homeland Security in the United States.

Fiscal year 2014 is defined as October 1, 2013 to September 30, 2014.

An alien is any person not a citizen or national of the United States.

Source: U.S. Department of Homeland Security, https://www.dhs.gov/yearbook-immigration-statistics-2014-lawful-permanent-residents

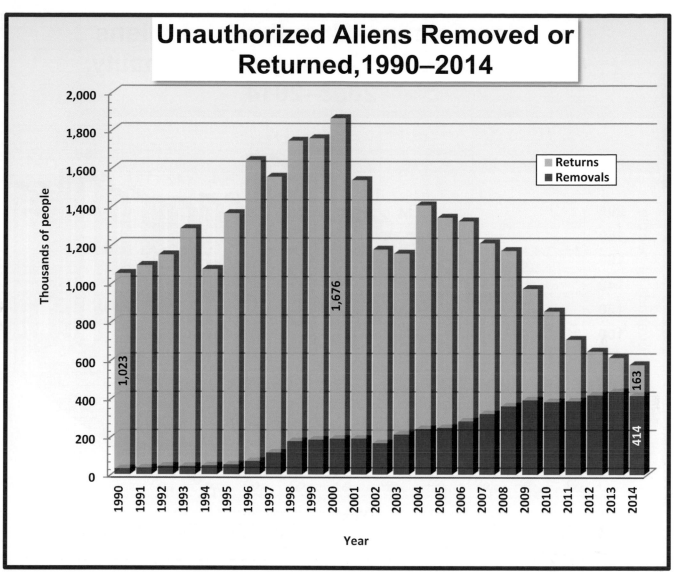

Unauthorized Aliens Removed or Returned,1990–2014

Between 2011–2014, annual removals of unauthorized aliens from the United States have exceeded returns.

The number of unauthorized immigrants returned from the U.S. peaked in 2000 at 1,675,876 persons and declined to 162,814 by fiscal year 2014. During that same period the number of aliens removed by court order increased from 188,467 to 414,481.

An alien is any person not a citizen or national of the United States.

Source: U.S. Department of Homeland Security, ENFORCE Alien Removal Module (EARM), October 2014, Enforcement Integrated Database (EID), October 2014, Table 41, https://www.dhs.gov/yearbook-immigration-statistics-2014-lawful-permanent-residents

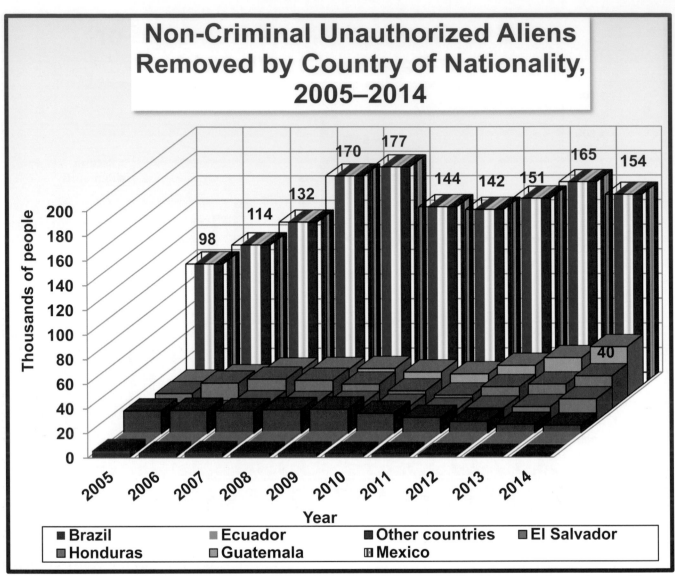

Non-Criminal Unauthorized Aliens Removed by Country of Nationality, 2005–2014

Legend: Brazil, Ecuador, Other countries, El Salvador, Honduras, Guatemala, Mexico

Values shown: 98, 114, 132, 170, 177, 144, 142, 151, 165, 154, 40

In 2014, six-of-ten non-criminal unauthorized alien removals were Mexican.

In fiscal year 2014, 154,161 noncriminal Mexican aliens were removed by court order, representing 62.4 percent of the total noncriminal removals. Guatemala was second highest with 40,455 (16.3 percent).

An alien is any person not a citizen or national of the United States.

Removals are the compulsory and confirmed movement of an inadmissible or deportable alien out of the United States based on an order of removal. An alien who is removed has administrative or criminal consequences placed on subsequent reentry owing to the fact of the removal.

Fiscal year 2014 is defined as October 1, 2013 to September 30, 2014.

Source: U.S. Department of Homeland Security, ENFORCE Alien Removal Module (EARM), October 2014, Enforcement Integrated Database (EID), October 2014, Table 41, https://www.dhs.gov/yearbook-immigration-statistics-2014-lawful-permanent-residents

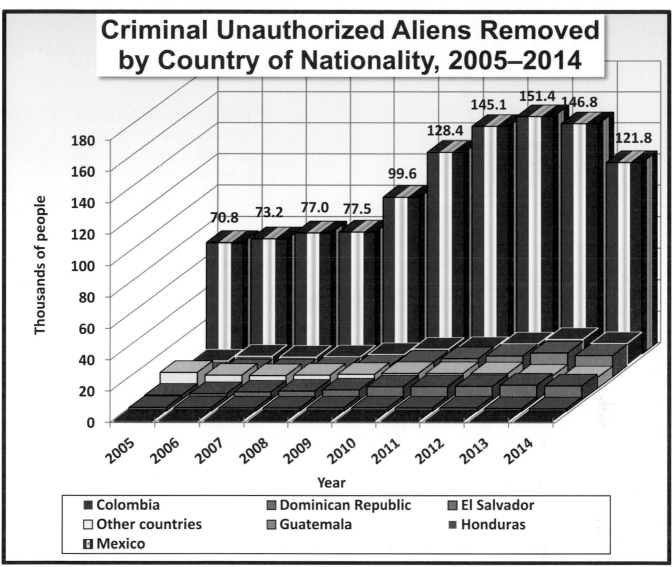

Criminal Unauthorized Aliens Removed by Country of Nationality, 2005–2014

Thousands of people

70.8 73.2 77.0 77.5 99.6 128.4 145.1 151.4 146.8 121.8

Year

- ■ Colombia
- □ Other countries
- ▣ Mexico
- ■ Dominican Republic
- ■ Guatemala
- ■ El Salvador
- ■ Honduras

In 2014, almost three-of-four of the 121,750 removals of criminal unauthorized aliens were Mexican.

In fiscal year 2014, 121,750 Mexican criminal aliens were removed by court order, representing 72.6 percent of the total criminal removals. Guatemala and Honduras were essentially tied for second highest number with 13,698 (8.2 percent) and 13,980 (8.3 percent), respectively. Fiscal year 2014 is defined as October 1, 2013 to September 30, 2014.

An alien is any person not a citizen or national of the United States.

Removals are the compulsory and confirmed movement of an inadmissible or deportable alien out of the United States based on an order of removal. An alien who is removed has administrative or criminal consequences placed on subsequent reentry owing to the fact of the removal.

Source: U.S. Department of Homeland Security, ENFORCE Alien Removal Module (EARM), October 2014, Enforcement Integrated Database (EID), October 2014, Table 41, https://www.dhs.gov/yearbook-immigration-statistics-2014-lawful-permanent-residents

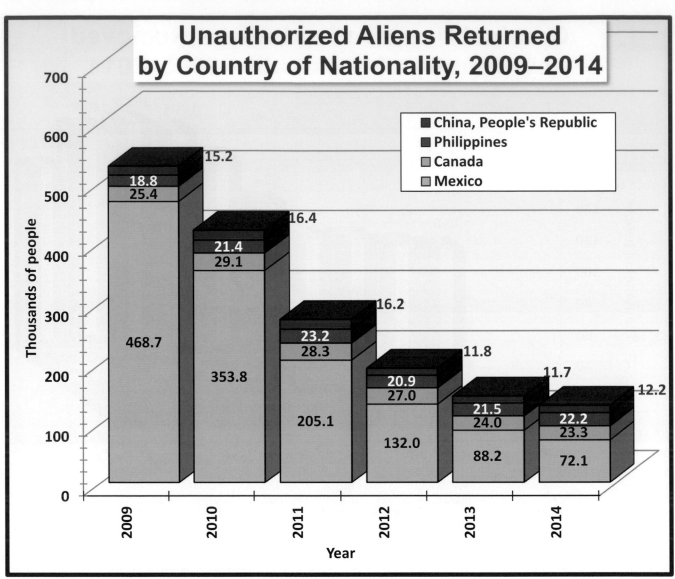

Unauthorized Aliens Returned by Country of Nationality, 2009–2014

Legend:
- ■ China, People's Republic
- ■ Philippines
- □ Canada
- □ Mexico

Y-axis: Thousands of people
X-axis: Year

Year	Mexico	Canada	Philippines	China
2009	468.7	25.4	18.8	15.2
2010	353.8	29.1	21.4	16.4
2011	205.1	28.3	23.2	16.2
2012	132.0	27.0	20.9	11.8
2013	88.2	24.0	21.5	11.7
2014	72.1	23.3	22.2	12.2

Returns of unauthorized aliens to Mexico have dropped six-fold, between 2009–2014.

The number of Mexicans apprehended in the U.S. and court-ordered to be returned to Mexico dropped from 469,000 in 2009 to 72,000 in fiscal year 2014.

An alien is any person not a citizen or national of the United States.

Returns are the confirmed movement of an inadmissible or deportable alien out of the United States not based on an order of removal.

Fiscal year 2014 is defined as October 1, 2013 to September 30, 2014.

Source: U.S. Department of Homeland Security, ENFORCE Alien Removal Module (EARM), October 2014, Enforcement Integrated Database (EID), October 2014, Table 40, https://www.dhs.gov/yearbook-immigration-statistics-2014-lawful-permanent-residents

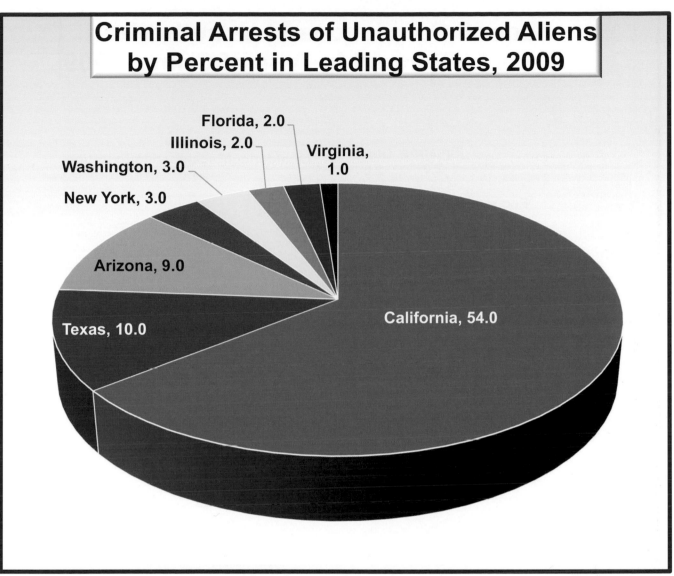

Criminal Arrests of Unauthorized Aliens by Percent in Leading States, 2009

Florida, 2.0
Illinois, 2.0
Virginia, 1.0
Washington, 3.0
New York, 3.0
Arizona, 9.0
Texas, 10.0
California, 54.0

In 2009, over one-half of all criminal arrests of unauthorized aliens occurred in California.

Arrests were made by federal, state and local authorities. About 75 percent of criminal aliens in the sample study population were arrested in one of three states—California, Texas, and Arizona.

An alien is any person not a citizen or national of the United States.

Source: United States Government Accountability Office: Accessible text file for GAO report number GAO-11-187, entitled 'Criminal Alien Statistics: Information on Incarcerations, Arrests, and Costs' which was released on April 21, 2011, accessed October 28, 2016 http://www.gao.gov/new.items/d11187.pdf

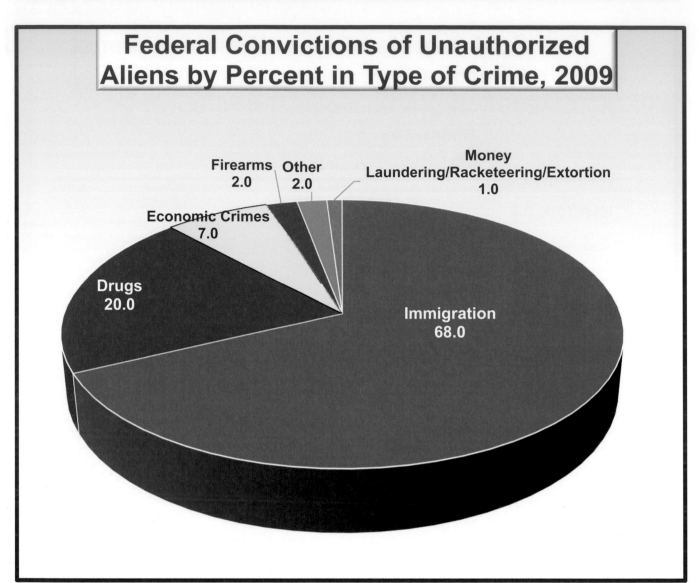

Federal Convictions of Unauthorized Aliens by Percent in Type of Crime, 2009

Firearms 2.0

Other 2.0

Money Laundering/Racketeering/Extortion 1.0

Economic Crimes 7.0

Drugs 20.0

Immigration 68.0

In 2009, over two-thirds of convictions of unauthorized aliens were for violations of immigration laws. Less than two percent of convictions were for crimes against persons.

The category "other" includes homicide, kidnapping, sex offenses, assault, arson, burglary and auto theft.

Arrests were made by federal, state and local authorities. About 75 percent of criminal aliens in the sample study population were arrested in one of three states–California, Texas, and Arizona.

An alien is any person not a citizen or national of the United States.

Source: United States Government Accountability Office: Accessible text file for GAO report number GAO-11-187, entitled 'Criminal Alien Statistics: Information on Incarcerations, Arrests, and Costs' which was released on April 21, 2011, accessed October 28, 2016 http://www.gao.gov/new.items/d11187.pdf

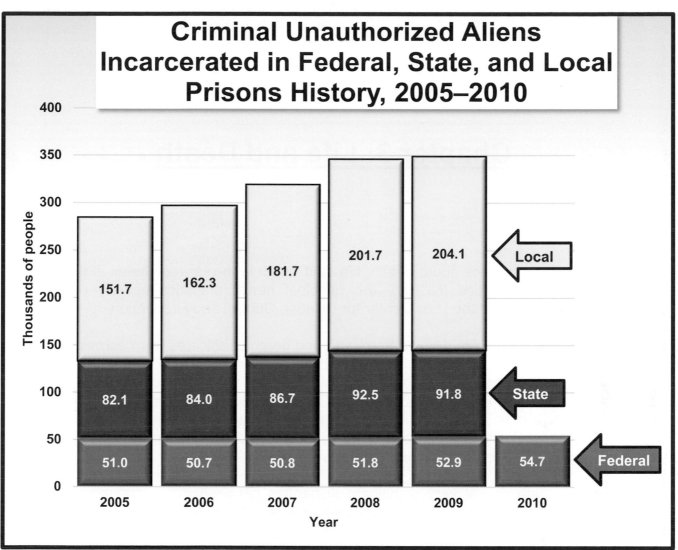

Criminal Unauthorized Aliens Incarcerated in Federal, State, and Local Prisons History, 2005–2010

In 2009, there were approximately 350,000 unauthorized aliens incarcerated in federal, state, or local prisons. Almost 60 percent of those incarcerated were held in local prisons.

Data are for fiscal years 2005–2010. In 2009, there were an estimated .14 million unauthorized immigrants (1.2 percent) incarcerated in federal and state prisons and at the same time there were 1.6 million (.5 percent) from the general population, according to the Bureau of Justice Statistics.

The federal government bears the incarceration costs for federal prisons and reimburses states and localities for portions of their costs through the Department of Justice's (DOJ) State Criminal Alien Assistance Program (SCAAP).

An alien is any person not a citizen or national of the United States.

Source: United States Government Accountability Office: Accessible text file for GAO report number GAO-11-187, entitled 'Criminal Alien Statistics: Information on Incarcerations, Arrests, and Costs' which was released on April 21, 2011, accessed October 28, 2016
http://www.gao.gov/new.items/d11187.pdf

Chapter 3: Life and Death

The primary source for data about health, life, and death in the United States is the National Center for Health Statistics (NCHS)—the principal health statistics agency of the U.S. government—a division of the U.S. Center for Disease Control and Prevention.

NCHS vital statistics data are derived from birth and death certificates from across the United States. These data include date of birth, sex of child, residence, as well as the age of mother, race, and Hispanic origin of both mother and father. Death data include residence, age, sex, race, and Hispanic origin of each decedent, and the date each death occurred. In general, the vital statistics data have a two-year lag. This means that the most recent data on births and deaths by geographic and demographic detail refer to the calendar year two years prior to the year of publication. The data published in 2016 was from calendar year 2014.

Life and death data reveal very significant disparities between races and ethnicities. For example, life expectancy at birth for Hispanic females in 2014 was 12.0 years greater than for non-Hispanic Black males—despite an increase in life expectancy for non-Hispanic Black males by 7.3 years between 1995 and 2014.

In order to compare death rates across races and ethnicities it is necessary to adjust the data to avoid distortions due to differences in age distributions. Death rates for most diseases generally increase with age—a population group with a relatively younger age distribution will tend to have fewer total deaths from a given disease than a comparably sized population group with an older age distribution. Similarly, even if the age-specific risks of dying for a group remain unchanged between two time points, the number of deaths will increase as the population ages. Therefore, in order to compare differences between population groups or for assessing change in mortality over time, adjustment for the inherent differences due to age is needed and these resulting data are referred to as age-adjusted.

The age-adjusted death rate per 100,000 persons, for all causes, was the highest among Black (or African American) persons compared with all other major races and ethnicities. Black persons also had the highest age-adjusted death rates for most of the leading causes of death, including heart disease, cancer, and diabetes. In 2014, the largest death rate disparity between Black persons and the other leading races and ethnicities, for a major disease, was for human immunodeficiency virus (HIV) disease. Black persons had the highest rate, at four times greater than for Hispanic persons, the second highest rate.

Non-Hispanic White persons had the second highest age-adjusted death rate for all causes and the highest rate for Alzheimer's disease, chronic lower respiratory disease, and suicide. American Indian or Alaska Natives led in age-adjusted death rate due to chronic liver disease—four times higher than the second highest group, Hispanic or Latino persons.

In 2014, poisoning had become the leading cause of injury death in the United States. Drug poisoning accounted for 47,055 deaths, of which 82 percent were unintentional. The most common drugs resulting in death were hydrocodone, morphine, oxycodone, fentanyl, and methadone.

The age-adjusted rate for deaths involving opioid analgesics nearly quadrupled, between 2000 to 2014. In that period, drug-poisoning death rates nearly tripled for non-Hispanic White persons while increasing 1.4-fold for non-Hispanic Black persons and Hispanic persons. Across all groups, the drug-poisoning death rate is highest for adults, ages 45–54.

Throughout 1999–2013, infant mortality rates were highest among infants born to non-Hispanic Black women and exceeded those born to non-Hispanic Asian or Pacific Islander women by a factor of 2.8.

~

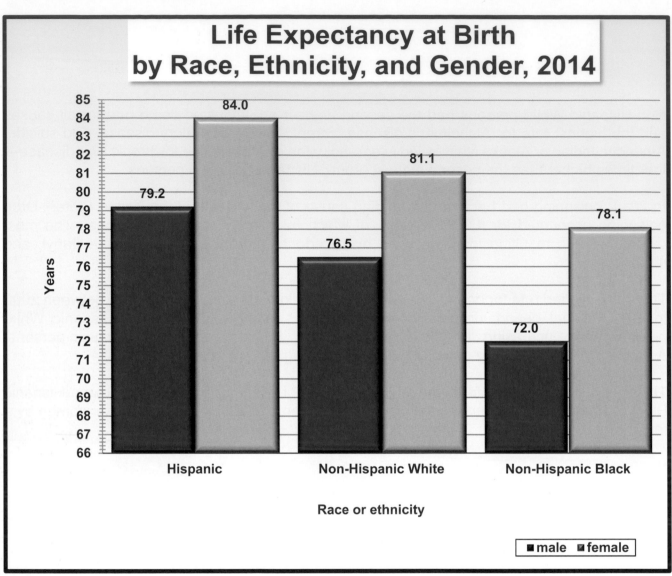

Life Expectancy at Birth by Race, Ethnicity, and Gender, 2014

Years

- Hispanic: male 79.2, female 84.0
- Non-Hispanic White: male 76.5, female 81.1
- Non-Hispanic Black: male 72.0, female 78.1

Race or ethnicity

■ male ■ female

Life expectancy for Hispanic females born in 2014 was 84 years and exceeded the life expectancy for Black males by 12 years.

Life expectancy was computed using 2010-based postcensal estimates.

Source: CDC/NCHS, 'National Vital Statistics System, public-use Mortality Files; table 15, http://www.cdc.gov/nchs/products/nvsr.htm

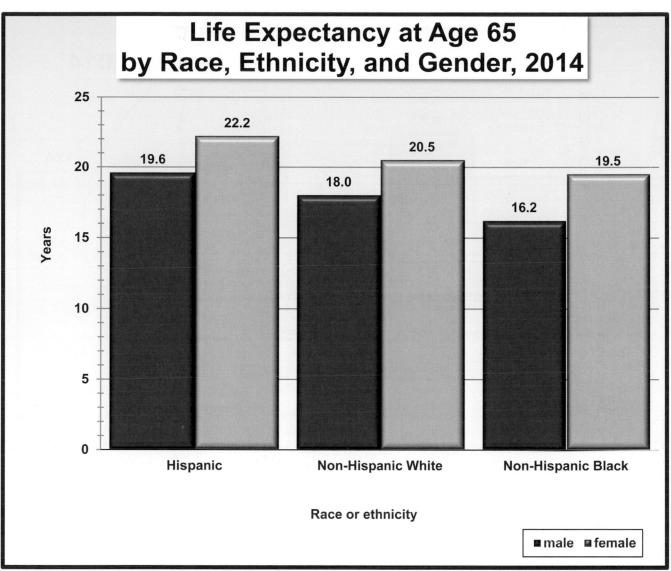

Life Expectancy at Age 65 by Race, Ethnicity, and Gender, 2014

Life expectancy for Hispanic females turning age 65 in 2014 was over 22 years, higher than either male or female non-Hispanic White or non-Hispanic Black persons.

Life expectancy was computed using 2010-based postcensal estimates.

Source: CDC/NCHS, 'National Vital Statistics System, public-use Mortality Files; table 15, http://www.cdc.gov/nchs/products/nvsr.htm

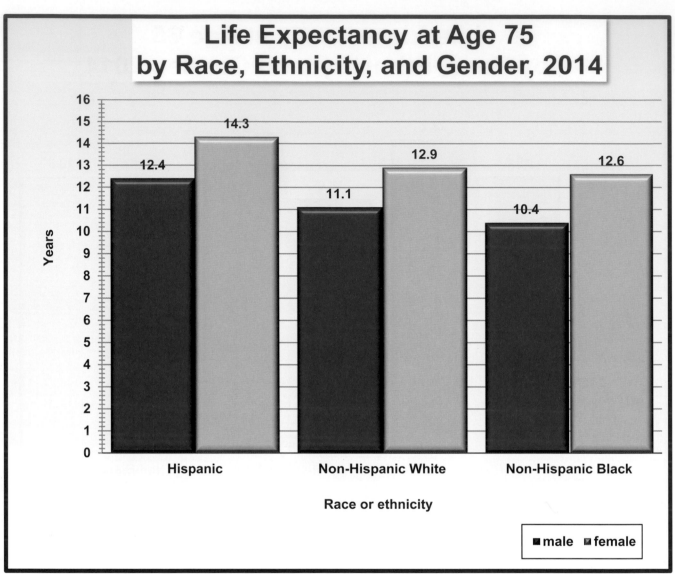

Life Expectancy at Age 75 by Race, Ethnicity, and Gender, 2014

Years

Hispanic: 12.4, 14.3

Non-Hispanic White: 11.1, 12.9

Non-Hispanic Black: 10.4, 12.6

Race or ethnicity

■ male ■ female

Life expectancy for Hispanic females turning age 75 in 2014 was over 14 years and higher than non-Hispanic White and non-Hispanic Black persons of either gender.

Life expectancy was computed using 2010-based postcensal estimates.

Source: CDC/NCHS, 'National Vital Statistics System, public-use Mortality Files; table 15, http://www.cdc.gov/nchs/products/nvsr.htm

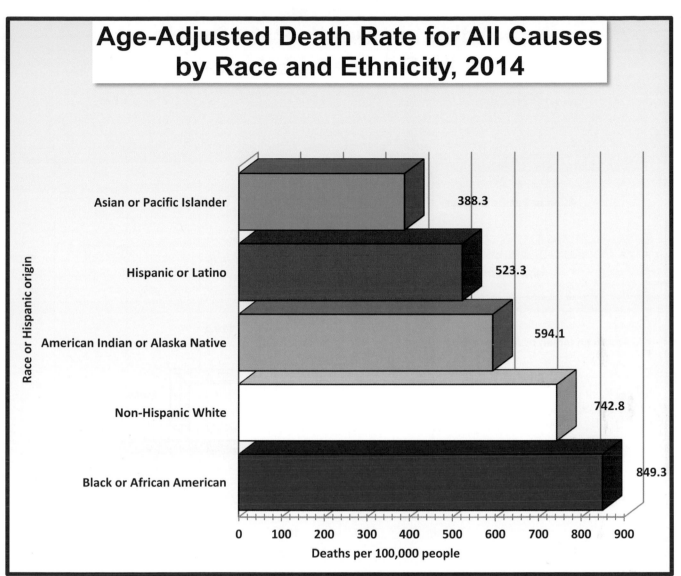

Age-Adjusted Death Rate for All Causes by Race and Ethnicity, 2014

Asian or Pacific Islander — 388.3

Hispanic or Latino — 523.3

American Indian or Alaska Native — 594.1

Non-Hispanic White — 742.8

Black or African American — 849.3

Race or Hispanic origin

0   100   200   300   400   500   600   700   800   900

Deaths per 100,000 people

In 2014, Black or African American age-adjusted death rates were the highest among all races and ethnicities and more than double the rate for Asian or Pacific Islanders.

Age-adjusted rates are calculated using the year 2000 standard population. Data are based on death certificates per 100,000 population.

Source: National Vital Statistics System, public-use Mortality File, public-use Birth File; 'Deaths: Final data for 2014, Table 17, Available from: http://www.cdc.gov/nchs/products/nvsr.htm, http://www.cdc.gov/nchs/hus/contents2015.htm#059

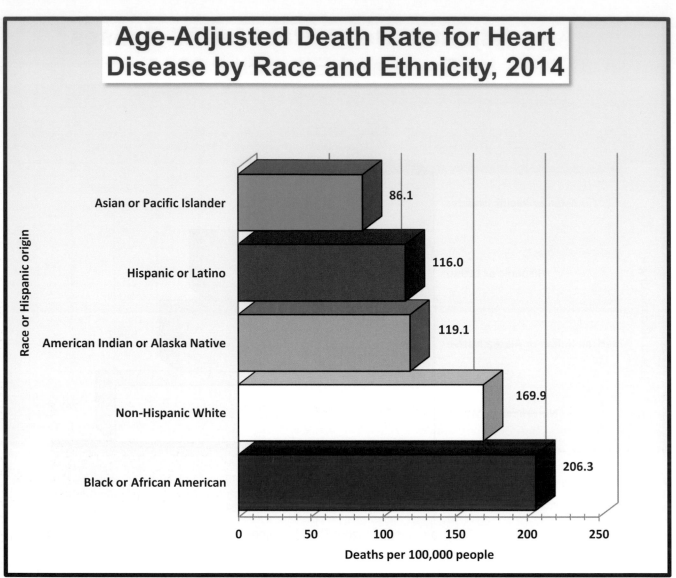

Age-Adjusted Death Rate for Heart Disease by Race and Ethnicity, 2014

Race or Hispanic origin

- Asian or Pacific Islander — 86.1
- Hispanic or Latino — 116.0
- American Indian or Alaska Native — 119.1
- Non-Hispanic White — 169.9
- Black or African American — 206.3

Deaths per 100,000 people

In 2014, Black or African Americans had the highest age-adjusted death rate for heart disease among all races and ethnicities.

Age-adjusted rates are calculated using the year 2000 standard population. Data are based on death certificates per 100,000 population.

Source: National Vital Statistics System, public-use Mortality File, public-use Birth File; 'Deaths: Final data for 2014, Table 17, Available from: http://www.cdc.gov/nchs/products/nvsr.htm, http://www.cdc.gov/nchs/hus/contents2015.htm#059

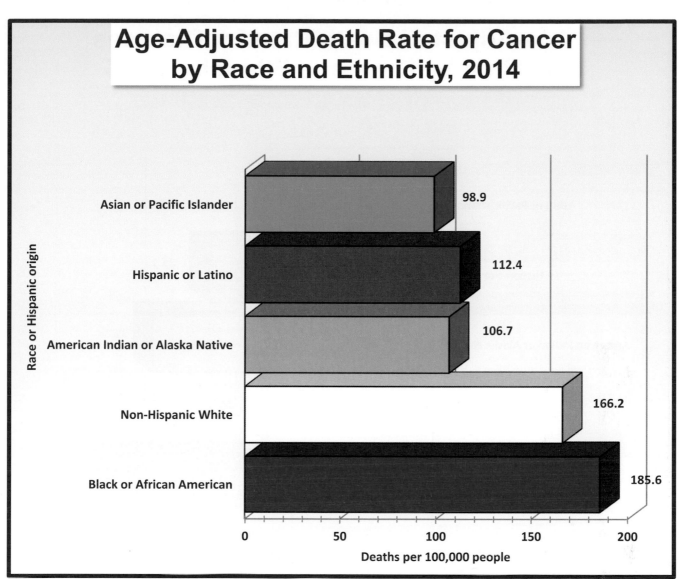

Age-Adjusted Death Rate for Cancer by Race and Ethnicity, 2014

Race or Hispanic origin

- Asian or Pacific Islander — 98.9
- Hispanic or Latino — 112.4
- American Indian or Alaska Native — 106.7
- Non-Hispanic White — 166.2
- Black or African American — 185.6

Deaths per 100,000 people

In 2014, Black or African Americans had the highest age-adjusted death rate for malignant neoplasms (cancer) among all races and ethnicities.

Age-adjusted rates are calculated using the year 2000 standard population. Data are based on death certificates per 100,000 population.

Source: National Vital Statistics System, public-use Mortality File, public-use Birth File; 'Deaths: Final data for 2014, Table 17, Available from: http://www.cdc.gov/nchs/products/nvsr.htm, http://www.cdc.gov/nchs/hus/contents2015.htm#059

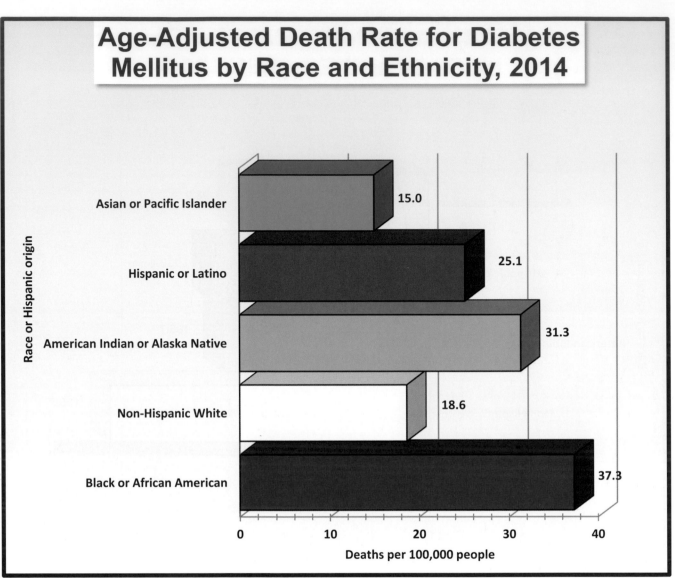

Age-Adjusted Death Rate for Diabetes Mellitus by Race and Ethnicity, 2014

In 2014, Asian or Pacific Islanders were least likely to die from diabetes mellitus compared with other races and ethnicities.

Age-adjusted rates are calculated using the year 2000 standard population. Data are based on death certificates per 100,000 population.

Source: National Vital Statistics System, public-use Mortality File, public-use Birth File; 'Deaths: Final data for 2014, Table 17, Available from: http://www.cdc.gov/nchs/products/nvsr.htm, http://www.cdc.gov/nchs/hus/contents2015.htm#059

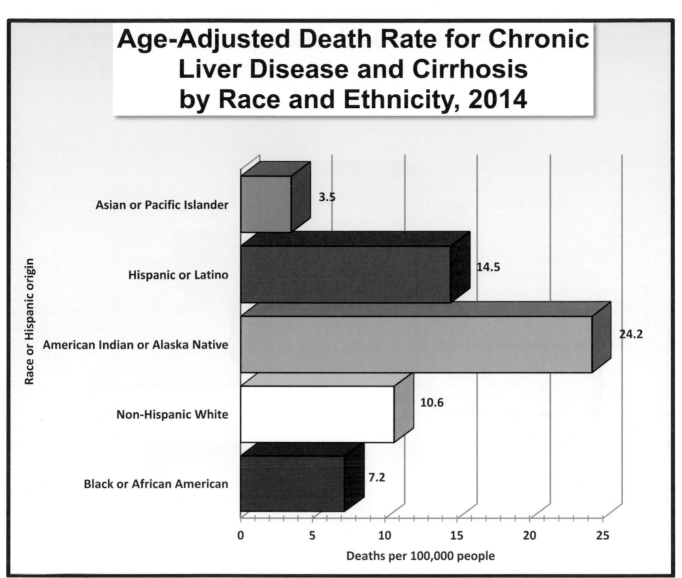

Age-Adjusted Death Rate for Chronic Liver Disease and Cirrhosis by Race and Ethnicity, 2014

In 2014, American Indian and Alaska Natives had the highest age-adjusted death rate for chronic liver disease and cirrhosis. It was nearly seven times higher than for Asian or Pacific Islanders.

Age-adjusted rates are calculated using the year 2000 standard population. Data are based on death certificates per 100,000 population.

Source: National Vital Statistics System, public-use Mortality File, public-use Birth File; 'Deaths: Final data for 2014, Table 17, Available from: http://www.cdc.gov/nchs/products/nvsr.htm, http://www.cdc.gov/nchs/hus/contents2015.htm#059

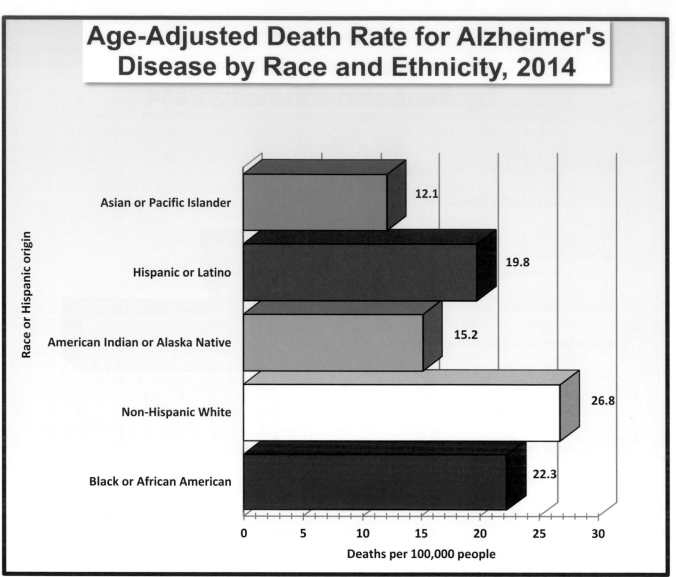

Age-Adjusted Death Rate for Alzheimer's Disease by Race and Ethnicity, 2014

Race or Hispanic origin

- Asian or Pacific Islander — 12.1
- Hispanic or Latino — 19.8
- American Indian or Alaska Native — 15.2
- Non-Hispanic White — 26.8
- Black or African American — 22.3

Deaths per 100,000 people

In 2014, non-Hispanic White persons had the highest age-adjusted death rate for Alzheimer's disease among all races. It was nearly double the rate for Asian and Pacific Islanders.

Age-adjusted rates are calculated using the year 2000 standard population. Data are based on death certificates per 100,000 population.

Source: National Vital Statistics System, public-use Mortality File, public-use Birth File; Deaths: Final data for 2014, Table 17, Available from: http://www.cdc.gov/nchs/products/nvsr.htm, http://www.cdc.gov/nchs/hus/contents2015.htm#059

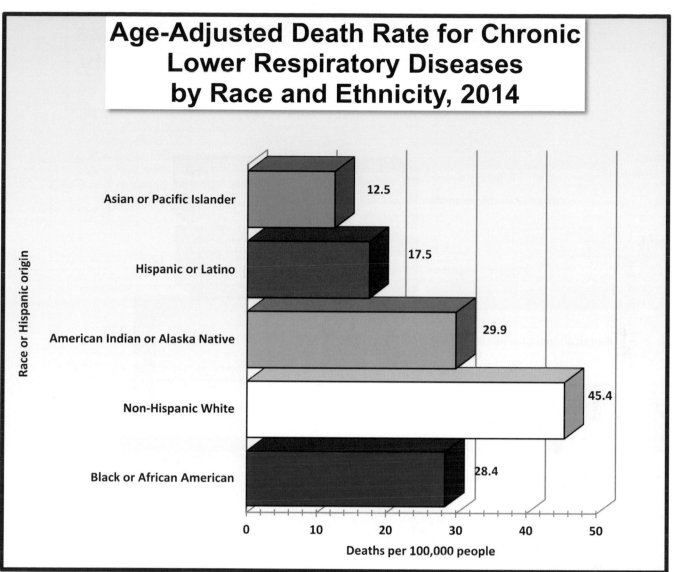

Age-Adjusted Death Rate for Chronic Lower Respiratory Diseases by Race and Ethnicity, 2014

Race or Hispanic origin

- Asian or Pacific Islander — 12.5
- Hispanic or Latino — 17.5
- American Indian or Alaska Native — 29.9
- Non-Hispanic White — 45.4
- Black or African American — 28.4

Deaths per 100,000 people

In 2014, non-Hispanic White persons had the highest age-adjusted death rate for lower respiratory diseases among all races and ethnicities. It was almost four times higher than the rate for Asian and Pacific Islanders.

Age-adjusted rates are calculated using the year 2000 standard population. Data are based on death certificates per 100,000 population.

Source: National Vital Statistics System, public-use Mortality File, public-use Birth File; Deaths: Final data for 2014, Table 17, Available from: http://www.cdc.gov/nchs/products/nvsr.htm, http://www.cdc.gov/nchs/hus/contents2015.htm#059

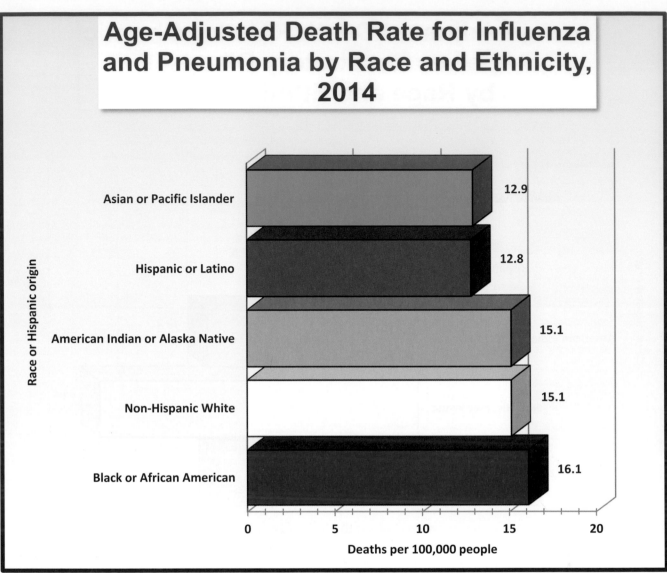

Age-Adjusted Death Rate for Influenza and Pneumonia by Race and Ethnicity, 2014

Race or Hispanic origin

- Asian or Pacific Islander — 12.9
- Hispanic or Latino — 12.8
- American Indian or Alaska Native — 15.1
- Non-Hispanic White — 15.1
- Black or African American — 16.1

0   5   10   15   20

Deaths per 100,000 people

In 2014, death rates due to influenza and pneumonia were within 25 percent among all races and ethnicities.

Age-adjusted rates are calculated using the year 2000 standard population. Data are based on death certificates per 100,000 population.

Source: National Vital Statistics System, public-use Mortality File, public-use Birth File; Deaths: Final data for 2014, Table 17, Available from: http://www.cdc.gov/nchs/products/nvsr.htm, http://www.cdc.gov/nchs/hus/contents2015.htm#059

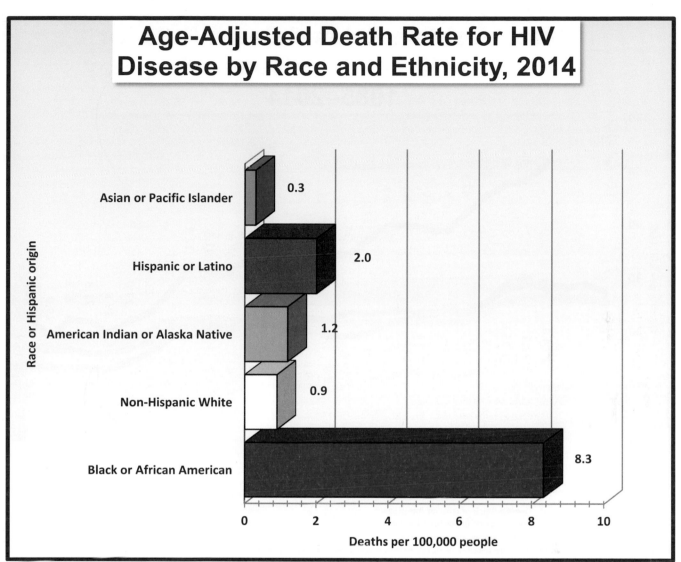

Age-Adjusted Death Rate for HIV Disease by Race and Ethnicity, 2014

Race or Hispanic origin

- Asian or Pacific Islander — 0.3
- Hispanic or Latino — 2.0
- American Indian or Alaska Native — 1.2
- Non-Hispanic White — 0.9
- Black or African American — 8.3

Deaths per 100,000 people

In 2014, the age-adjusted death rate for human immunodeficiency virus (HIV) disease was highest among Black or African Americans and was 27 times higher than the rate for Asian or Pacific Islanders.

Age-adjusted rates are calculated using the year 2000 standard population. Data are based on death certificates per 100,000 population.

Source: National Vital Statistics System, public-use Mortality File, public-use Birth File; Deaths: Final data for 2014, Table 17, Available from: http://www.cdc.gov/nchs/products/nvsr.htm, http://www.cdc.gov/nchs/hus/contents2015.htm#059

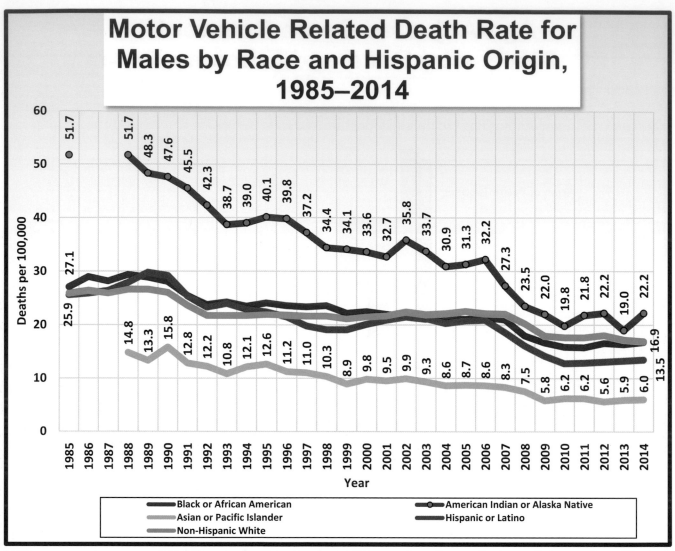

Motor Vehicle Related Death Rate for Males by Race and Hispanic Origin, 1985–2014

The motor vehicle related death rate for American Indian, Alaska Native, Asian, and Pacific Islander males decreased by approximately a factor of two between 1998–2014.

Data are based on death certificates. Underlying cause of death was coded according to the 6th Revision of the International Classification of Diseases (ICD) in 1950, 7th Revision in 1960, 8th Revision in 1970, and 9th Revision in 1980–1998.

Source: National Vital Statistics System, public-use Mortality File, public-use Birth File; Deaths: Final data for 2014, Table 28, Available from: http://www.cdc.gov/nchs/products/nvsr.htm, http://www.cdc.gov/nchs/hus/contents2015.htm#059, Available from: http://www.cdc.gov/mmwr/preview/mmwrhtml/mm6450a3.htm?s_cid=mm6450a3_w

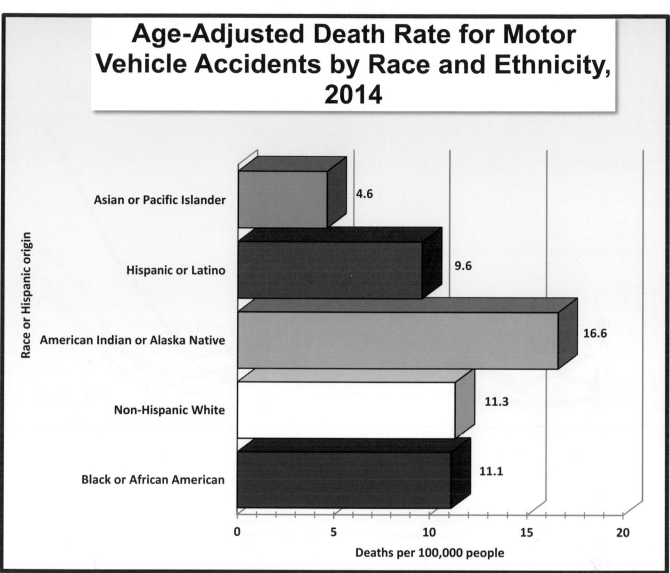

Age-Adjusted Death Rate for Motor Vehicle Accidents by Race and Ethnicity, 2014

In 2014, American Indian and Alaska Natives had the highest motor vehicle accident death rate among all races. It was almost four times higher than the rate for Asian and Pacific Islanders.

Age-adjusted rates are calculated using the year 2000 standard population. Data are based on death certificates per 100,000 population.

Source: National Vital Statistics System, public-use Mortality File, public-use Birth File; Deaths: Final data for 2014, Table 17, Available from: http://www.cdc.gov/nchs/products/nvsr.htm, http://www.cdc.gov/nchs/hus/contents2015.htm#059

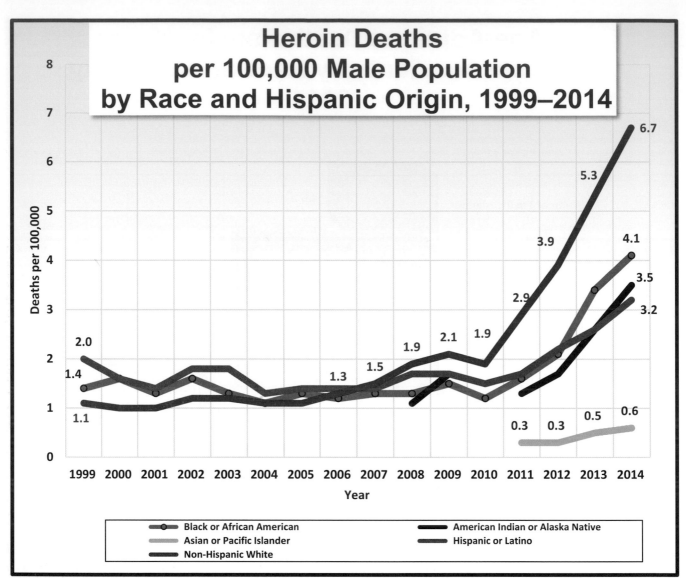

Heroin Deaths per 100,000 Male Population by Race and Hispanic Origin, 1999–2014

Legend:
- Black or African American
- Asian or Pacific Islander
- Non-Hispanic White
- American Indian or Alaska Native
- Hispanic or Latino

Heroin deaths for non-Hispanic White males climbed approximately 350 percent between 2010 and 2014—the steepest rise for males among all races and ethnicities.

Data are based on death certificates. Drug poisoning was coded using underlying cause of death according to the 10th Revision of the International Classification of Diseases (ICD-10). Drug poisoning deaths include those resulting from accidental or intentional overdoses of a drug, being given the wrong drug, taking the wrong drug in error, taking a drug inadvertently, or other misuses of drugs. These deaths are from all manners and intents, including unintentional, suicide, homicide, undetermined intent, legal intervention, and operations of war.

Source: National Vital Statistics System, public-use Mortality File, public-use Birth File; Deaths: Final data for 2014, Table 27, Available from: http://www.cdc.gov/nchs/products/nvsr.htm, http://www.cdc.gov/nchs/hus/contents2015.htm#059, Available from: http://www.cdc.gov/mmwr/preview/mmwrhtml/mm6450a3.htm?s_cid=mm6450a3_w

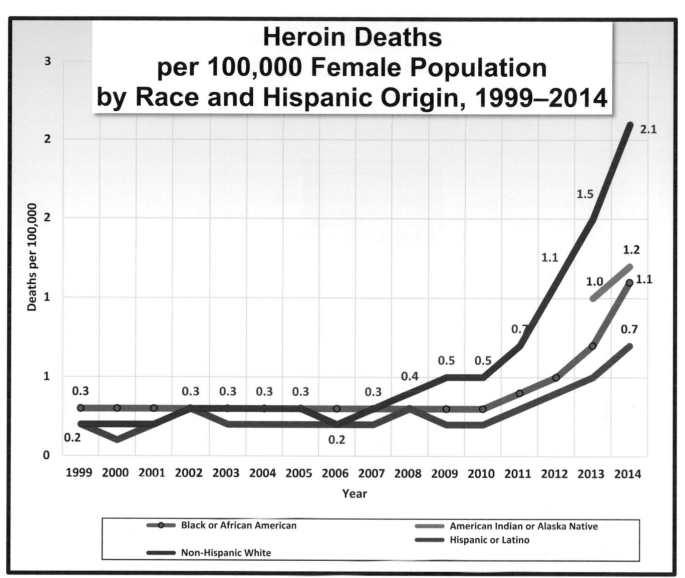

Heroin Deaths per 100,000 Female Population by Race and Hispanic Origin, 1999–2014

Deaths per 100,000

Year

Legend:
- ●— Black or African American
- ═══ American Indian or Alaska Native
- ─── Non-Hispanic White
- ─── Hispanic or Latino

Heroin deaths for non-Hispanic White females climbed 420 percent between 2010 and 2014—the steepest rise among all races and ethnicities for either gender.

Data are based on death certificates. Drug poisoning was coded using underlying cause of death according to the 10th Revision of the International Classification of Diseases (ICD-10). Drug poisoning deaths include those resulting from accidental or intentional overdoses of a drug, being given the wrong drug, taking the wrong drug in error, taking a drug inadvertently, or other misuses of drugs. These deaths are from all manners and intents, including unintentional, suicide, homicide, undetermined intent, legal intervention, and operations of war.

Source: National Vital Statistics System, public-use Mortality File, public-use Birth File; Deaths: Final data for 2014, Table 27, Available from: http://www.cdc.gov/nchs/products/nvsr.htm, http://www.cdc.gov/nchs/hus/contents2015.htm#059, Available from: http://www.cdc.gov/mmwr/preview/mmwrhtml/mm6450a3.htm?s_cid=mm6450a3_w

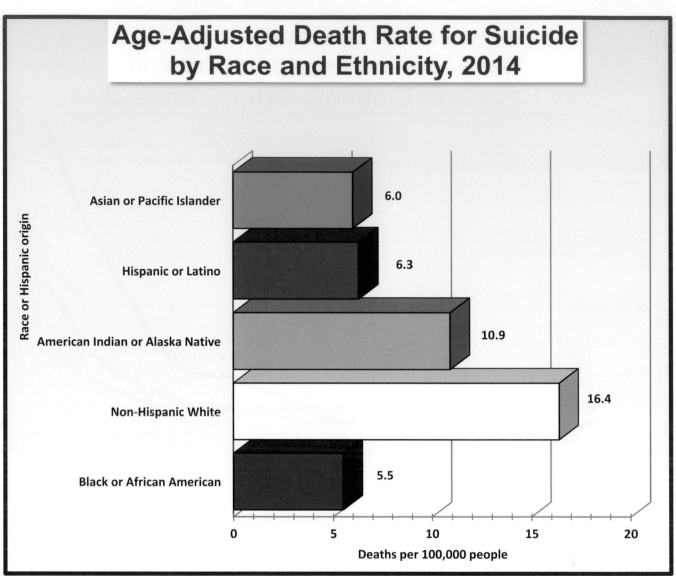

Age-Adjusted Death Rate for Suicide by Race and Ethnicity, 2014

Race or Hispanic origin

- Asian or Pacific Islander — 6.0
- Hispanic or Latino — 6.3
- American Indian or Alaska Native — 10.9
- Non-Hispanic White — 16.4
- Black or African American — 5.5

Deaths per 100,000 people

In 2014, non-Hispanic White persons had the highest age-adjusted suicide rate among all races and ethnicities. It was triple the rate for Black and African Americans.

Age-adjusted rates are calculated using the year 2000 standard population. Data are based on death certificates.

Source: National Vital Statistics System, public-use Mortality File, public-use Birth File; Deaths: Final data for 2014, Table 17, Available from: http://www.cdc.gov/nchs/products/nvsr.htm, http://www.cdc.gov/nchs/hus/contents2015.htm#059

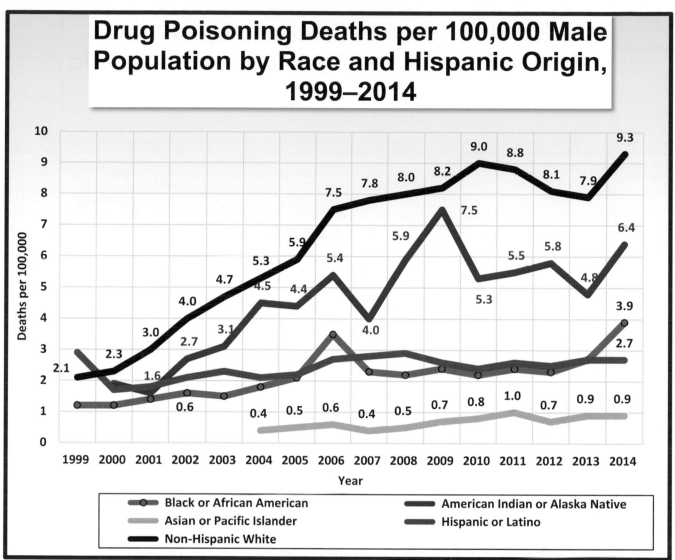

Drug Poisoning Deaths per 100,000 Male Population by Race and Hispanic Origin, 1999–2014

Drug poisoning deaths of non-Hispanic White males increased almost five-fold between 1999 and 2014. Non-Hispanic White males had highest drug poisoning death rate among males of all races and ethnicities.

Data are based on death certificates. Drug poisoning was coded using underlying cause of death according to the 10th Revision of the International Classification of Diseases (ICD-10). Drug poisoning deaths include those resulting from accidental or intentional overdoses of a drug, being given the wrong drug, taking the wrong drug in error, taking a drug inadvertently, or other misuses of drugs. These deaths are from all manners and intents, including unintentional, suicide, homicide, undetermined intent, legal intervention, and operations of war.

Source: National Vital Statistics System, public-use Mortality File, public-use Birth File; Deaths: Final data for 2014, Table 27, Available from: http://www.cdc.gov/nchs/products/nvsr.htm, http://www.cdc.gov/nchs/hus/contents2015.htm#059, Available from: http://www.cdc.gov/mmwr/preview/mmwrhtml/mm6450a3.htm?s_cid=mm6450a3_w

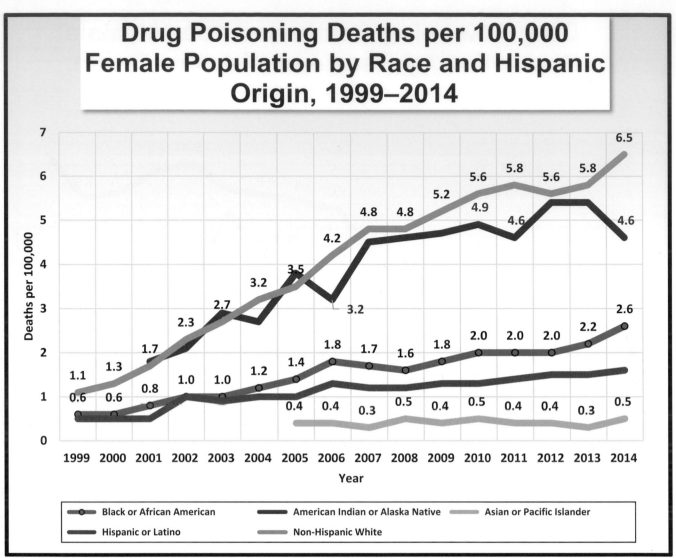

Drug Poisoning Deaths per 100,000 Female Population by Race and Hispanic Origin, 1999–2014

Legend:
- Black or African American
- American Indian or Alaska Native
- Asian or Pacific Islander
- Hispanic or Latino
- Non-Hispanic White

Drug poisoning deaths have increased six-fold for non-Hispanic White females between 1999 and 2014. Non-Hispanic White females had the highest drug poisoning rate of deaths among females of all races and ethnicities.

Data are based on death certificates. Drug poisoning was coded using underlying cause of death according to the 10th Revision of the International Classification of Diseases (ICD-10). Drug poisoning deaths include those resulting from accidental or intentional overdoses of a drug, being given the wrong drug, taking the wrong drug in error, taking a drug inadvertently, or other misuses of drugs. These deaths are from all manners and intents, including unintentional, suicide, homicide, undetermined intent, legal intervention, and operations of war.

Source: National Vital Statistics System, public-use Mortality File, public-use Birth File; Deaths: Final data for 2014, Table 27, Available from: http://www.cdc.gov/nchs/products/nvsr.htm, http://www.cdc.gov/nchs/hus/contents2015.htm#059, Available from: http://www.cdc.gov/mmwr/preview/mmwrhtml/mm6450a3.htm?s_cid=mm6450a3_w

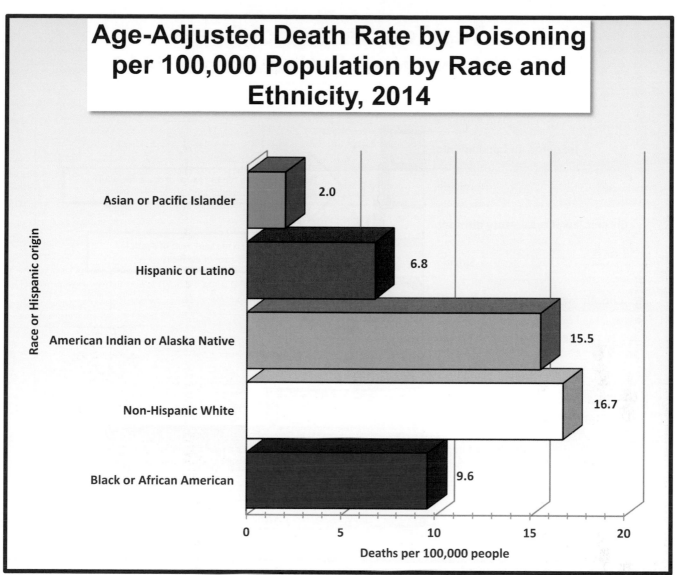

Age-Adjusted Death Rate by Poisoning per 100,000 Population by Race and Ethnicity, 2014

Race or Hispanic origin

- Asian or Pacific Islander — 2.0
- Hispanic or Latino — 6.8
- American Indian or Alaska Native — 15.5
- Non-Hispanic White — 16.7
- Black or African American — 9.6

0   5   10   15   20

Deaths per 100,000 people

In 2014, the death rate due to poisoning was highest among non-Hispanic White persons, American Indian, and Alaska Natives—approximately eight times higher than for Asian or Pacific Islanders.

Age-adjusted rates are calculated using the year 2000 standard population. Data are based on death certificates.

Source: National Vital Statistics System, public-use Mortality File, public-use Birth File; Deaths: Final data for 2014, Table 17, Available from: http://www.cdc.gov/nchs/products/nvsr.htm, http://www.cdc.gov/nchs/hus/contents2015.htm#059

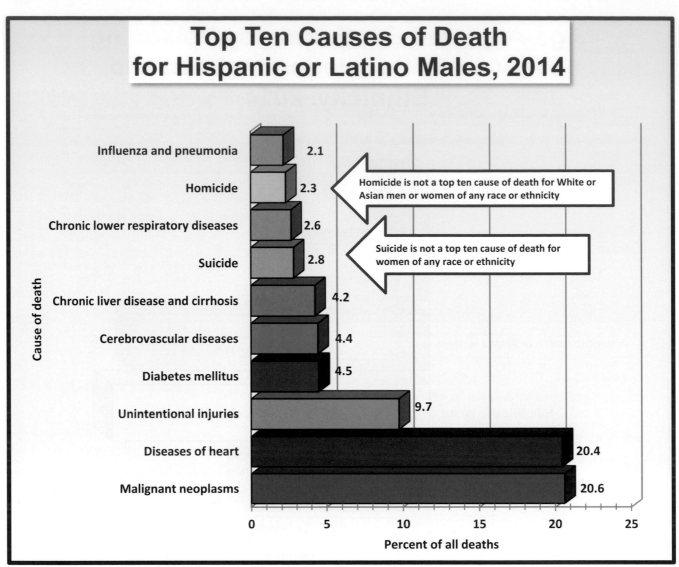

Top Ten Causes of Death for Hispanic or Latino Males, 2014

Cause of death	Percent of all deaths
Influenza and pneumonia	2.1
Homicide	2.3
Chronic lower respiratory diseases	2.6
Suicide	2.8
Chronic liver disease and cirrhosis	4.2
Cerebrovascular diseases	4.4
Diabetes mellitus	4.5
Unintentional injuries	9.7
Diseases of heart	20.4
Malignant neoplasms	20.6

Homicide is not a top ten cause of death for White or Asian men or women of any race or ethnicity

Suicide is not a top ten cause of death for women of any race or ethnicity

In 2014, suicide and homicide accounted for 1-of-20 deaths among Hispanic or Latino males.

Data are based on death certificates per 100,000 population.

Source: National Vital Statistics System, public-use Mortality File, public-use Birth File; Deaths: Final data for 2014, Table 19, Available from: http://www.cdc.gov/nchs/products/nvsr.htm, http://www.cdc.gov/nchs/hus/contents2015.htm#059

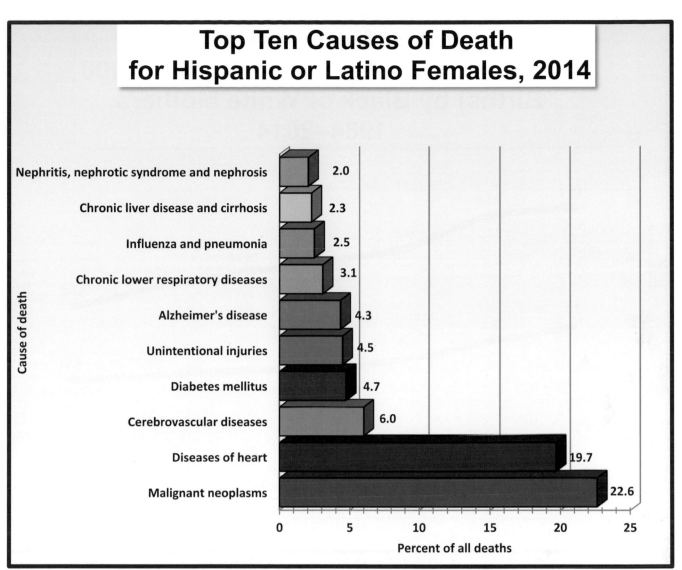

Top Ten Causes of Death
for Hispanic or Latino Females, 2014

Cause of death

Cause	Value
Nephritis, nephrotic syndrome and nephrosis	2.0
Chronic liver disease and cirrhosis	2.3
Influenza and pneumonia	2.5
Chronic lower respiratory diseases	3.1
Alzheimer's disease	4.3
Unintentional injuries	4.5
Diabetes mellitus	4.7
Cerebrovascular diseases	6.0
Diseases of heart	19.7
Malignant neoplasms	22.6

Percent of all deaths

One-of-twenty Hispanic or Latino females who died in 2014, died from influenza, pneumonia, or chronic lower respiratory disease.

Data are based on death certificates per 100,000 population.

Source: National Vital Statistics System, public-use Mortality File, public-use Birth File; Deaths: Final data for 2014, Table 19, Available from: http://www.cdc.gov/nchs/products/nvsr.htm, http://www.cdc.gov/nchs/hus/contents2015.htm#059

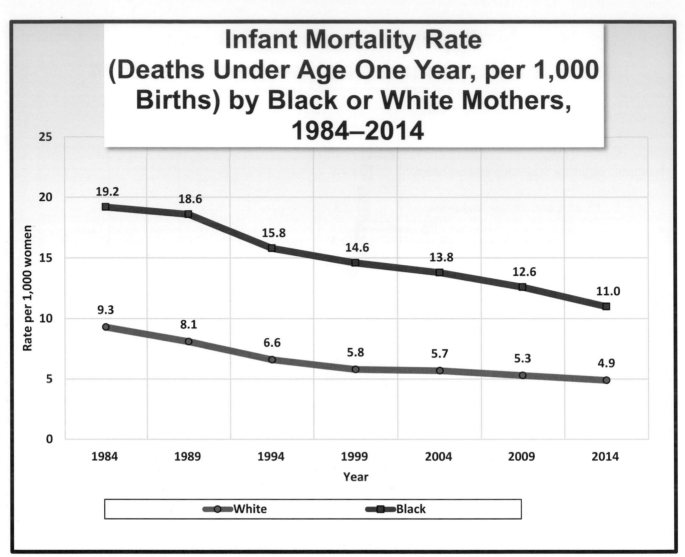

Infant Mortality Rate (Deaths Under Age One Year, per 1,000 Births) by Black or White Mothers, 1984–2014

Between 1980 and 2014, the mortality rate for Black or African American infants—under one year old—was more than double the rate of White infants.

Infants are under one year old.

Includes births and deaths of persons who were not residents of the 50 states and the District of Columbia. Infant deaths are tabulated by race of infant.

Source: National Vital Statistics System, public-use Mortality File, public-use Birth File; Deaths: Final data for 2014, Table 11, Available from: http://www.cdc.gov/nchs/products/nvsr.htm,http://www.cdc.gov/nchs/hus/contents2015.htm#059

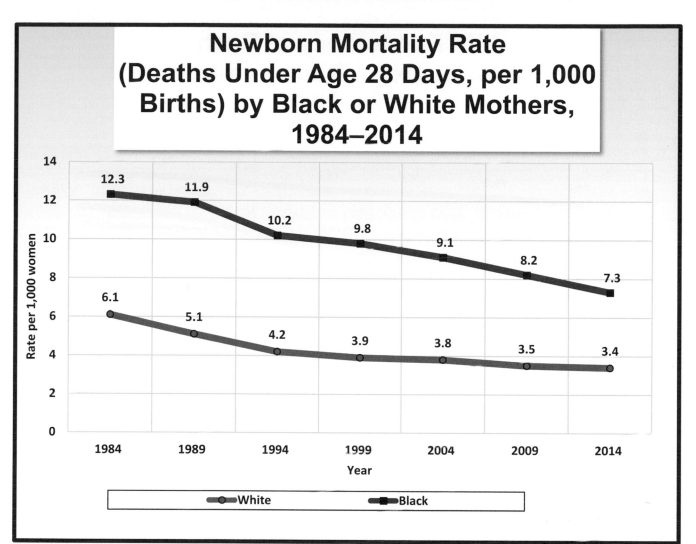

Newborn Mortality Rate (Deaths Under Age 28 Days, per 1,000 Births) by Black or White Mothers, 1984–2014

Between 1980 and 2014, Black infants under 28 days old died at more than double the rate as White infants.

Newborns are under 28 days old.

Includes births and deaths of persons who were not residents of the 50 states and the District of Columbia. Infant deaths are tabulated by race of infant.

Source: National Vital Statistics System, public-use Mortality File, public-use Birth File; Deaths: Final data for 2014, Table 11, Available from: http://www.cdc.gov/nchs/products/nvsr.htm
http://www.cdc.gov/nchs/hus/contents2015.htm#059

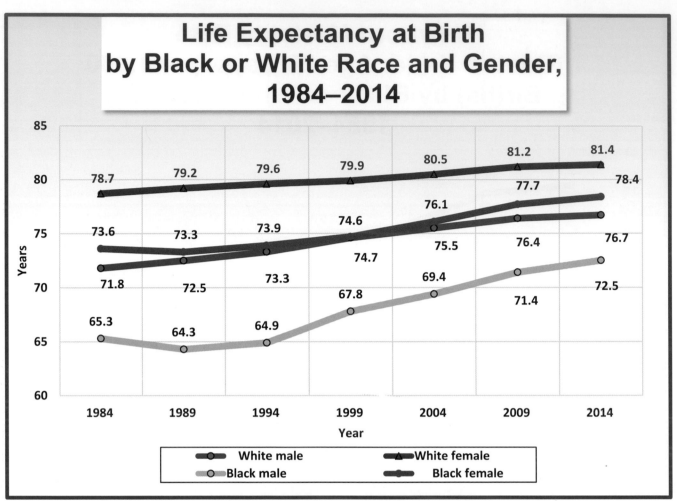

Life Expectancy at Birth by Black or White Race and Gender, 1984–2014

Between 1990 and 2014, life expectancy at birth for Black and African American males increased by nearly eight years.

Data are based on death certificates.

Source: National Vital Statistics System, public-use Mortality File, public-use Birth File; Deaths: Final data for 2014, Table 15, Available from: http://www.cdc.gov/nchs/products/nvsr.htm, http://www.cdc.gov/nchs/hus/contents2015.htm#059

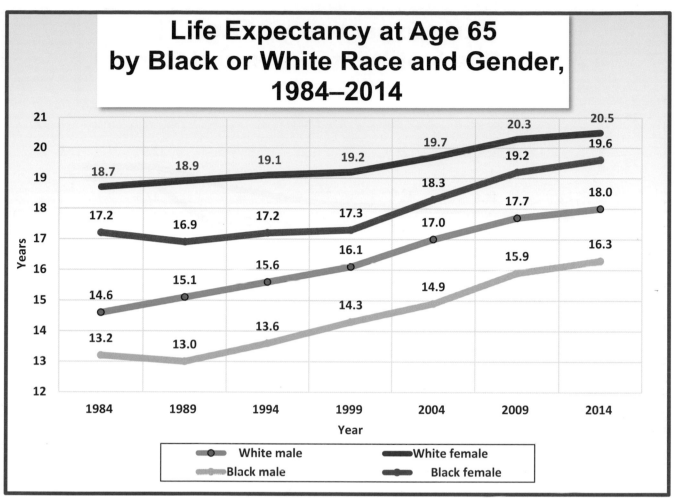

Life Expectancy at Age 65 by Black or White Race and Gender, 1984–2014

In 2014, White females at age 65 had a life expectancy of over 20 years. This was four years more than Black or African American males.

Data are based on death certificates.

Source: National Vital Statistics System, public-use Mortality File, public-use Birth File; Deaths: Final data for 2014, Table 15, Available from: http://www.cdc.gov/nchs/products/nvsr.htm, http://www.cdc.gov/nchs/hus/contents2015.htm#059

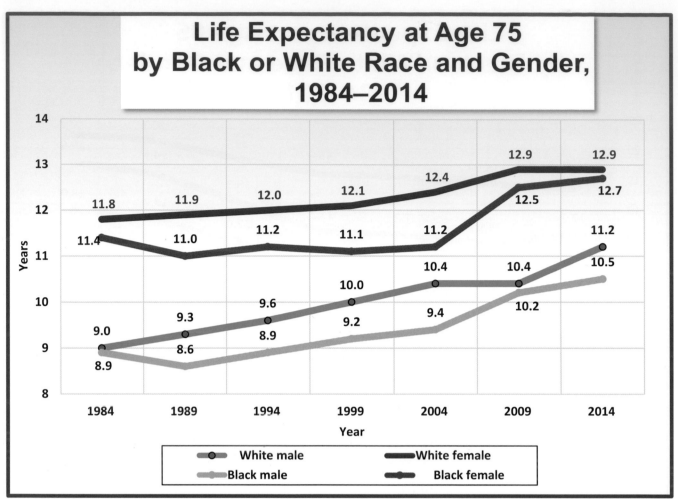

Life Expectancy at Age 75 by Black or White Race and Gender, 1984–2014

In 2014, White females at age 75 had a life expectancy of 12.9 years. This was almost two years greater than White males.

Data are based on death certificates.

Source: National Vital Statistics System, public-use Mortality File, public-use Birth File; Deaths: Final data for 2014, Table 15, Available from: http://www.cdc.gov/nchs/products/nvsr.htm, http://www.cdc.gov/nchs/hus/contents2015.htm#059

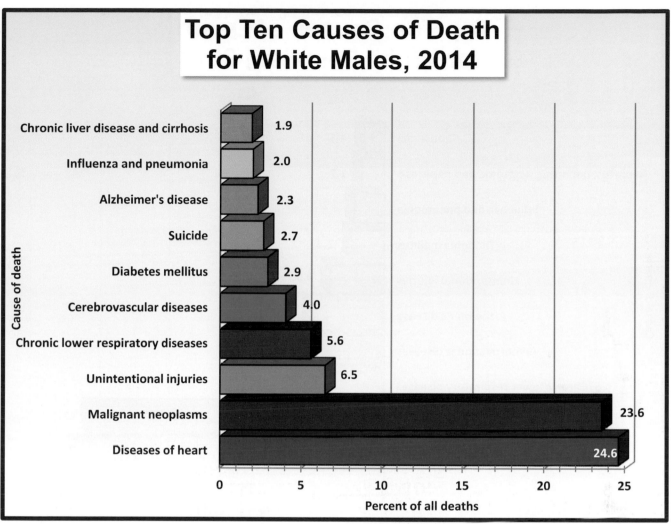

Top Ten Causes of Death for White Males, 2014

Cause of death	Percent of all deaths
Chronic liver disease and cirrhosis	1.9
Influenza and pneumonia	2.0
Alzheimer's disease	2.3
Suicide	2.7
Diabetes mellitus	2.9
Cerebrovascular diseases	4.0
Chronic lower respiratory diseases	5.6
Unintentional injuries	6.5
Malignant neoplasms	23.6
Diseases of heart	24.6

In 2014, suicide plus unintentional injuries were responsible for nine percent of all deaths of White males.

Data are based on death certificates per 100,000 population.

Source: National Vital Statistics System, public-use Mortality File, public-use Birth File; Deaths: Final data for 2014, Table 19, Available from: http://www.cdc.gov/nchs/products/nvsr.htm, http://www.cdc.gov/nchs/hus/contents2015.htm#059

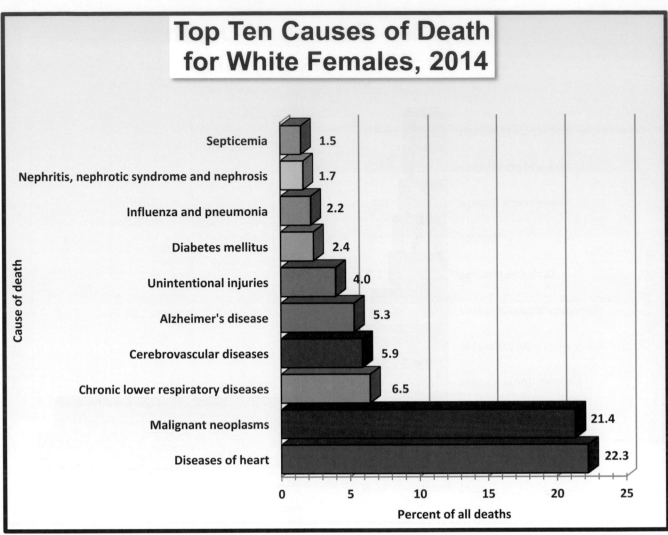

Top Ten Causes of Death for White Females, 2014

Cause of death	Percent of all deaths
Septicemia	1.5
Nephritis, nephrotic syndrome and nephrosis	1.7
Influenza and pneumonia	2.2
Diabetes mellitus	2.4
Unintentional injuries	4.0
Alzheimer's disease	5.3
Cerebrovascular diseases	5.9
Chronic lower respiratory diseases	6.5
Malignant neoplasms	21.4
Diseases of heart	22.3

In 2014, one-of-twenty White female deaths was due to Alzheimer's disease.

Data are based on death certificates per 100,000 population.

Source: National Vital Statistics System, public-use Mortality File, public-use Birth File; Deaths: Final data for 2014, Table 19, Available from: http://www.cdc.gov/nchs/products/nvsr.htm, http://www.cdc.gov/nchs/hus/contents2015.htm#059

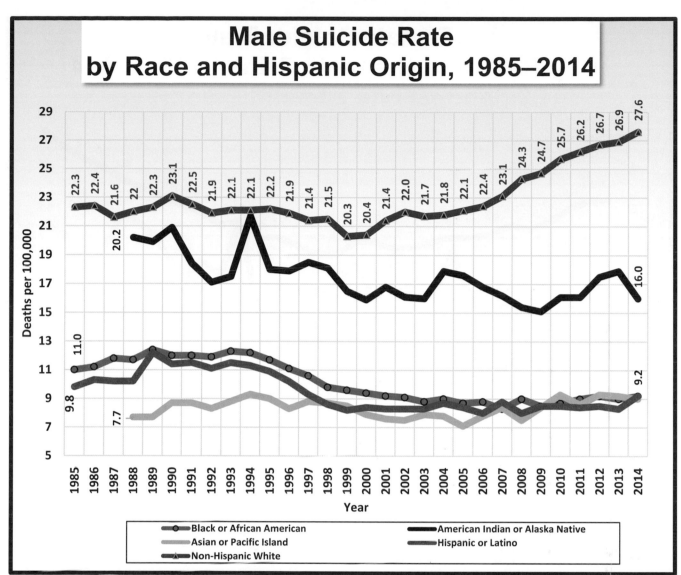

Male Suicide Rate by Race and Hispanic Origin, 1985–2014

The non-Hispanic White male death rate by suicide steadily increased by approximately one-third between 2000 and 2014 and was highest among males of all races and ethnicities.

Data are based on death certificates. Underlying cause of death was coded according to the 6th Revision of the International Classification of Diseases (ICD) in 1950, 7th Revision in 1960, 8th Revision in 1970, and 9th Revision in 1980–1998.

Source: National Vital Statistics System, public-use Mortality File, public-use Birth File; Deaths: Final data for 2014, Table 30, Available from: http://www.cdc.gov/nchs/products/nvsr.htm, http://www.cdc.gov/nchs/hus/contents2015.htm#059, Available from: http://www.cdc.gov/mmwr/preview/mmwrhtml/mm6450a3.htm?s_cid=mm6450a3_w

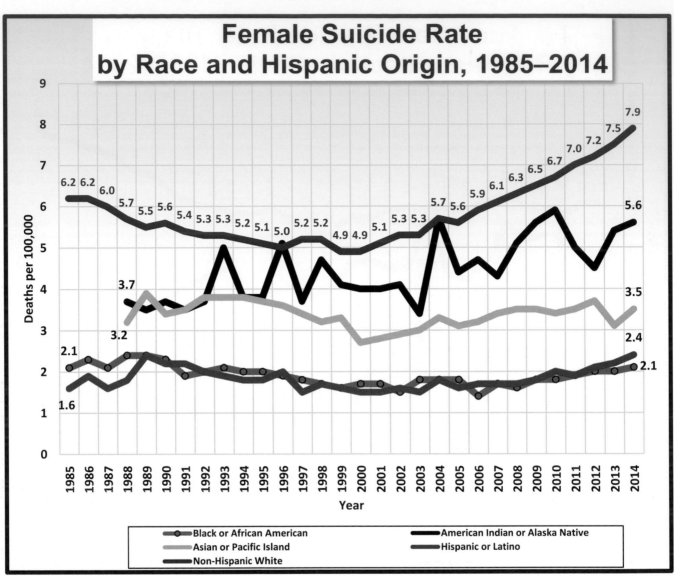

Female Suicide Rate by Race and Hispanic Origin, 1985–2014

Between 2000 and 2014, the non-Hispanic White female suicide rate increased by 60 percent—the highest among females of all races and ethnicities.

Data are based on death certificates. Underlying cause of death was coded according to the 6th Revision of the International Classification of Diseases (ICD) in 1950, 7th Revision in 1960, 8th Revision in 1970, and 9th Revision in 1980–1998.

Source: National Vital Statistics System, public-use Mortality File, public-use Birth File; Deaths: Final data for 2014, Table 30, Available from: http://www.cdc.gov/nchs/products/nvsr.htm, http://www.cdc.gov/nchs/hus/contents2015.htm#059, Available from: http://www.cdc.gov/mmwr/preview/mmwrhtml/mm6450a3.htm?s_cid=mm6450a3_w

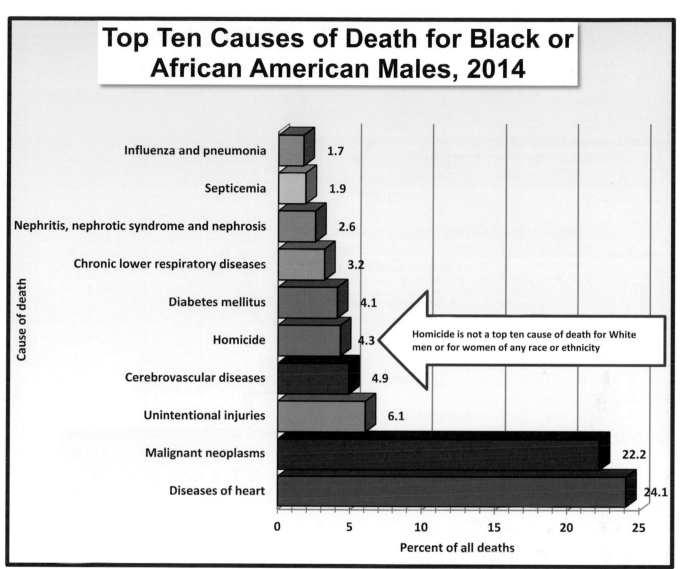

Top Ten Causes of Death for Black or African American Males, 2014

Cause of death

Cause	Value
Influenza and pneumonia	1.7
Septicemia	1.9
Nephritis, nephrotic syndrome and nephrosis	2.6
Chronic lower respiratory diseases	3.2
Diabetes mellitus	4.1
Homicide	4.3
Cerebrovascular diseases	4.9
Unintentional injuries	6.1
Malignant neoplasms	22.2
Diseases of heart	24.1

Homicide is not a top ten cause of death for White men or for women of any race or ethnicity

Percent of all deaths

Homicides killed 1-of-22 Black or African American males in 2014—the fifth leading cause of their deaths.

Data are based on death certificates per 100,000 population.

Source: National Vital Statistics System, public-use Mortality File, public-use Birth File; Deaths: Final data for 2014, Table 19, Available from: http://www.cdc.gov/nchs/products/nvsr.htm, http://www.cdc.gov/nchs/hus/contents2015.htm#059

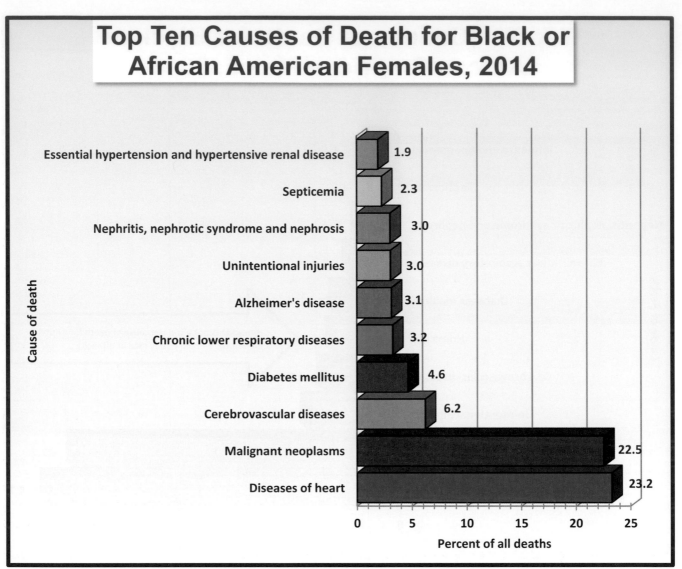

Top Ten Causes of Death for Black or African American Females, 2014

Cause of death:
- Essential hypertension and hypertensive renal disease — 1.9
- Septicemia — 2.3
- Nephritis, nephrotic syndrome and nephrosis — 3.0
- Unintentional injuries — 3.0
- Alzheimer's disease — 3.1
- Chronic lower respiratory diseases — 3.2
- Diabetes mellitus — 4.6
- Cerebrovascular diseases — 6.2
- Malignant neoplasms — 22.5
- Diseases of heart — 23.2

Percent of all deaths (0, 5, 10, 15, 20, 25)

In 2014, Black or African American females were twice as likely to die from cerebrovascular disease as from Alzheimer's disease.

Data are based on death certificates per 100,000 population.

Source: National Vital Statistics System, public-use Mortality File, public-use Birth File; Deaths: Final data for 2014, Table 19, Available from: http://www.cdc.gov/nchs/products/nvsr.htm, http://www.cdc.gov/nchs/hus/contents2015.htm#059

Chapter 3: Life and Death

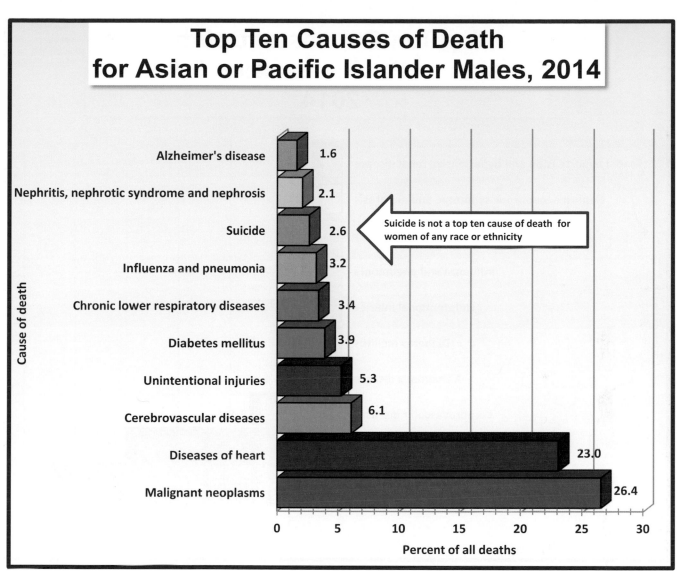

Top Ten Causes of Death for Asian or Pacific Islander Males, 2014

Cause of death:
- Alzheimer's disease — 1.6
- Nephritis, nephrotic syndrome and nephrosis — 2.1
- Suicide — 2.6
- Influenza and pneumonia — 3.2
- Chronic lower respiratory diseases — 3.4
- Diabetes mellitus — 3.9
- Unintentional injuries — 5.3
- Cerebrovascular diseases — 6.1
- Diseases of heart — 23.0
- Malignant neoplasms — 26.4

Suicide is not a top ten cause of death for women of any race or ethnicity

Percent of all deaths

In 2014, over 1-of-20 deaths of male Asian or Pacific Islanders were due to unintentional injuries.

Data are based on death certificates per 100,000 population.

Source: National Vital Statistics System, public-use Mortality File, public-use Birth File; Deaths: Final data for 2014, Table 19, Available from: http://www.cdc.gov/nchs/products/nvsr.htm, http://www.cdc.gov/nchs/hus/contents2015.htm#059

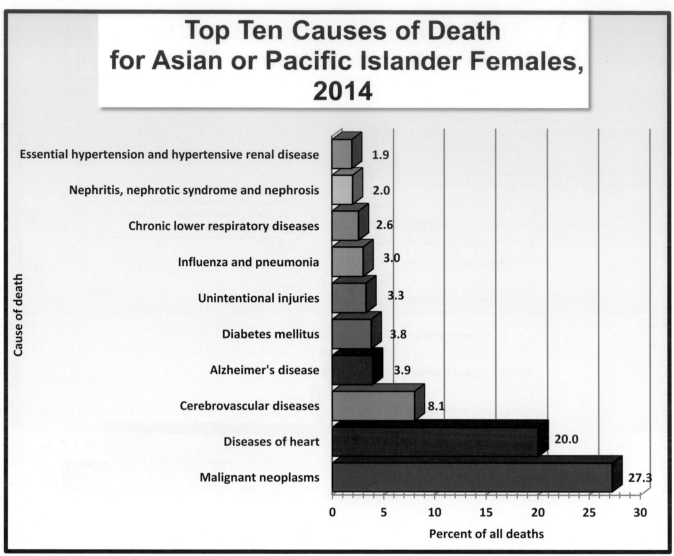

Top Ten Causes of Death for Asian or Pacific Islander Females, 2014

Cause of death	Percent of all deaths
Essential hypertension and hypertensive renal disease	1.9
Nephritis, nephrotic syndrome and nephrosis	2.0
Chronic lower respiratory diseases	2.6
Influenza and pneumonia	3.0
Unintentional injuries	3.3
Diabetes mellitus	3.8
Alzheimer's disease	3.9
Cerebrovascular diseases	8.1
Diseases of heart	20.0
Malignant neoplasms	27.3

In 2014, one-of-five Asian or Pacific Islander female deaths were due to heart disease.

Data are based on death certificates per 100,000 population.

Source: National Vital Statistics System, public-use Mortality File, public-use Birth File; Deaths: Final data for 2014, Table 19, Available from: http://www.cdc.gov/nchs/products/nvsr.htm, http://www.cdc.gov/nchs/hus/contents2015.htm#059

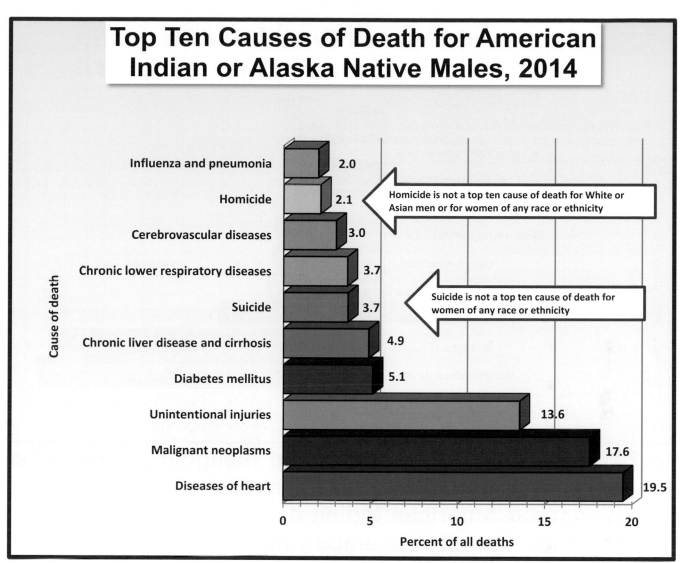

Top Ten Causes of Death for American Indian or Alaska Native Males, 2014

Cause of death

Cause	Percent
Influenza and pneumonia	2.0
Homicide	2.1
Cerebrovascular diseases	3.0
Chronic lower respiratory diseases	3.7
Suicide	3.7
Chronic liver disease and cirrhosis	4.9
Diabetes mellitus	5.1
Unintentional injuries	13.6
Malignant neoplasms	17.6
Diseases of heart	19.5

Homicide is not a top ten cause of death for White or Asian men or for women of any race or ethnicity

Suicide is not a top ten cause of death for women of any race or ethnicity

Percent of all deaths

In 2014, suicide and homicide accounted for 1-of-18 deaths of American Indian or Alaska Natives.

Data are based on death certificates per 100,000 population.

Source: National Vital Statistics System, public-use Mortality File, public-use Birth File; Deaths: Final data for 2014, Table 19, Available from: http://www.cdc.gov/nchs/products/nvsr.htm, http://www.cdc.gov/nchs/hus/contents2015.htm#059

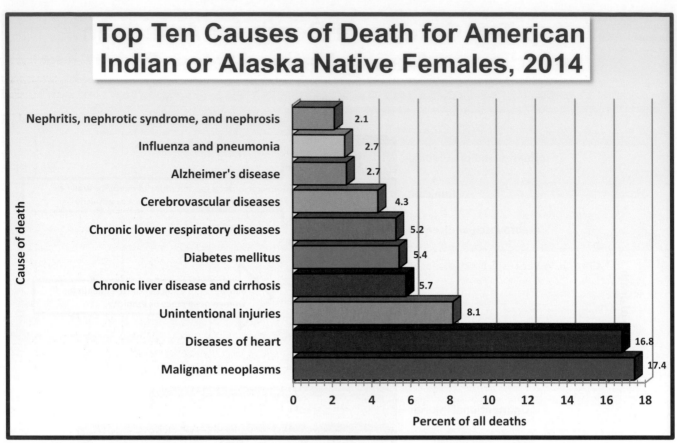

Top Ten Causes of Death for American Indian or Alaska Native Females, 2014

Cause of death

Cause	Percent of all deaths
Nephritis, nephrotic syndrome, and nephrosis	2.1
Influenza and pneumonia	2.7
Alzheimer's disease	2.7
Cerebrovascular diseases	4.3
Chronic lower respiratory diseases	5.2
Diabetes mellitus	5.4
Chronic liver disease and cirrhosis	5.7
Unintentional injuries	8.1
Diseases of heart	16.8
Malignant neoplasms	17.4

Percent of all deaths

In 2014, diseases of the heart and malignant neoplasms (cancers) accounted for approximately one-third of all deaths among American Indian or Alaska Native females. This was the lowest rate among males or females of any racial or ethnic group.

Data are based on death certificates per 100,000 population.

Source: National Vital Statistics System, public-use Mortality File, public-use Birth File; Deaths: Final data for 2014, Table 19, Available from: http://www.cdc.gov/nchs/products/nvsr.htm, http://www.cdc.gov/nchs/hus/contents2015.htm#059

Chapter 4: Health

The National Center for Health Statistics (NCHS), a division of the U.S. Center for Disease Control and Prevention, compiles statistical information to guide actions and policies to improve the health of the American people.

Across many indicators of health and health care, data based on race and ethnicity show significant differences between groups, and below were some of the greatest disparities in the 2014 survey.

Black or African Americans females experienced the highest rate of morbid obesity at 16.7 percent—a rate more than double the rate for Black or African American males, or White and Hispanic persons of either gender. Morbid obesity is diagnosed by determining body mass index (BMI). BMI is defined by the ratio of an individual's height to his or her weight. Normal BMI ranges from 20–25. An individual is considered morbidly obese if he or she is 100 pounds over his/her ideal body weight, has a BMI of 40 or more, or 35 or more and experiencing obesity-related health conditions, such as high blood pressure or diabetes. Those who are morbidly obese are at greater risk for illnesses including diabetes, high blood pressure, and heart disease.

Black or African Americans also experienced the highest pre-term birth rate among the leading races and ethnicities, at 11.1 percent, a rate 1.6 times higher than for Asian or non-Hispanic White babies.

One-of-three American Indian and Alaska Natives under age 65 had private insurance and another one-third were on Medicaid. This compares with three-of-four non-Hispanic White and Asian persons with private health insurance and 15 percent on Medicaid.

One-of-four Hispanic females of high school age seriously considered suicide, a rate 2.6 times higher than for Black or African American males.

Asian children, ages 12-to-17, used illicit drugs at one-half the rate of other leading races or ethnicities.

~

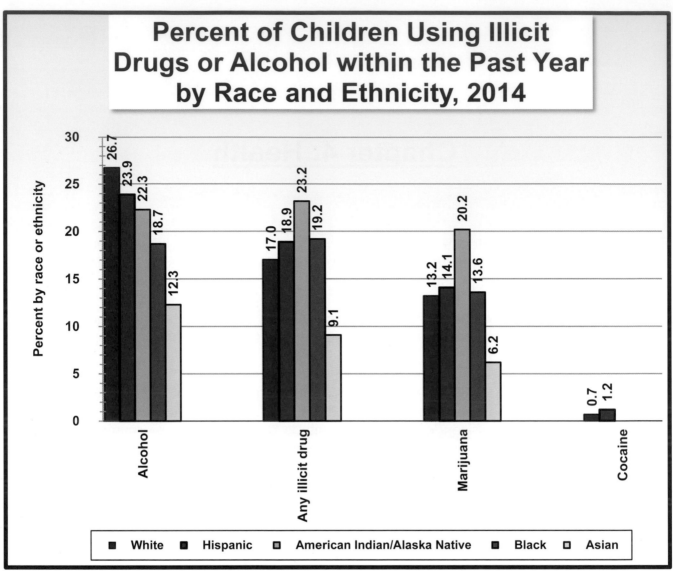

Percent of Children Using Illicit Drugs or Alcohol within the Past Year by Race and Ethnicity, 2014

White ■ Hispanic □ American Indian/Alaska Native ■ Black □ Asian

In 2014, Asian children ages 12 to 17 used illicit drugs at one-half the rate of other races or Hispanic children.

Percentage of 12 to 17 years old children reporting use of illicit drugs or alcohol within the past year in 2014.

Illicit drugs include other illegal drug use not shown separately—specifically, the use of heroin, hallucinogens, and inhalants, as well as the nonmedical use of prescription-type pain relievers, tranquilizers, stimulants, and sedatives. Marijuana includes hashish usage.

Race categories exclude persons of Hispanic ethnicity.

Source: U.S. Department of Health and Human Services, Substance Abuse and Mental Health Services Administration, National Household Survey on Drug Abuse: Main Findings, selected years, 1985 through 2001, and National Survey on Drug Use and Health, 2002 through 2014. Retrieved March 4, 2016, from http://www.samhsa.gov/data/population-data-nsduh/reports?tab=38. (This table was prepared March 2016.), Table 232.95, https://nces.ed.gov/programs/digest/2015menu_tables.asp

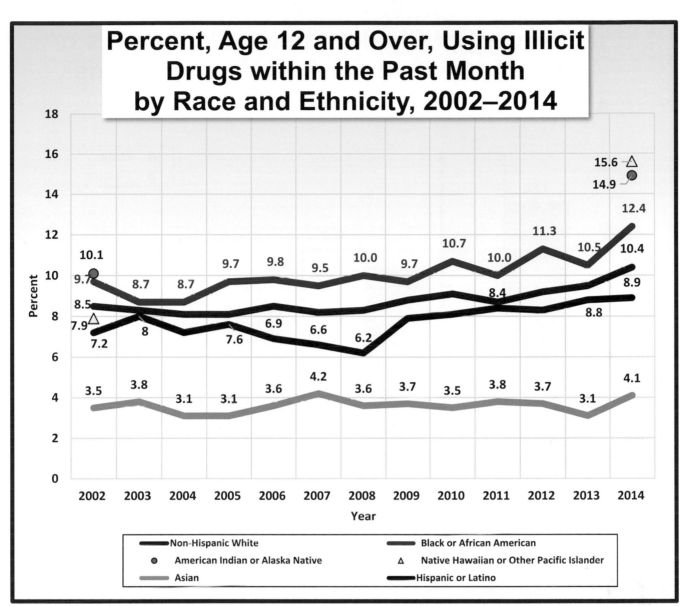

Percent, Age 12 and Over, Using Illicit Drugs within the Past Month by Race and Ethnicity, 2002–2014

Legend:
- Non-Hispanic White
- Black or African American
- ● American Indian or Alaska Native
- △ Native Hawaiian or Other Pacific Islander
- Asian
- Hispanic or Latino

In 2014, approximately one-of-seven American Indian, Alaska Native, Native Hawaiian, or Pacific Islander used illicit drugs. This rate was nearly double the rate in 2002 and four times higher than the rate for Asians.

Use of selected substances in the past month among persons aged 12 and over. Data are based on household interviews of a sample of the civilian noninstitutionalized population. Any illicit drug includes marijuana/hashish, cocaine (including crack), heroin, hallucinogens (including LSD and PCP), inhalants, or any prescription-type psychotherapeutic drug used nonmedically.

Source: National Vital Statistics System, public-use Mortality File, public-use Birth File; 'Deaths: Final data for 2014, Table 50, Available from: http://www.cdc.gov/nchs/products/nvsr.htm, http://www.cdc.gov/nchs/hus/contents2015.htm#059, Available from: http://www.cdc.gov/mmwr/preview/mmwrhtml/mm6450a3.htm?s_cid=mm6450a3_w

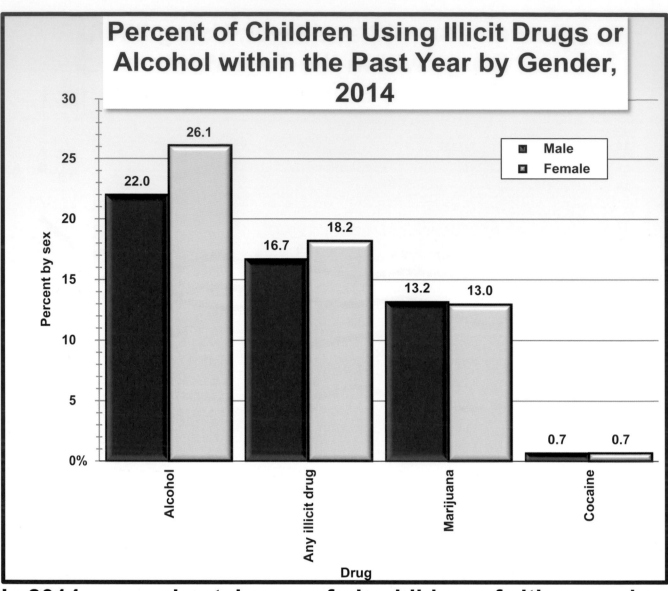

Percent of Children Using Illicit Drugs or Alcohol within the Past Year by Gender, 2014

In 2014, approximately one-of-six children of either gender, ages 12 to 17, admitted to using illicit drugs.

Percentage of 12 to 17 years old reporting use of illicit drugs or alcohol within the past year in 2014.

Illicit drugs include the use of heroin, hallucinogens, and inhalants, as well as the nonmedical use of prescription-type pain relievers, tranquilizers, stimulants, and sedatives.

Marijuana includes hashish usage.

Source: U.S. Department of Health and Human Services, Substance Abuse and Mental Health Services Administration, National Household Survey on Drug Abuse: Main Findings, selected years, 1985 through 2001, and National Survey on Drug Use and Health, 2002 through 2014. Retrieved March 4, 2016, from http://www.samhsa.gov/data/population-data-nsduh/reports?tab=38. (This table was prepared March 2016.), Table 232.95, https://nces.ed.gov/programs/digest/2015menu_tables.asp

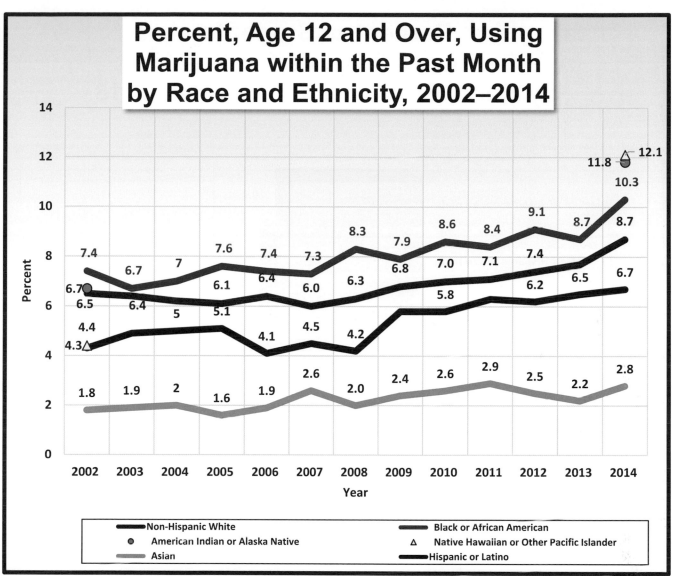

Percent, Age 12 and Over, Using Marijuana within the Past Month by Race and Ethnicity, 2002–2014

In 2014, nearly one-of-eight American Indian, Alaska Native, Native Hawaiian, or Other Pacific Islander used marijuana.

Use of selected substances in the past month among persons aged 12 and over. Data are based on household interviews of a sample of the civilian noninstitutionalized population.

Source: Substance Abuse and Mental Health Services Administration, Center for Behavioral Health Statistics, Table 50, Available from: http://www.cdc.gov/nchs/products/nvsr.htm, http://www.cdc.gov/nchs/hus/contents2015.htm#059, Available from: http://www.cdc.gov/mmwr/preview/mmwrhtml/mm6450a3.htm?s_cid=mm6450a3_w

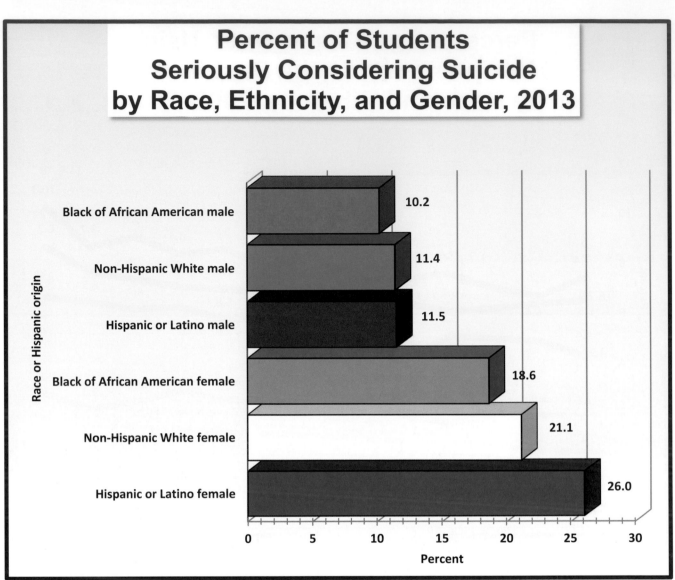

Percent of Students Seriously Considering Suicide by Race, Ethnicity, and Gender, 2013

Race or Hispanic origin

Black of African American male	10.2
Non-Hispanic White male	11.4
Hispanic or Latino male	11.5
Black of African American female	18.6
Non-Hispanic White female	21.1
Hispanic or Latino female	26.0

Percent: 0   5   10   15   20   25   30

In 2013, one-of-four high school age Hispanic or Latino females seriously considered suicide, the highest rate among all races or ethnicities.

Students grades 9-12 surveyed. Only youths attending school participated in the survey.

Source: CDC/National Center for HIV, Hepatitis, STD, and TB Prevention, Youth Risk Behavior Survey. See Youth Online website at http://nccd.cdc.gov/youthonline. Table 52, Available from: http://www.cdc.gov/nchs/products/nvsr.htm, http://www.cdc.gov/nchs/hus/contents2015.htm#059

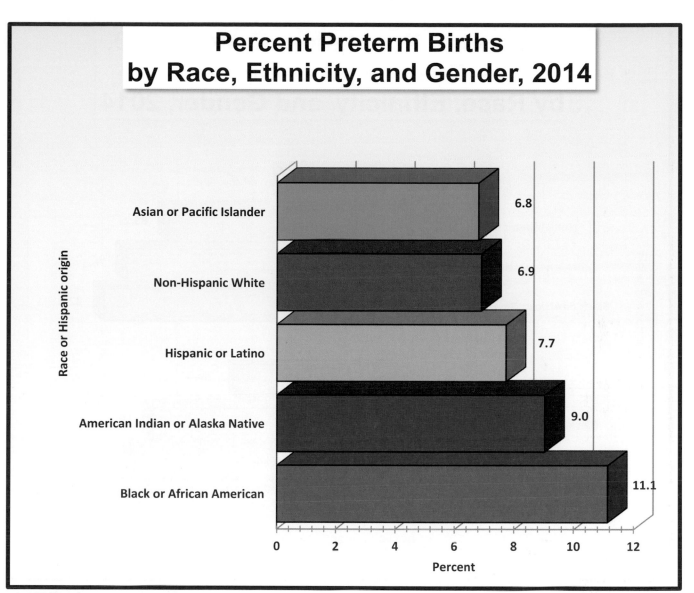

Percent Preterm Births by Race, Ethnicity, and Gender, 2014

Race or Hispanic origin

- Asian or Pacific Islander: 6.8
- Non-Hispanic White: 6.9
- Hispanic or Latino: 7.7
- American Indian or Alaska Native: 9.0
- Black or African American: 11.1

Percent

In 2014, more than 11 percent of Black or African American births were preterm. This was more than any other race or ethnicity, and 63 percent more than births of Asian or Pacific Islanders.

Source: CDC/NCHS, National Vital Statistics System, public-use Birth File, http://www.cdc.gov/nchs/hus/contents2015.htm#059, Figure 20

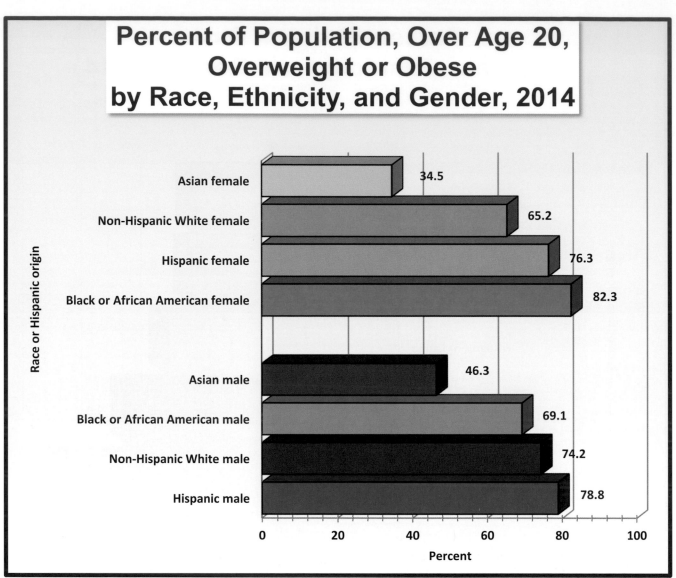

Percent of Population, Over Age 20, Overweight or Obese by Race, Ethnicity, and Gender, 2014

Race or Hispanic origin

Asian female	34.5
Non-Hispanic White female	65.2
Hispanic female	76.3
Black or African American female	82.3
Asian male	46.3
Black or African American male	69.1
Non-Hispanic White male	74.2
Hispanic male	78.8

Percent

In 2014, approximately four-of-five Black or African American females over the age of 20 were overweight or obese. This was more than double the rate for Asian females.

Body mass index (BMI) equals weight in kilograms divided by height in meters squared. Overweight or obese is having a BMI greater than 24. Data are based on measured height and weight of a sample of the civilian noninstitutionalized population. Data for ages 20 and older.

Source: CDC/National Center for HIV, Hepatitis, STD, and TB Prevention, Youth Risk Behavior Survey. See Youth Online website at http://nccd.cdc.gov/youthonline. Table 58, Available from: http://www.cdc.gov/nchs/products/nvsr.htm, http://www.cdc.gov/nchs/hus/contents2015.htm#059

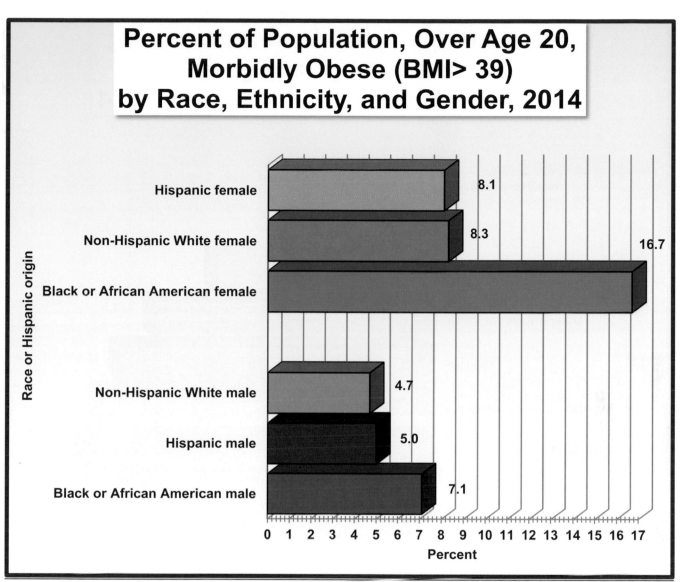

Percent of Population, Over Age 20, Morbidly Obese (BMI> 39) by Race, Ethnicity, and Gender, 2014

Race or Hispanic origin

- Hispanic female — 8.1
- Non-Hispanic White female — 8.3
- Black or African American female — 16.7
- Non-Hispanic White male — 4.7
- Hispanic male — 5.0
- Black or African American male — 7.1

0 1 2 3 4 5 6 7 8 9 10 11 12 13 14 15 16 17

Percent

In 2014, approximately one-of-six Black or African American females over age 20 were morbidly obese. This was more than double the rate for Hispanic or non-Hispanic White females.

Data are based on measured height and weight of a sample of the civilian noninstitutionalized population. Data for ages 20 and older. Body mass index (BMI) equals weight in kilograms divided by height in meters squared. Morbid obesity is diagnosed by determining body mass index (BMI). BMI is defined by the ratio of an individual's height to his or her weight. Normal BMI ranges from 20–25. An individual is considered morbidly obese if he or she is 100 pounds over his/her ideal body weight, has a BMI of 40 or more, or 35 or more and experiencing obesity-related health conditions, such as high blood pressure or diabetes.

Source: CDC/NCHS, National Health and Nutrition Examination Survey, http://www.cdc.gov/nchs/hus/contents2015.htm#059, Table 58

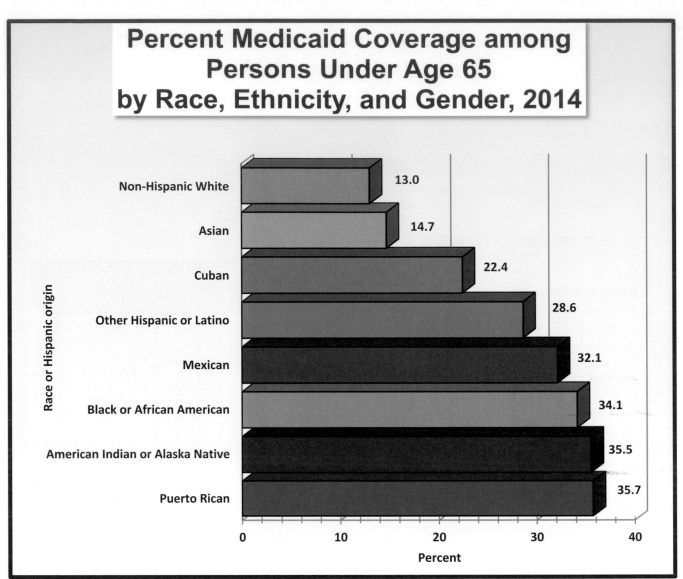

Percent Medicaid Coverage among Persons Under Age 65 by Race, Ethnicity, and Gender, 2014

In 2014, approximately one-of-three Black, African Americans, America Indian, Alaska Natives, Puerto Rican, and Mexican persons were enrolled in Medicaid.

Medicaid is a U.S. government program, financed by federal, state, and local funds, for hospitalization and medical insurance for persons of all ages below certain income limits. Data are based on household interviews of a sample of the civilian noninstitutionalized population.

The category Medicaid coverage includes persons who had any of the following at the time of interview: Medicaid, other public assistance through 1996, state-sponsored health plan starting in 1997, or Children's Health Insurance Program (CHIP) starting in 1999; it includes those who also had another type of coverage in addition to one of these.

Source: National Health Interview Survey, http://www.cdc.gov/nchs/hus/contents2015.htm#059, Table 104

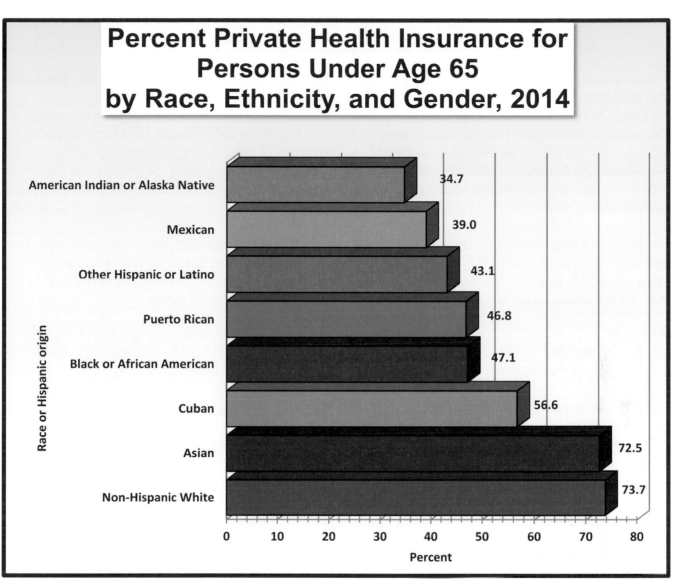

Percent Private Health Insurance for Persons Under Age 65 by Race, Ethnicity, and Gender, 2014

American Indian or Alaska Native — 34.7
Mexican — 39.0
Other Hispanic or Latino — 43.1
Puerto Rican — 46.8
Black or African American — 47.1
Cuban — 56.6
Asian — 72.5
Non-Hispanic White — 73.7

Race or Hispanic origin (vertical axis)

0   10   20   30   40   50   60   70   80

Percent

In 2014, most Hispanic ethnicities along with more than one half of Blacks, American Indians, and Alaska Natives under the age of 65 did not have private health insurance.

Private health insurance coverage among persons under age 65. Data are based on household interviews of a sample of the civilian noninstitutionalized population. Any private health insurance coverage (both individual and insurance obtained through the workplace. Private health insurance coverage is at the time of interview.

Chapter 5: Society

Society, according to one of the definitions by the Merriam-Webster dictionary, are people in general thought of as living together in organized communities with shared laws, traditions, and values. America consists of many societies co-habiting the same nation, and while all Americans are subject to the same laws to govern behavior that affects others, the traditions and social norms of acceptable behavior in some racial, ethnic, or religious groups can be substantially different than for others. For example, there are very significant differences between races and ethnicities regarding permissive sexual behavior and what constitutes a typical family unit.

In 1990, 49 out of 10,000 non-Hispanic Black or African American girls, ages 10–14, had babies—double the rate for Hispanic girls and 10 times greater than for non-Hispanic White girls. By 2014, the rate for non-Hispanic Black or African American girls had declined to 6 births per 10,000—six times greater than for non-Hispanic White or Asian girls.

In 2014:

- 30 percent of Black or African American households with children under the age of six included a married couple, compared with 85 percent of Asian households.

- The percentage of women giving birth who were unmarried was highest among non-Hispanic Black or African American women, at 70 percent, compared to 16 percent for Asian women, the lowest rate of the leading races and ethnicities.

- One-in-four American Indian and Alaska Native persons, over age 12, admitted to binge drinking of alcohol—five or more drinks at one occasion—compared to one-of-seven Asian persons.

- Approximately 23 percent of the population who responded to a PEW Research survey stated they were not affiliated with any religion. Among those born after 1990 the percentage was 36.

- In the 2014 mid-term, national election only 27 percent of Hispanics eligible to vote, voted, compared with 46 percent of non-Hispanic White persons. In the 2016 presidential election, 75.2 percent of those who voted in Lincoln County, West Virginia—the county with the highest percentage of non-Hispanic White population—voted for the Republican candidate, Donald Trump, whereas 79.1 percent who voted in Starr County, Texas —the county with the highest percentage of Hispanic population— voted for the Democrat candidate, Hillary Clinton.

- 85 percent of Asian households with children under age six, had both married parents present compared with 30 percent of Black or African American households.

- Of 783,000 same-sex couple households in the United States, 75 percent were non-Hispanic White although non-Hispanic White persons are only 62 percent of the general population.

~

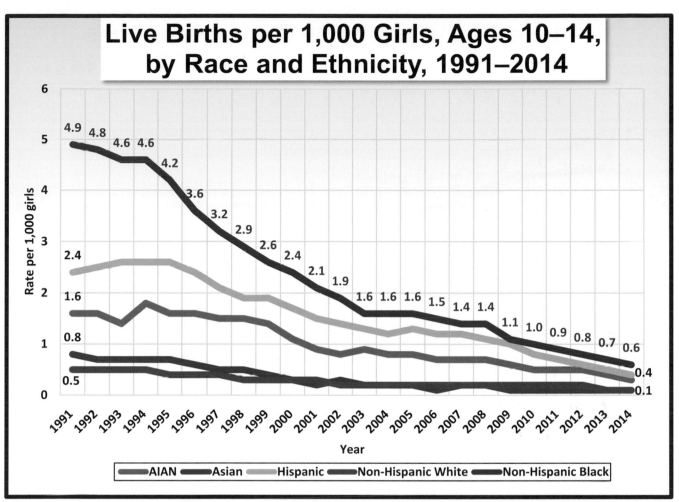

Live Births per 1,000 Girls, Ages 10–14, by Race and Ethnicity, 1991–2014

Non-Hispanic Black girls, ages 10–14, experienced a reduction in birth rate by a factor of nine, between 1990 and 2014. In 2014, the rate was six times greater than for Asian or non-Hispanic White girls.

Births refers to live births.

Source: CDC/NCHS, National Vital Statistics System, public-use Birth File. Hamilton BE, Martin JA, Osterman MJK, et al. Births: Final data for 2014. National vital statistics reports; volume 64, no. 12. Hyattsville, MD: NCHS. 2015; Available from: http://www.cdc.gov/nchs/data/nvsr/nvsr64/nvsr64_12.pdf, http://www.cdc.gov/nchs/hus/contents2015.htm#059

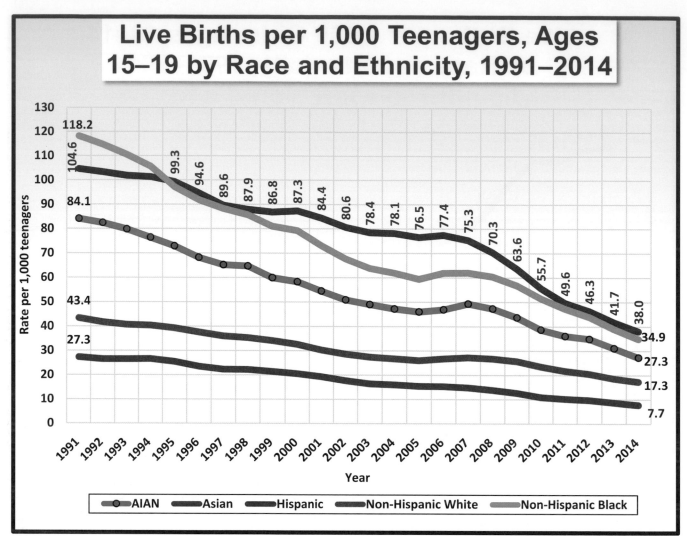

Live Births per 1,000 Teenagers, Ages 15–19 by Race and Ethnicity, 1991–2014

Rate per 1,000 teenagers

Legend: AIAN, Asian, Hispanic, Non-Hispanic White, Non-Hispanic Black

Hispanic, non-Hispanic Black, American Indian and Alaska Native teenagers, ages 15–19, experienced a reduction in birth rate by two-thirds, between 1990 and 2014. In 2014, the birth rate for Hispanics was five times higher than it was for Asians.

Source: CDC/NCHS, National Vital Statistics System, public-use Birth File. Hamilton BE, Martin JA, Osterman MJK, et al. Births: Final data for 2014. National vital statistics reports; volume 64, no. 12. Hyattsville, MD: NCHS. 2015;
Available from: http://www.cdc.gov/nchs/data/nvsr/nvsr64/nvsr64_12.pdf, http://www.cdc.gov/nchs/hus/contents2015.htm#059

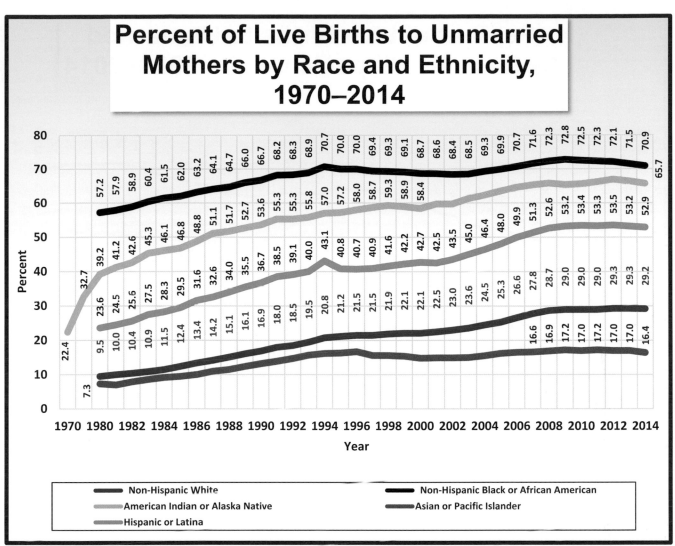

Percent of Live Births to Unmarried Mothers by Race and Ethnicity, 1970–2014

In 2014, approximately two-of-three Black, American Indian, and Alaska Native women who gave birth were unmarried compared with one-of-six Asian or Pacific Island women.

Rates were computed by dividing number of live births to number of unmarried mothers, regardless of age of mother, by the population of unmarried women aged 15–44.

For 1970 and 1975, birth rates are by race of child.

Prior to 1993, data from states that did not report Hispanic origin on the birth certificate were excluded. Data for non-Hispanic White and non-Hispanic Black women for years prior to 1989 are not nationally representative and are provided solely for comparison with Hispanic data.

Source: CDC/NCHS, National Vital Statistics System, public-use Birth File. Hamilton BE, Martin JA, Osterman MJK, et al. Births: Final data for 2014. National vital statistics reports; volume 64, no. 12. Hyattsville, MD. NCHS. 2015; Available from: http://www.cdc.gov/nchs/data/nvsr/nvsr64/nvsr64_12.pdf, http://www.cdc.gov/nchs/hus/contents2015.htm#004

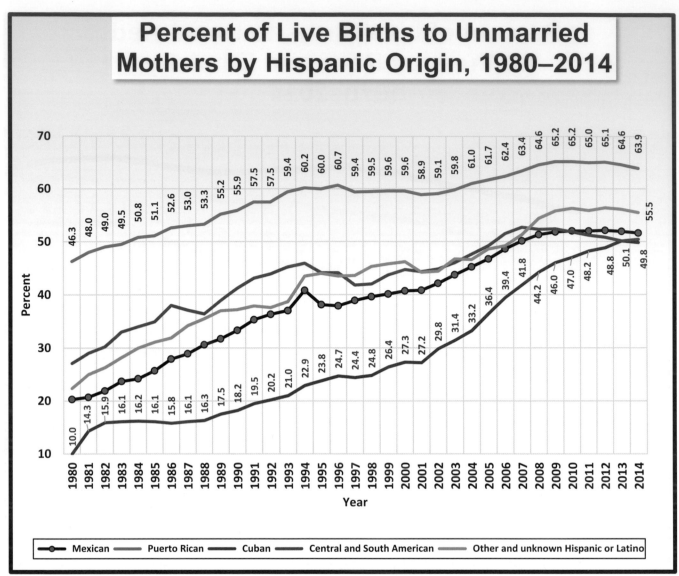

Percent of Live Births to Unmarried Mothers by Hispanic Origin, 1980–2014

In 2014, almost two-of-three Puerto Rican women who gave birth were unmarried compared with one-of-two Cuban women.

Source: CDC/NCHS, National Vital Statistics System, public-use Birth File. Hamilton BE, Martin JA, Osterman MJK, et al. Births: Final data for 2014. National vital statistics reports; volume 64, no. 12. Hyattsville, MD: NCHS. 2015;
Available from: http://www.cdc.gov/nchs/data/nvsr/nvsr64/nvsr64_12.pdf, http://www.cdc.gov/nchs/hus/contents2015.htm#004

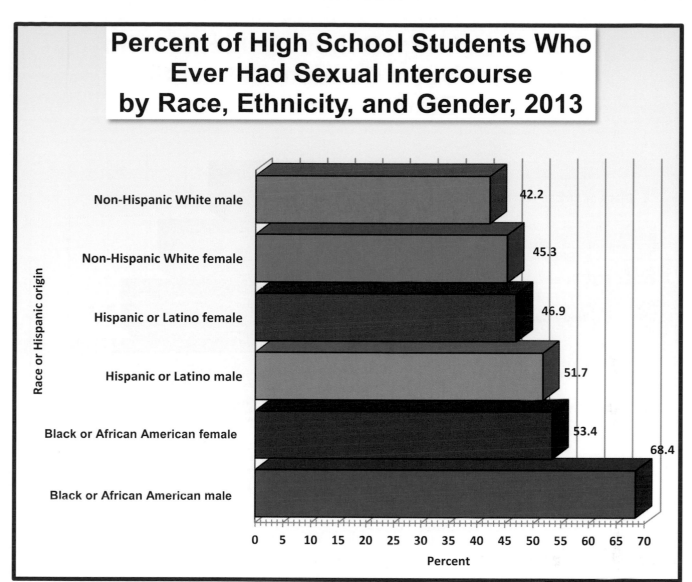

Percent of High School Students Who Ever Had Sexual Intercourse by Race, Ethnicity, and Gender, 2013

In 2013, 68 percent of Black or African American high school age males reported they had had sexual intercourse, compared with 42 percent non-Hispanic White males.

Survey among students grades 9-12.

Source: CDC/National Center for HIV, Hepatitis, STD, and TB Prevention, Youth Risk Behavior Survey. See Youth Online website at http://nccd.cdc.gov/youthonline. Table 52, Available from: http://www.cdc.gov/nchs/products/nvsr.htm, http://www.cdc.gov/nchs/hus/contents2015.htm#059

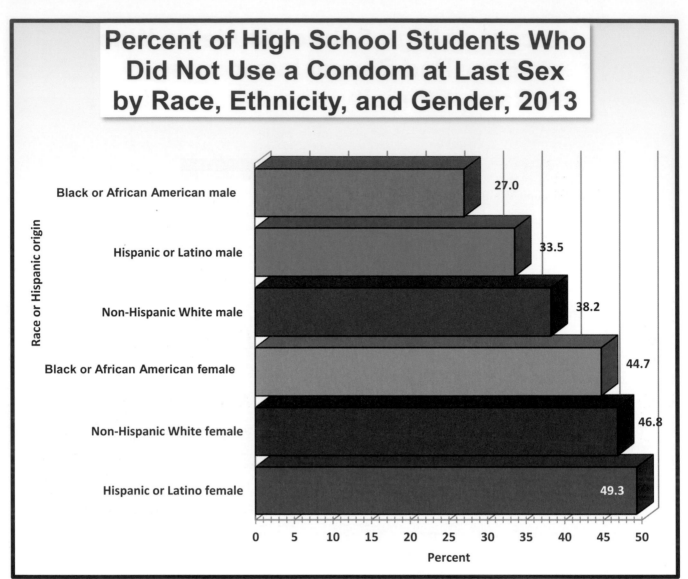

Percent of High School Students Who Did Not Use a Condom at Last Sex by Race, Ethnicity, and Gender, 2013

Race or Hispanic origin

Black or African American male	27.0
Hispanic or Latino male	33.5
Non-Hispanic White male	38.2
Black or African American female	44.7
Non-Hispanic White female	46.8
Hispanic or Latino female	49.3

Percent

In 2013, one-half of high school age Hispanic or Latino females reported they did not use a condom during sexual intercourse.

Among students grades 9-12 who had sexual intercourse during the past 3 months.

Source: CDC/National Center for HIV, Hepatitis, STD, and TB Prevention, Youth Risk Behavior Survey. See Youth Online website at http://nccd.cdc.gov/youthonline. Table 52, Available from: http://www.cdc.gov/nchs/products/nvsr.htm, http://www.cdc.gov/nchs/hus/contents2015.htm#059

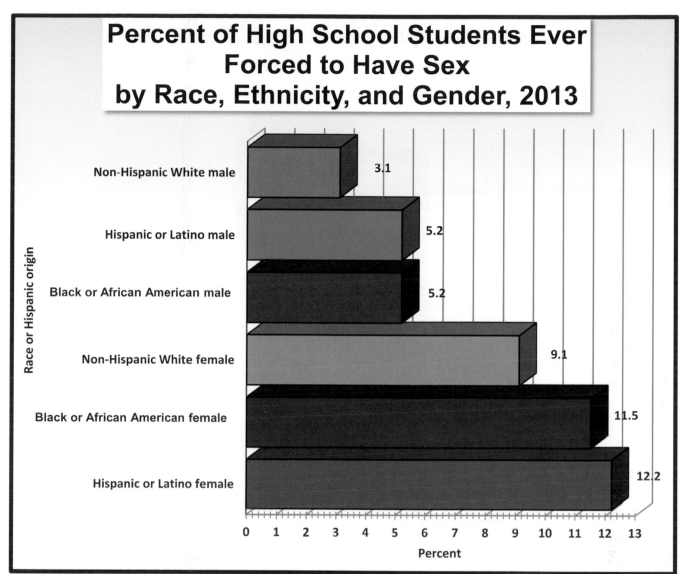

Percent of High School Students Ever Forced to Have Sex by Race, Ethnicity, and Gender, 2013

Race or Hispanic origin

Non-Hispanic White male — 3.1

Hispanic or Latino male — 5.2

Black or African American male — 5.2

Non-Hispanic White female — 9.1

Black or African American female — 11.5

Hispanic or Latino female — 12.2

Percent

In 2013, one-of-eight high school age Hispanic or Latino females reported they were forced to have sex—the highest percent among all races and ethnicities.

Among students grades 9-12.

Source: CDC/National Center for HIV, Hepatitis, STD, and TB Prevention, Youth Risk Behavior Survey. See Youth Online website at http://nccd.cdc.gov/youthonline. Table 52, Available from: http://www.cdc.gov/nchs/products/nvsr.htm, http://www.cdc.gov/nchs/hus/contents2015.htm#059

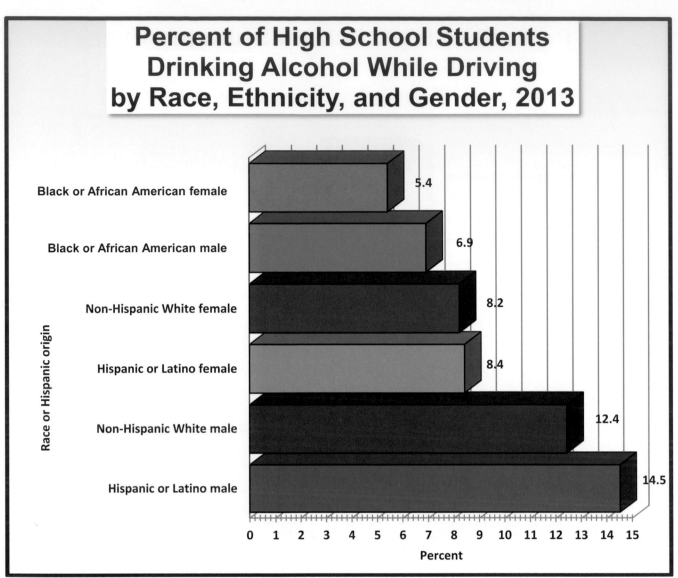

Percent of High School Students Drinking Alcohol While Driving by Race, Ethnicity, and Gender, 2013

Black or African American female — 5.4
Black or African American male — 6.9
Non-Hispanic White female — 8.2
Hispanic or Latino female — 8.4
Non-Hispanic White male — 12.4
Hispanic or Latino male — 14.5

Race or Hispanic origin

Percent

In 2013, one-in-seven Hispanic or Latino high school age male drivers drank alcohol while driving—the highest rate among all races and ethnicities.

Among students grades 9-12 in the past 30 days.

Source: CDC/National Center for HIV, Hepatitis, STD, and TB Prevention, Youth Risk Behavior Survey. See Youth Online website at http://nccd.cdc.gov/youthonline. Table 52, Available from: http://www.cdc.gov/nchs/products/nvsr.htm, http://www.cdc.gov/nchs/hus/contents2015.htm#059

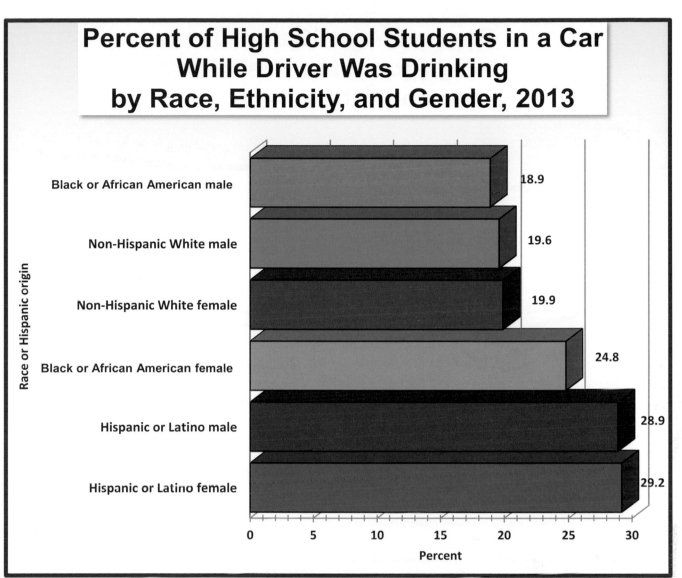

Percent of High School Students in a Car While Driver Was Drinking by Race, Ethnicity, and Gender, 2013

Black or African American male — 18.9

Non-Hispanic White male — 19.6

Non-Hispanic White female — 19.9

Black or African American female — 24.8

Hispanic or Latino male — 28.9

Hispanic or Latino female — 29.2

Race or Hispanic origin

Percent

In 2013, approximately 20 percent of high school age non-Hispanic White males and females rode with someone who was drinking. In comparison, 30 percent of Hispanics rode with a driver who was drinking.

Among students grades 9-12, when riding in a car driven by someone else, in the past 30 days.

Source: CDC/National Center for HIV, Hepatitis, STD, and TB Prevention, Youth Risk Behavior Survey. See Youth Online website at http://nccd.cdc.gov/youthonline. Table 52, Available from: http://www.cdc.gov/nchs/products/nvsr.htm, http://www.cdc.gov/nchs/hus/contents2015.htm#059

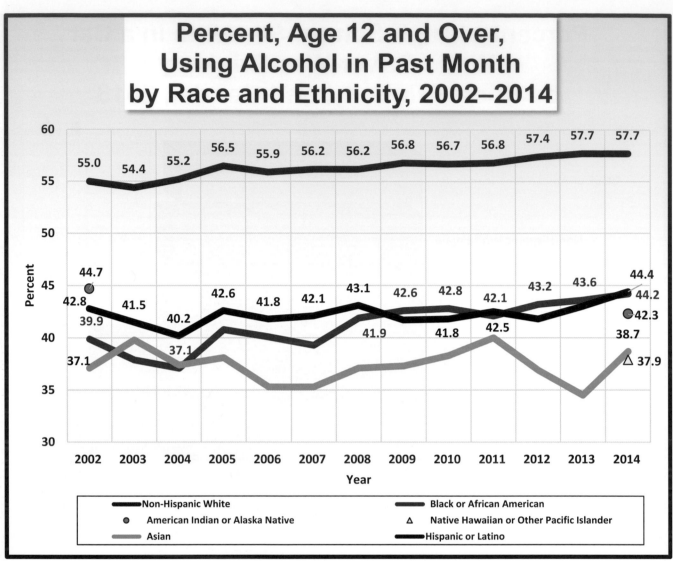

Percent, Age 12 and Over, Using Alcohol in Past Month by Race and Ethnicity, 2002–2014

Legend:
- Non-Hispanic White
- Black or African American
- American Indian or Alaska Native
- Native Hawaiian or Other Pacific Islander
- Asian
- Hispanic or Latino

Nearly six-of-ten non-Hispanic White persons over the age of twelve used alcohol in 2014. This rate was approximately 50 percent higher than any other race and virtually unchanged since 2002.

Use of selected substances in the past month among persons aged 12 and over. Data are based on household interviews of a sample of the civilian noninstitutionalized population.

Source: Substance Abuse and Mental Health Services Administration, Center for Behavioral Health Statistics, Table 50, Available from: http://www.cdc.gov/nchs/products/nvsr.htm, http://www.cdc.gov/nchs/hus/contents2015.htm#059, Available from: http://www.cdc.gov/mmwr/preview/mmwrhtml/mm6450a3.htm?s_cid=mm6450a3_w

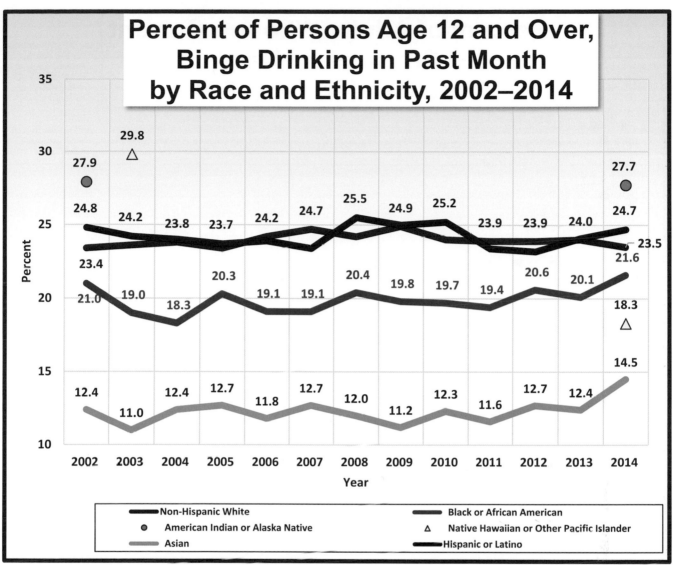

Percent of Persons Age 12 and Over, Binge Drinking in Past Month by Race and Ethnicity, 2002–2014

One-of-four American Indian or Alaska Native persons over the age of 12 admitted to binge drinking in 2014— double the rate of Asian persons.

Binge alcohol use is defined as drinking five or more drinks on the same occasion on at least 1 day in the past 30 days. Data are based on household interviews of a sample of the civilian noninstitutionalized population.

Source: Substance Abuse and Mental Health Services Administration, Center for Behavioral Health Statistics, Table 50, Available from: http://www.cdc.gov/nchs/products/nvsr.htm, http://www.cdc.gov/nchs/hus/contents2015.htm#059, Available from: http://www.cdc.gov/mmwr/preview/mmwrhtml/mm6450a3.htm?s_cid=mm6450a3_w

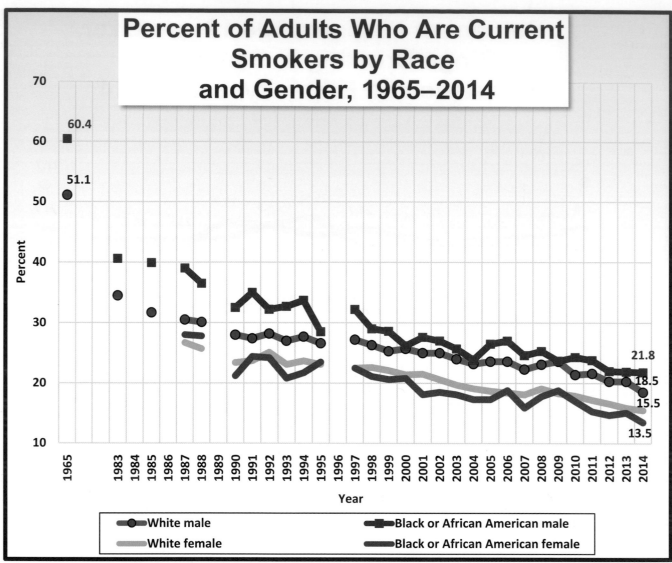

Percent of Adults Who Are Current Smokers by Race and Gender, 1965–2014

Smoking rates by White, Black or African Americans, both male and female, have been reduced by two-thirds between 1965 and 2014.

Data are based on household interviews of a sample of the civilian noninstitutionalized population.

Source: National Vital Statistics System, public-use Mortality File, public-use Birth File; 'Deaths: Final data for 2014, Table 47, Available from: http://www.cdc.gov/nchs/products/nvsr.htm, http://www.cdc.gov/nchs/hus/contents2015.htm#059, Available from: http://www.cdc.gov/mmwr/preview/mmwrhtml/mm6450a3.htm?s_cid=mm6450a3_w

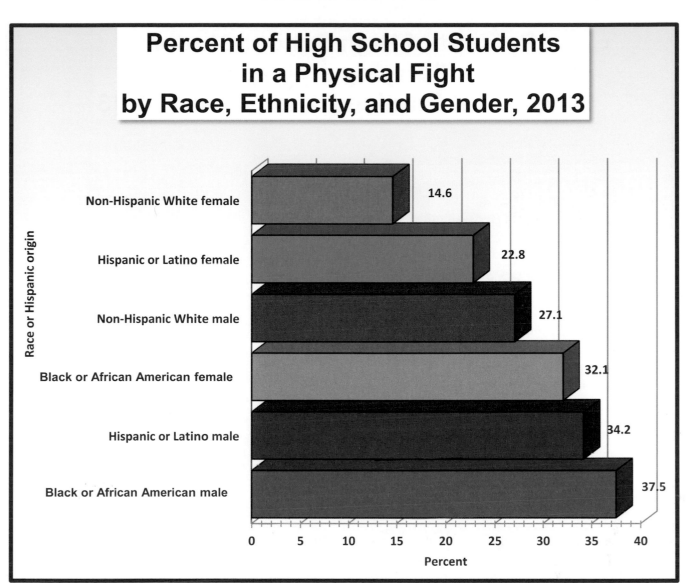

Percent of High School Students in a Physical Fight by Race, Ethnicity, and Gender, 2013

Race or Hispanic origin	Percent
Non-Hispanic White female	14.6
Hispanic or Latino female	22.8
Non-Hispanic White male	27.1
Black or African American female	32.1
Hispanic or Latino male	34.2
Black or African American male	37.5

In 2013, nearly one-of-three Black or African American high school females was in a physical fight—approximately 20 percent higher rate than for non-Hispanic White males.

Only youths attending school participated in the survey, grades 9–12.

Source: CDC/National Center for HIV, Hepatitis, STD, and TB Prevention, Youth Risk Behavior Survey. See Youth Online website at http://nccd.cdc.gov/youthonline. Table 52, Available from: http://www.cdc.gov/nchs/products/nvsr.htm, http://www.cdc.gov/nchs/hus/contents2015.htm#059

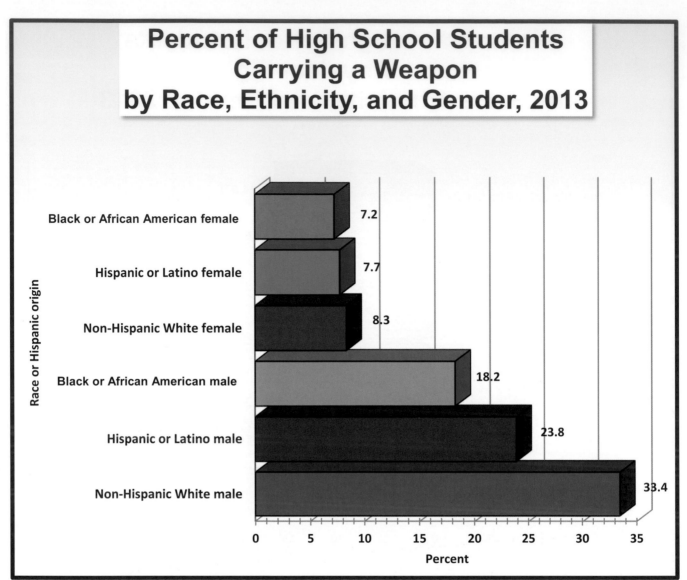

Percent of High School Students Carrying a Weapon by Race, Ethnicity, and Gender, 2013

Race or Hispanic origin

- Black or African American female — 7.2
- Hispanic or Latino female — 7.7
- Non-Hispanic White female — 8.3
- Black or African American male — 18.2
- Hispanic or Latino male — 23.8
- Non-Hispanic White male — 33.4

Percent

In 2013, one-of-three non-Hispanic White males in high school carried a weapon—the highest rate among all races and ethnicities.

Only youths attending school participated in the survey, grade 9-12. Weapons such as a gun, knife, or club carried within the past 30 days.

Source: CDC/National Center for HIV, Hepatitis, STD, and TB Prevention, Youth Risk Behavior Survey. See Youth Online website at http://nccd.cdc.gov/youthonline. Table 52, Available from: http://www.cdc.gov/nchs/products/nvsr.htm, http://www.cdc.gov/nchs/hus/contents2015.htm#059

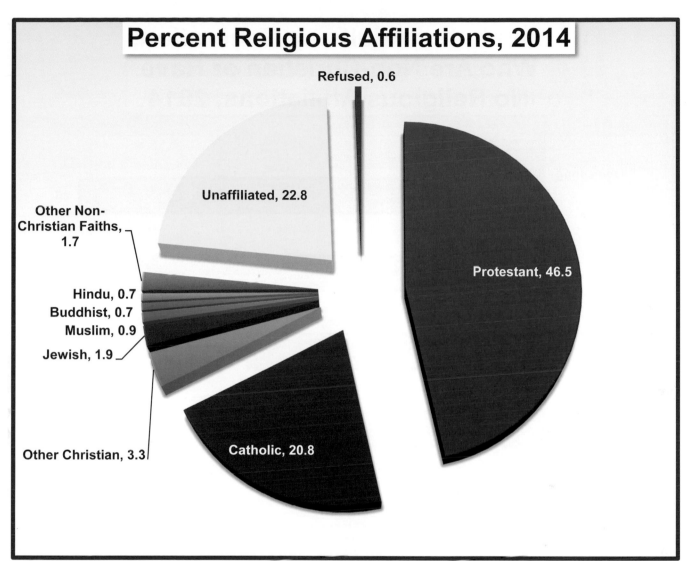

Percent Religious Affiliations, 2014

Refused, 0.6

Unaffiliated, 22.8

Other Non-Christian Faiths, 1.7

Hindu, 0.7

Buddhist, 0.7

Muslim, 0.9

Jewish, 1.9

Other Christian, 3.3

Catholic, 20.8

Protestant, 46.5

In 2014, over 70 percent of the population was affiliated with the Christian religion and approximately 23 percent was not affiliated with any religion.

According to the PEW Research Center in 2014, 70.6 percent of the population surveyed were affiliated with a Christian religious sect compared with 78.4 percent in their 2007 survey.

Pew Research Center estimates that there were about 3.3 million Muslims of all ages living in the United States in 2015 and projects that the Muslim share of the total population will increase to approximately two percent by 2050.

Source: PEW Research Center http://www.pewforum.org/2015/05/12/americas-changing-religious-landscape/, http://www.pewresearch.org/fact-tank/2016/01/06/a-new-estimate-of-the-u-s-muslim-population/

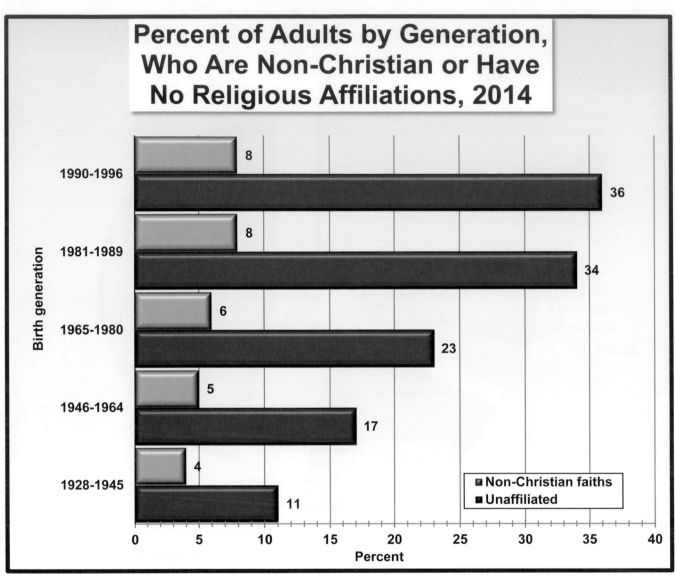

Percent of Adults by Generation, Who Are Non-Christian or Have No Religious Affiliations, 2014

Birth generation

Generation	Non-Christian faiths	Unaffiliated
1990-1996	8	36
1981-1989	8	34
1965-1980	6	23
1946-1964	5	17
1928-1945	4	11

Percent: 0, 5, 10, 15, 20, 25, 30, 35, 40

■ Non-Christian faiths
■ Unaffiliated

In 2014, more than one-third of those born after 1990 were not affiliated with any religion.

According to the PEW Research Center the percentage of persons with no religious affiliation has grown larger than any other religious sector.

Source: PEW Research Center, 2014 Religious Landscape Study, http://www.pewforum.org/2015/05/12/americas-changing-religious-landscape/pr_15-05-12_rls-01/

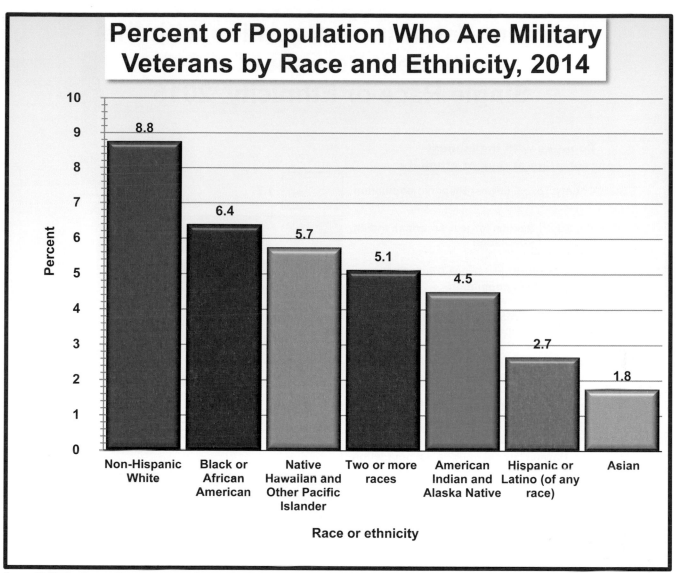

Percent of Population Who Are Military Veterans by Race and Ethnicity, 2014

In 2014, almost 1-of-11 non-Hispanic White persons were military veterans, a rate higher than any other race or ethnic group and almost five times higher than Asian persons.

Source: U.S. Department of Veteran Affairs, http://www.va.gov/vetdata/

Percent Veterans in Counties with the Highest Percent of a Single Race or Ethnicity, 2015

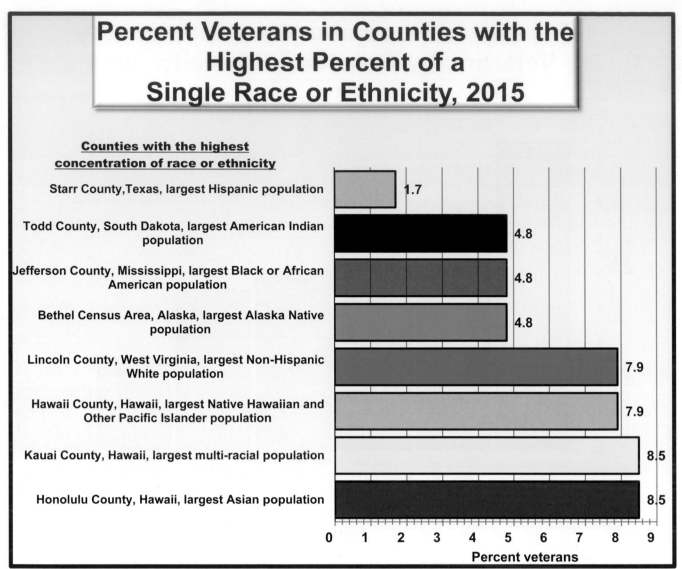

Counties with the highest concentration of race or ethnicity

County	Percent veterans
Starr County, Texas, largest Hispanic population	1.7
Todd County, South Dakota, largest American Indian population	4.8
Jefferson County, Mississippi, largest Black or African American population	4.8
Bethel Census Area, Alaska, largest Alaska Native population	4.8
Lincoln County, West Virginia, largest Non-Hispanic White population	7.9
Hawaii County, Hawaii, largest Native Hawaiian and Other Pacific Islander population	7.9
Kauai County, Hawaii, largest multi-racial population	8.5
Honolulu County, Hawaii, largest Asian population	8.5

Percent veterans

In 2015, three counties in Hawaii had the highest percent of military veterans among all counties where a single racial or ethnic group had the highest concentration. One-of-eleven persons in these three counties was a veteran.

The United States is comprised of 3,142 counties. A county is a political and geographic subdivision of a state. The Census Bureau considers the parishes of Louisiana and the boroughs of Alaska and the District of Columbia to be equivalent to counties for statistical purposes. Hispanic origin is considered an ethnicity, not a race. Hispanics may be of any race.

Source: U.S. Census Bureau, American Fact Finder, Community Facts, 2015 Population Estimates Program, accessed 10/17/16, http://factfinder.census.gov/faces/nav/jsf/pages/community_facts.xhtml#

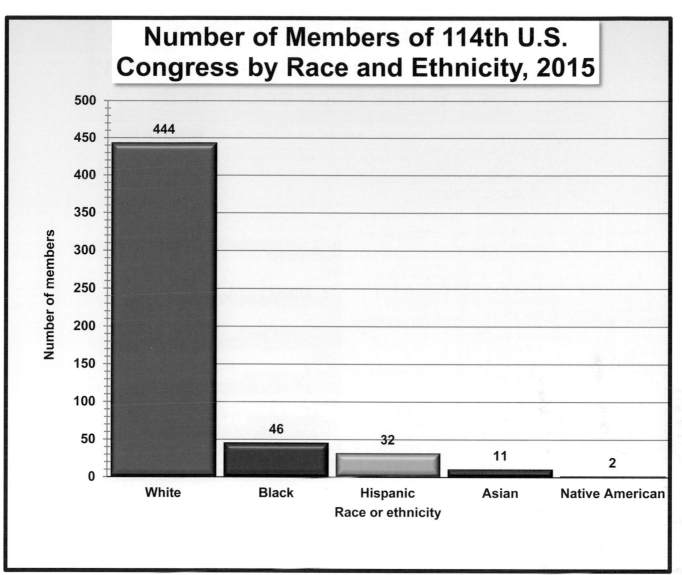

Number of Members of 114th U.S. Congress by Race and Ethnicity, 2015

(Chart: Number of members vs. Race or ethnicity)

- White: 444
- Black: 46
- Hispanic: 32
- Asian: 11
- Native American: 2

Eighty-three percent of the members of the 114th U.S. Congress were non-Hispanic White. Non-Hispanic White persons comprised 62.2 percent of the United States population in 2014. The members of the 114th Congress were elected to office in November 2014.

The 114th Congress election occurred in November 2014. Race categories exclude persons of Hispanic ethnicity.

Source: PEW Research Center, Washington D.C., published January 12, 2015, http://www.pewresearch.org/fact-tank/2015/01/12/114th-congress-is-most-diverse-ever/

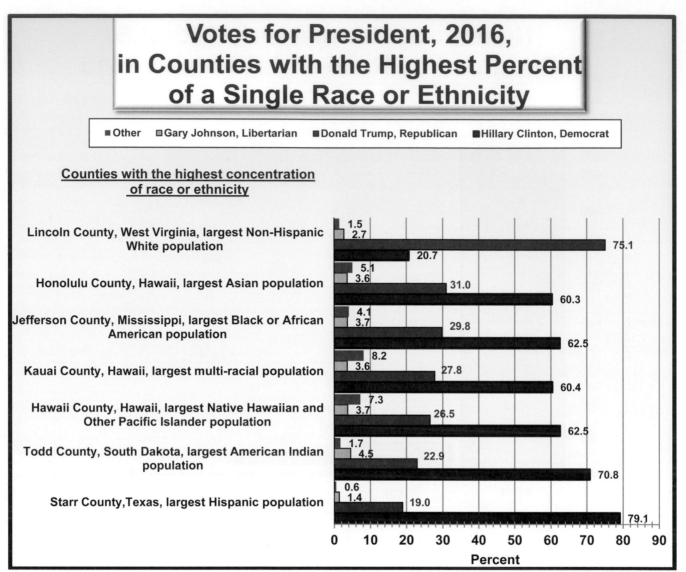

Votes for President, 2016, in Counties with the Highest Percent of a Single Race or Ethnicity

■ Other   ▫ Gary Johnson, Libertarian   ■ Donald Trump, Republican   ■ Hillary Clinton, Democrat

Counties with the highest concentration of race or ethnicity

Lincoln County, West Virginia, largest Non-Hispanic White population
- 1.5
- 2.7
- 20.7
- 75.1

Honolulu County, Hawaii, largest Asian population
- 5.1
- 3.6
- 31.0
- 60.3

Jefferson County, Mississippi, largest Black or African American population
- 4.1
- 3.7
- 29.8
- 62.5

Kauai County, Hawaii, largest multi-racial population
- 8.2
- 3.6
- 27.8
- 60.4

Hawaii County, Hawaii, largest Native Hawaiian and Other Pacific Islander population
- 7.3
- 3.7
- 26.5
- 62.5

Todd County, South Dakota, largest American Indian population
- 1.7
- 4.5
- 22.9
- 70.8

Starr County, Texas, largest Hispanic population
- 0.6
- 1.4
- 19.0
- 79.1

Percent (0, 10, 20, 30, 40, 50, 60, 70, 80, 90)

In 2016, 75.1 percent of voters in Lincoln County, West Virginia—the county with the highest proportion of non-Hispanic White persons—voted for Donald Trump. The counties with the highest concentrations of Hispanic or minority races voted between 60–79 percent for Hillary Clinton.

Hispanic is an ethnicity and can be of any race.

Source: https://results.vote.wa.gov/results/current/jefferson/,
http://services.sos.wv.gov/apps/elections/results/results.aspx?year=2016&eid=23&county=Lincoln,
http://www.co.starr.tx.us/default.aspx?Starr_County/Elections, http://files.hawaii.gov/elections/files/results/2016/general/coh.pdf,
http://electionresults.sd.gov/resultsCTY.aspx?type=SWR&pty=0&rid=5039&osn=100&map=CTY

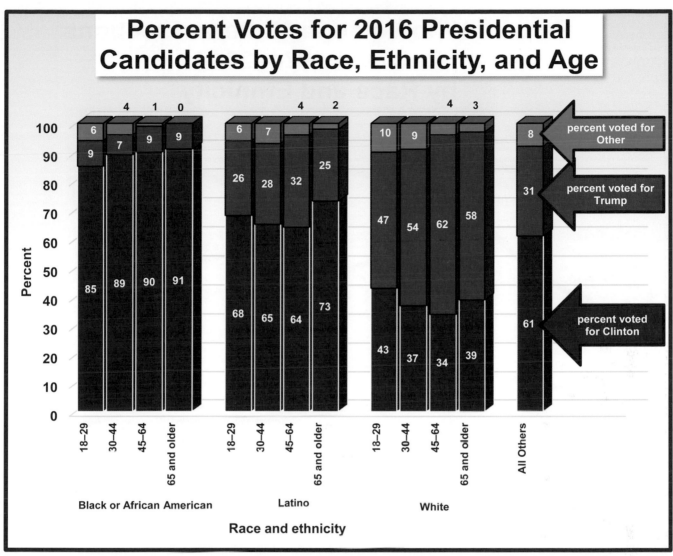

Percent Votes for 2016 Presidential Candidates by Race, Ethnicity, and Age

In the 2016 presidential election, Hillary Clinton received over 85 percent of the Black or African American vote while Donald Trump received 54–62 percent of votes by White voters, over age 30. Ten percent of White voters, ages 18–29, voted for candidates "other" than Clinton or Trump.

The voter survey by Edison Research is based on questionnaires completed by 24,537 voters leaving 350 voting places throughout the United States on election day including 4,398 telephone interviews with early and absentee voters.

Source: Edison Research 2016 Exit Poll, http://www.edisonresearch.com/

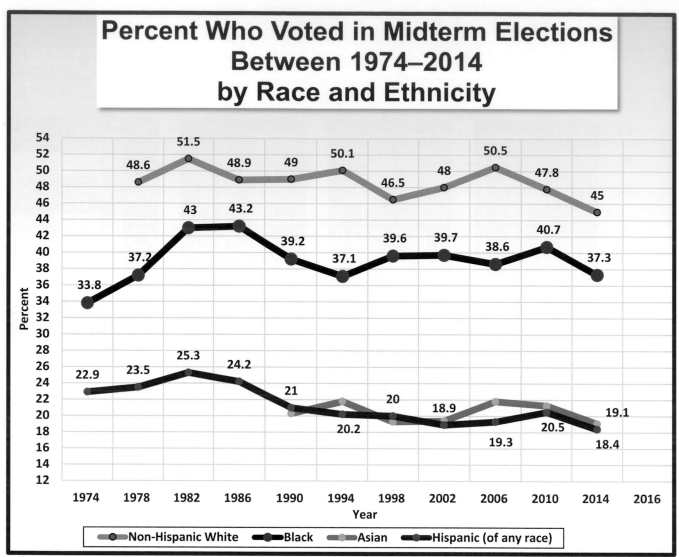

Percent Who Voted in Midterm Elections Between 1974–2014 by Race and Ethnicity

Legend: Non-Hispanic White · Black · Asian · Hispanic (of any race)

Non-Hispanic White: 48.6, 51.5, 48.9, 49, 50.1, 46.5, 48, 50.5, 47.8, 45

Black: 33.8, 37.2, 43, 43.2, 39.2, 37.1, 39.6, 39.7, 38.6, 40.7, 37.3

Asian / Hispanic: 22.9, 23.5, 25.3, 24.2, 21, 20.2, 20, 18.9, 19.3, 20.5, 19.1, 18.4

The percent of persons over the age of 18 who have voted in midterm national elections between 1982–2014, has declined by two-to-six percentage points for all races and ethnicities.

Hispanic is an ethnicity and can be of any race.

Source: U.S. Census Bureau, Current Population Survey, November 2014 and earlier years, www2.census.gov/programs-surveys/cps/tables/time-series/voting-historical.../a1.xls

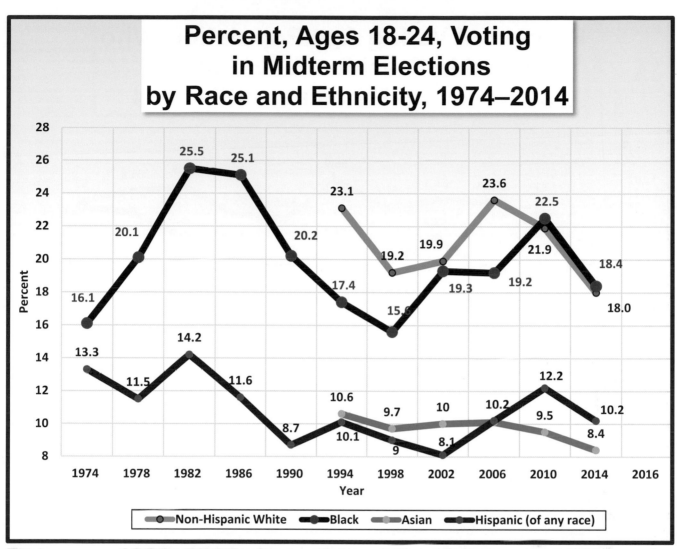

Percent, Ages 18-24, Voting in Midterm Elections by Race and Ethnicity, 1974–2014

Non-Hispanic White — **Black** — **Asian** — **Hispanic (of any race)**

Non-Hispanic White values: 23.1, 19.2, 19.9, 23.6, 22.5, 18.4
Black values: 16.1, 20.1, 25.5, 25.1, 20.2, 17.4, 15.6, 19.3, 19.2, 21.9, 18.0
Hispanic values: 13.3, 11.5, 14.2, 11.6, 8.7, 10.1, 9, 8.1, 10.2, 12.2, 8.4
Asian values: 10.6, 9.7, 10, 10.2, 9.5, 10.2

Between 1986–2014, less than one-of-four non-Hispanic White and Black or African American persons between the ages of 18 and 24 voted in midterm elections. In comparison, less than one-of-ten Hispanic or Asian persons aged 18 to 24 voted.

Hispanic is an ethnicity and can be of any race.

Source: U.S. Census Bureau, Current Population Survey, November 2014 and earlier years, www2.census.gov/programs-surveys/cps/tables/time-series/voting-historical.../a1.xls

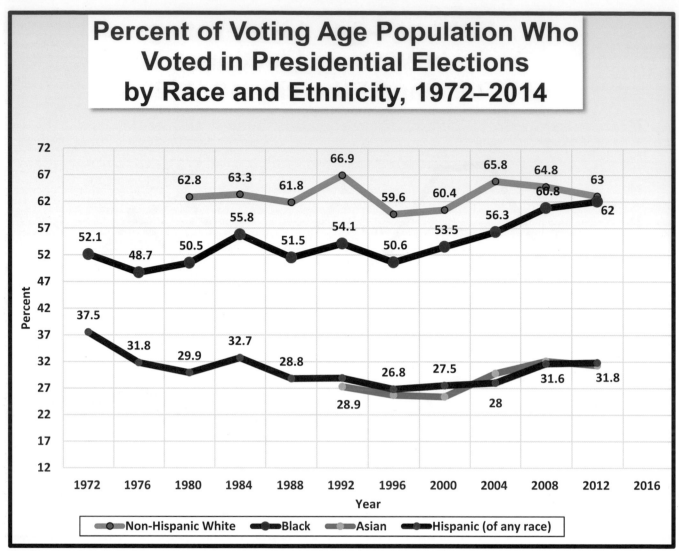

Percent of Voting Age Population Who Voted in Presidential Elections by Race and Ethnicity, 1972–2014

The percent of non-Hispanic White and Black or African American persons who voted in the 2012 presidential election was approximately the same. It was double the rate of Hispanic or Asian voters.

Hispanic is an ethnicity and can be of any race.

Source: U.S. Census Bureau, Current Population Survey, November 2014 and earlier years, www2.census.gov/programs-surveys/cps/tables/time-series/voting-historical.../a1.xls

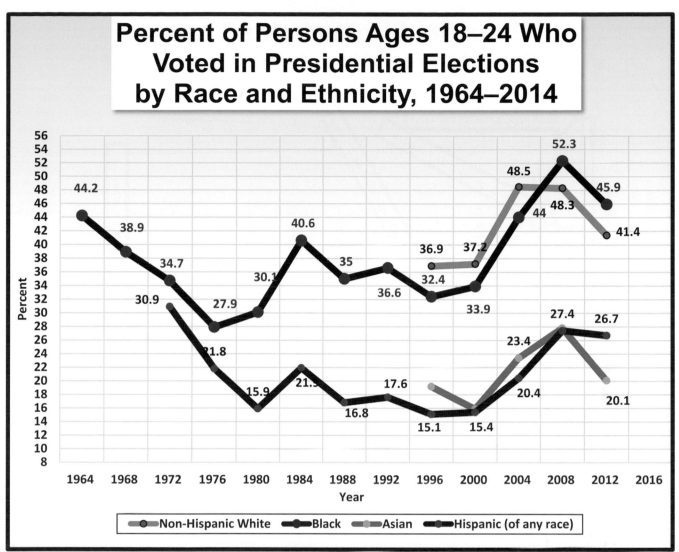

Percent of Persons Ages 18–24 Who Voted in Presidential Elections by Race and Ethnicity, 1964–2014

The percent of persons aged 18–24 years old who voted in the 2012 presidential election was highest for Black or African Americans at 45.9 percent and least for Asians at 20.1 percent.

Hispanic is an ethnicity and can be of any race.

Source: U.S. Census Bureau, Current Population Survey, November 2014 and earlier years, www2.census.gov/programs-surveys/cps/tables/time-series/voting-historical.../a1.xls

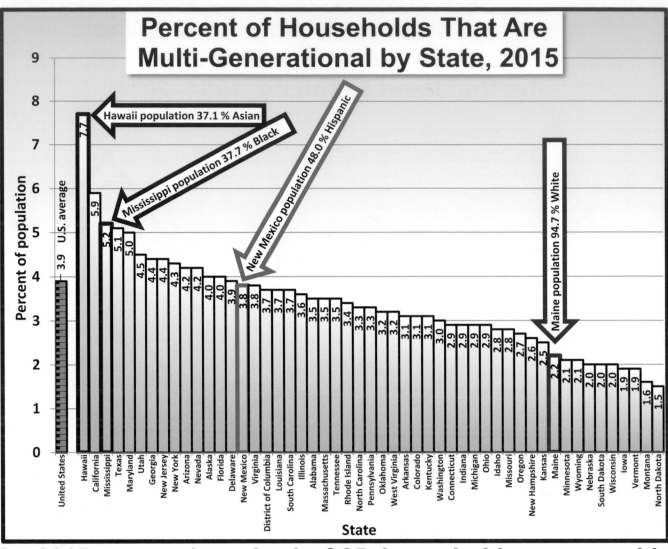

Percent of Households That Are Multi-Generational by State, 2015

In 2015, approximately 1-of-25 households were multi-generational, led by Hawaii with almost double the national average.

Although the American Community Survey (ACS) produces population, demographic, and housing unit estimates, it is the Census Bureau's Population Estimates Program that produces and disseminates the official estimates of the population for the nation, states, counties, cities, and towns as well as estimates of housing units for states and counties.

Source: U.S. Census Bureau, 2015 American Community Survey 1-Year Estimates Table R1106, http://www.census.gov/programs-surveys/acs/data/summary-file.html

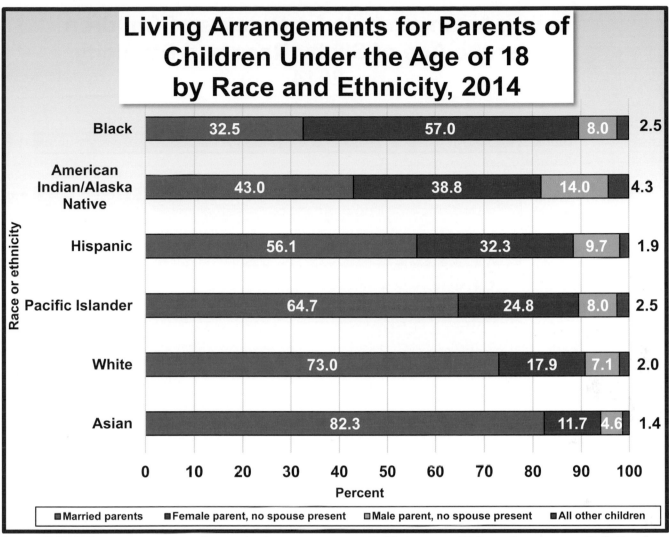

Living Arrangements for Parents of Children Under the Age of 18 by Race and Ethnicity, 2014

Race or ethnicity	Married parents	Female parent, no spouse present	Male parent, no spouse present	All other children
Black	32.5	57.0	8.0	2.5
American Indian/Alaska Native	43.0	38.8	14.0	4.3
Hispanic	56.1	32.3	9.7	1.9
Pacific Islander	64.7	24.8	8.0	2.5
White	73.0	17.9	7.1	2.0
Asian	82.3	11.7	4.6	1.4

Percent

■ Married parents ■ Female parent, no spouse present ▢ Male parent, no spouse present ■ All other children

In 2014, approximately one-of-three Black or African American children under the age of 18 lived in households with two married parents—the lowest percentage of any race or ethnicity.

Race categories exclude persons of Hispanic ethnicity.

Includes all children who live either with their parent(s) or with a householder to whom they are related by birth, marriage, or adoption (except a child who is the spouse of the householder), including foster children, children in unrelated subfamilies, children living in group quarters, and children who were reported as the householder or spouse of the householder.

Children are classified by their parents' marital status or, if no parents are present in the household, by the marital status of the householder who is related to the children. Living arrangements with only a "female parent" or "male parent" are those in which the parent or the householder who is related to the child does not have a spouse living in the household. The householder is the person (or one of the people) who owns or rents (maintains) the housing unit.

Source: U.S. Department of Commerce, Census Bureau, American Community Survey (ACS), 2009 and 2014. (This table was prepared January 2016.), Digest 2015, Table 102.20, https://nces.cd.gov/programs/digest/2015menu_tables.asp

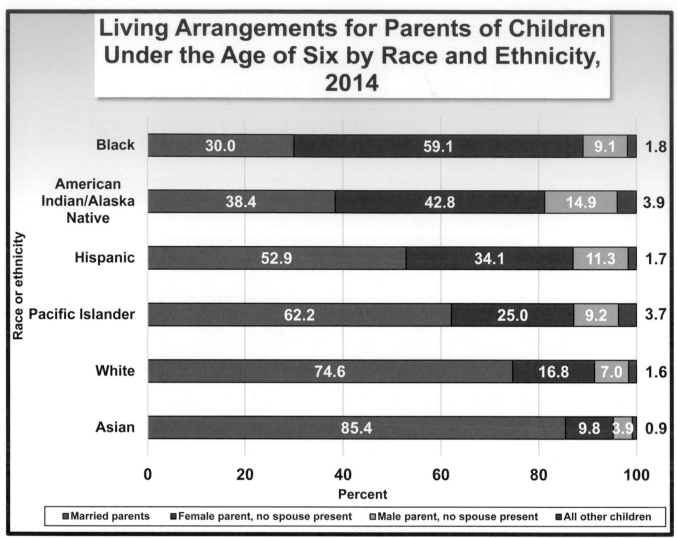

Living Arrangements for Parents of Children Under the Age of Six by Race and Ethnicity, 2014

Race or ethnicity	Married parents	Female parent, no spouse present	Male parent, no spouse present	All other children
Black	30.0	59.1	9.1	1.8
American Indian/Alaska Native	38.4	42.8	14.9	3.9
Hispanic	52.9	34.1	11.3	1.7
Pacific Islander	62.2	25.0	9.2	3.7
White	74.6	16.8	7.0	1.6
Asian	85.4	9.8	3.9	0.9

Legend: ■ Married parents ■ Female parent, no spouse present ▫ Male parent, no spouse present ■ All other children

In 2014, 30 percent of Black or African American children, under the age of 6, lived in a household with both married parents compared with 85 percent of Asian children.

Race categories exclude persons of Hispanic ethnicity.

Includes all children who live either with their parent(s) or with a householder to whom they are related by birth, marriage, or adoption (except a child who is the spouse of the householder), including foster children, children in unrelated subfamilies, children living in group quarters, and children who were reported as the householder or spouse of the householder.

Children are classified by their parents' marital status or, if no parents are present in the household, by the marital status of the householder who is related to the children. Living arrangements with only a "female parent" or "male parent" are those in which the parent or the householder who is related to the child does not have a spouse living in the household. The householder is the person (or one of the people) who owns or rents (maintains) the housing unit.

Source: U.S. Department of Commerce, Census Bureau, American Community Survey (ACS), 2009 and 2014. (This table was prepared January 2016.), Digest 2015, Table 102.20, https://nces.ed.gov/programs/digest/2015menu_tables.asp

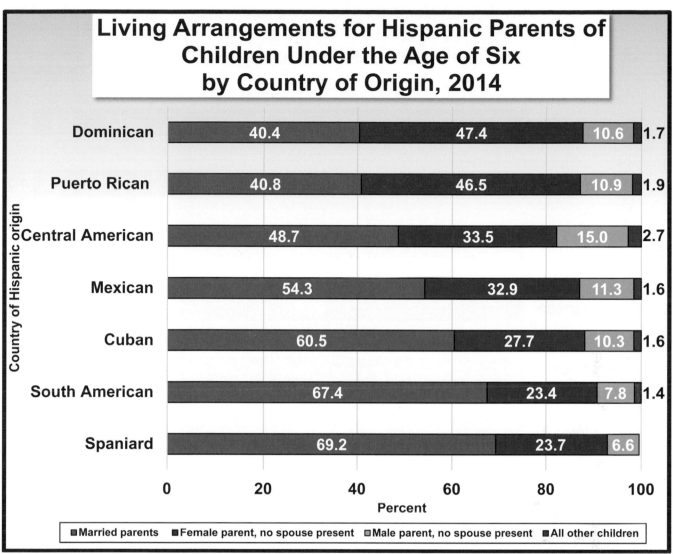

Living Arrangements for Hispanic Parents of Children Under the Age of Six by Country of Origin, 2014

Country of Hispanic origin	Married parents	Female parent, no spouse present	Male parent, no spouse present	All other children
Dominican	40.4	47.4	10.6	1.7
Puerto Rican	40.8	46.5	10.9	1.9
Central American	48.7	33.5	15.0	2.7
Mexican	54.3	32.9	11.3	1.6
Cuban	60.5	27.7	10.3	1.6
South American	67.4	23.4	7.8	1.4
Spaniard	69.2	23.7	6.6	

In 2014, 69 percent of children under the age of six, whose parents were born in Spain, lived in households with both married parents present.

Race categories exclude persons of Hispanic ethnicity.

Includes all children who live either with their parent(s) or with a householder to whom they are related by birth, marriage, or adoption (except a child who is the spouse of the householder), including foster children, children in unrelated subfamilies, children living in group quarters, and children who were reported as the householder or spouse of the householder.

Children are classified by their parents' marital status or, if no parents are present in the household, by the marital status of the householder who is related to the children. Living arrangements with only a "female parent" or "male parent" are those in which the parent or the householder who is related to the child does not have a spouse living in the household. The householder is the person (or one of the people) who owns or rents (maintains) the housing unit.

Source: U.S. Department of Commerce, Census Bureau, American Community Survey (ACS), 2009 and 2014. (This table was prepared January 2016.), Digest 2015, Table 102.20, https://nces.ed.gov/programs/digest/2015menu_tables.asp

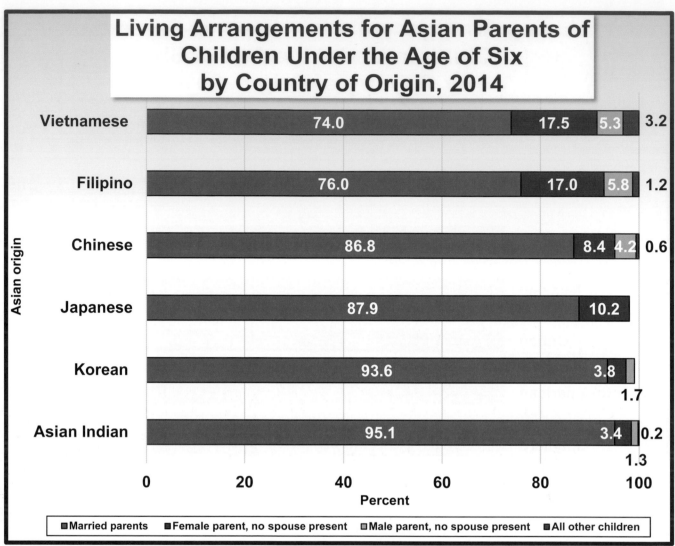

Living Arrangements for Asian Parents of Children Under the Age of Six by Country of Origin, 2014

Asian origin:

Vietnamese 74.0 | 17.5 | 5.3 | 3.2
Filipino 76.0 | 17.0 | 5.8 | 1.2
Chinese 86.8 | 8.4 | 4.2 | 0.6
Japanese 87.9 | 10.2
Korean 93.6 | 3.8 | 1.7
Asian Indian 95.1 | 3.4 | 0.2 | 1.3

Percent: 0, 20, 40, 60, 80, 100

Legend: ■ Married parents   ■ Female parent, no spouse present   ■ Male parent, no spouse present   ■ All other children

In 2014, 95 percent of children under the age of six, whose parents were both born in India, lived in a household with both parents present.

Race categories exclude persons of Hispanic ethnicity.
Includes all children who live either with their parent(s) or with a householder to whom they are related by birth, marriage, or adoption (except a child who is the spouse of the householder), including foster children, children in unrelated subfamilies, children living in group quarters, and children who were reported as the householder or spouse of the householder.

Children are classified by their parents' marital status or, if no parents are present in the household, by the marital status of the householder who is related to the children. Living arrangements with only a "female parent" or "male parent" are those in which the parent or the householder who is related to the child does not have a spouse living in the household. The householder is the person (or one of the people) who owns or rents (maintains) the housing unit.

Source: U.S. Department of Commerce, Census Bureau, American Community Survey (ACS), 2009 and 2014. (This table was prepared January 2016.), Digest 2015, Table 102.20, https://nces.ed.gov/programs/digest/2015menu_tables.asp

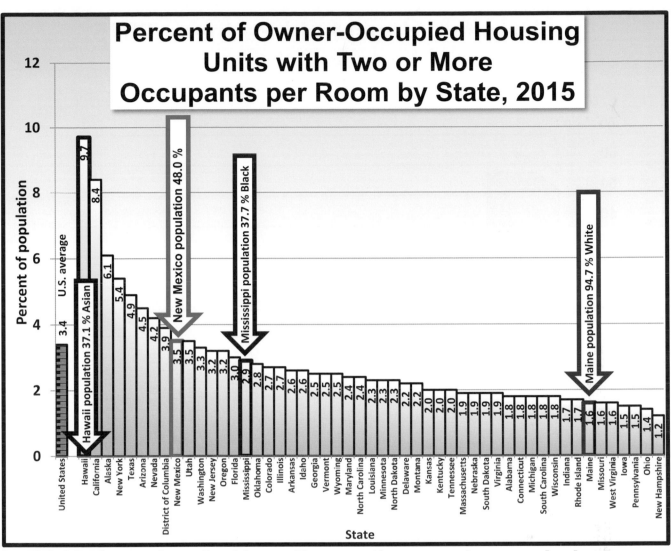

Percent of Owner-Occupied Housing Units with Two or More Occupants per Room by State, 2015

In 2015, housing in Hawaii was the most crowded among all the states with approximately 10 percent of all owner-occupied housing averaging at least two people per room. Hawaii has the highest concentration of Asian persons at 37.1 percent of the population.

Although the American Community Survey (ACS) produces population, demographic, and housing unit estimates, it is the Census Bureau's Population Estimates Program that produces and disseminates the official estimates of the population for the nation, states, counties, cities, and towns as well as estimates of housing units for states and counties.

Source: U.S. Census Bureau, 2015 American Community Survey 1-Year Estimates Table R2509, http://www.census.gov/programs-surveys/acs/data/summary-file.html

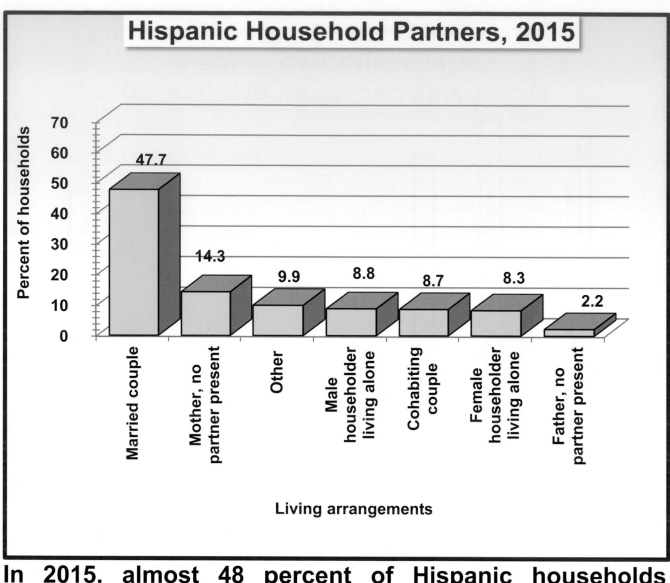

Hispanic Household Partners, 2015

Percent of households

- Married couple: 47.7
- Mother, no partner present: 14.3
- Other: 9.9
- Male householder living alone: 8.8
- Cohabiting couple: 8.7
- Female householder living alone: 8.3
- Father, no partner present: 2.2

Living arrangements

In 2015, almost 48 percent of Hispanic households included a married couple.

Persons of Hispanic origin may be of any race.

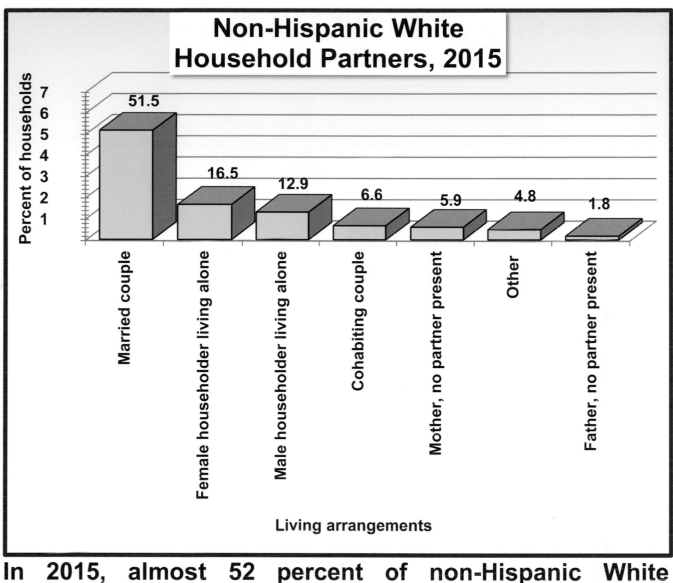

Non-Hispanic White Household Partners, 2015

Percent of households

- Married couple: 51.5
- Female householder living alone: 16.5
- Male householder living alone: 12.9
- Cohabiting couple: 6.6
- Mother, no partner present: 5.9
- Other: 4.8
- Father, no partner present: 1.8

Living arrangements

In 2015, almost 52 percent of non-Hispanic White households included a married couple.

Persons of Hispanic origin may be of any race.

Source: U.S. Census Bureau, https://www.census.gov/hhes/families/files/hh7.csv

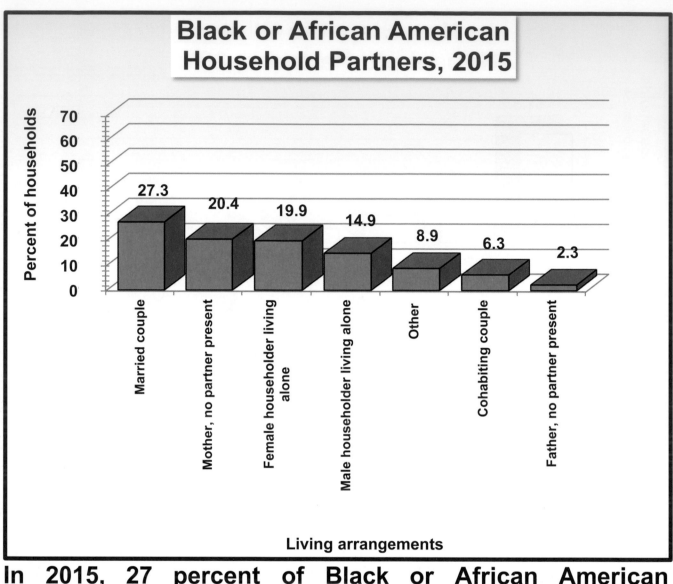

Black or African American Household Partners, 2015

Percent of households

- Married couple: 27.3
- Mother, no partner present: 20.4
- Female householder living alone: 19.9
- Male householder living alone: 14.9
- Other: 8.9
- Cohabiting couple: 6.3
- Father, no partner present: 2.3

Living arrangements

In 2015, 27 percent of Black or African American households included a married couple.

Source: U.S. Census Bureau, https://www.census.gov/hhes/families/files/hh7.csv

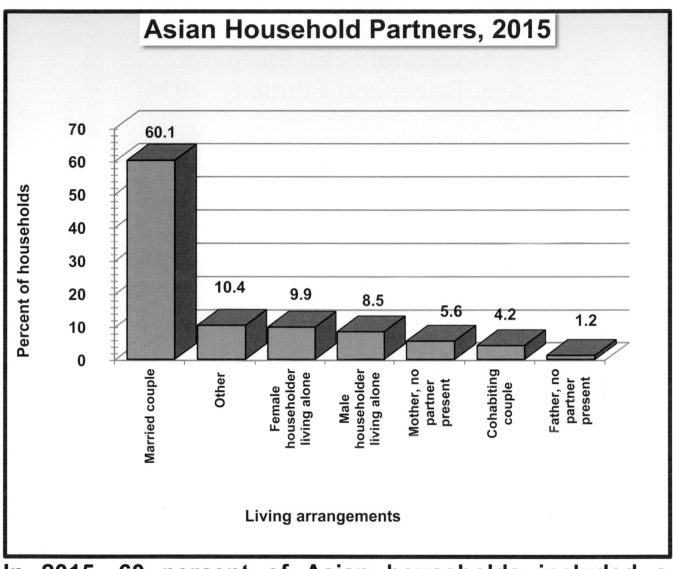

Asian Household Partners, 2015

Percent of households

- Married couple: 60.1
- Other: 10.4
- Female householder living alone: 9.9
- Male householder living alone: 8.5
- Mother, no partner present: 5.6
- Cohabiting couple: 4.2
- Father, no partner present: 1.2

Living arrangements

In 2015, 60 percent of Asian households included a married couple.

Source: U.S. Census Bureau, https://www.census.gov/hhes/families/files/hh7.csv

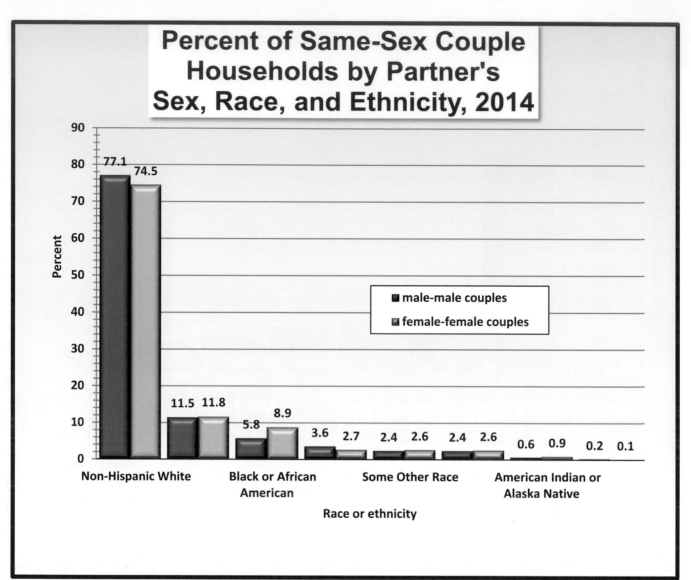

Percent of Same-Sex Couple Households by Partner's Sex, Race, and Ethnicity, 2014

male-male couples
female-female couples

Non-Hispanic White: 77.1, 74.5
Black or African American: 11.5, 11.8
5.8, 8.9
Some Other Race: 3.6, 2.7
2.4, 2.6
2.4, 2.6
American Indian or Alaska Native: 0.6, 0.9
0.2, 0.1

Race or ethnicity

In 2014, there were almost equal numbers of male-male households as female-female households among all non-Hispanic White same-sex couple households.

In 2014, there were 783,100 same-sex occupied households in the United States of all races and ethnicities.

Source: U.S. Census Bureau, 2014 American Community Survey 1-year data file, Table 1, http://www.census.gov/hhes/samesex/index.html

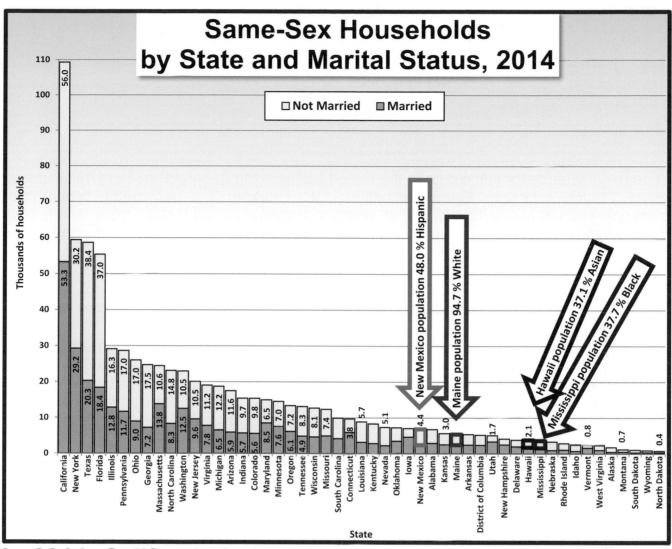

Same-Sex Households by State and Marital Status, 2014

In 2014, California led the nation in the number of same-sex households at 109,000. There were an estimated 783,000 nationwide.

Source: U.S. Census Bureau, 2014 American Community Survey 1-year data file, Table 3, http://www.census.gov/hhes/samesex/index.html

Chapter 6: Crime

A primary resource for crime data in the United States is the Federal Bureau of Investigation (FBI). The FBI's Uniform Crime Reporting (UCR) Program is a nationwide, cooperative, statistical effort of nearly 18,000 city, university and college, county, state, tribal, and federal law enforcement agencies voluntarily reporting data on crimes brought to their attention. Since 1930, the FBI has administered the UCR Program and continues to assess and monitor the nature and type of crime in the nation. The program's primary objective is to generate reliable information for use in law enforcement administration, operation, and management. However, its data over the years has also become one of the country's leading social indicators.

To ensure data are uniformly reported, the FBI provides contributing law enforcement agencies with a handbook that explains how to classify and score offenses and provides uniform crime offense definitions. Acknowledging that offense definitions may vary from state to state, the FBI cautions agencies to report offenses not according to local or state statutes but according to those guidelines provided in the handbook. Most agencies make a good faith effort to comply with established guidelines.

Crime is generally classified as to whether the victim is a person (as in homicide, rape, assault, etc.); a possession (robbery, fraud, arson, etc.); or against society (driving while intoxicated, disorderly conduct, liquor law violations, etc.).

The crime rates for both perpetrators and victims across the races and ethnicities vary significantly, and in general the Asian, Native Hawaiian, or Other Pacific Islander populations have the lowest rates—as victims and perpetrators—for most categories of crime while the Black or African American populations have the highest rates.

The homicide death rate in 2014 was more than 11 times greater for Black or African Americans than Asians. Ninety percent of the time when the victim was Black or African American so was the offender.

The representation of Black or African Americans and Hispanic persons among sworn personnel in local police departments has continually increased between 1987 and 2013. In 2013, in departments serving cities of over one million persons, nearly one-of-four officers were Hispanic and one-of-seven were Black or African American. However, for police departments serving smaller cities the representation by these minority groups was generally only five-to-ten percent.

~

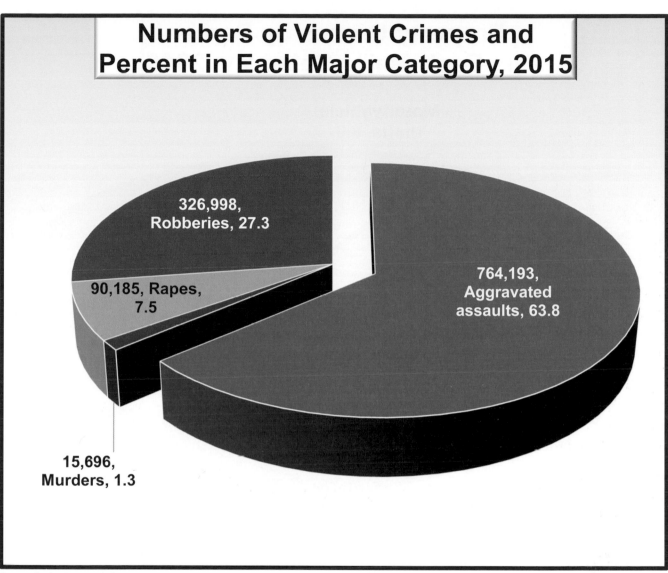

Numbers of Violent Crimes and Percent in Each Major Category, 2015

326,998, Robberies, 27.3

90,185, Rapes, 7.5

15,696, Murders, 1.3

764,193, Aggravated assaults, 63.8

In 2015, there were almost 16,000 murders in the United States—averaging 43 per day.

There were an estimated 1,197,704 violent crimes committed around the nation. While that was an increase from 2014 figures, the 2015 violent crime total was 0.7 percent lower than the 2011 level and 16.5 percent below the 2006 level.

The estimated number of murders in the nation was 15,696. During the year, there were an estimated 90,185 rapes. (This figure currently reflects UCR's legacy definition. Learn more about the revised rape definition.)

Firearms were used in 71.5 percent of the nation's murders, 40.8 percent of robberies, and 24.2 percent of aggravated assaults.

Source: Federal Bureau of Investigation, https://www.fbi.gov/news/stories/latest-crime-statistics-released

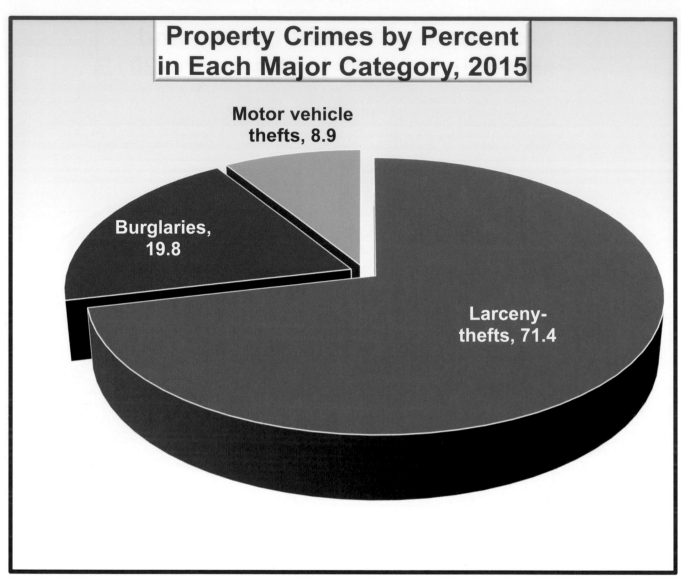

Property Crimes by Percent in Each Major Category, 2015

Motor vehicle thefts, 8.9

Burglaries, 19.8

Larceny-thefts, 71.4

In 2015, over 70 percent of property crimes was for larceny-theft.

There were an estimated 327,374 robberies nationwide in 2015, which accounted for an estimated $390 million in losses (average dollar value of stolen property per reported robbery was $1,190).

Property crimes resulted in losses estimated at $14.3 billion. The total value of reported stolen property (i.e., currency, jewelry, motor vehicles, electronics, firearms) was over $12 billion.

Source: Federal Bureau of Investigation, https://www.fbi.gov/news/stories/latest-crime-statistics-released

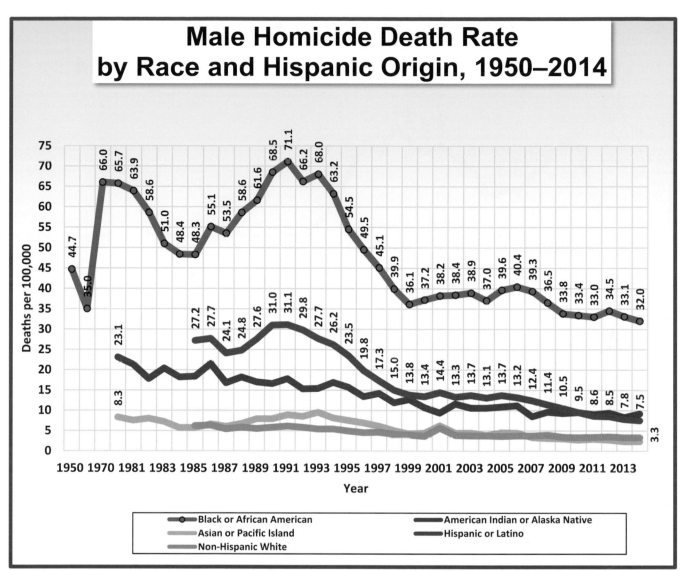

Male Homicide Death Rate by Race and Hispanic Origin, 1950–2014

The homicide death rate among Black or African males declined by more than a factor of two between 1990 and 2014.

Data are based on death certificates. Deaths per 100,000 population. Underlying cause of death was coded according to the 6th Revision of the International Classification of Diseases (ICD) in 1950, 7th Revision in 1960, 8th Revision in 1970, and 9th Revision in 1980–1998.

Source: National Vital Statistics System, public-use Mortality File, public-use Birth File; Deaths: Final data for 2014, Table 29, Available from: http://www.cdc.gov/nchs/products/nvsr.htm, http://www.cdc.gov/nchs/hus/contents2015.htm#059, Available from: http://www.cdc.gov/mmwr/preview/mmwrhtml/mm6450a3.htm?s_cid=mm6450a3_w

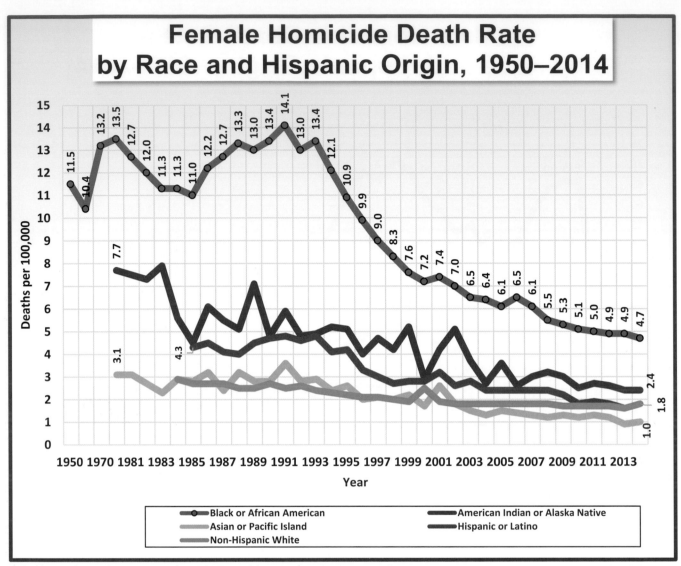

Female Homicide Death Rate by Race and Hispanic Origin, 1950–2014

The homicide death rate among Black or African American females declined by a factor of three between 1991 and 2014.

Data are based on death certificates. Deaths per 100,000 population. Underlying cause of death was coded according to the 6th Revision of the International Classification of Diseases (ICD) in 1950, 7th Revision in 1960, 8th Revision in 1970, and 9th Revision in 1980–1998.

Source: National Vital Statistics System, public-use Mortality File, public-use Birth File; Deaths: Final data for 2014, Table 29, Available from: http://www.cdc.gov/nchs/products/nvsr.htm, http://www.cdc.gov/nchs/hus/contents2015.htm#059, Available from: http://www.cdc.gov/mmwr/preview/mmwrhtml/mm6450a3.htm?s_cid=mm6450a3_w

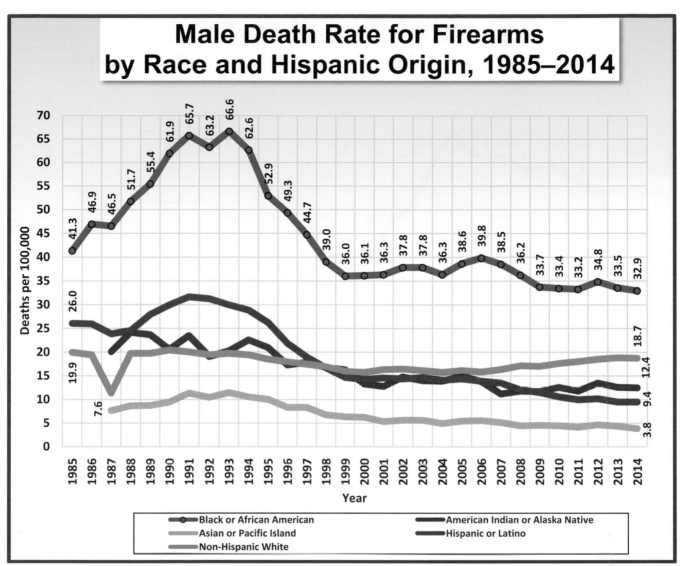

Male Death Rate for Firearms by Race and Hispanic Origin, 1985–2014

The death rate from gun violence for Black or African American males decreased by a factor of two between 1993 and 2014.

Data are based on death certificates. Deaths per 100,000 population. Underlying cause of death was coded according to the 6th Revision of the International Classification of Diseases (ICD) in 1950, 7th Revision in 1960, 8th Revision in 1970, and 9th Revision in 1980–1998.

Source: National Vital Statistics System, public-use Mortality File, public-use Birth File; Deaths: Final data for 2014, Table 31, Available from: http://www.cdc.gov/nchs/products/nvsr.htm, http://www.cdc.gov/nchs/hus/contents2015.htm#059, Available from: http://www.cdc.gov/mmwr/preview/mmwrhtml/mm6450a3.htm?s_cid=mm6450a3_w

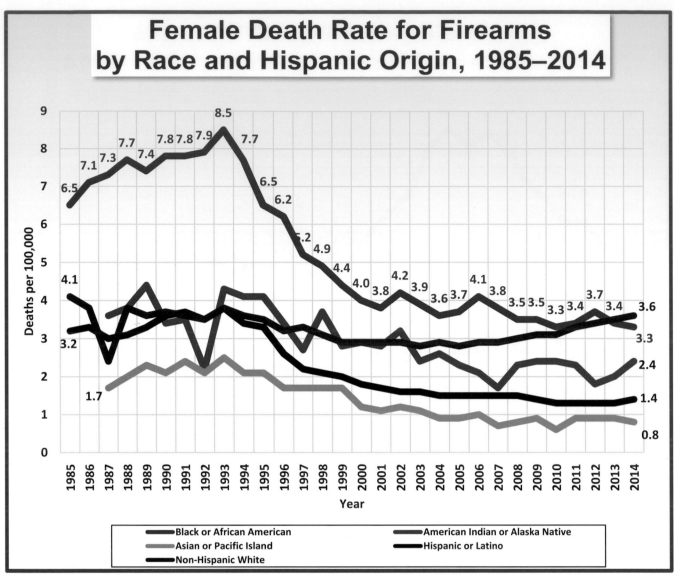

Female Death Rate for Firearms by Race and Hispanic Origin, 1985–2014

Deaths per 100,000

Black or African American values: 6.5, 7.1, 7.3, 7.7, 7.4, 7.8, 7.8, 7.9, 8.5, 7.7, 6.5, 6.2, .2, 4.9, 4.4, 4.0, 3.8, 4.2, 3.9, 3.6, 3.7, 4.1, 3.8, 3.5, 3.5, 3.3, 3.4, 3.7, 3.4, 3.6

Other series start values: 4.1, 3.2, 1.7

End values: 3.6, 3.3, 2.4, 1.4, 0.8

Year

Legend:
- Black or African American
- Asian or Pacific Island
- Non-Hispanic White
- American Indian or Alaska Native
- Hispanic or Latino

The death rate for Black or African American females from gun violence declined by almost of factor of three between 1993 and 2014.

Data are based on death certificates. Deaths per 100,000 population. Underlying cause of death was coded according to the 6th Revision of the International Classification of Diseases (ICD) in 1950, 7th Revision in 1960, 8th Revision in 1970, and 9th Revision in 1980–1998.

Source: National Vital Statistics System, public-use Mortality File, public-use Birth File; Deaths: Final data for 2014, Table 31, Available from: http://www.cdc.gov/nchs/products/nvsr.htm, http://www.cdc.gov/nchs/hus/contents2015.htm#059, Available from: http://www.cdc.gov/mmwr/preview/mmwrhtml/mm6450a3.htm?s_cid=mm6450a3_w

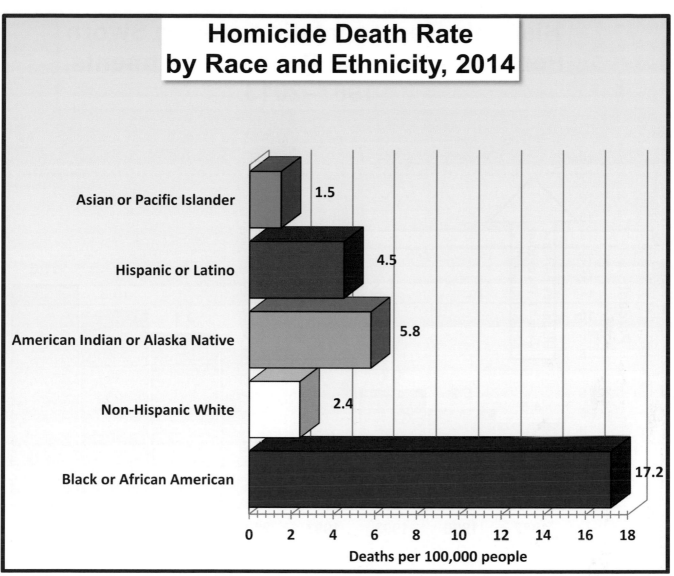

Homicide Death Rate by Race and Ethnicity, 2014

Asian or Pacific Islander — 1.5

Hispanic or Latino — 4.5

American Indian or Alaska Native — 5.8

Non-Hispanic White — 2.4

Black or African American — 17.2

Deaths per 100,000 people

In 2014, the homicide rate for Black or African Americans was more than 11 times higher than Asian or Pacific Islanders.

Data are based on death certificates.

Source: National Vital Statistics System, public-use Mortality File, public-use Birth File; Deaths: Final data for 2014, Table 17, Available from: http://www.cdc.gov/nchs/products/nvsr.htm, http://www.cdc.gov/nchs/hus/contents2015.htm#059

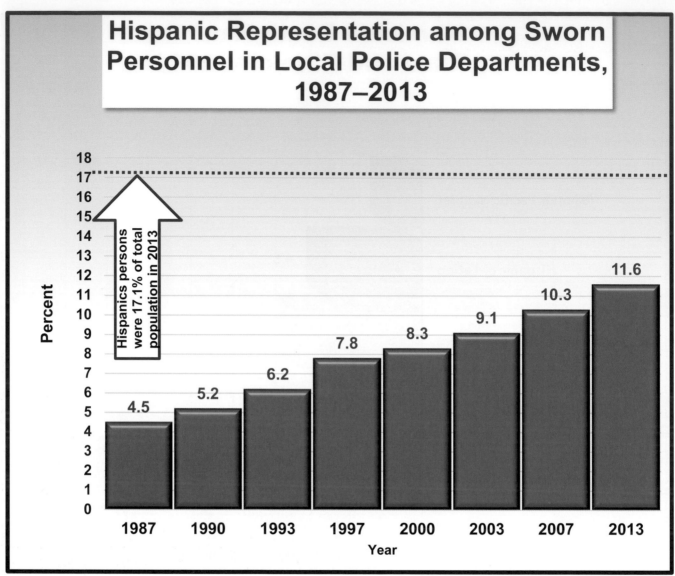

Hispanic Representation among Sworn Personnel in Local Police Departments, 1987–2013

Hispanics persons were 17.1% of total population in 2013

Year	Percent
1987	4.5
1990	5.2
1993	6.2
1997	7.8
2000	8.3
2003	9.1
2007	10.3
2013	11.6

People of Hispanic origin doubled their representation in local police departments between 1990 and 2013, but were still under-represented by about one-third.

As of January 1, 2013, the more than 12,000 local police departments in the United States employed an estimated 605,000 persons on a full-time basis. This total included about 477,000 sworn officers (those with general arrest powers) and about 128,000 nonsworn employees. Approximately 55,000 Hispanic or Latino officers were employed by local police departments in 2013, which was about 8,000 (up 16 percent) more than in 2007. From 2007 to 2013, the percent of Hispanic officers increased from 10.3 percent to 11.6 percent. In 1987, 4.5 percent of officers were Hispanic.

In 2013, more than a quarter (27 percent) of full-time local police officers were members of a racial or ethnic minority. About 130,000 minority local police were employed in 2013.

Source: Bureau of Justice Statistics, Law Enforcement Management and Administrative Statistics Survey, 2013, Report title: Local Police Departments, 2013: Personnel, Policies, and Practices NCJ 248677, http://www.bjs.gov/content/pub/pdf/lpd13ppp.pdf

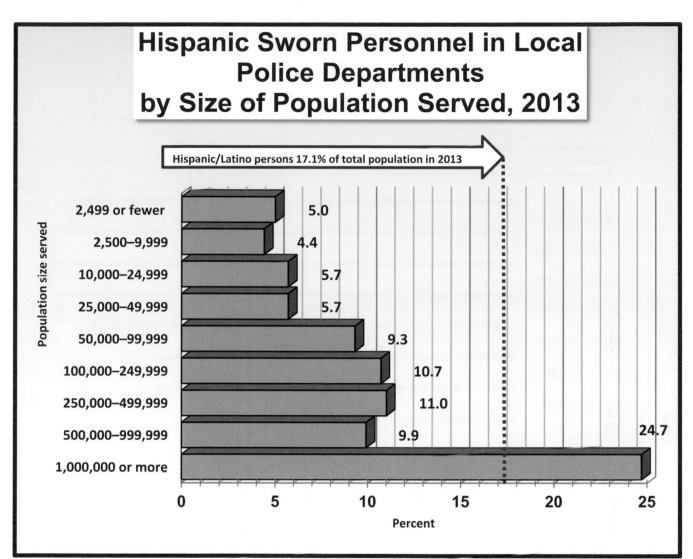

Hispanic Sworn Personnel in Local Police Departments by Size of Population Served, 2013

Hispanic/Latino persons 17.1% of total population in 2013

Population size served

Population size served	Percent
2,499 or fewer	5.0
2,500–9,999	4.4
10,000–24,999	5.7
25,000–49,999	5.7
50,000–99,999	9.3
100,000–249,999	10.7
250,000–499,999	11.0
500,000–999,999	9.9
1,000,000 or more	24.7

Percent

In 2013, Hispanic and Latino representation in local police departments was approximately 25 percent in cities of one million or more people, and under six percent in cities with populations under 50,000.

From 2007 to 2013, the number of full-time Hispanic or Latino local police officers increased by 16 percent.

Departments serving larger jurisdictions were more diverse than departments serving smaller jurisdictions. Consistent with prior LEMAS Surveys, departments in larger jurisdictions were more diverse than those in smaller ones. Findings are based on the 2013 Law Enforcement Management and Administrative Statistics (LEMAS) Survey sponsored by the Bureau of Justice Statistics (BJS). The LEMAS Survey, conducted periodically since 1987, collects data on a range of topics from a nationally representative sample of state and local law enforcement agencies. Prior to the 2013 survey, the most recent LEMAS Survey was conducted in 2007.

Source: Bureau of Justice Statistics, Law Enforcement Management and Administrative Statistics Survey, 2013, Report title: Local Police Departments, 2013: Personnel, Policies, and Practices NCJ 248677, http://www.bjs.gov/content/pub/pdf/lpd13ppp.pdf

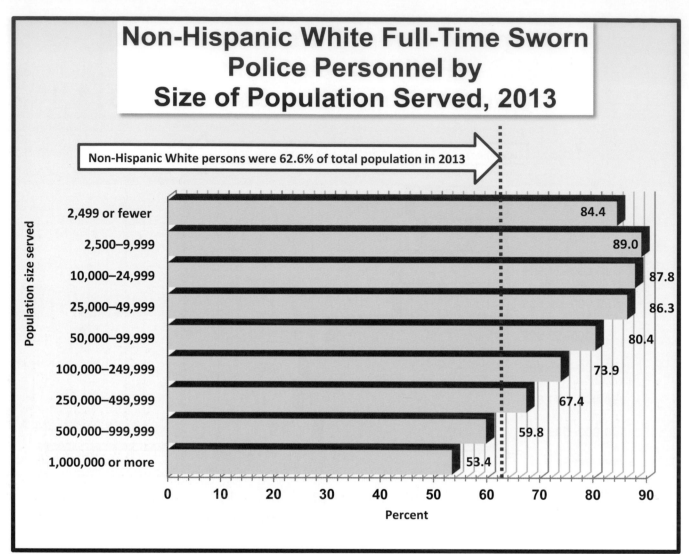

Non-Hispanic White Full-Time Sworn Police Personnel by Size of Population Served, 2013

Non-Hispanic White persons were 62.6% of total population in 2013

Population size served

Population size served	Percent
2,499 or fewer	84.4
2,500–9,999	89.0
10,000–24,999	87.8
25,000–49,999	86.3
50,000–99,999	80.4
100,000–249,999	73.9
250,000–499,999	67.4
500,000–999,999	59.8
1,000,000 or more	53.4

0 10 20 30 40 50 60 70 80 90

Percent

In 2013, over 80 percent of law enforcement officers in local police departments—serving populations under 100,000—were non-Hispanic White, compared with 53 percent for departments serving populations greater than one million.

As of January 1, 2013, the more than 12,000 local police departments in the United States employed an estimated 605,000 persons on a full-time basis. This total included about 477,000 sworn officers (those with general arrest powers) and about 128,000 nonsworn employees.

LEMAS is the Law Enforcement Management and Administrative Statistics Survey. Consistent with prior LEMAS Surveys, departments in larger jurisdictions were more diverse than those in smaller ones. In 2013, more than 2 in 5 officers in jurisdictions with 500,000 or more residents were members of a racial or ethnic minority, compared to fewer than 1 in 5 officers in jurisdictions with a population of less than 50,000. In 2013, the lowest percentage in population categories below 50,000 was 11 percent (2,500 to 9,999 residents).

Source: Bureau of Justice Statistics, Law Enforcement Management and Administrative Statistics Survey, 2013, Report title: Local Police Departments, 2013: Personnel, Policies, and Practices NCJ 248677, http://www.bjs.gov/content/pub/pdf/lpd13ppp.pdf

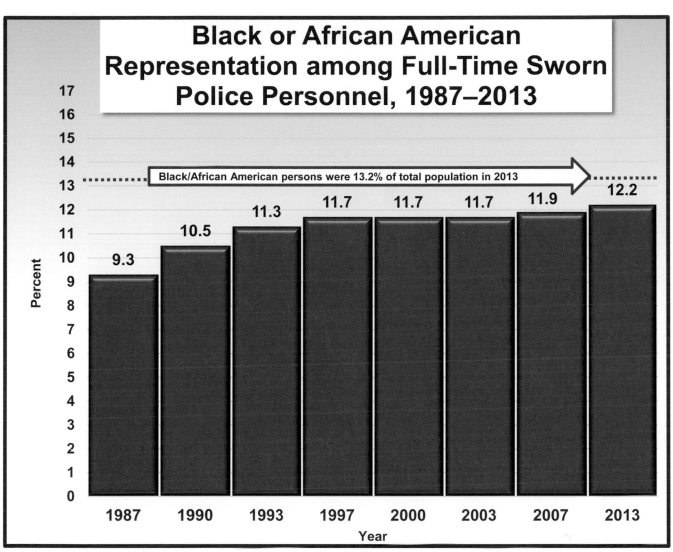

Black or African American Representation among Full-Time Sworn Police Personnel, 1987–2013

Black/African American persons were 13.2% of total population in 2013

Year	Percent
1987	9.3
1990	10.5
1993	11.3
1997	11.7
2000	11.7
2003	11.7
2007	11.9
2013	12.2

Between 2007 and 2013, the representation of Black or African American persons in local police departments increased from 70 percent to 92 percent of their proportion in the general population.

Black and African American excludes persons of Hispanic or Latino origin.

As of January 1, 2013, the more than 12,000 local police departments in the United States employed an estimated 605,000 persons on a full-time basis. This total included about 477,000 sworn officers (those with general arrest powers) and about 128,000 nonsworn employees. About 58,000 Black or African American officers were employed by local police departments in 2013. About 9 percent of officers were Black in 1987. In 2013, more than a quarter (27 percent) of full-time local police officers were members of a racial or ethnic minority. About 130,000 minority local police were employed in 2013. The total represented an increase of about 78,000 (up 150 percent) since 1987. From 2007 to 2013, minority representation among local police officers increased from 25.3 percent to 27.3 percent. Minorities made up 14.6 percent of officers in 1987.

Source: Bureau of Justice Statistics, Law Enforcement Management and Administrative Statistics Survey, 2013, Report title: Local Police Departments, 2013: Personnel, Policies, and Practices NCJ 248677, http://www.bjs.gov/content/pub/pdf/lpd13ppp.pdf

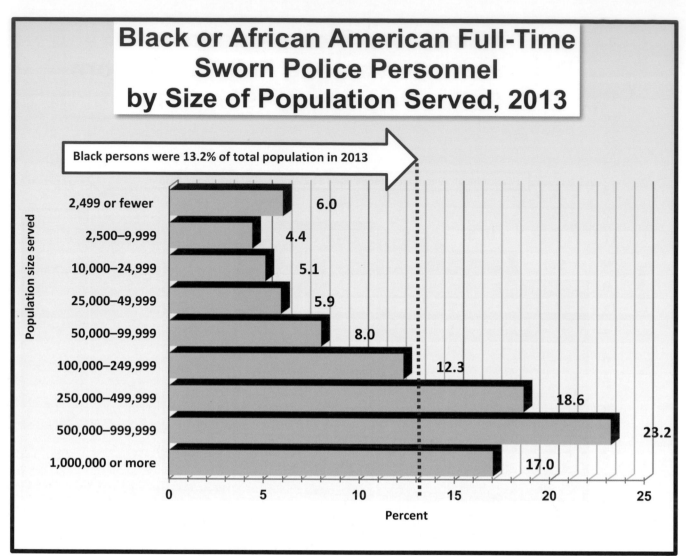

Black or African American Full-Time Sworn Police Personnel by Size of Population Served, 2013

Black persons were 13.2% of total population in 2013

Population size served

Population size served	Percent
2,499 or fewer	6.0
2,500–9,999	4.4
10,000–24,999	5.1
25,000–49,999	5.9
50,000–99,999	8.0
100,000–249,999	12.3
250,000–499,999	18.6
500,000–999,999	23.2
1,000,000 or more	17.0

Percent

In 2013, over 17 percent of law enforcement officers in local police departments—serving populations over 250,000—were Black or African American, compared with less than eight percent in departments serving populations less than 100,000.

Black and African American excludes persons of Hispanic or Latino origin.

Departments serving larger jurisdictions were more diverse than departments serving smaller jurisdictions Consistent with prior LEMAS Surveys, departments in larger jurisdictions were more diverse than those in smaller ones. In 2013, more than two in five officers in jurisdictions with 500,000 or more residents were members of a racial or ethnic minority, compared to fewer than one in five officers in jurisdictions with a population of less than 50,000. Since 1987, diversity has increased in all population categories. In 2013, the lowest percentage in population categories below 50,000 was 11 percent (2,500 to 9,999 residents). LEMAS is the Law Enforcement Management and Administrative Statistics Survey.

Source: Bureau of Justice Statistics, Law Enforcement Management and Administrative Statistics Survey, 2013, Report title: Local Police Departments, 2013: Personnel, Policies, and Practices NCJ 248677, http://www.bjs.gov/content/pub/pdf/lpd13ppp.pdf

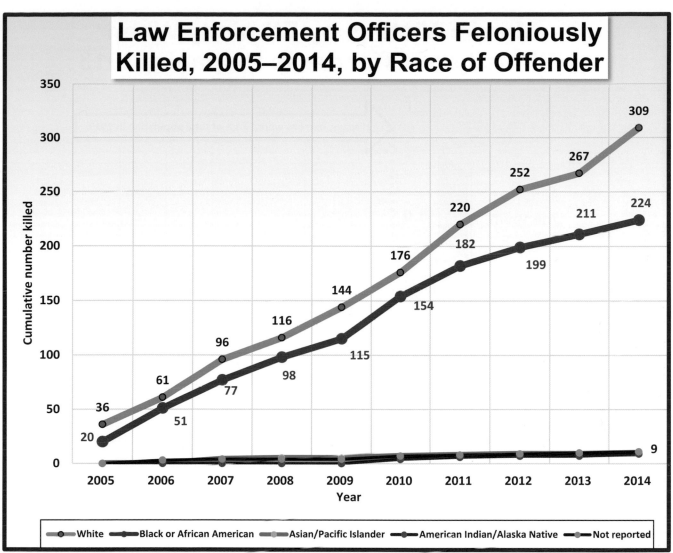

Law Enforcement Officers Feloniously Killed, 2005–2014, by Race of Offender

Legend: White, Black or African American, Asian/Pacific Islander, American Indian/Alaska Native, Not reported

In the period 2005–2014, 563 law enforcement officers were feloniously killed. Black or African Americans—comprising approximately 13 percent of the population—were the offenders in 40 percent of the killings.

Of the 563 offenders, 545 (97 percent) were male.

The FBI publishes the Law Enforcement Officers Killed and Assaulted report each year to provide information about officers who were killed, feloniously or accidentally, and officers who were assaulted while performing their duties. The FBI collects these data through the Uniform Crime Reporting (UCR) Program.

Source: Federal Bureau of Investigation (FBI) Uniform Crime Reporting program, accessed February, 2017, https://ucr.fbi.gov/leoka/2014/tables/table_47_leos_fk_race_and_sex_of_known_offender_2005-2014.xls

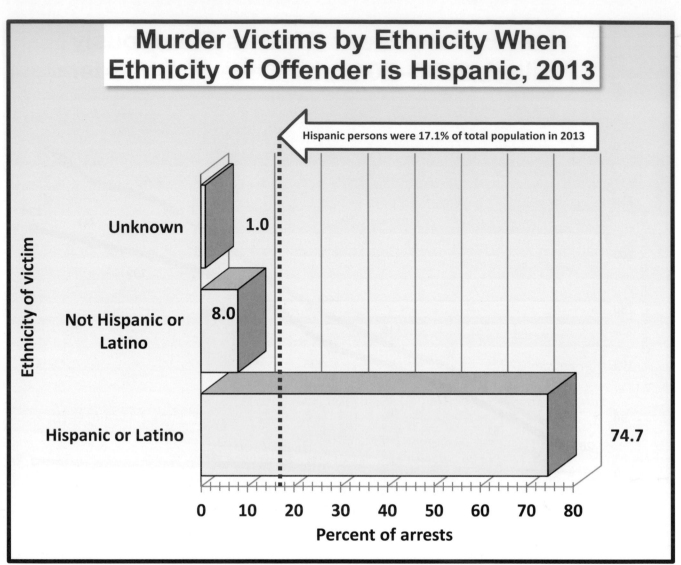

Murder Victims by Ethnicity When Ethnicity of Offender is Hispanic, 2013

Hispanic persons were 17.1% of total population in 2013

Ethnicity of victim

Unknown — 1.0

Not Hispanic or Latino — 8.0

Hispanic or Latino — 74.7

0 10 20 30 40 50 60 70 80

Percent of arrests

In 2013, approximately three-of-four Hispanic persons murdered were murdered by Hispanic persons.

Data are limited to single victim with single offender and based upon sampling 5,623 murders.

Hispanic origin can be of any race. The ethnicity totals are representative of those agencies that provided ethnicity breakdowns. Not all agencies provide ethnicity data, therefore the race and ethnicity totals will not equal.

This table is based on incidents where some information about the offender is known by law enforcement; therefore, when the offender age, sex, and race are all reported as unknown, these data are excluded from the table.

Source: FBI, https://ucr.fbi.gov/crime-in-the-u.s/2013/crime-in-the-u.s.-2013/offenses-known-to-law-enforcement/expanded-homicide/expanded_homicide_data_table_6_murder_race_and_sex_of_vicitm_by_race_and_sex_of_offender_2013.xls

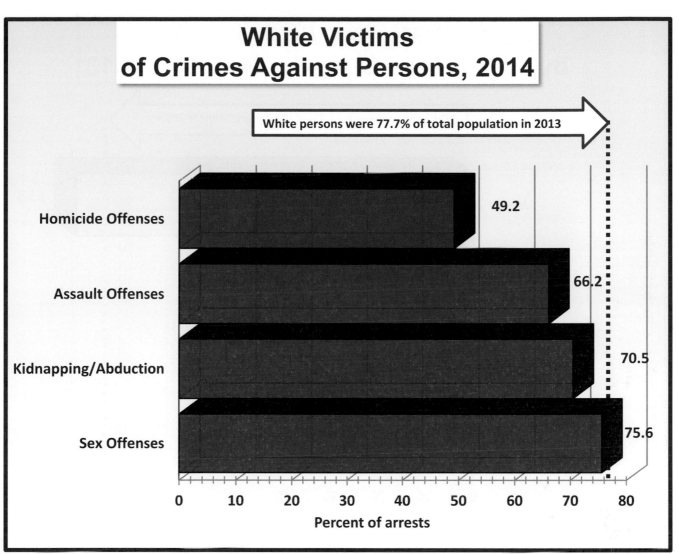

White Victims of Crimes Against Persons, 2014

White persons were 77.7% of total population in 2013

Offense	Percent
Homicide Offenses	49.2
Assault Offenses	66.2
Kidnapping/Abduction	70.5
Sex Offenses	75.6

Percent of arrests

In 2014, almost one-half of all victims of homicide were White persons.

The definition of the racial designation of White is: A person having origins in any of the original peoples of Europe, the Middle East, or North Africa.

The FBI collected these data through the Uniform Crime Reporting (UCR) Program's National Incident-Based Reporting System (NIBRS).

Source: FBI, The Uniform Crime Reporting (UCR) Program, The FBI collected these data through the Uniform Crime Reporting (UCR) Program's National Incident-Based Reporting System (NIBRS).
https://ucr.fbi.gov/about-us/cjis/ucr/nibrs/2014/tables/main

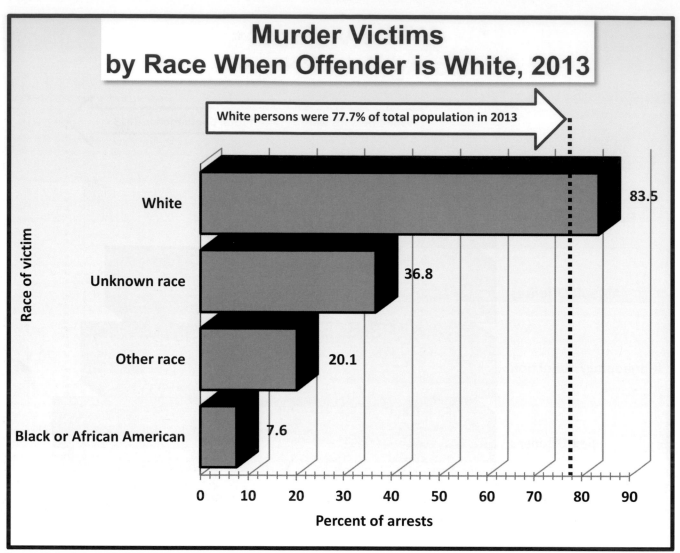

Murder Victims by Race When Offender is White, 2013

White persons were 77.7% of total population in 2013

Race of victim

White	83.5
Unknown race	36.8
Other race	20.1
Black or African American	7.6

0 10 20 30 40 50 60 70 80 90

Percent of arrests

In 2013, 83 percent of the White persons murdered were murdered by White persons.

Data are limited to single victim with single offender and based upon sampling 5,623 murders.

Race is shown without consideration to Hispanic origin. Hispanic origin can be of any race. The ethnicity totals are representative of those agencies that provided ethnicity breakdowns. Not all agencies provide ethnicity data, therefore the race and ethnicity totals will not equal. "Other race" includes American Indian or Alaska Native; Asian; Native Hawaiian or Other Pacific Islander.

This table is based on incidents where some information about the offender is known by law enforcement; therefore, when the offender age, sex, and race are all reported as unknown, these data are excluded from the table.

Source: FBI, https://ucr.fbi.gov/crime-in-the-u.s/2013/crime-in-the-u.s.-2013/offenses-known-to-law-enforcement/expanded-homicide/expanded_homicide_data_table_6_murder_race_and_sex_of_vicitm_by_race_and_sex_of_offender_2013.xls

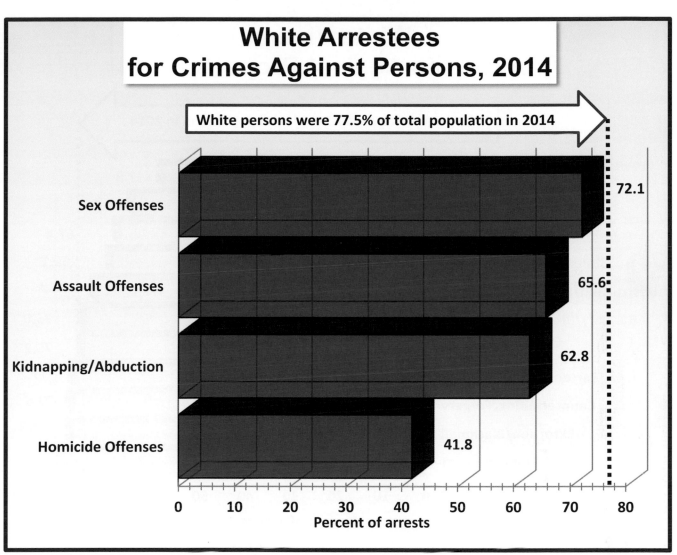

White Arrestees for Crimes Against Persons, 2014

White persons were 77.5% of total population in 2014

	Percent of arrests
Sex Offenses	72.1
Assault Offenses	65.6
Kidnapping/Abduction	62.8
Homicide Offenses	41.8

Percent of arrests

In 2014, 72 percent of crimes against persons resulted in the arrest of a White person.

The FBI collected these data through the Uniform Crime Reporting (UCR) Program's National Incident-Based Reporting System (NIBRS). The data are shown by race without distinction of ethnicity.

The UCR Program counted each arrestee associated with an incident. In addition, for 2014, the UCR Program counted each arrestee reported through only an arrest report. The arrestee data were aggregated by the race categories presented and broken down by their associated arrest offense categories. These data do not include duplicate data for arrestees who were reported to have been involved in more than one incident and, therefore, had arrestee reports submitted with multiple incident reports.

Source: FBI, The Uniform Crime Reporting (UCR) Program, The FBI collected these data through the Uniform Crime Reporting (UCR) Program's National Incident-Based Reporting System (NIBRS).
https://ucr.fbi.gov/about-us/cjis/ucr/nibrs/2014/tables/main

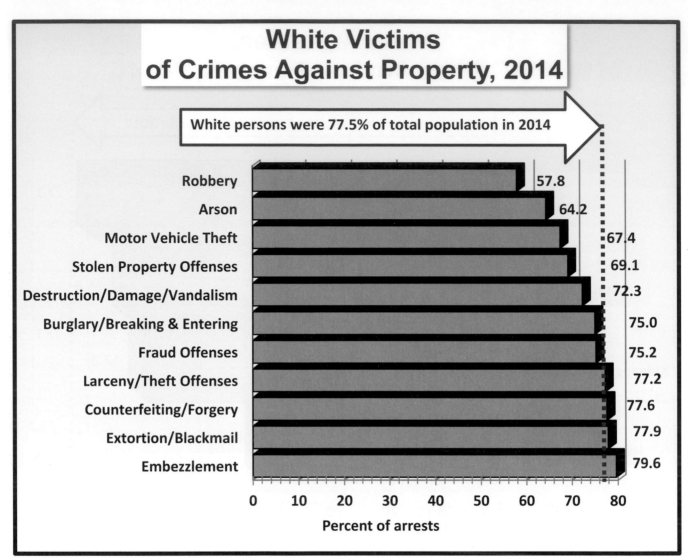

White Victims of Crimes Against Property, 2014

White persons were 77.5% of total population in 2014

Category	Percent of arrests
Robbery	57.8
Arson	64.2
Motor Vehicle Theft	67.4
Stolen Property Offenses	69.1
Destruction/Damage/Vandalism	72.3
Burglary/Breaking & Entering	75.0
Fraud Offenses	75.2
Larceny/Theft Offenses	77.2
Counterfeiting/Forgery	77.6
Extortion/Blackmail	77.9
Embezzlement	79.6

Percent of arrests

In 2014, White persons were victims of 80 percent of the embezzlements.

The definition of the racial designation of White is: A person having origins in any of the original peoples of Europe, the Middle East, or North Africa.

The FBI collected these data through the Uniform Crime Reporting (UCR) Program's National Incident-Based Reporting System (NIBRS).

Source: FBI, The Uniform Crime Reporting (UCR) Program, The FBI collected these data through the Uniform Crime Reporting (UCR) Program's National Incident-Based Reporting System (NIBRS).
https://ucr.fbi.gov/about-us/cjis/ucr/nibrs/2014/tables/main

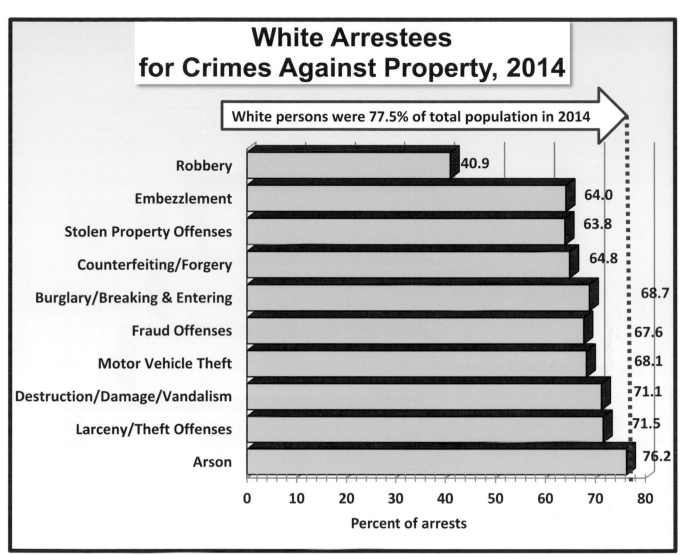

White Arrestees for Crimes Against Property, 2014

White persons were 77.5% of total population in 2014

Category	Percent
Robbery	40.9
Embezzlement	64.0
Stolen Property Offenses	63.8
Counterfeiting/Forgery	64.8
Burglary/Breaking & Entering	68.7
Fraud Offenses	67.6
Motor Vehicle Theft	68.1
Destruction/Damage/Vandalism	71.1
Larceny/Theft Offenses	71.5
Arson	76.2

Percent of arrests

In 2014, White persons were arrested for 76 percent of all arsons and 40 percent of all robberies.

The FBI collected these data through the Uniform Crime Reporting (UCR) Program's National Incident-Based Reporting System (NIBRS). The data are shown by race without distinction of ethnicity.

The UCR Program counted each arrestee associated with an incident. In addition, for 2014, the UCR Program counted each arrestee reported through only an arrest report. The arrestee data were aggregated by the race categories presented and broken down by their associated arrest offense categories. These data do not include duplicate data for arrestees who were reported to have been involved in more than one incident and, therefore, had arrestee reports submitted with multiple incident reports.

Source: FBI, The Uniform Crime Reporting (UCR) Program, The FBI collected these data through the Uniform Crime Reporting (UCR) Program's National Incident-Based Reporting System (NIBRS). https://ucr.fbi.gov/about-us/cjis/ucr/nibrs/2014/tables/main

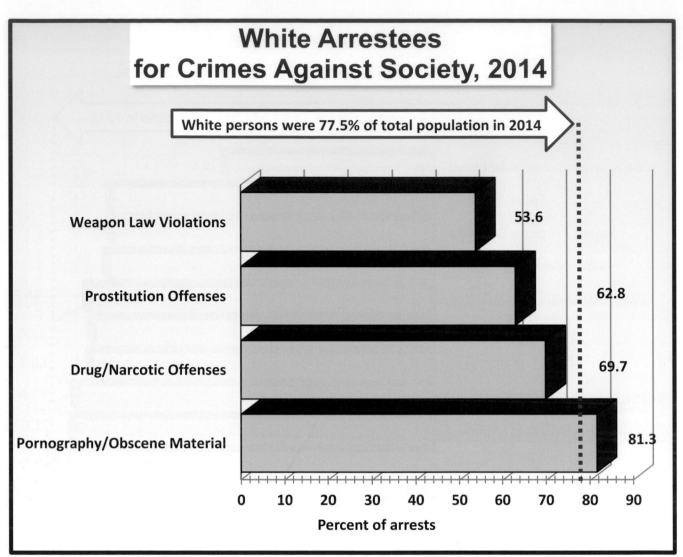

White Arrestees for Crimes Against Society, 2014

White persons were 77.5% of total population in 2014

Category	Percent
Weapon Law Violations	53.6
Prostitution Offenses	62.8
Drug/Narcotic Offenses	69.7
Pornography/Obscene Material	81.3

Percent of arrests

In 2014, 81 percent of arrests for pornography were White persons, as were 53 percent of weapons law violations.

The FBI collected these data through the Uniform Crime Reporting (UCR) Program's National Incident-Based Reporting System (NIBRS). The data are shown by race without distinction of ethnicity.

The UCR Program counted each arrestee associated with an incident. In addition, for 2014, the UCR Program counted each arrestee reported through only an arrest report. The arrestee data were aggregated by the race categories presented and broken down by their associated arrest offense categories. These data do not include duplicate data for arrestees who were reported to have been involved in more than one incident and, therefore, had arrestee reports submitted with multiple incident reports.

Source: FBI, The Uniform Crime Reporting (UCR) Program, The FBI collected these data through the Uniform Crime Reporting (UCR) Program's National Incident-Based Reporting System (NIBRS).
https://ucr.fbi.gov/about-us/cjis/ucr/nibrs/2014/tables/main

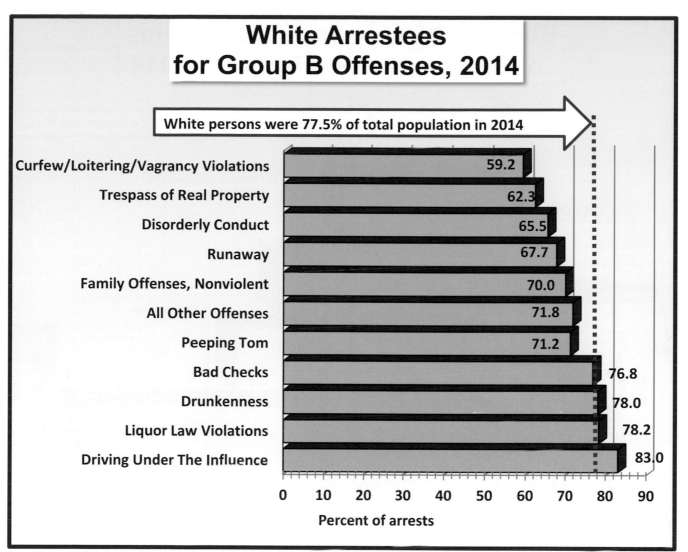

White Arrestees for Group B Offenses, 2014

White persons were 77.5% of total population in 2014

Offense	Percent of arrests
Curfew/Loitering/Vagrancy Violations	59.2
Trespass of Real Property	62.3
Disorderly Conduct	65.5
Runaway	67.7
Family Offenses, Nonviolent	70.0
All Other Offenses	71.8
Peeping Tom	71.2
Bad Checks	76.8
Drunkenness	78.0
Liquor Law Violations	78.2
Driving Under The Influence	83.0

Percent of arrests

In 2014, 83 percent of arrests for driving under the influence were White persons.

Group B offenses are all offenses other than those classified as Group A, which are crimes against persons, property or society. The following criteria were used determine if a crime should be designated as a Group A offense: 1.) The seriousness or significance of the offense. 2.) The frequency or volume of its occurrence. 3.) The prevalence of the offense nationwide. 4.) The probability law enforcement becomes aware of the offense. 5.) The likelihood law enforcement is the best channel for collecting data regarding the offense. 6.) The burden placed on law enforcement in collecting data on the offense. 7.) The national statistical validity and usefulness of the collected data.

The definition of the racial designation of White is: A person having origins in any of the original peoples of Europe, the Middle East, or North Africa.

Source: FBI, The Uniform Crime Reporting (UCR) Program, The FBI collected these data through the Uniform Crime Reporting (UCR) Program's National Incident-Based Reporting System (NIBRS). https://ucr.fbi.gov/about-us/cjis/ucr/nibrs/2014/tables/main

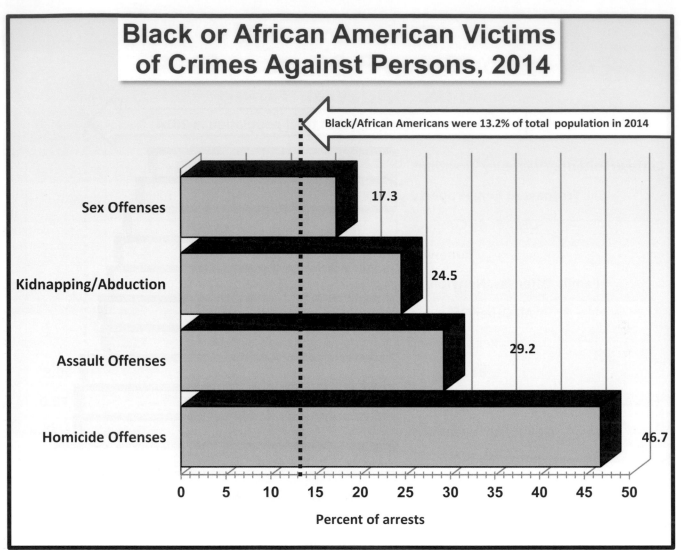

Black or African American Victims of Crimes Against Persons, 2014

Black/African Americans were 13.2% of total population in 2014

Offense	Percent
Sex Offenses	17.3
Kidnapping/Abduction	24.5
Assault Offenses	29.2
Homicide Offenses	46.7

Percent of arrests

In 2014, almost one-half of all victims of homicide were Black or African Americans.

The definition of the racial designation Black or African American is: A person having origins in any of the Black racial groups of Africa. The FBI collected these data through the Uniform Crime Reporting (UCR) Program's National Incident-Based Reporting System (NIBRS).

The UCR Program counted each arrestee associated with an incident. In addition, for 2014, the UCR Program counted each arrestee reported through only an arrest report. Arrest offense categories include the offense types for which agencies arrested individuals, but they are not necessarily the same offense types as initially reported in the incidents. The data does not include duplicate data for arrestees who were reported to have been involved in more than one incident and, therefore, had arrestee reports submitted with multiple incident reports.

Source: FBI, The Uniform Crime Reporting (UCR) Program, The FBI collected these data through the Uniform Crime Reporting (UCR) Program's National Incident-Based Reporting System (NIBRS).
https://ucr.fbi.gov/about-us/cjis/ucr/nibrs/2014/tables/main

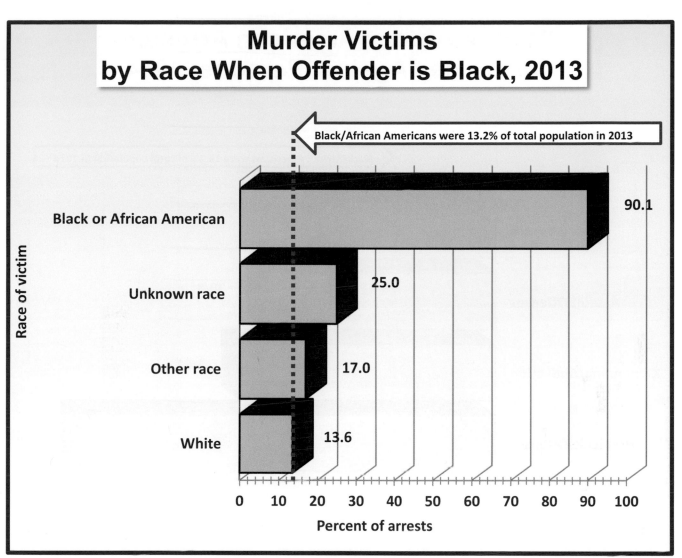

Murder Victims
by Race When Offender is Black, 2013

Black/African Americans were 13.2% of total population in 2013

Race of victim

Black or African American	90.1
Unknown race	25.0
Other race	17.0
White	13.6

0   10   20   30   40   50   60   70   80   90   100

Percent of arrests

In 2013, 90 percent of Black or African Americans murdered were murdered by Black or African Americans.

Data are limited to single victim with single offender and based upon sampling 5,623 murders.

Race is shown without consideration to Hispanic origin. Hispanic origin can be of any race. The ethnicity totals are representative of those agencies that provided ethnicity breakdowns. Not all agencies provide ethnicity data, therefore the race and ethnicity totals will not equal. "Other race" includes American Indian or Alaska Native; Asian; Native Hawaiian or Other Pacific Islander.

This table is based on incidents where some information about the offender is known by law enforcement; therefore, when the offender age, sex, and race are all reported as unknown, these data are excluded from the table.

Source: FBI, https://ucr.fbi.gov/crime-in-the-u.s/2013/crime-in-the-u.s.-2013/offenses-known-to-law-enforcement/expanded-homicide/expanded_homicide_data_table_6_murder_race_and_sex_of_vicitm_by_race_and_sex_of_offender_2013.xls

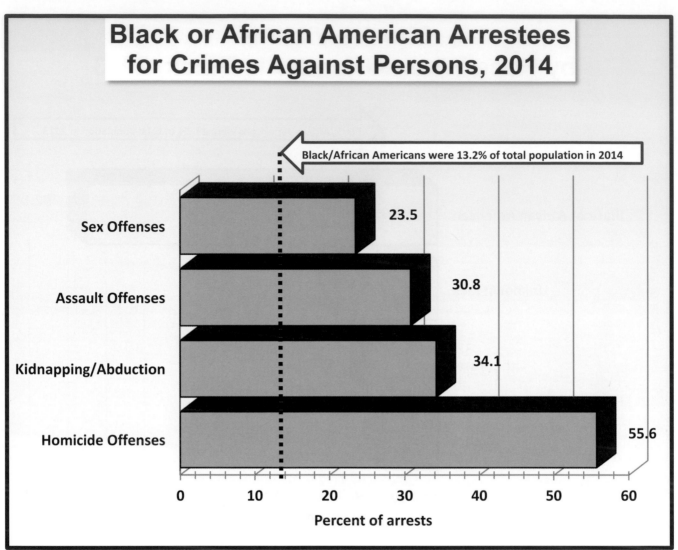

Black or African American Arrestees for Crimes Against Persons, 2014

Black/African Americans were 13.2% of total population in 2014

Sex Offenses — 23.5

Assault Offenses — 30.8

Kidnapping/Abduction — 34.1

Homicide Offenses — 55.6

Percent of arrests

0   10   20   30   40   50   60

In 2014, 55 percent of homicides resulted in the arrest of a Black or African American person.

The definition of the racial designation Black or African American is: A person having origins in any of the Black racial groups of Africa. The FBI collected these data through the Uniform Crime Reporting (UCR) Program's National Incident-Based Reporting System (NIBRS).

The UCR Program counted each arrestee associated with an incident. In addition, for 2014, the UCR Program counted each arrestee reported through only an arrest report. Arrest offense categories include the offense types for which agencies arrested individuals, but they are not necessarily the same offense types as initially reported in the incidents. The data does not include duplicate data for arrestees who were reported to have been involved in more than one incident and, therefore, had arrestee reports submitted with multiple incident reports.

Source: FBI, The Uniform Crime Reporting (UCR) Program, The FBI collected these data through the Uniform Crime Reporting (UCR) Program's National Incident-Based Reporting System (NIBRS). https://ucr.fbi.gov/about-us/cjis/ucr/nibrs/2014/tables/main

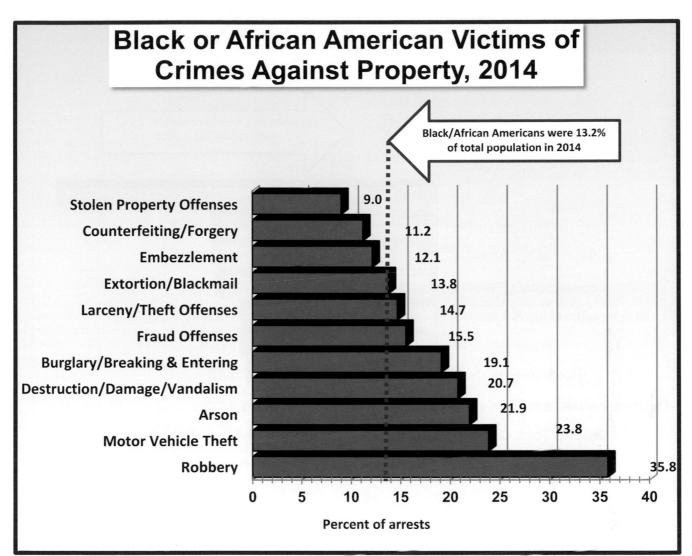

Black or African American Victims of Crimes Against Property, 2014

Black/African Americans were 13.2% of total population in 2014

	Percent of arrests
Stolen Property Offenses	9.0
Counterfeiting/Forgery	11.2
Embezzlement	12.1
Extortion/Blackmail	13.8
Larceny/Theft Offenses	14.7
Fraud Offenses	15.5
Burglary/Breaking & Entering	19.1
Destruction/Damage/Vandalism	20.7
Arson	21.9
Motor Vehicle Theft	23.8
Robbery	35.8

In 2014, Black or African Americans were victims of one-third of the robberies.

The definition of the racial designation Black or African American is: A person having origins in any of the Black racial groups of Africa. The FBI collected these data through the Uniform Crime Reporting (UCR) Program's National Incident-Based Reporting System (NIBRS). Data are for individual (person) victims and business, financial institution, government, religious organizations, or other victim types.

The UCR Program counted each arrestee associated with an incident. In addition, for 2014, the UCR Program counted each arrestee reported through only an arrest report. These data do not include duplicate data for arrestees who were reported to have been involved in more than one incident and, therefore, had arrestee reports submitted with multiple incident reports.

Source: FBI, The Uniform Crime Reporting (UCR) Program, The FBI collected these data through the Uniform Crime Reporting (UCR) Program's National Incident-Based Reporting System (NIBRS).
https://ucr.fbi.gov/about-us/cjis/ucr/nibrs/2014/tables/main

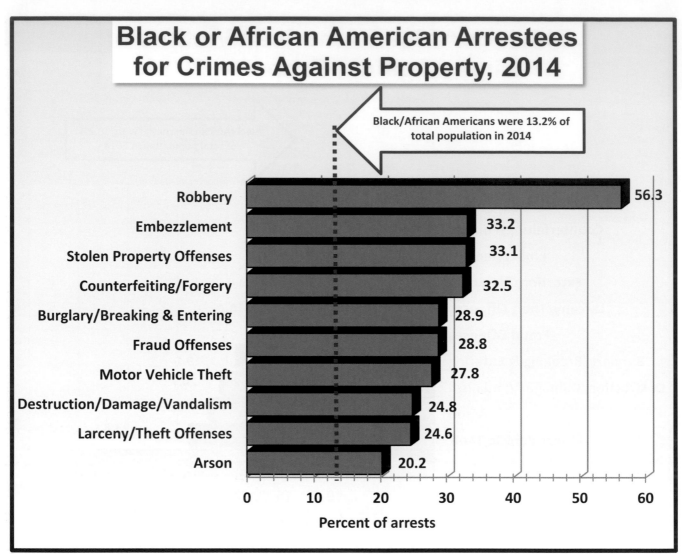

Black or African American Arrestees for Crimes Against Property, 2014

Black/African Americans were 13.2% of total population in 2014

Crime	Percent of arrests
Robbery	56.3
Embezzlement	33.2
Stolen Property Offenses	33.1
Counterfeiting/Forgery	32.5
Burglary/Breaking & Entering	28.9
Fraud Offenses	28.8
Motor Vehicle Theft	27.8
Destruction/Damage/Vandalism	24.8
Larceny/Theft Offenses	24.6
Arson	20.2

Percent of arrests

In 2014, Black or African Americans were arrested for 56 percent of all robberies and 20 percent of the arsons.

The definition of the racial designation Black or African American is: A person having origins in any of the Black racial groups of Africa. The FBI collected these data through the Uniform Crime Reporting (UCR) Program's National Incident-Based Reporting System (NIBRS). Data are for individual (person) victims and business, financial institution, government, religious organizations, or other victim types.

The UCR Program counted each arrestee associated with an incident. In addition, for 2014, the UCR Program counted each arrestee reported through only an arrest report. These data do not include duplicate data for arrestees who were reported to have been involved in more than one incident and, therefore, had arrestee reports submitted with multiple incident reports.

Source: FBI, The Uniform Crime Reporting (UCR) Program, The FBI collected these data through the Uniform Crime Reporting (UCR) Program's National Incident-Based Reporting System (NIBRS).
https://ucr.fbi.gov/about-us/cjis/ucr/nibrs/2014/tables/main

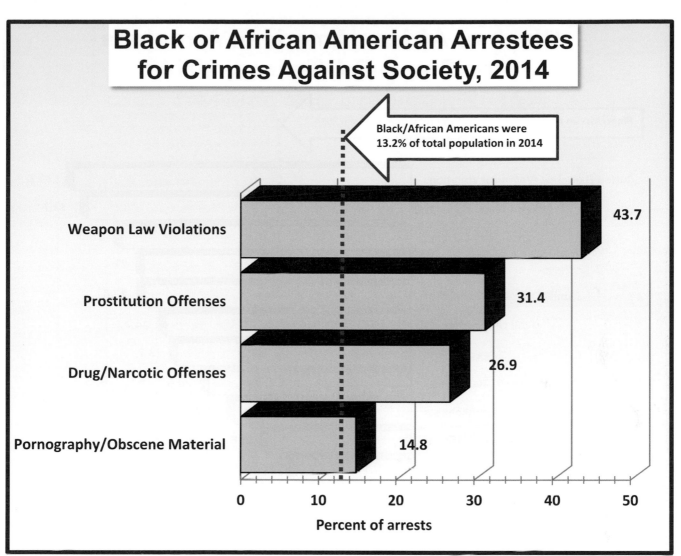

Black or African American Arrestees for Crimes Against Society, 2014

Black/African Americans were 13.2% of total population in 2014

Weapon Law Violations	43.7
Prostitution Offenses	31.4
Drug/Narcotic Offenses	26.9
Pornography/Obscene Material	14.8

Percent of arrests

In 2014, Black or African Americans were arrested for 15 percent of all arrests for pornography and 44 percent of all arrests for weapons law violations.

The definition of the racial designation Black or African American is: A person having origins in any of the Black racial groups of Africa. The FBI collected these data through the Uniform Crime Reporting (UCR) Program's National Incident-Based Reporting System (NIBRS). Data are for individual (person) victims and business, financial institution, government, religious organizations, or other victim types.

The UCR Program counted each arrestee associated with an incident. In addition, for 2014, the UCR Program counted each arrestee reported through only an arrest report. These data do not include duplicate data for arrestees who were reported to have been involved in more than one incident and, therefore, had arrestee reports submitted with multiple incident reports.

Source: FBI, The Uniform Crime Reporting (UCR) Program, The FBI collected these data through the Uniform Crime Reporting (UCR) Program's National Incident-Based Reporting System (NIBRS).
https://ucr.fbi.gov/about-us/cjis/ucr/nibrs/2014/tables/main

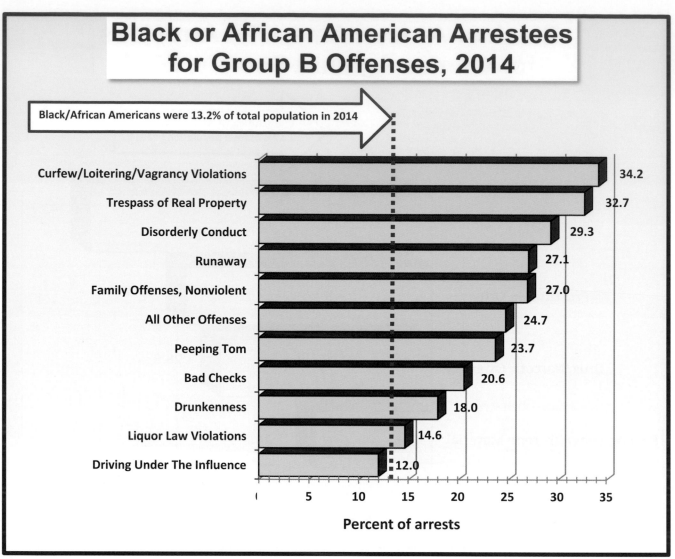

Black or African American Arrestees for Group B Offenses, 2014

Black/African Americans were 13.2% of total population in 2014

Offense	Percent
Curfew/Loitering/Vagrancy Violations	34.2
Trespass of Real Property	32.7
Disorderly Conduct	29.3
Runaway	27.1
Family Offenses, Nonviolent	27.0
All Other Offenses	24.7
Peeping Tom	23.7
Bad Checks	20.6
Drunkenness	18.0
Liquor Law Violations	14.6
Driving Under The Influence	12.0

Percent of arrests

In 2014, 12 percent of persons arrested for driving under the influence were Black or African American.

Group B offenses are all offenses other than those classified as Group A, which are crimes against persons, property or society. NIBRS developers used the following criteria to determine if a crime should be designated as a Group A offense: 1.) The seriousness or significance of the offense. 2.) The frequency or volume of its occurrence. 3.) The prevalence of the offense nationwide. 4.) The probability law enforcement becomes aware of the offense. 5.) The likelihood law enforcement is the best channel for collecting data regarding the offense. 6.) The burden placed on law enforcement in collecting data on the offense. 7.) The national statistical validity and usefulness of the collected data.

The definition of the racial designation Black or African American is: A person having origins in any of the Black racial groups of Africa.

Source: FBI, The Uniform Crime Reporting (UCR) Program, The FBI collected these data through the Uniform Crime Reporting (UCR) Program's National Incident-Based Reporting System (NIBRS), https://ucr.fbi.gov/about-us/cjis/ucr/nibrs/2014/tables/main

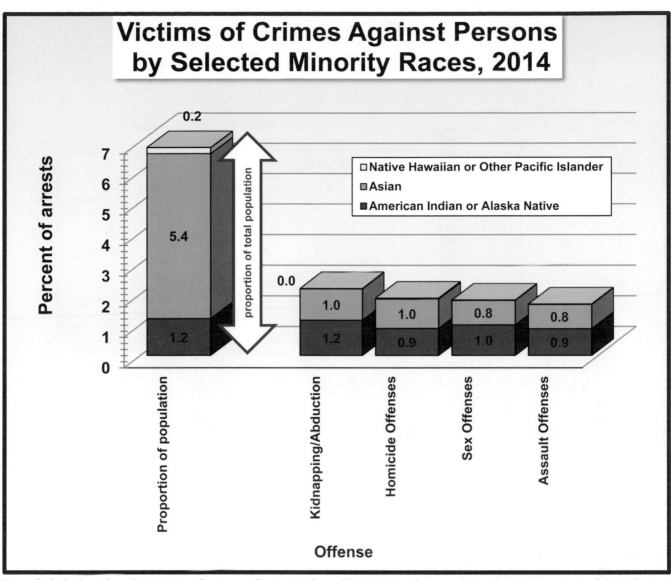

Victims of Crimes Against Persons by Selected Minority Races, 2014

Percent of arrests

0.2

Native Hawaiian or Other Pacific Islander
Asian
American Indian or Alaska Native

5.4

proportion of total population

0.0

1.0 1.0 0.8 0.8

1.2 1.2 0.9 1.0 0.9

Proportion of population

Kidnapping/Abduction

Homicide Offenses

Sex Offenses

Assault Offenses

Offense

In 2014, Asians, American Indians, Alaska Natives, Native Hawaiians, and Other Pacific Islanders, combined, accounted for less than two percent of all victims of homicide.

The definitions of the racial designations are: American Indian or Alaska Native—A person having origins in any of the original peoples of North and South America (including Central America) and who maintains tribal affiliation or community attachment. Asian—A person having origins in any of the original peoples of the Far East, Southeast Asia, the Indian subcontinent.

The term "Native Hawaiian" does not include individuals who are native to the state of Hawaii simply by virtue of being born there.

Source: FBI, The Uniform Crime Reporting (UCR) Program, The FBI collected these data through the Uniform Crime Reporting (UCR) Program's National Incident-Based Reporting System (NIBRS).
https://ucr.fbi.gov/about-us/cjis/ucr/nibrs/2014/tables/main

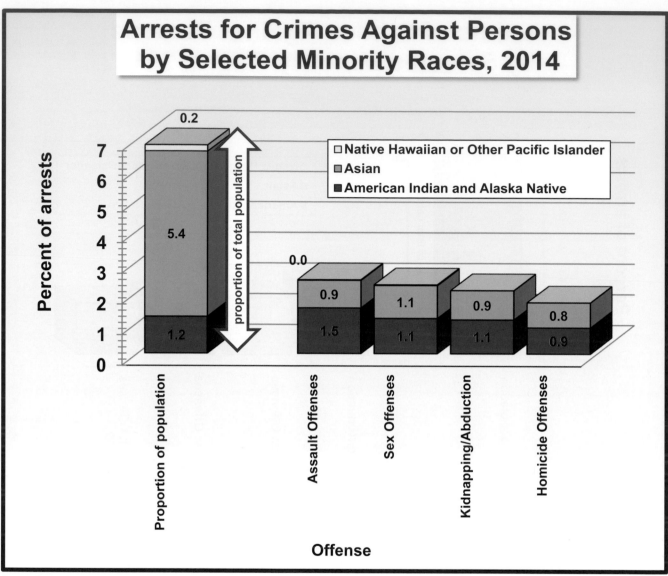

Arrests for Crimes Against Persons by Selected Minority Races, 2014

Percent of arrests

- ☐ Native Hawaiian or Other Pacific Islander
- ◼ Asian
- ◼ American Indian and Alaska Native

proportion of total population

Proportion of population: 0.2, 5.4, 1.2

Assault Offenses: 0.0, 0.9, 1.5

Sex Offenses: 1.1, 1.1

Kidnapping/Abduction: 0.9, 1.1

Homicide Offenses: 0.8, 0.9

Offense

In 2014, Native Hawaiian or Other Pacific Islanders were arrested for crimes against persons at rates below one-tenth of their proportion in the general population.

The definitions of the racial designations are: American Indian or Alaska Native(AIAN) —a person having origins in any of the original peoples of North and South America (including Central America) and who maintains tribal affiliation or community attachment; Asian—A person having origins in any of the original peoples of the Far East, Southeast Asia, the Indian subcontinent including, for example, Cambodia, China, India, Japan, Korea, Malaysia, Pakistan, the Philippine Islands, Thailand, and Vietnam Native; Hawaiian or Other Pacific Islander—a person having origins in any of the original peoples of Hawaii, Guam, Samoa, or other Pacific Islands. Note: The term "Native Hawaiian" does not include individuals who are native to the state of Hawaii simply by virtue of being born there.

Source: FBI, The Uniform Crime Reporting (UCR) Program, The FBI collected these data through the Uniform Crime Reporting (UCR) Program's National Incident-Based Reporting System (NIBRS).
https://ucr.fbi.gov/about-us/cjis/ucr/nibrs/2014/tables/main

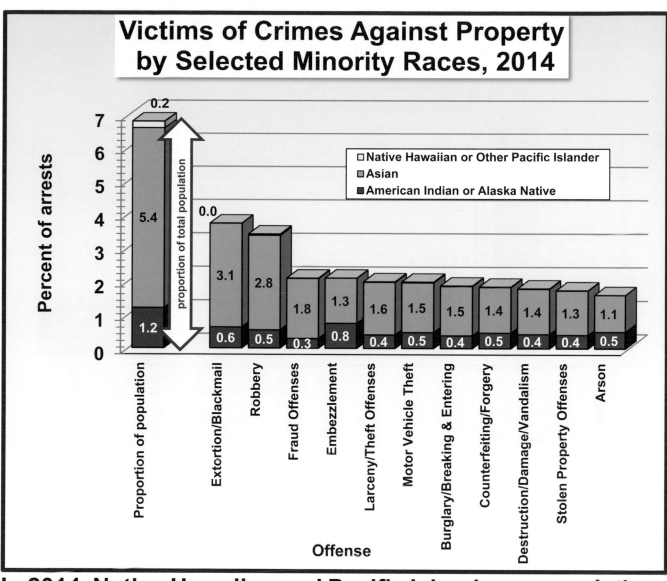

Victims of Crimes Against Property by Selected Minority Races, 2014

Percent of arrests (y-axis)

proportion of total population

Legend:
- ☐ Native Hawaiian or Other Pacific Islander
- ☐ Asian
- ■ American Indian or Alaska Native

Offense	Native Hawaiian or Other Pacific Islander	Asian	American Indian or Alaska Native
Proportion of population	0.2	5.4	1.2
Extortion/Blackmail	0.0	3.1	0.6
Robbery		2.8	0.5
Fraud Offenses		1.8	0.3
Embezzlement		1.3	0.8
Larceny/Theft Offenses		1.6	0.4
Motor Vehicle Theft		1.5	0.5
Burglary/Breaking & Entering		1.5	0.4
Counterfeiting/Forgery		1.4	0.5
Destruction/Damage/Vandalism		1.4	0.4
Stolen Property Offenses		1.3	0.4
Arson		1.1	0.5

Offense

In 2014, Native Hawaiian and Pacific Islanders were victims of property crimes at rates generally below one-fifth of their proportion in the general population.

The definitions of the racial designations are: American Indian or Alaska Native—a person having origins in any of the original peoples of North and South America (including Central America) and who maintains tribal affiliation or community attachment Asian—A person having origins in any of the original peoples of the Far East, Southeast Asia, the Indian subcontinent. Native Hawaiian or Other Pacific Islander—a person having origins in any of the original peoples of Hawaii, Guam, Samoa, or other Pacific Islands, e.g., individuals who are Carolinian, Fijian, Kosraean, Melanesian, Micronesian, Northern Mariana Islander, Palauan, Papua New Guinean, Ponapean (Pohnpelan), Polynesian, Solomon Islander, Tahitian, Tarawa Islander, Tokelauan, Tongan, Trukese (Chuukese), and Yapese. Note: The term "Native Hawaiian" does not include individuals who are native to the state of Hawaii simply by virtue of being born there.

Source: FBI, The Uniform Crime Reporting (UCR) Program, The FBI collected these data through the Uniform Crime Reporting (UCR) Program's National Incident-Based Reporting System (NIBRS).
https://ucr.fbi.gov/about-us/cjis/ucr/nibrs/2014/tables/main

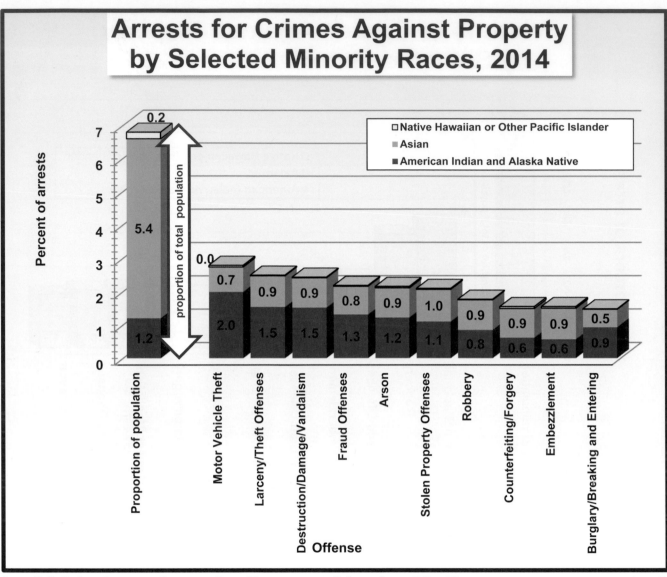

Arrests for Crimes Against Property by Selected Minority Races, 2014

Legend:
- □ Native Hawaiian or Other Pacific Islander
- ▨ Asian
- ■ American Indian and Alaska Native

Y-axis: Percent of arrests

Category	NHOPI	Asian	AIAN
Proportion of population	0.2	5.4	1.2
Motor Vehicle Theft	0.0	0.7	2.0
Larceny/Theft Offenses		0.9	1.5
Destruction/Damage/Vandalism		0.9	1.5
Fraud Offenses		0.8	1.3
Arson		0.9	1.2
Stolen Property Offenses		1.0	1.1
Robbery		0.9	0.8
Counterfeiting/Forgery		0.9	0.6
Embezzlement		0.9	0.6
Burglary/Breaking and Entering		0.5	0.9

Offense

In 2014, American Indian or Alaska Natives were arrested for two percent of all motor vehicle thefts.

The definitions of the racial designations are: American Indian or Alaska Native (AIAN) —a person having origins in any of the original peoples of North and South America (including Central America) and who maintains tribal affiliation or community attachment; Asian—a person having origins in any of the original peoples of the Far East, Southeast Asia, the Indian subcontinent. Hawaiian or Other Pacific Islander—a person having origins in any of the original peoples of Hawaii, Guam, Samoa, or other Pacific Islands. Note: The term "Native Hawaiian" does not include individuals who are native to the state of Hawaii simply by virtue of being born there.

Source: FBI, The Uniform Crime Reporting (UCR) Program, The FBI collected these data through the Uniform Crime Reporting (UCR) Program's National Incident-Based Reporting System (NIBRS). https://ucr.fbi.gov/about-us/cjis/ucr/nibrs/2014/tables/main

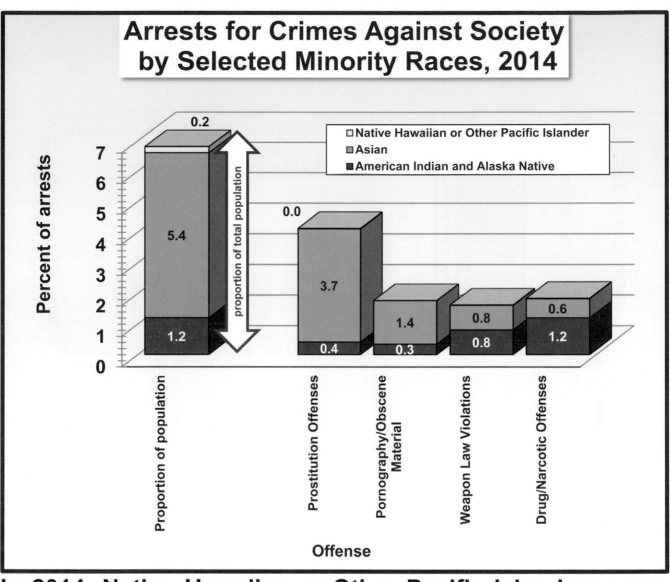

Arrests for Crimes Against Society by Selected Minority Races, 2014

Percent of arrests (y-axis)

Legend:
- ☐ Native Hawaiian or Other Pacific Islander
- ▨ Asian
- ■ American Indian and Alaska Native

Proportion of population: 0.2, 5.4, 1.2 (proportion of total population)
Prostitution Offenses: 0.0, 3.7, 0.4
Pornography/Obscene Material: 1.4, 0.3
Weapon Law Violations: 0.8, 0.8
Drug/Narcotic Offenses: 0.6, 1.2

Offense (x-axis)

In 2014, Native Hawaiian or Other Pacific Islanders were arrested for crimes against society at rates below one-tenth of their proportion of the general population.

The definitions of the racial designations are: American Indian or Alaska Native—a person having origins in any of the original peoples of North and South America (including Central America) and who maintains tribal affiliation or community attachment Asian—a person having origins in any of the original peoples of the Far East, Southeast Asia, the Indian subcontinent. Native Hawaiian or Other Pacific Islander—a person having origins in any of the original peoples of Hawaii, Guam, Samoa, or other Pacific Islands, e.g., individuals who are Carolinian, Fijian, Kosraean, Melanesian, Micronesian, Northern Mariana Islander, Palauan, Papua New Guinean, Ponapean (Pohnpelan), Polynesian, Solomon Islander, Tahitian, Tarawa Islander, Tokelauan, Tongan, Trukese (Chuukese), and Yapese. Note: The term "Native Hawaiian" does not include individuals who are native to the state of Hawaii simply by virtue of being born there.

Source: FBI, The Uniform Crime Reporting (UCR) Program, The FBI collected these data through the Uniform Crime Reporting (UCR) Program's National Incident-Based Reporting System (NIBRS).
https://ucr.fbi.gov/about-us/cjis/ucr/nibrs/2014/tables/main

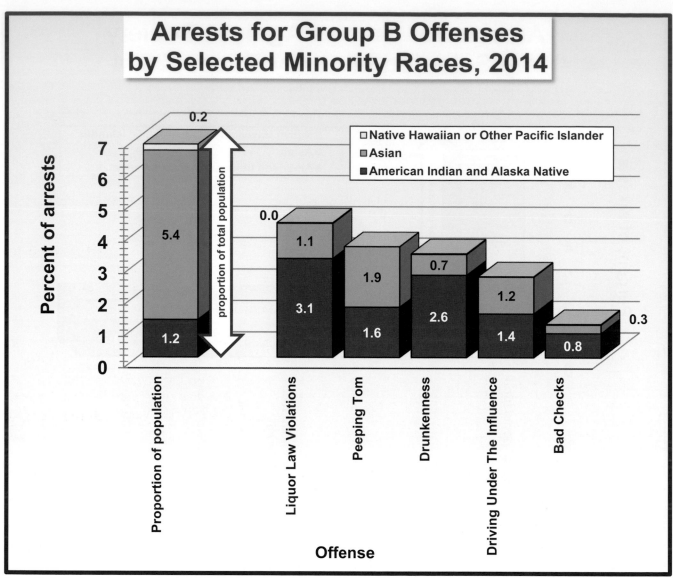

Arrests for Group B Offenses by Selected Minority Races, 2014

In 2014, American Indian and Alaska Natives were arrested for liquor law and drunkenness offenses at rates more than double their proportion in the general population.

Group B offenses are all offenses other than those classified as Group A, which are crimes against persons, property or society. NIBRS developers used the following criteria to determine if a crime should be designated as a Group A offense: 1.) The seriousness or significance of the offense. 2.) The frequency or volume of its occurrence. 3.) The prevalence of the offense nationwide. 4.) The probability law enforcement becomes aware of the offense. 5.) The likelihood law enforcement is the best channel for collecting data regarding the offense. 6.) The burden placed on law enforcement in collecting data on the offense. 7.) The national statistical validity and usefulness of the collected data.

Source: FBI, The Uniform Crime Reporting (UCR) Program, The FBI collected these data through the Uniform Crime Reporting (UCR) Program's National Incident-Based Reporting System (NIBRS). https://ucr.fbi.gov/about-us/cjis/ucr/nibrs/2014/tables/main

Chapter 7: Correctional System

Most correctional control in the United States is conducted at the state level. In 2016, the Prison Policy Initiative estimated that there were 2.3 million persons incarcerated in all prisons; twice as many in state prisons as in local jails and more than seven times as many in state prisons as in federal prisons.

In 2014, across all 50 states the incarceration rate for Black or African Americans was significantly greater than for non-Hispanic White persons, ranging from 2.4 times greater in Hawaii to 12.1 times greater in New Jersey. The incarceration rate for Hispanic persons was higher than for non-Hispanic White persons in 27 states, led by Massachusetts at 4.3 times greater, whereas the incarceration rate of non-Hispanic White persons was 10 times greater than for Hispanics in Louisiana.

Oklahoma had the highest incarceration rate for non-Hispanic White persons in 2014 among all states. It was seven times the rate of Massachusetts—the state with the lowest rate.

Black or African American juvenile offenders are housed in residential facilities at much higher rates than juveniles of other races or ethnicities. In 2013, Black or African American juveniles were incarcerated at 16.5 times the rate of Asian juveniles. That year there were also six times as many male juvenile offenders housed as female.

~

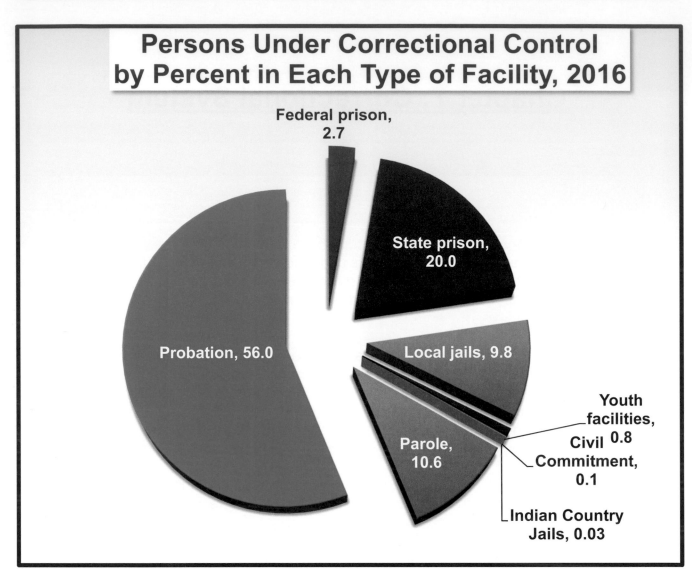

Persons Under Correctional Control by Percent in Each Type of Facility, 2016

- Federal prison, 2.7
- State prison, 20.0
- Local jails, 9.8
- Youth facilities, 0.8
- Civil Commitment, 0.1
- Probation, 56.0
- Parole, 10.6
- Indian Country Jails, 0.03

In 2016, state prisons and local jails held approximately 11 times as many prisoners as federal prisons.

The Prison Policy Initiative estimates that more than 2.3 million people were incarcerated in 2016, in 1,719 state prisons, 102 federal prisons, 2,259 juvenile correctional facilities, 3,283 local jails, and 79 Indian Country jails, military prisons, immigration detention facilities, civil commitment centers, and prisons in the U.S. territories.

Also, according to the Prison Policy Initiative: Almost half a million adults and children are locked up because their most significant offense was a drug offense.

Source: Prison Policy Initiative, http://www.prisonpolicy.org/reports/pie2015.html

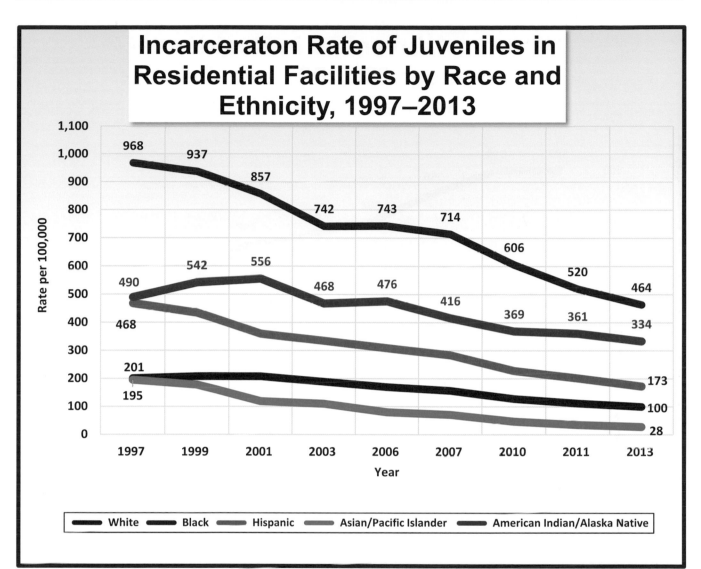

Incarceraton Rate of Juveniles in Residential Facilities by Race and Ethnicity, 1997–2013

The rate at which Black juvenile offenders were placed in residential facilities decreased by approximately a factor of two between 1997–2013. This was a reduction greater than any other group but still higher in 2013 than any other group.

Residential placement rate calculated per 100,000 persons, age 10 through the upper age at which those charged with a criminal law violation were under original jurisdiction of the juvenile courts in each state in the given year (through age 17 in most states). Data do not include adult prisons, jails, federal facilities, or facilities exclusively for drug or mental health treatment or for abused or neglected youth. The data provide 1-day population counts of juveniles in residential placement facilities.

Race categories exclude persons of Hispanic ethnicity.

Source: U.S. Department of Justice, Office of Juvenile Justice and Delinquency Prevention, Census of Juveniles in Residential Placement (CJRP), retrieved October 20, 2015, from http://www.ojjdp.gov/ojstatbb/ezacjrp/. (This table was prepared October 2015.), from http://www.samhsa.gov/data/population-data-nsduh/reports?tab=38., Table 233.92, https://nces.ed.gov/programs/digest/2015menu_tables.asp

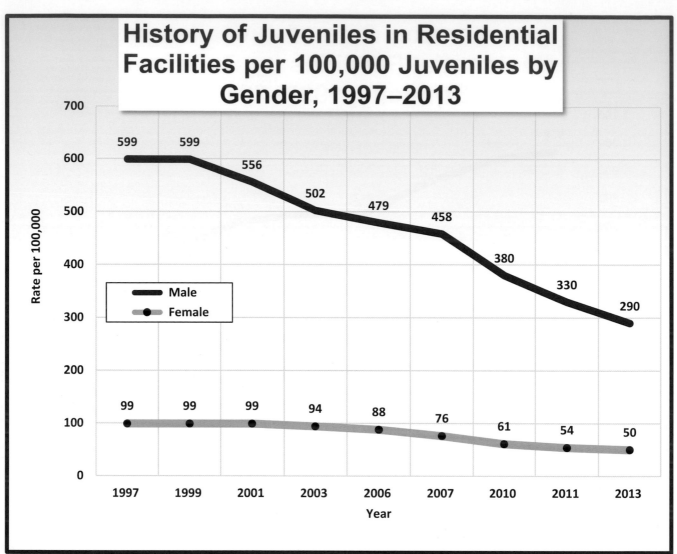

History of Juveniles in Residential Facilities per 100,000 Juveniles by Gender, 1997–2013

The rate at which both male and female juvenile offenders were placed in residential facilities decreased by a factor of two between 1997–2013. Males were placed at six times the rate as females throughout the period.

Residential placement rate calculated per 100,000 population, age 10 through the upper age at which those charged with a criminal law violation were under original jurisdiction of the juvenile courts in each state in the given year (through age 17 in most states). Data do not include adult prisons, jails, federal facilities, or facilities exclusively for drug or mental health treatment or for abused or neglected youth. The data provide 1-day population counts of juveniles in residential placement facilities; 1-day counts differ substantially from the annual admission and release data used to measure facility population flow.

Source: U.S. Department of Justice, Office of Juvenile Justice and Delinquency Prevention, Census of Juveniles in Residential Placement (CJRP), retrieved October 20, 2015, from http://www.ojjdp.gov/ojstatbb/ezacjrp/. (This table was prepared October 2015.), from http://www.samhsa.gov/data/population-data-nsduh/reports?tab=38., Table 233.92, https://nces.ed.gov/programs/digest/2015menu_tables.asp

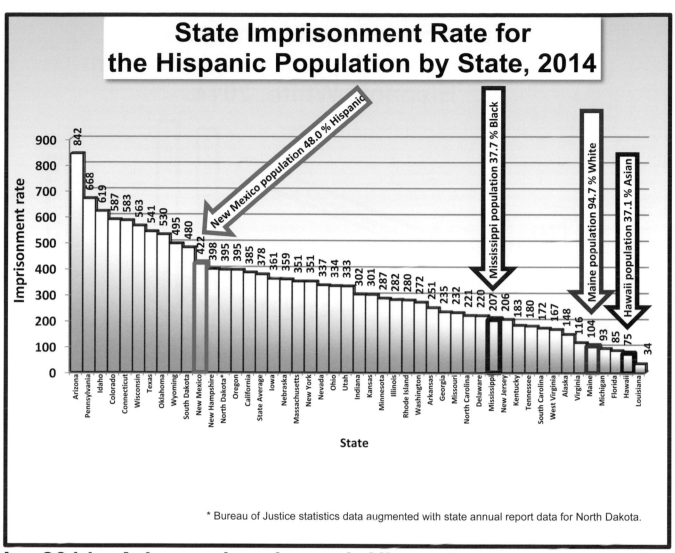

State Imprisonment Rate for the Hispanic Population by State, 2014

New Mexico population 48.0 % Hispanic

Mississippi population 37.7 % Black

Maine population 94.7 % White

Hawaii population 37.1 % Asian

Imprisonment rate / State

Arizona 842, Pennsylvania 668, Idaho 619, Colorado 587, Connecticut 583, Wisconsin 563, Texas 541, Oklahoma 530, Wyoming 495, South Dakota 480, New Mexico 422, New Hampshire 398, North Dakota* 395, Oregon 395, California 385, State Average 378, Iowa 361, Nebraska 359, Massachusetts 351, New York 351, Nevada 337, Ohio 334, Utah 333, Indiana 302, Kansas 301, Minnesota 287, Illinois 282, Rhode Island 280, Washington 272, Arkansas 251, Georgia 235, Missouri 232, North Carolina 221, Delaware 220, Mississippi 207, New Jersey 206, Kentucky 183, Tennessee 180, South Carolina 172, West Virginia 167, Alaska 148, Virginia 116, Maine 104, Michigan 93, Florida 85, Hawaii 75, Louisiana 34

* Bureau of Justice statistics data augmented with state annual report data for North Dakota.

In 2014, Arizona imprisoned Hispanic persons at the highest rate of any state and approximately 25 times the rate in Louisiana.

The imprisonment rate is the number of persons of Hispanic origin imprisoned in states prisons per 100,000 of person of Hispanic origin in the general population.

Data for Alabama, Maryland, Montana, and Vermont are not provided.

Source: The Sentencing Project publication The Color of Justice: Racial and Ethnic Disparity in State Prisons, Tables Appendix Tables A, B, States Imprisonment 2014 and Tables 1, and 2, Incarceration rates. http://www.sentencingproject.org/wp-content/uploads/2016/06/The-Color-of-Justice-Racial-and-Ethnic-Disparity-in-State-Prisons.pdf

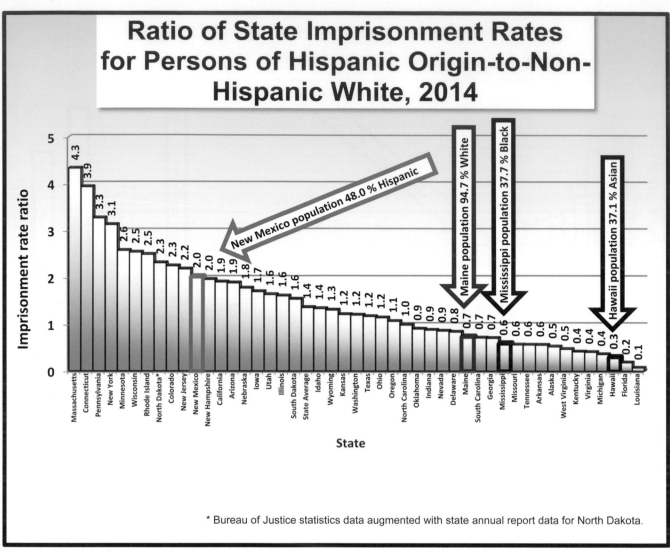

Ratio of State Imprisonment Rates for Persons of Hispanic Origin-to-Non-Hispanic White, 2014

In 2014, Massachusetts imprisoned Hispanic persons at approximately four times the rate as non-Hispanic White persons—the highest disparity of all states.

Data for Alabama, Maryland, Montana, and Vermont not provided.

The imprisonment rate ratio is calculated as the number of Hispanic prisoners per 100,000 Hispanic persons in the general population divided by the number of non-Hispanic White prisoners per 100,000 non-Hispanic White persons in the general population, for state prisons within each state.

Source: The Sentencing Project publication The Color of Justice: Racial and Ethnic Disparity in State Prisons, Tables Appendix Tables A, B, States Imprisonment 2014 and Tables 1, and 2, Incarceration rates. http://www.sentencingproject.org/wp-content/uploads/2016/06/The-Color-of-Justice-Racial-and-Ethnic-Disparity-in-State-Prisons.pdf

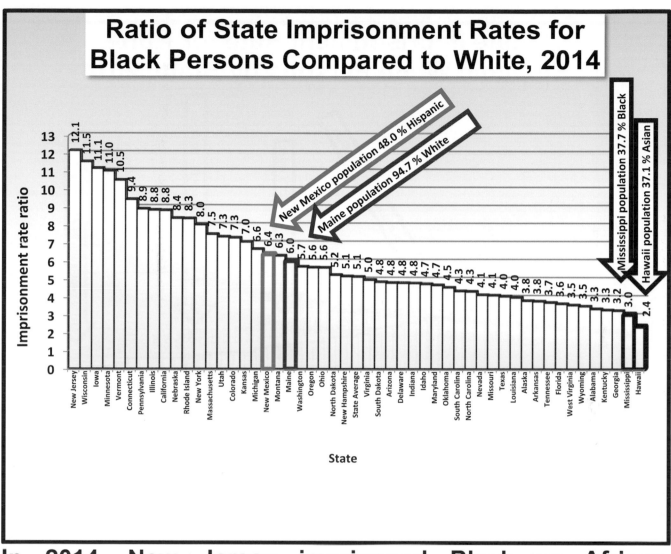

Ratio of State Imprisonment Rates for Black Persons Compared to White, 2014

In 2014, New Jersey imprisoned Black or African Americans at 12 times the rate of White persons—the highest disparity of all states.

The imprisonment rate ratio is calculated as the number of Black prisoners per 100,000 Black persons in the general population divided by the number of non-Hispanic White prisoners per 100,000 non-Hispanic White persons in the general population, for state prisons within each state.

Source: The Sentencing Project publication The Color of Justice: Racial and Ethnic Disparity in State Prisons, Tables Appendix Tables A, B, States Imprisonment 2014 and Tables 1, and 2, Incarceration rates. http://www.sentencingproject.org/wp-content/uploads/2016/06/The-Color-of-Justice-Racial-and-Ethnic-Disparity-in-State-Prisons.pdf

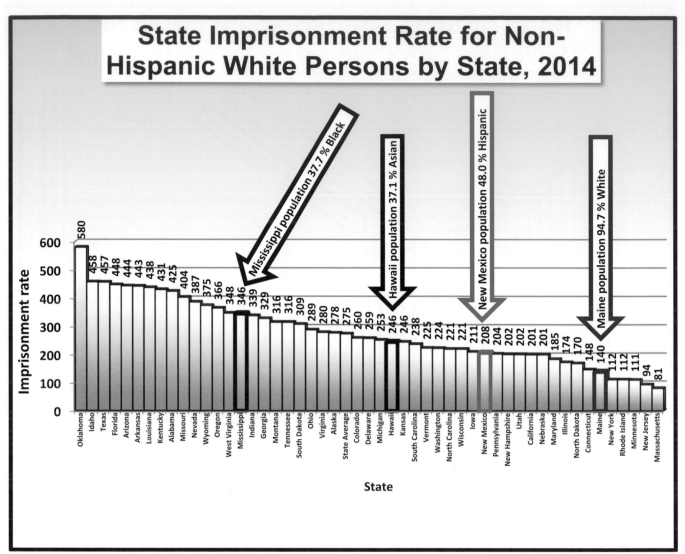

State Imprisonment Rate for Non-Hispanic White Persons by State, 2014

In 2014, Oklahoma imprisoned non-Hispanic White persons at the highest rate of any other state, and seven times the rate of Massachusetts.

The imprisonment rate is the number of non-Hispanic White persons imprisoned in states prison per 100,000 of Non-Hispanic White persons in the general population.

Source: The Sentencing Project publication The Color of Justice: Racial and Ethnic Disparity in State Prisons, Tables Appendix Tables A, B, States Imprisonment 2014 and Tables 1, and 2, Incarceration rates. http://www.sentencingproject.org/wp-content/uploads/2016/06/The-Color-of-Justice-Racial-and-Ethnic-Disparity-in-State-Prisons.pdf

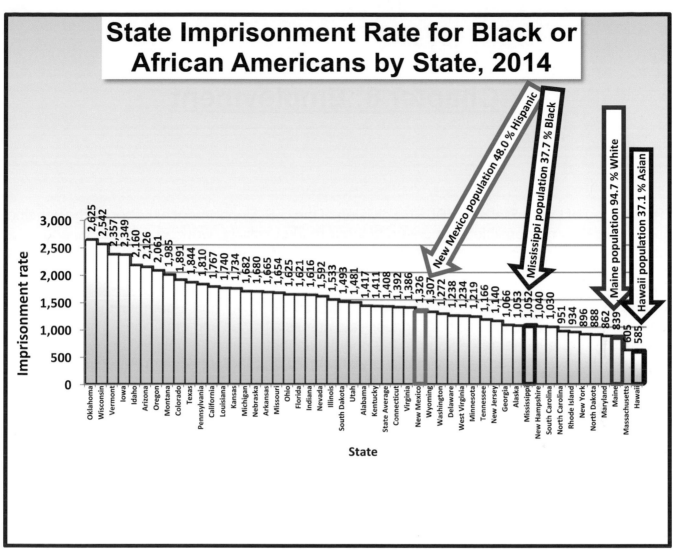

State Imprisonment Rate for Black or African Americans by State, 2014

In 2014, Oklahoma imprisoned Black or African American persons at the highest rate of any state—more than four times the rate of non-Hispanic White persons.

The imprisonment rate is the number of Black and African American persons imprisoned in state prisons per 100,000 of Black and African American persons in the general population.

Source: The Sentencing Project publication The Color of Justice: Racial and Ethnic Disparity in State Prisons, Tables Appendix Tables A, B, States Imprisonment 2014 and Tables 1, and 2, Incarceration rates. http://www.sentencingproject.org/wp-content/uploads/2016/06/The-Color-of-Justice-Racial-and-Ethnic-Disparity-in-State-Prisons.pdf

Chapter 8: Employment

The Bureau of Labor Statistics (BLS), a division of the U.S. Department of Labor, is the principal federal agency responsible for measuring labor market activity, working conditions, and price changes in the economy. Its mission is to collect, analyze, and disseminate essential economic information to support public and private decision-making.

There exists a strong relationship between education level and unemployment rate, and education level and workforce participation rate across all races and ethnicities. The labor force participation rate is the percentage of the population that is either employed or unemployed— that is, either working or actively seeking work. In 2015, Black or African American men had the lowest participation rate at 64 percent. By comparison, 72 percent of Asian men were participants, the group with the highest.

Black or African American workers with post-bachelor's degrees experienced a 4.0 percent unemployment rate compared with 15.9 percent for Black or African Americans without a high school diploma. Asian persons with post-bachelor's degrees experienced an even lower unemployment rate of 2.3 percent.

Men who are veterans and under the age 35 experienced an unemployment rate approximately one percentage point higher than non-veterans while veteran women experienced a similar one percentage point disparity across all age groups.

Thirty-eight percent of American Indian and Alaska Natives, between the ages of 18–24, were neither in school or working in 2015, compared with nine percent of Asians.

Nearly 16 percent of Black or African American men were represented by a union in 2015, compared with 10 percent of Asians.

In 2015, approximately one-half of all maids and housekeeping cleaners were Hispanic, and 90 percent were women. Black or African Americans accounted for 40 percent of all barbers, while 56 percent of all medical scientists were Asian. Ninety-seven percent of all kindergarten teachers were women.

~

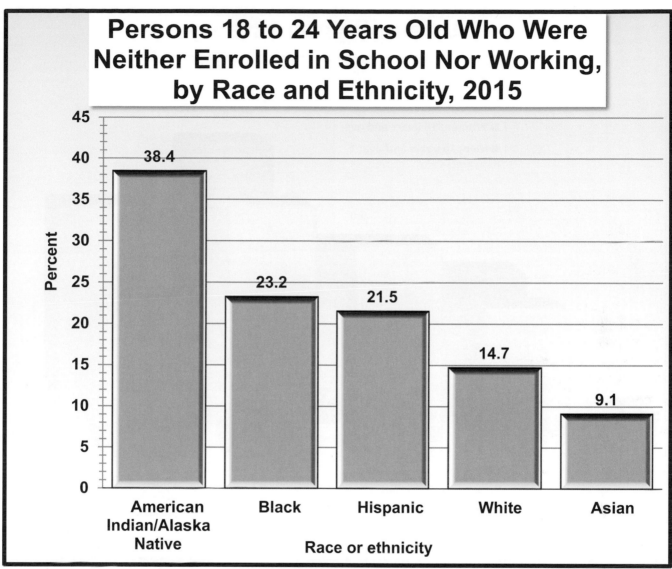

Persons 18 to 24 Years Old Who Were Neither Enrolled in School Nor Working, by Race and Ethnicity, 2015

In 2015, approximately two-of-five American Indian or Alaska Native persons aged 18–24 years old were neither enrolled in school or working. This was the highest rate among all races and ethnicities.

Race categories exclude persons of Hispanic ethnicity.

Source: U.S. Department of Commerce, Census Bureau, American Community Survey (ACS), 2009 and 2014. (This table was prepared December 2015.) Digest 2015, Table 501.30, https://nces.ed.gov/programs/digest/2015menu_tables.asp, http://www.census.gov/hhes/www/poverty/about/overview/measure.html

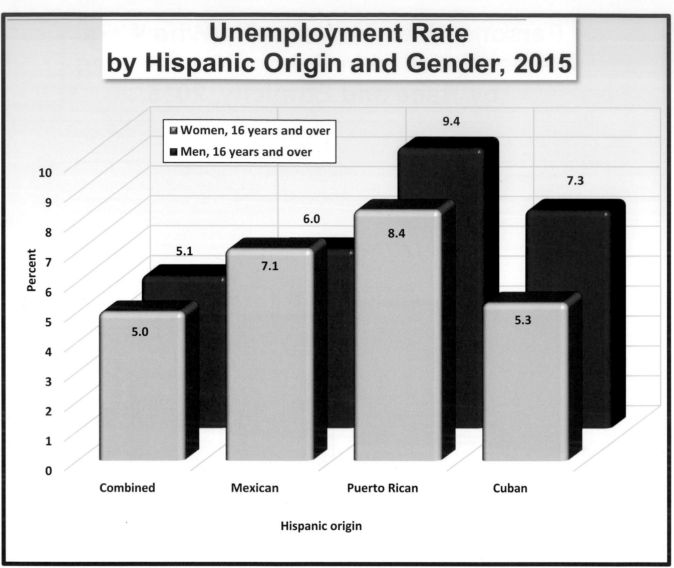

Unemployment Rate by Hispanic Origin and Gender, 2015

In 2015, Puerto Rican men had the highest unemployment rate at 9.4 percent compared with Mexicans and Cubans of either gender.

Annual average Hispanic workforce participation rate is for the civilian non-institutional population in 2015.

Includes persons of Central or South American origin and of other Hispanic or Latino ethnicity, not shown separately.

Estimates for the above race groups (White, Black or African American, and Asian) do not sum to totals because data are not presented for all races. Persons whose ethnicity is identified as Hispanic or Latino may be of any race.

Source: U.S. Department of Labor, Bureau of Labor Statistics, Table CPSAAT06, http://www.bls.gov/cps/tables.htm

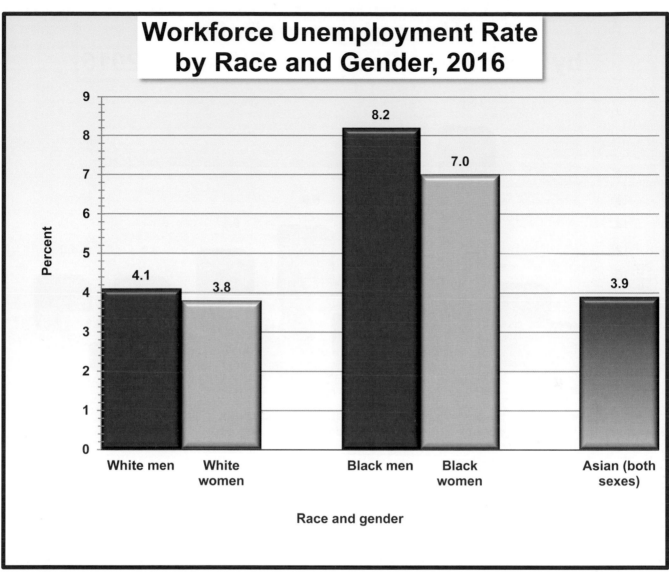

Workforce Unemployment Rate by Race and Gender, 2016

In October 2016, the unemployment rate for Black or African American men was 8.2 percent—double the rate for White men.

Source: U.S. Bureau of Labor Statistics, http://www.bls.gov/news.release/empsit.t02.htm,Table A2

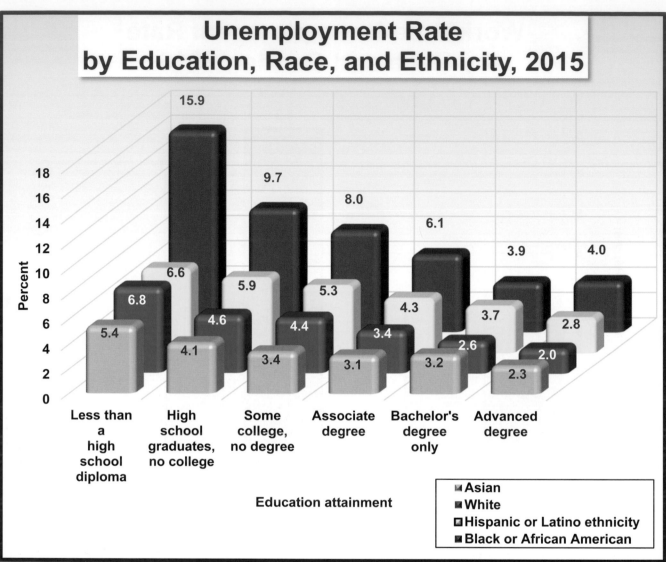

Unemployment Rate by Education, Race, and Ethnicity, 2015

Percent

Education attainment	Less than a high school diploma	High school graduates, no college	Some college, no degree	Associate degree	Bachelor's degree only	Advanced degree
Asian	5.4	4.1	3.4	3.1	3.2	2.3
White	6.8	4.6	4.4	3.4	2.6	2.0
Hispanic or Latino ethnicity	6.6	5.9	5.3	4.3	3.7	2.8
Black or African American	15.9	9.7	8.0	6.1	3.9	4.0

Legend:
- Asian
- White
- Hispanic or Latino ethnicity
- Black or African American

In 2015, the unemployment rate for Black or African Americans without high school diplomas was four times higher than for those with advanced degrees. This was the largest disparity among all races and ethnicities.

Annual average unemployment rate of the civilian non-institutional population 25 years and over by educational attainment in 2015.

Estimates for the above race groups (White, Black or African American, and Asian) do not sum to totals because data are not presented for all races. Persons whose ethnicity is identified as Hispanic or Latino may be of any race.

High school includes persons with a high school diploma or equivalent.

Advanced degree Includes persons with bachelor's master`s, professional, and doctoral degrees.

Source: U.S. Department of Labor, Bureau of Labor Statistics, Table CPSAAT07, http://www.bls.gov/cps/tables.htm

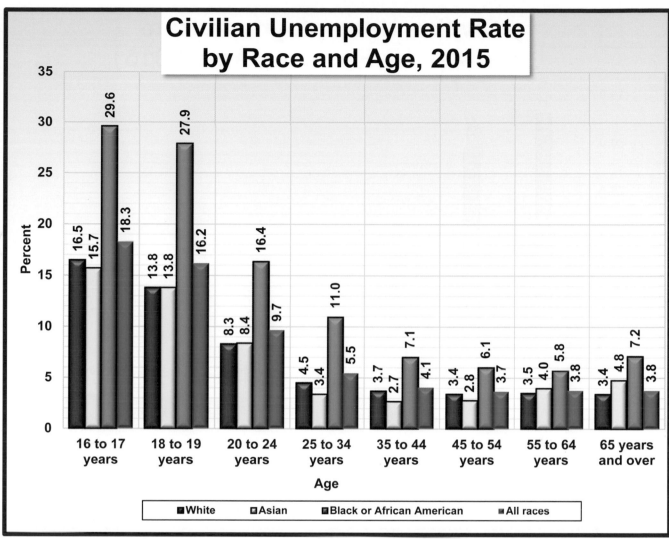

Civilian Unemployment Rate by Race and Age, 2015

In 2015, Black or African American teenage workers had an unemployment rate near 30 percent, the highest among all age groups, races and ethnicities. The rate was approximately 10 times higher than for middle-age Asians.

Annual average unemployment rate is for the civilian non-institutional population in 2015.

Estimates for the above race groups (White, Black or African American, and Asian) do not sum to totals because data are not presented for all races. Persons whose ethnicity is identified as Hispanic or Latino may be of any race.

Source: U.S. Department of Labor, Bureau of Labor Statistics, Table CPSAAT03, http://www.bls.gov/cps/tables.htm

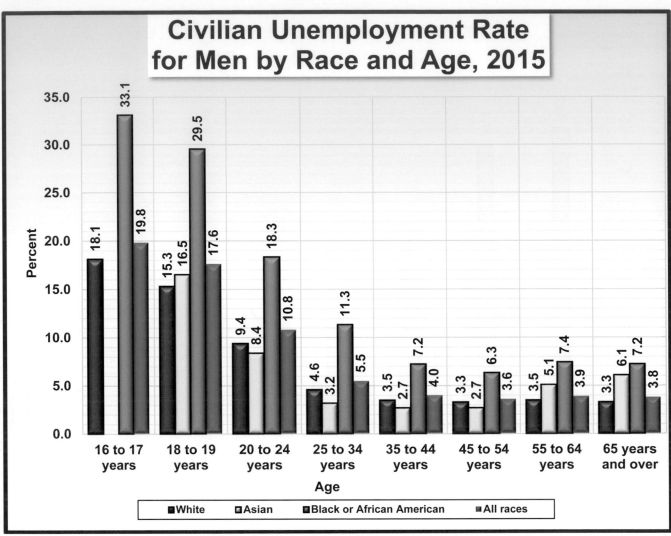

Civilian Unemployment Rate for Men by Race and Age, 2015

In 2015, Black or African American male workers had the highest unemployment rate for males of any race or ethnicity, across all age groups.

Annual average unemployment rate is for the civilian non-institutional population in 2015.

Estimates for the above race groups (White, Black or African American, and Asian) do not sum to totals because data are not presented for all races. Persons whose ethnicity is identified as Hispanic or Latino may be of any race.

Source: U.S. Department of Labor, Bureau of Labor Statistics, Table CPSAAT03, http://www.bls.gov/cps/tables.htm

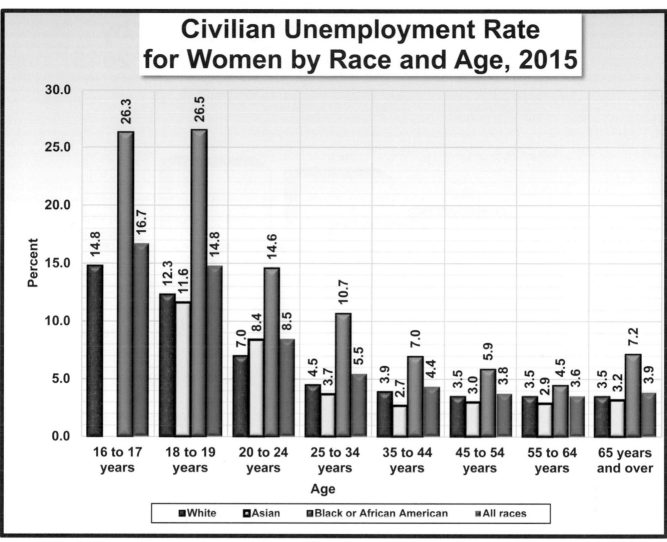

Civilian Unemployment Rate for Women by Race and Age, 2015

In 2015, Black or African American female civilian workers had the highest unemployment rate for females of any race or ethnicity, across all age groups.

Annual average unemployment rate is for the civilian non-institutional population in 2015.

Estimates for the above race groups (White, Black or African American, and Asian) do not sum to totals because data are not presented for all races. Persons whose ethnicity is identified as Hispanic or Latino may be of any race.

Source: U.S. Department of Labor, Bureau of Labor Statistics, Table CPSAAT03, http://www.bls.gov/cps/tables.htm

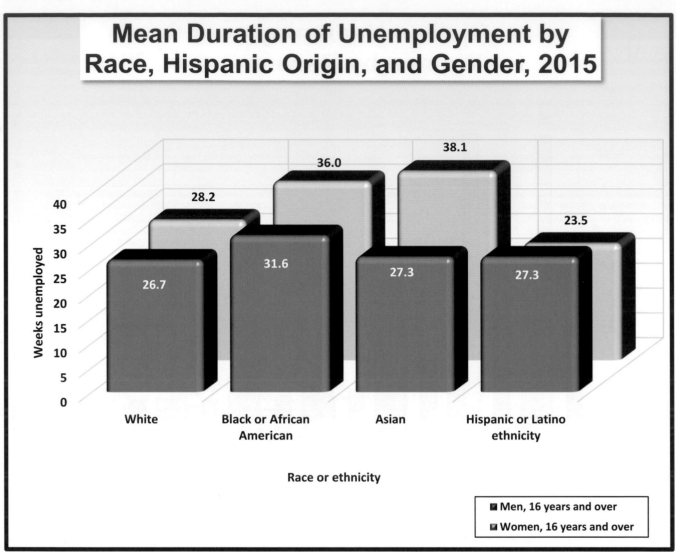

Mean Duration of Unemployment by Race, Hispanic Origin, and Gender, 2015

Weeks unemployed

White: 26.7, 28.2
Black or African American: 31.6, 36.0
Asian: 27.3, 38.1
Hispanic or Latino ethnicity: 27.3, 23.5

Race or ethnicity

■ Men, 16 years and over
■ Women, 16 years and over

In 2015, Asian women had the highest unemployment duration compared with Black or African American, White, or Hispanic persons of either gender.

Estimates for the above race groups (White, Black or African American, and Asian) do not sum to totals because data are not presented for all races. Persons whose ethnicity is identified as Hispanic or Latino may be of any race.

Source: U.S. Department of Labor, Bureau of Labor Statistics, Table CPSAAT31, http://www.bls.gov/cps/tables.htm, http://www.bls.gov/cps/tables.htm

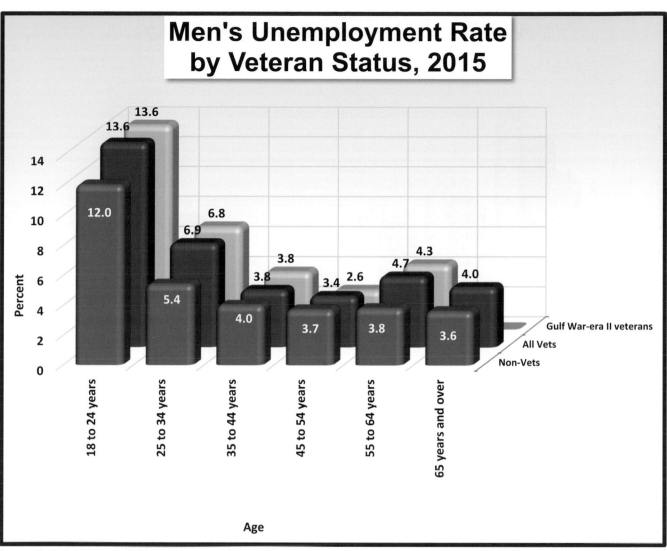

Men's Unemployment Rate by Veteran Status, 2015

In 2015, military veterans—under the age of 35—had an unemployment rate that was approximately 1.5 percentage points higher than non-veterans.

Veterans are men and women who served on active duty in the U.S. Armed Forces and were not on active duty at the time of the survey. Gulf War-era II veterans served on active duty anywhere in the world sometime since September 2001.

Source: U.S. Department of Labor, Bureau of Labor Statistics, Table CPSAAT48, http://www.bls.gov/cps/tables.htm, http://www.bls.gov/cps/tables.htm

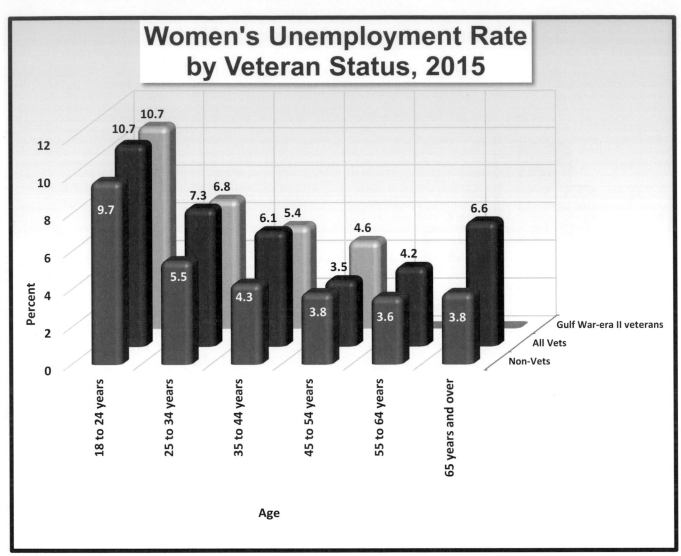

Women's Unemployment Rate by Veteran Status, 2015

In 2015, women who were veterans had between a one-to-three percentage point higher unemployment rate than non-veterans, depending on age.

Veterans are men and women who served on active duty in the U.S. Armed Forces and were not on active duty at the time of the survey. Gulf War-era II veterans served on active duty anywhere in the world sometime since September 2001.

Source: U.S. Department of Labor, Bureau of Labor Statistics, Table CPSAAT48, http://www.bls.gov/cps/tables.htm, http://www.bls.gov/cps/tables.htm

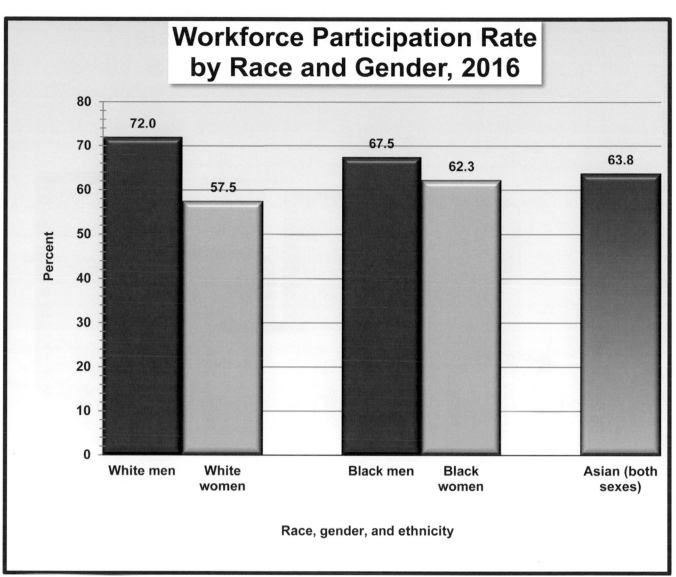

Workforce Participation Rate by Race and Gender, 2016

Percent

- White men: 72.0
- White women: 57.5
- Black men: 67.5
- Black women: 62.3
- Asian (both sexes): 63.8

Race, gender, and ethnicity

In October 2016, 72 percent of White men were either employed or looking for work compared with 57 percent of White women.

The labor force participation rate is the percentage of the population that is either employed or unemployed (that is, either working or actively seeking work)

Source: U.S. Bureau of Labor Statistics, http://www.bls.gov/news.release/empsit.t02.htm,Table A2

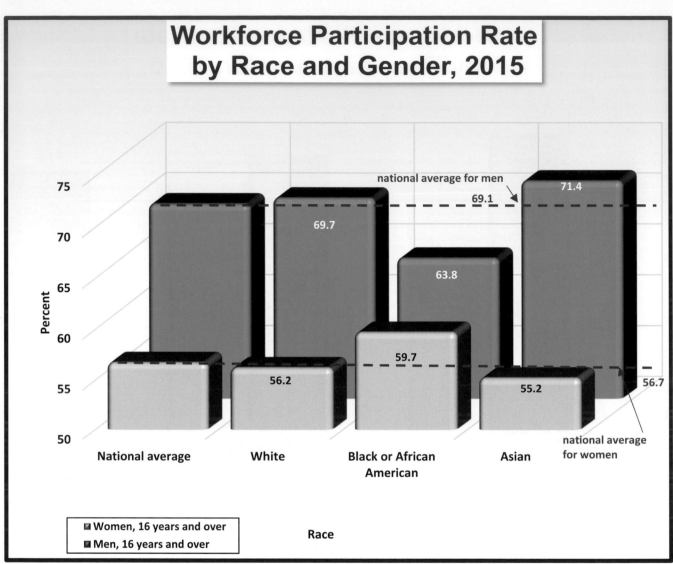

Workforce Participation Rate by Race and Gender, 2015

national average for men 69.1

| National average | White | Black or African American | Asian |

- Women, 16 years and over
- Men, 16 years and over

Race

White: 69.7 (men), 56.2 (women)
Black or African American: 63.8 (men), 59.7 (women)
Asian: 71.4 (men), 55.2 (women)
national average for women: 56.7

In 2015, Asian men had the highest workforce participation rate compared with men or women of other races.

Annual average workforce participation rate is for the civilian non-institutional population in 2015.

Estimates for the above race groups (White, Black or African American, and Asian) do not sum to totals because data are not presented for all races. Persons whose ethnicity is identified as Hispanic or Latino may be of any race.

Source: U.S. Department of Labor, Bureau of Labor Statistics, Table CPSAAT03, http://www.bls.gov/cps/tables.htm

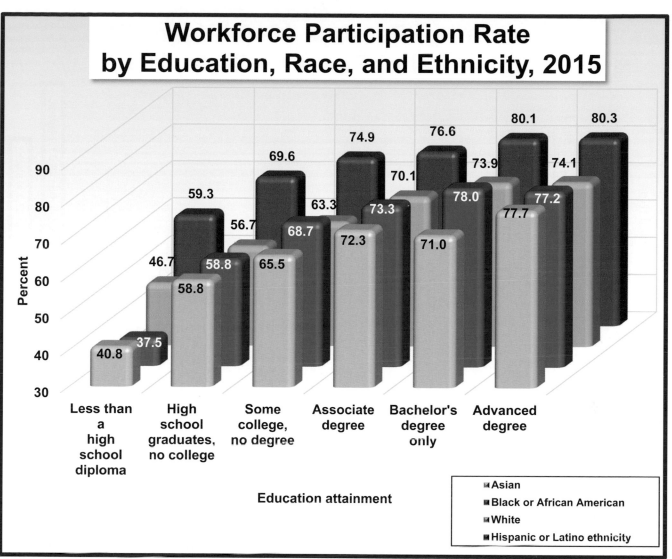

Workforce Participation Rate by Education, Race, and Ethnicity, 2015

Percent

| Education attainment | Asian | Black or African American | White | Hispanic or Latino ethnicity |

- Less than a high school diploma: 40.8, 37.5, 46.7, 58.8
- High school graduates, no college: 58.8, 59.3, 56.7, 65.5
- Some college, no degree: 65.5, 69.6, 68.7, 63.3
- Associate degree: 72.3, 74.9, 73.3, 70.1
- Bachelor's degree only: 71.0, 76.6, 73.9, 78.0
- Advanced degree: 77.7, 80.1, 74.1, 77.2, 80.3

Legend:
- Asian
- Black or African American
- White
- Hispanic or Latino ethnicity

In 2015, increased workforce participation rates were associated with higher education levels by up to a factor of two—from non-high school completion to advanced degrees—regardless of race or ethnicity.

Annual average unemployment rate of the civilian non-institutional population 25 years and over by educational attainment in 2015.

Estimates for the above race groups (White, Black or African American, and Asian) do not sum to totals because data are not presented for all races. Persons whose ethnicity is identified as Hispanic or Latino may be of any race.

High school includes persons with a high school diploma or equivalent.

Advanced degree Includes persons with bachelor's master`s, professional, and doctoral degrees.

Source: U.S. Department of Labor, Bureau of Labor Statistics, Table CPSAAT07, http://www.bls.gov/cps/tables.htm

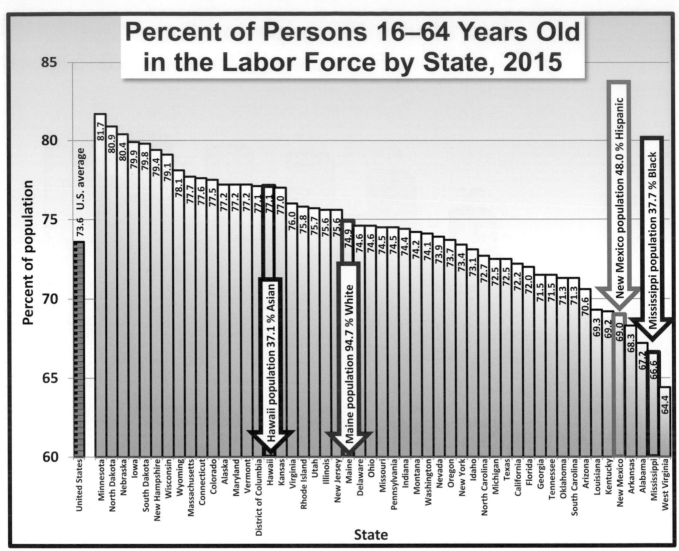

Percent of Persons 16–64 Years Old in the Labor Force by State, 2015

Percent of population (y-axis)

State (x-axis)

State	Value
United States (U.S. average)	73.6
Minnesota	81.7
North Dakota	80.9
Nebraska	80.4
Iowa	79.9
South Dakota	79.8
New Hampshire	79.4
Wisconsin	79.1
Wyoming	78.1
Massachusetts	77.7
Connecticut	77.6
Colorado	77.5
Alaska	77.2
Maryland	77.2
Vermont	77.2
District of Columbia	77.1
Hawaii	77.1
Kansas	77.0
Virginia	76.0
Rhode Island	75.8
Utah	75.7
Illinois	75.6
New Jersey	75.6
Maine	74.9
Delaware	74.6
Ohio	74.6
Missouri	74.5
Pennsylvania	74.5
Indiana	74.4
Montana	74.2
Washington	74.1
Nevada	73.9
Oregon	73.7
New York	73.4
Idaho	73.1
North Carolina	72.7
Michigan	72.5
Texas	72.5
California	72.2
Florida	72.0
Georgia	71.5
Tennessee	71.5
Oklahoma	71.3
South Carolina	71.3
Arizona	70.6
Louisiana	69.3
Kentucky	69.2
New Mexico	69.0
Arkansas	68.3
Alabama	67.2
Mississippi	66.6
West Virginia	64.4

Hawaii population 37.1 % Asian

Maine population 94.7 % White

New Mexico population 48.0 % Hispanic

Mississippi population 37.7 % Black

In 2015, approximately two-of-three people in West Virginia between the ages of 16–64 and were eligible to work were working. This was the lowest participation rate among the states.

Although the American Community Survey (ACS) produces population, demographic and housing unit estimates, it is the Census Bureau's Population Estimates Program that produces and disseminates the official estimates of the population for the nation, states, counties, cities, and towns and estimates of housing units for states and counties.

Source: U.S. Census Bureau, 2015 American Community Survey 1-Year Estimates Table R2301, http://www.census.gov/programs-surveys/acs/data/summary-file.html

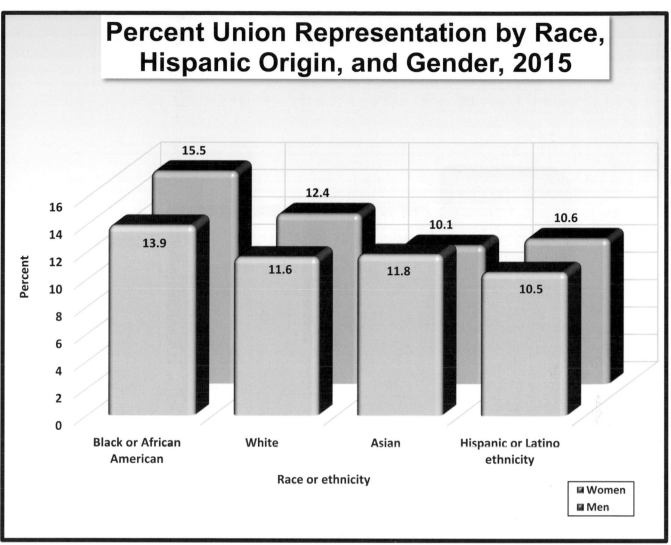

Percent Union Representation by Race, Hispanic Origin, and Gender, 2015

In 2015, one-of-seven Black or African Americans were represented by a union, the highest level among the races and ethnicities of either gender.

Estimates for the above race groups (White, Black or African American, and Asian) do not sum to totals because data are not presented for all races. Persons whose ethnicity is identified as Hispanic or Latino may be of any race.

Source: U.S. Department of Labor, Bureau of Labor Statistics, Table CPSAAT40, http://www.bls.gov/cps/tables.htm, http://www.bls.gov/cps/tables.htm

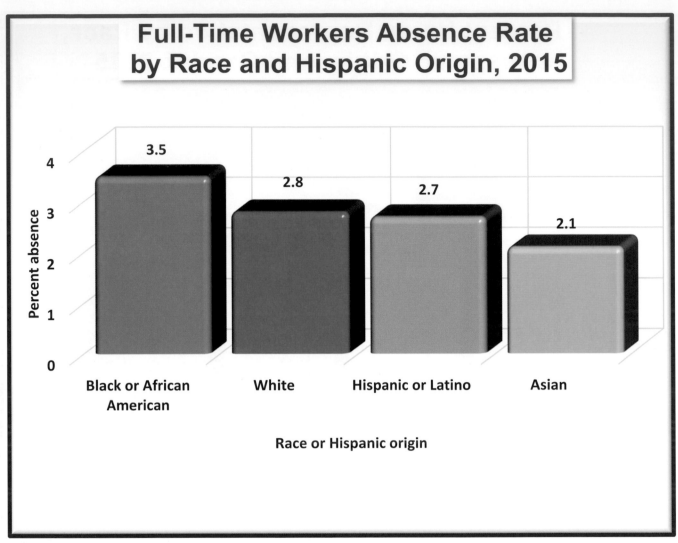

Full-Time Workers Absence Rate by Race and Hispanic Origin, 2015

In 2015, Asian workers had the lowest absence rate from work among all races and ethnicities.

Chart shows absences from work of employed full-time wage and salary workers by age, sex, race, and Hispanic or Latino ethnicity. Hours absent as a percent of hours usually worked.

Absences are defined as instances when persons who usually work 35 or more hours per week (full time) worked less than 35 hours during the reference week for one of the following reasons: own illness, injury, or medical problems; child care problems; other family or personal obligations; civic or military duty; and maternity or paternity leave. Excluded are situations in which work was missed due to vacation or personal days, holiday, labor dispute, and other reasons. For multiple jobholders, absence data refer only to work missed at their main jobs. The absence rate is the ratio of workers with absences to total full-time wage and salary employment.

Source: U.S. Department of Labor, Bureau of Labor Statistics, Table CPSAAT46, http://www.bls.gov/cps/tables.htm, http://www.bls.gov/cps/tables.htm

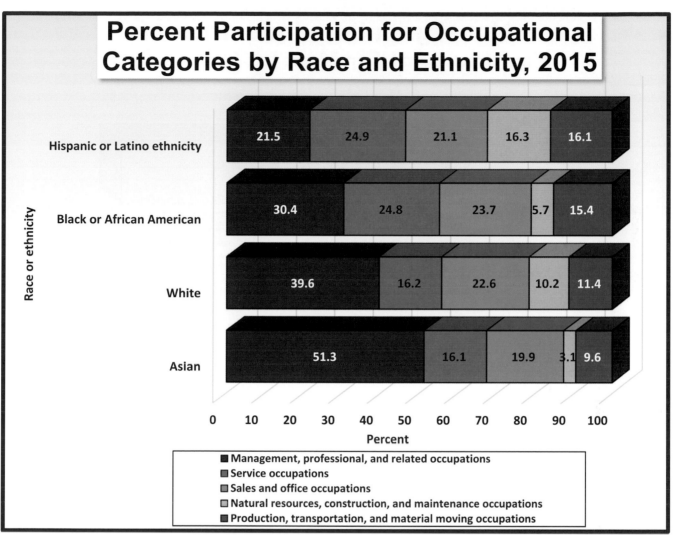

Percent Participation for Occupational Categories by Race and Ethnicity, 2015

Race or ethnicity

Hispanic or Latino ethnicity: 21.5 | 24.9 | 21.1 | 16.3 | 16.1

Black or African American: 30.4 | 24.8 | 23.7 | 5.7 | 15.4

White: 39.6 | 16.2 | 22.6 | 10.2 | 11.4

Asian: 51.3 | 16.1 | 19.9 | 3.1 | 9.6

Percent: 0 10 20 30 40 50 60 70 80 90 100

- ■ Management, professional, and related occupations
- ■ Service occupations
- ■ Sales and office occupations
- □ Natural resources, construction, and maintenance occupations
- ■ Production, transportation, and material moving occupations

In 2015, approximately one-half of all Asian workers worked in management, professional, and related occupations.

Estimates for the above race groups (White, Black or African American, and Asian) do not sum to totals because data are not presented for all races. Persons whose ethnicity is identified as Hispanic or Latino may be of any race.

Source: U.S. Department of Labor, Bureau of Labor Statistics, Table CPSAAT10, http://www.bls.gov/cps/tables.htm

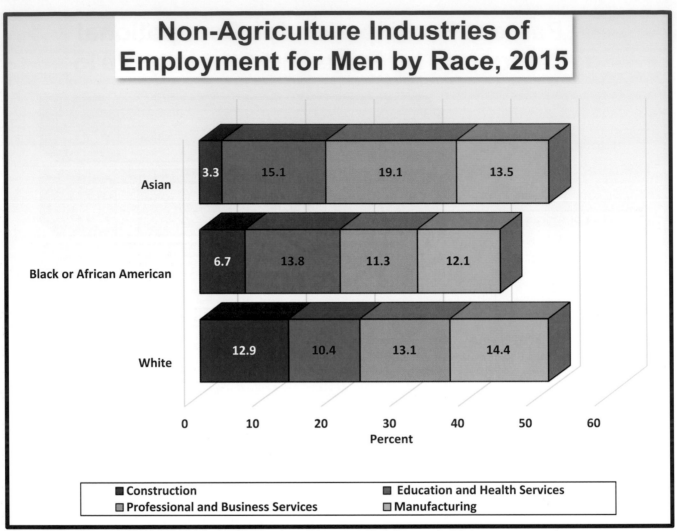

Non-Agriculture Industries of Employment for Men by Race, 2015

Asian: Construction 3.3, Professional and Business Services 15.1, Education and Health Services 19.1, Manufacturing 13.5

Black or African American: Construction 6.7, Professional and Business Services 13.8, Education and Health Services 11.3, Manufacturing 12.1

White: Construction 12.9, Professional and Business Services 10.4, Education and Health Services 13.1, Manufacturing 14.4

Percent (0 10 20 30 40 50 60)

■ Construction
■ Professional and Business Services
■ Education and Health Services
■ Manufacturing

In 2015, approximately one-of-five Asian workers were professional or business services workers.

Estimates for the above race groups (White, Black or African American, and Asian) do not sum to totals because data are not presented for all races. Persons whose ethnicity is identified as Hispanic or Latino may be of any race.

Source: U.S. Department of Labor, Bureau of Labor Statistics, Table CPSAAT14, http://www.bls.gov/cps/tables.htm

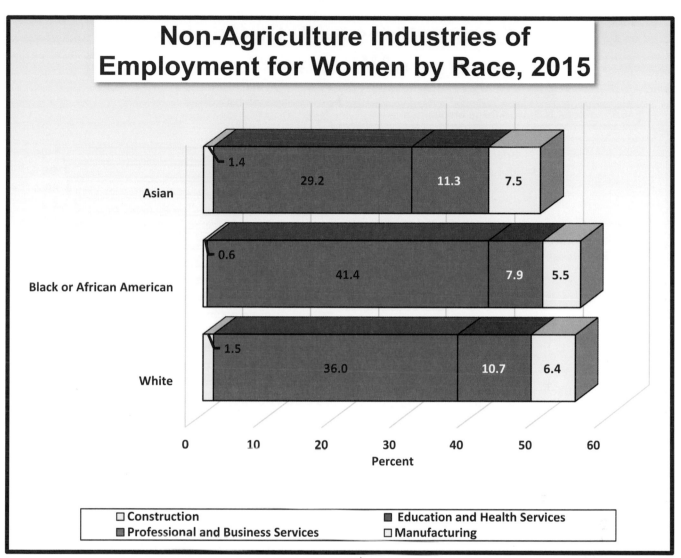

Non-Agriculture Industries of Employment for Women by Race, 2015

Asian	1.4	29.2	11.3	7.5
Black or African American	0.6	41.4	7.9	5.5
White	1.5	36.0	10.7	6.4

Percent

☐ Construction   ■ Education and Health Services
■ Professional and Business Services   ☐ Manufacturing

In 2015, less than two percent of women worked in construction, while 41 percent of Black or African American women worked in education and health services.

Estimates for the above race groups (White, Black or African American, and Asian) do not sum to totals because data are not presented for all races. Persons whose ethnicity is identified as Hispanic or Latino may be of any race.

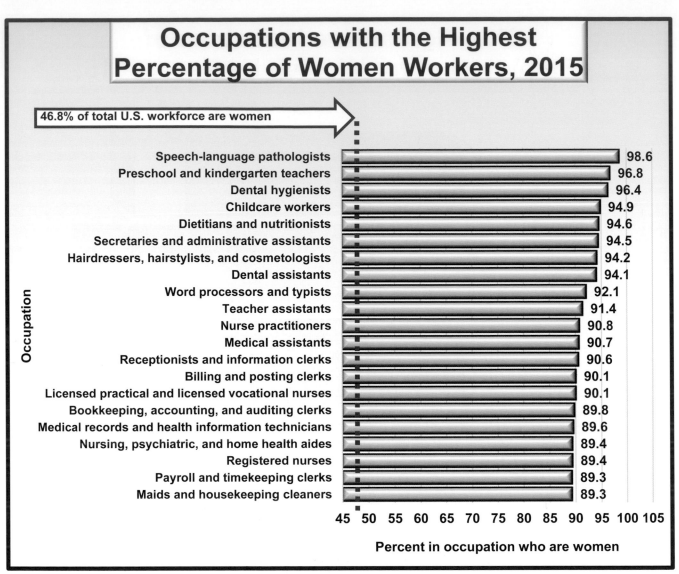

Occupations with the Highest Percentage of Women Workers, 2015

46.8% of total U.S. workforce are women

Occupation	Percent in occupation who are women
Speech-language pathologists	98.6
Preschool and kindergarten teachers	96.8
Dental hygienists	96.4
Childcare workers	94.9
Dietitians and nutritionists	94.6
Secretaries and administrative assistants	94.5
Hairdressers, hairstylists, and cosmetologists	94.2
Dental assistants	94.1
Word processors and typists	92.1
Teacher assistants	91.4
Nurse practitioners	90.8
Medical assistants	90.7
Receptionists and information clerks	90.6
Billing and posting clerks	90.1
Licensed practical and licensed vocational nurses	90.1
Bookkeeping, accounting, and auditing clerks	89.8
Medical records and health information technicians	89.6
Nursing, psychiatric, and home health aides	89.4
Registered nurses	89.4
Payroll and timekeeping clerks	89.3
Maids and housekeeping cleaners	89.3

In 2015, 97 percent of kindergarten teachers and almost 99 percent of speech-language pathologists were women.

Data are for age 16 and older. Total employed are 148.8 million, including 46.8 million women, 11.7 million Black or African American, 5.8 million Asian and 16.4 million Hispanic or Latino Origin. Data as of February 2016.

Estimates for the above race groups (White, Black or African American, and Asian) do not sum to totals because data are not presented for all races. Persons whose ethnicity is identified as Hispanic or Latino may be of any race.

Source: Bureau of Labor Statistics, http://www.bls.gov/cps/cpsaat11.htm

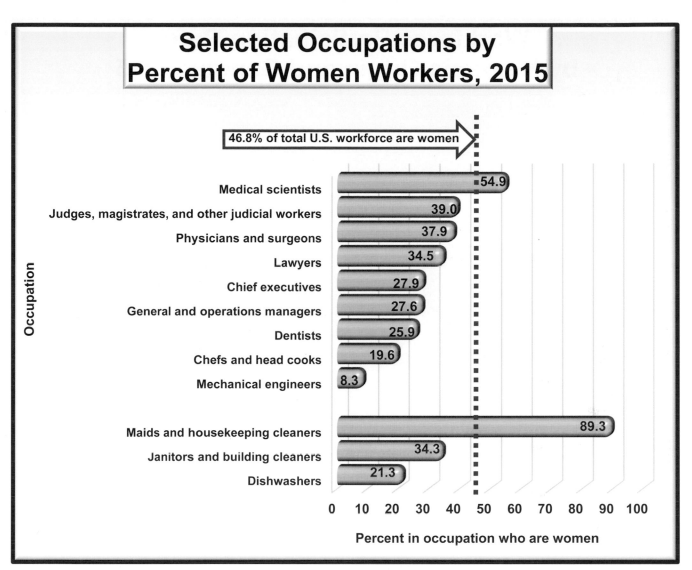

Selected Occupations by Percent of Women Workers, 2015

46.8% of total U.S. workforce are women

Occupation	Percent
Medical scientists	54.9
Judges, magistrates, and other judicial workers	39.0
Physicians and surgeons	37.9
Lawyers	34.5
Chief executives	27.9
General and operations managers	27.6
Dentists	25.9
Chefs and head cooks	19.6
Mechanical engineers	8.3
Maids and housekeeping cleaners	89.3
Janitors and building cleaners	34.3
Dishwashers	21.3

Percent in occupation who are women

In 2015, almost nine-of-ten maids and housekeeping cleaners were women and one-of-four were dentists.

Data are for age 16 and older. Total employed are 148.8 million, including 46.8 million women, 11.7 million Black or African American, 5.8 million Asian and 16.4 million Hispanic or Latino Origin. Data as of February 2016.

Estimates for the above race groups (White, Black or African American, and Asian) do not sum to totals because data are not presented for all races. Persons whose ethnicity is identified as Hispanic or Latino may be of any race.

Source: Bureau of Labor Statistics, http://www.bls.gov/cps/cpsaat11.htm

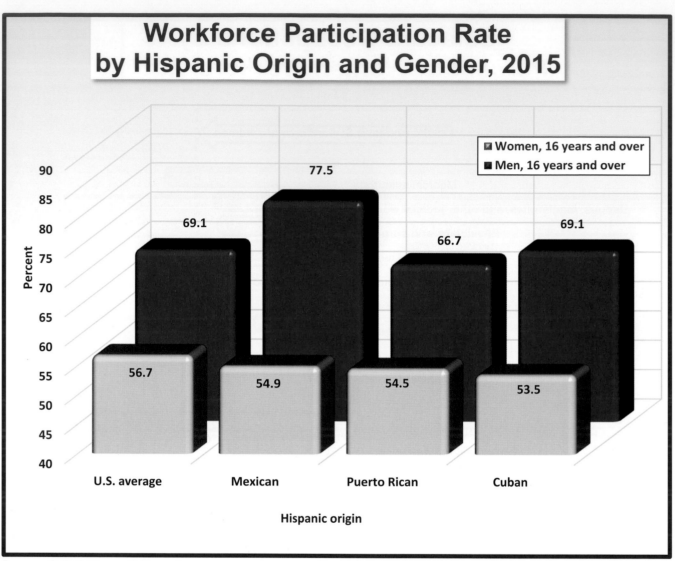

Workforce Participation Rate by Hispanic Origin and Gender, 2015

In 2015, Mexican men had the highest workforce participation rate compared with Mexican women or Puerto Rican and Cuban men.

Annual average Hispanic workforce participation rate is for the civilian non-institutional population in 2015.

Includes persons of Central or South American origin and of other Hispanic or Latino ethnicity, not shown separately.

Estimates for the above race groups (White, Black or African American, and Asian) do not sum to totals because data are not presented for all races. Persons whose ethnicity is identified as Hispanic or Latino may be of any race.

Source: U.S. Department of Labor, Bureau of Labor Statistics, Table CPSAAT06, http://www.bls.gov/cps/tables.htm

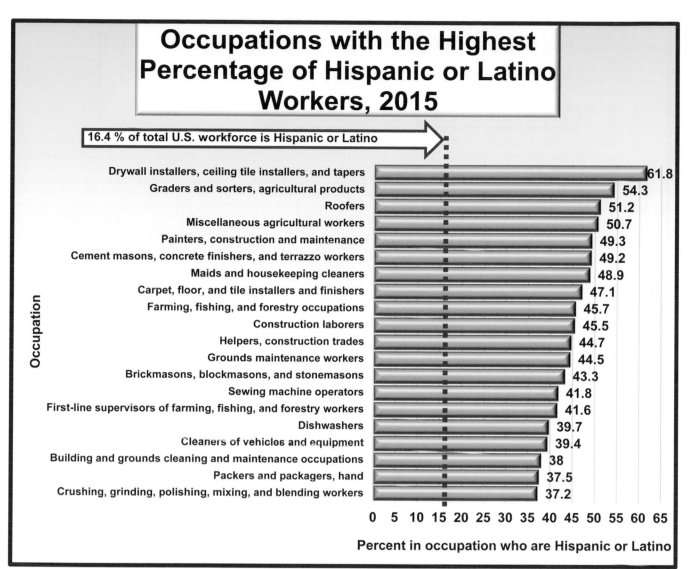

Occupations with the Highest Percentage of Hispanic or Latino Workers, 2015

16.4 % of total U.S. workforce is Hispanic or Latino

Occupation	Percent
Drywall installers, ceiling tile installers, and tapers	61.8
Graders and sorters, agricultural products	54.3
Roofers	51.2
Miscellaneous agricultural workers	50.7
Painters, construction and maintenance	49.3
Cement masons, concrete finishers, and terrazzo workers	49.2
Maids and housekeeping cleaners	48.9
Carpet, floor, and tile installers and finishers	47.1
Farming, fishing, and forestry occupations	45.7
Construction laborers	45.5
Helpers, construction trades	44.7
Grounds maintenance workers	44.5
Brickmasons, blockmasons, and stonemasons	43.3
Sewing machine operators	41.8
First-line supervisors of farming, fishing, and forestry workers	41.6
Dishwashers	39.7
Cleaners of vehicles and equipment	39.4
Building and grounds cleaning and maintenance occupations	38
Packers and packagers, hand	37.5
Crushing, grinding, polishing, mixing, and blending workers	37.2

Percent in occupation who are Hispanic or Latino

In 2015, over one-half of workers in the drywall installation industry were Hispanic or Latino.

Data are for age 16 and older. Total employed are 148.8 million, including 46.8 million women, 11.7 million Black or African American, 5.8 million Asian and 16.4 million Hispanic or Latino Origin. Data as of February 2016.

Estimates for the above race groups (White, Black or African American, and Asian) do not sum to totals because data are not presented for all races. Persons whose ethnicity is identified as Hispanic or Latino may be of any race.

Source: Bureau of Labor Statistics, http://www.bls.gov/cps/cpsaat11.htm

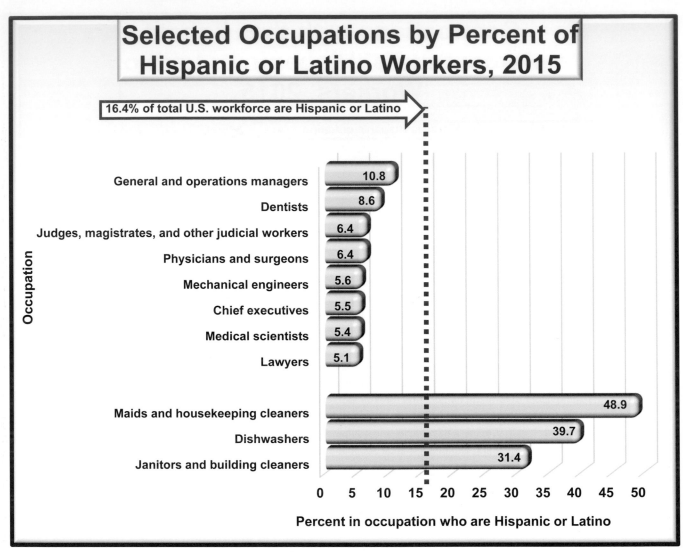

Selected Occupations by Percent of Hispanic or Latino Workers, 2015

16.4% of total U.S. workforce are Hispanic or Latino

Occupation

General and operations managers	10.8
Dentists	8.6
Judges, magistrates, and other judicial workers	6.4
Physicians and surgeons	6.4
Mechanical engineers	5.6
Chief executives	5.5
Medical scientists	5.4
Lawyers	5.1
Maids and housekeeping cleaners	48.9
Dishwashers	39.7
Janitors and building cleaners	31.4

0   5   10   15   20   25   30   35   40   45   50

Percent in occupation who are Hispanic or Latino

In 2015, approximately one-half of all maids and housekeeping cleaners were Hispanic or Latino.

Data are for age 16 and older. Total employed are 148.8 million, including 46.8 million women, 11.7 million Black or African American, 5.8 million Asian and 16.4 million Hispanic or Latino Origin. Data as of February 2016.

Estimates for the above race groups (White, Black or African American, and Asian) do not sum to totals because data are not presented for all races. Persons whose ethnicity is identified as Hispanic or Latino may be of any race.

Source: Bureau of Labor Statistics, http://www.bls.gov/cps/cpsaat11.htm

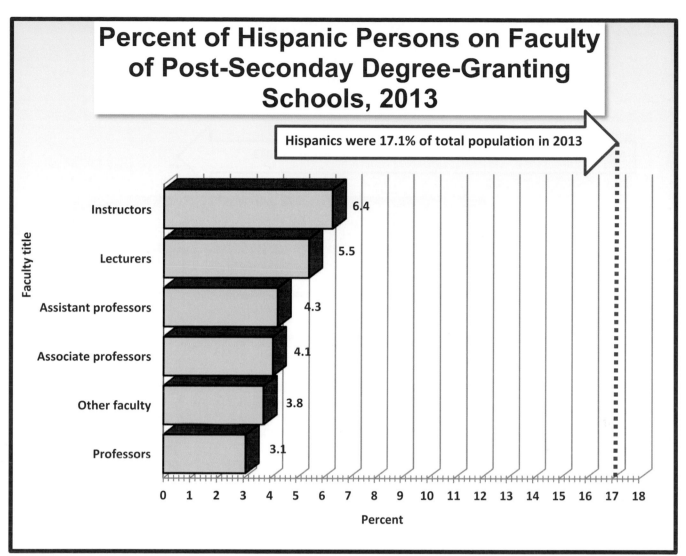

Percent of Hispanic Persons on Faculty of Post-Seconday Degree-Granting Schools, 2013

Hispanics were 17.1% of total population in 2013

Faculty title

Faculty title	Percent
Instructors	6.4
Lecturers	5.5
Assistant professors	4.3
Associate professors	4.1
Other faculty	3.8
Professors	3.1

Percent: 0 1 2 3 4 5 6 7 8 9 10 11 12 13 14 15 16 17 18

In 2013, less than seven percent of the top teaching positions in post-secondary schools were held by Hispanic persons while they made up 17.1 percent of the general population.

Full-time Hispanic faculty in degree-granting postsecondary institutions, by academic rank in the fall semester of 2013. Note: Degree-granting institutions grant associate's or higher degrees and participate in Title IV federal financial aid programs. Includes institutions with fewer than 15 full-time employees.

Excludes race/ethnicity unknown and nonresident alien. Hispanic origin is of any race.

Source: U.S. Department of Education, National Center for Education Statistics, Integrated Postsecondary Education Data System (IPEDS), Spring 2014, Human Resources component, Fall Staff section. (This table was prepared March 2015.), Table 315.20
https://nces.ed.gov/programs/digest/d14/tables/dt14_315.20.asp

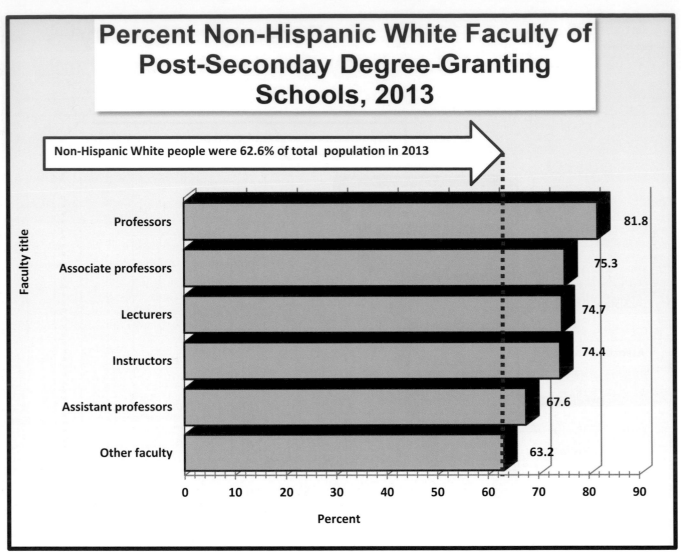

Percent Non-Hispanic White Faculty of Post-Seconday Degree-Granting Schools, 2013

Non-Hispanic White people were 62.6% of total population in 2013

Faculty title

Professors	81.8
Associate professors	75.3
Lecturers	74.7
Instructors	74.4
Assistant professors	67.6
Other faculty	63.2

Percent

In 2013, approximately three-quarters of the top teaching positions in post-secondary schools were held by non-Hispanic White persons.

Full-time non-Hispanic White faculty in degree-granting postsecondary institutions, by academic rank in the fall semester of 2013. Note: Degree-granting institutions grant associate's or higher degrees and participate in Title IV federal financial aid programs. Includes institutions with fewer than 15 full-time employees.

Excludes race/ethnicity unknown and nonresident alien and race excludes Hispanic origin.

Source: U.S. Department of Education, National Center for Education Statistics, Integrated Postsecondary Education Data System (IPEDS), Spring 2014, Human Resources component, Fall Staff section. (This table was prepared March 2015.), Table 315.20
https://nces.ed.gov/programs/digest/d14/tables/dt14_315.20.asp

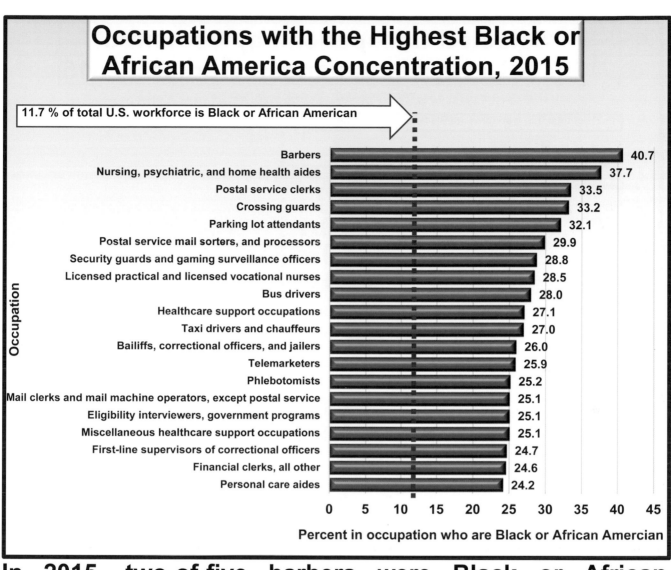

Occupations with the Highest Black or African America Concentration, 2015

11.7 % of total U.S. workforce is Black or African American

Occupation	Percent
Barbers	40.7
Nursing, psychiatric, and home health aides	37.7
Postal service clerks	33.5
Crossing guards	33.2
Parking lot attendants	32.1
Postal service mail sorters, and processors	29.9
Security guards and gaming surveillance officers	28.8
Licensed practical and licensed vocational nurses	28.5
Bus drivers	28.0
Healthcare support occupations	27.1
Taxi drivers and chauffeurs	27.0
Bailiffs, correctional officers, and jailers	26.0
Telemarketers	25.9
Phlebotomists	25.2
Mail clerks and mail machine operators, except postal service	25.1
Eligibility interviewers, government programs	25.1
Miscellaneous healthcare support occupations	25.1
First-line supervisors of correctional officers	24.7
Financial clerks, all other	24.6
Personal care aides	24.2

Percent in occupation who are Black or African Amercian

In 2015, two-of-five barbers were Black or African American.

Data are for age 16 and older. Total employed are 148.8 million, including 46.8 million women, 11.7 million Black or African American, 5.8 million Asian and 16.4 million Hispanic or Latino Origin. Data as of February 2016.

Estimates for the above race groups (White, Black or African American, and Asian) do not sum to totals because data are not presented for all races. Persons whose ethnicity is identified as Hispanic or Latino may be of any race.

Source: Bureau of Labor Statistics, http://www.bls.gov/cps/cpsaat11.htm

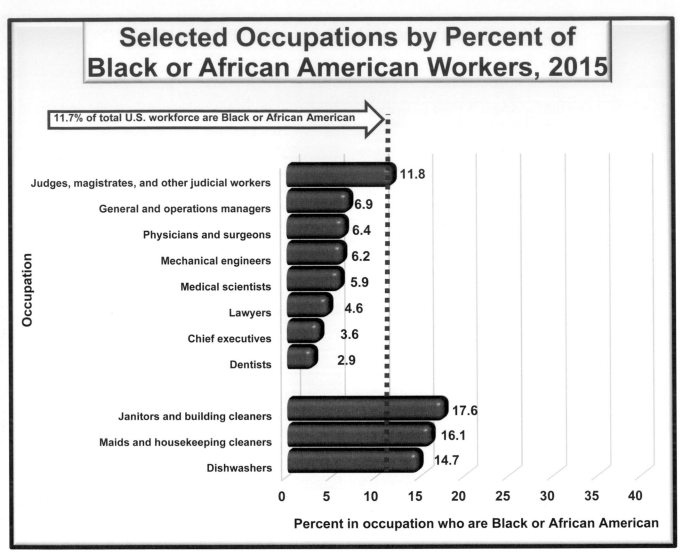

Selected Occupations by Percent of Black or African American Workers, 2015

11.7% of total U.S. workforce are Black or African American

Occupation

Occupation	Percent
Judges, magistrates, and other judicial workers	11.8
General and operations managers	6.9
Physicians and surgeons	6.4
Mechanical engineers	6.2
Medical scientists	5.9
Lawyers	4.6
Chief executives	3.6
Dentists	2.9
Janitors and building cleaners	17.6
Maids and housekeeping cleaners	16.1
Dishwashers	14.7

0   5   10   15   20   25   30   35   40

Percent in occupation who are Black or African American

In 2015, approximately 3-of-100 dentists and one-of-six janitors were Black or African American.

Data are for age 16 and older. Total employed are 148.8 million, including 46.8 million women, 11.7 million Black or African American, 5.8 million Asian and 16.4 million Hispanic or Latino Origin. Data as of February 2016.

Estimates for the above race groups (White, Black or African American, and Asian) do not sum to totals because data are not presented for all races. Persons whose ethnicity is identified as Hispanic or Latino may be of any race.

Source: Bureau of Labor Statistics, http://www.bls.gov/cps/cpsaat11.htm

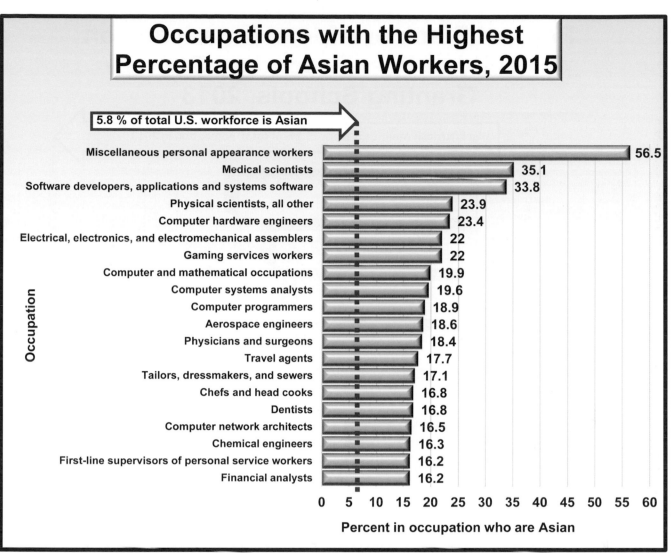

Occupations with the Highest Percentage of Asian Workers, 2015

5.8 % of total U.S. workforce is Asian

Occupation	Percent
Miscellaneous personal appearance workers	56.5
Medical scientists	35.1
Software developers, applications and systems software	33.8
Physical scientists, all other	23.9
Computer hardware engineers	23.4
Electrical, electronics, and electromechanical assemblers	22
Gaming services workers	22
Computer and mathematical occupations	19.9
Computer systems analysts	19.6
Computer programmers	18.9
Aerospace engineers	18.6
Physicians and surgeons	18.4
Travel agents	17.7
Tailors, dressmakers, and sewers	17.1
Chefs and head cooks	16.8
Dentists	16.8
Computer network architects	16.5
Chemical engineers	16.3
First-line supervisors of personal service workers	16.2
Financial analysts	16.2

Percent in occupation who are Asian

In 2015, over one-half of persons working in the personal appearance industry, and one-third of medical scientists, were Asian.

Data are for age 16 and older. Total employed are 148.8 million, including 46.8 million women, 11.7 million Black or African American, 5.8 million Asian and 16.4 million Hispanic or Latino Origin. Data as of February 2016.

Estimates for the above race groups (White, Black or African American, and Asian) do not sum to totals because data are not presented for all races. Persons whose ethnicity is identified as Hispanic or Latino may be of any race.

Source: Bureau of Labor Statistics, http://www.bls.gov/cps/cpsaat11.htm

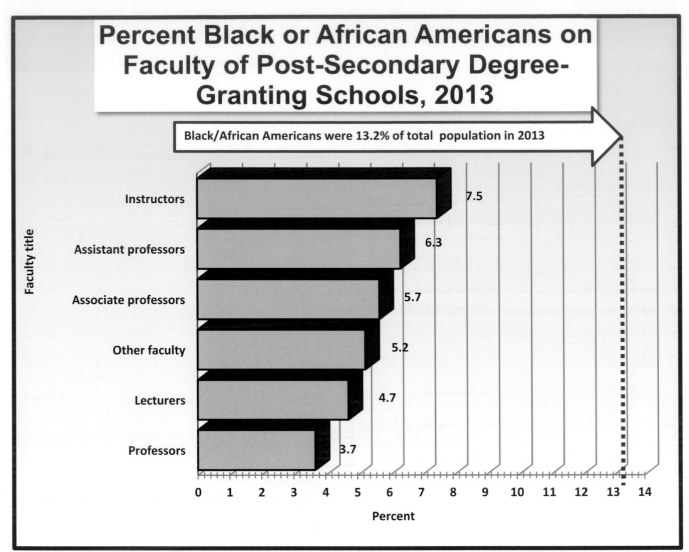

Percent Black or African Americans on Faculty of Post-Secondary Degree-Granting Schools, 2013

Black/African Americans were 13.2% of total population in 2013

Faculty title

- Instructors — 7.5
- Assistant professors — 6.3
- Associate professors — 5.7
- Other faculty — 5.2
- Lecturers — 4.7
- Professors — 3.7

Percent

0 1 2 3 4 5 6 7 8 9 10 11 12 13 14

In 2013, less than seven percent of the top teaching positions in post-secondary schools were held by Black or African American persons—approximately one-half of their 13.2 percent portion of the general population.

Full-time Black or African American faculty in degree-granting postsecondary institutions, by academic rank in the fall semester of 2013. Note: Degree-granting institutions grant associate's or higher degrees and participate in Title IV federal financial aid programs. Includes institutions with fewer than 15 full-time employees.

Excludes race/ethnicity unknown and nonresident alien and race excludes Hispanic origin.

Source: U.S. Department of Education, National Center for Education Statistics, Integrated Postsecondary Education Data System (IPEDS), Spring 2014, Human Resources component, Fall Staff section. (This table was prepared March 2015.), Table 315.20
https://nces.ed.gov/programs/digest/d14/tables/dt14_315.20.asp

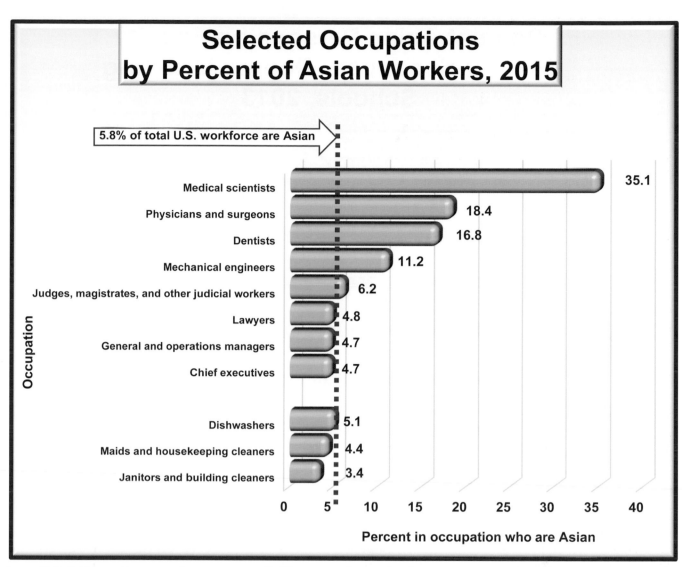

Selected Occupations by Percent of Asian Workers, 2015

5.8% of total U.S. workforce are Asian

Occupation	Percent in occupation who are Asian
Medical scientists	35.1
Physicians and surgeons	18.4
Dentists	16.8
Mechanical engineers	11.2
Judges, magistrates, and other judicial workers	6.2
Lawyers	4.8
General and operations managers	4.7
Chief executives	4.7
Dishwashers	5.1
Maids and housekeeping cleaners	4.4
Janitors and building cleaners	3.4

In 2015, almost one-of-five physicians or surgeons, and less than 1-of-20 maids or janitors, were Asian.

Data are for age 16 and older. Total employed are 148.8 million, including 46.8 million women, 11.7 million Black or African American, 5.8 million Asian and 16.4 million Hispanic or Latino Origin. Data as of February 2016.

Estimates for the above race groups (White, Black or African American, and Asian) do not sum to totals because data are not presented for all races. Persons whose ethnicity is identified as Hispanic or Latino may be of any race.

Source: Bureau of Labor Statistics, http://www.bls.gov/cps/cpsaat11.htm

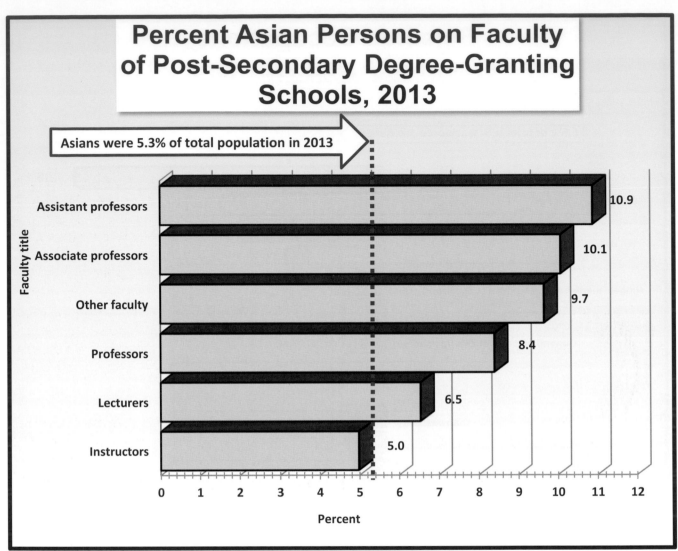

Percent Asian Persons on Faculty of Post-Secondary Degree-Granting Schools, 2013

Asians were 5.3% of total population in 2013

Faculty title	Percent
Assistant professors	10.9
Associate professors	10.1
Other faculty	9.7
Professors	8.4
Lecturers	6.5
Instructors	5.0

Percent

In 2013, Asians held approximately double the proportion of top teaching positions in post-secondary schools compared with their 5.3 percent portion of the general population.

Full-time Asian faculty in degree-granting postsecondary institutions, by academic rank in the fall semester of 2013. Note: Degree-granting institutions grant associate's or higher degrees and participate in Title IV federal financial aid programs. Includes institutions with fewer than 15 full-time employees.

Excludes race/ethnicity unknown and nonresident alien and race excludes Hispanic origin.

Source: U.S. Department of Education, National Center for Education Statistics, Integrated Postsecondary Education Data System (IPEDS), Spring 2014, Human Resources component, Fall Staff section. (This table was prepared March 2015.), Table 315.20
https://nces.ed.gov/programs/digest/d14/tables/dt14_315.20.asp

Chapter 9: Income, Poverty, and Wealth

The primary source of data for income and poverty is provided by the U.S. Census Bureau. The U.S. government official poverty data are published in the Current Population Survey, which is sponsored jointly by the U.S. Census Bureau and the Bureau of Labor Statistics (BLS). They utilize a poverty threshold formula for annual income, based primarily on family size, which ranged from $12,082 for a single member family to $49,111 for a family of nine or more in 2015. The threshold formula was developed in the early 1960s and was derived from the cost of a minimum diet multiplied by three—to allow for expenditures on other goods and services. Although the threshold is adjusted annually for inflation it has not been updated to reflect current government programs, payroll taxes, or Supplemental Nutrition Assistance Program (SNAP, formerly known as food stamps), nor does it reflect the large differences in cost of living across different regions. For all these reasons, the threshold may not be indicative of poverty but may be a useful yardstick to compare differences in the ability persons of different races and ethnicities to stay above a basic sustenance level.

The official poverty rate in 2015 was 13.5 percent with 43.1 million people in poverty. However, there was a wide disparity between the racial and ethnic groups. Nearly one-of-four (24.1 percent) Black or African Americans were below poverty compared with 9.1 percent of non-Hispanic Whites. The group with the lowest poverty level was Asian Indian children, at 5.9 percent.

In 2015, the average poverty rate distribution among states ranged from a low average of 8.2 percent in New Hampshire to a high of almost 20 percent in New Mexico, Kentucky, and Mississippi. Not included in these poverty statistics, however, are cash values of public assistance income or SNAP payments.

In 2015, 2.5 percent of households received cash public assistance. Alaska had the highest rate at 6.5 percent while South Carolina had the lowest rate at 1.3 percent. Nationally, 12.8 percent of households received SNAP funds, led by Oregon with 18.6 percent compared with 4.7 percent in Wyoming, the state with the lowest rate.

In 2015, household income varied by almost two to one among states with Maryland having the highest income and Mississippi having the lowest income. Asian men had the highest weekly earnings. They were 79 percent above the lowest paid group—Hispanics. This disparity was reduced to 38 percent when comparing only those with bachelor's degrees.

Another measure of income published by the Census Bureau is "money income", which attempts to account for all sources of income, not just wages and salaries. Between 1990 and 2015, mean money income for men appeared to coalesce into two primary racial/ethnic groups, Asian plus non-Hispanic White compared with Black plus Hispanic. The mean money income for the first group was 60 percent higher than the latter, throughout that time period.

Money income consists of the following 23 income components:

1) Earnings (wages, salaries, and self-employment income)
2) Interest income
3) Dividend income
4) Rents, royalties, estate, and trust income
5) Non-government retirement pensions and annuities
6) Non-government survivor pensions and annuities
7) Non-government disability pensions and annuities
8) Social Security
9) Unemployment compensation
10) Workers' compensation
11) Veterans' payments other than pensions
12) Government retirement pensions and annuities
13) Government survivor pensions and annuities
14) Government disability pensions and annuities
15) Public assistance (includes TANF and other cash welfare)
16) Supplemental Security Income (SSI)
17) Veterans' pensions
18) Government educational assistance
19) Non-government educational assistance
20) Child Support
21) Alimony
22) Regular contributions from persons not living in the household
23) Money income not elsewhere classified

The Merriam-Webster dictionary defines wealth as "all property that has a money value or an exchangeable value". Wealth includes all types of property and since the market value of property is always in a state of flux measuring it is very problematic. More meaningful than wealth is net worth, which reduces the value of possessions by the amount of indebtedness. The federal reserve estimated U.S. household net worth, in September 2016, at $89.1 trillion dollars.

In 2011, comparisons of household mean net worth between race and ethnic groups revealed that the mean net worth for the bottom quintile of all leading racial and ethnic groups was similar. They all had debt that exceeded assets by $21,000 to $31,000.

In 2013, the largest disparity in household median net worth between races and ethnicities was for non-Hispanic White households, with 12.9 times higher value than non-Hispanic Black households.

The value of housing, a major component of household wealth, varied five to one based on location. In 2015, the median value of owner-occupied homes was $567,000 in Hawaii compared with $112,000 in West Virginia.

~

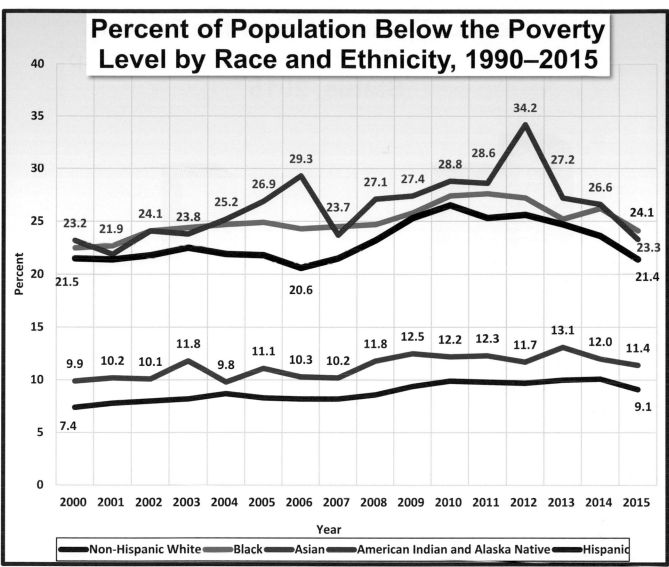

Percent of Population Below the Poverty Level by Race and Ethnicity, 1990–2015

Legend: Non-Hispanic White, Black, Asian, American Indian and Alaska Native, Hispanic

The percent of persons below the poverty level was essentially unchanged for all races and ethnicities between 2000 and 2015. Throughout that period Black or African Americans, American Indians, Alaska Natives, and Hispanic persons were below the poverty level at more than double the rate of non-Hispanic White and Asian persons.

Excludes race/ethnicity unknown and nonresident alien and race excludes Hispanic origin.

Source: U.S. Bureau of the Census, Current Population Survey, Annual Social and Economic Supplements, accessed November 18, 2016, http://www.census.gov/data/tables/time-series/demo/income-poverty/historical-poverty-people.html

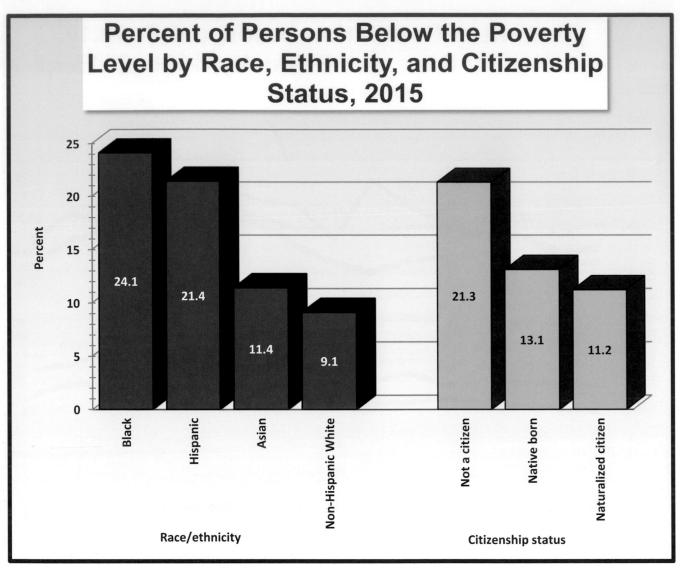

Percent of Persons Below the Poverty Level by Race, Ethnicity, and Citizenship Status, 2015

In 2015, approximately one-of-four Black or African Americans was below the poverty level, a rate similar to non-citizens of all races and ethnicities.

Poverty based on income in 2015 dollars.

Source: U.S. Census Bureau, Source: U.S. Census Bureau, Current Population Survey, People in Poverty by Selected Characteristics: 2014 and 2015, Table 3, http://www.census.gov/data/tables/2016/demo/income-poverty/p60-256.html

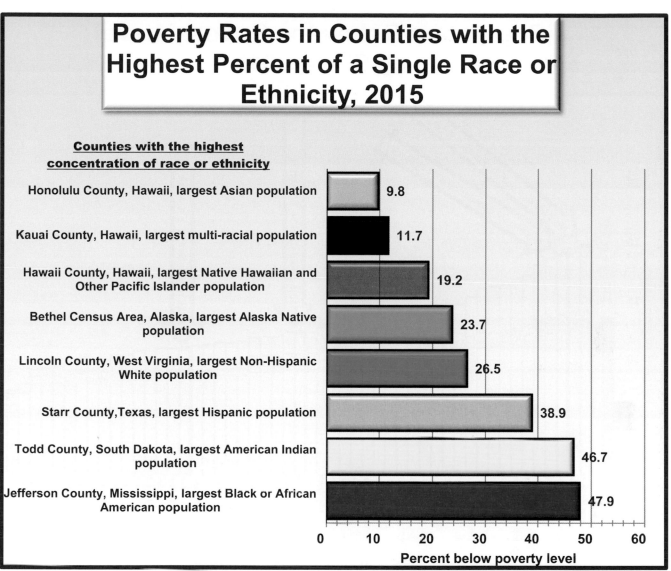

Poverty Rates in Counties with the Highest Percent of a Single Race or Ethnicity, 2015

Counties with the highest concentration of race or ethnicity

County	Percent below poverty level
Honolulu County, Hawaii, largest Asian population	9.8
Kauai County, Hawaii, largest multi-racial population	11.7
Hawaii County, Hawaii, largest Native Hawaiian and Other Pacific Islander population	19.2
Bethel Census Area, Alaska, largest Alaska Native population	23.7
Lincoln County, West Virginia, largest Non-Hispanic White population	26.5
Starr County, Texas, largest Hispanic population	38.9
Todd County, South Dakota, largest American Indian population	46.7
Jefferson County, Mississippi, largest Black or African American population	47.9

Percent below poverty level

In 2015, approximately one-half of residents in Jefferson county, Mississippi—the county with the highest percent of Black or African American residents—were below the poverty level. Honolulu County, Hawaii—the county with the highest percent of Asian residents—had 10 percent of its population below the poverty level.

The United States is comprised of 3,142 counties. A county is a political and geographic subdivision of a state. The Census Bureau considers the parishes of Louisiana and the boroughs of Alaska and the District of Columbia to be equivalent to counties for statistical purposes.

Hispanic origin is considered an ethnicity, not a race. Hispanics may be of any race.

Source: U.S. Census Bureau, American Fact Finder, Community Facts, 2015 Population Estimates Program, accessed 10/17/16, http://factfinder.census.gov/faces/nav/jsf/pages/community_facts.xhtml#

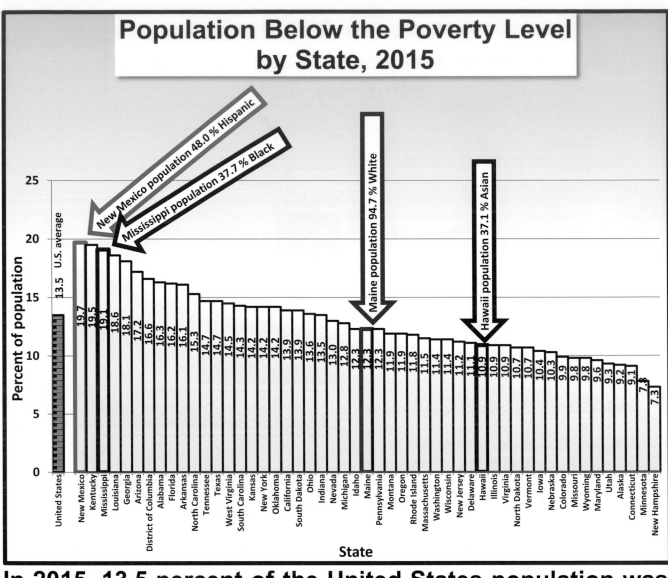

Population Below the Poverty Level by State, 2015

In 2015, 13.5 percent of the United States population was below the poverty level as were one-of-five persons living in New Mexico, Kentucky, and Mississippi.

Hispanic origin is considered an ethnicity, not a race. Hispanics may be of any race.

Source: U.S. Census Bureau, American Fact Finder, Community Facts, 2015 Population Estimates Program, Last Revised: September 1, 2016, accessed 11/17/16, http://www.census.gov/data/tables/time-series/demo/income-poverty/historical-poverty-people.html

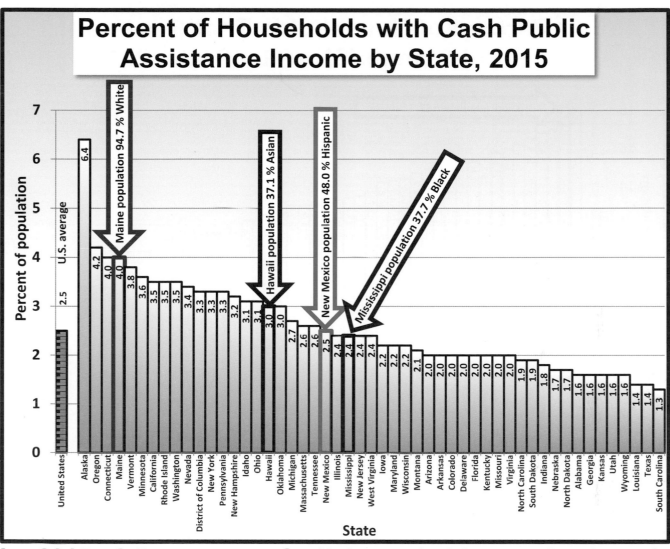

Percent of Households with Cash Public Assistance Income by State, 2015

In 2015, 2.5 percent of all households received cash assistance. Alaska ranked highest among all states at 6.4 percent.

Although the American Community Survey (ACS) produces population, demographic and housing unit estimates, it is the Census Bureau's Population Estimates Program that produces and disseminates the official estimates of the population for the nation, states, counties, cities, and towns and estimates of housing units for states and counties.

Source: U.S. Census Bureau, 2015 American Community Survey 1-Year Estimates Table R1904, http://www.census.gov/programs-surveys/acs/data/summary-file.html

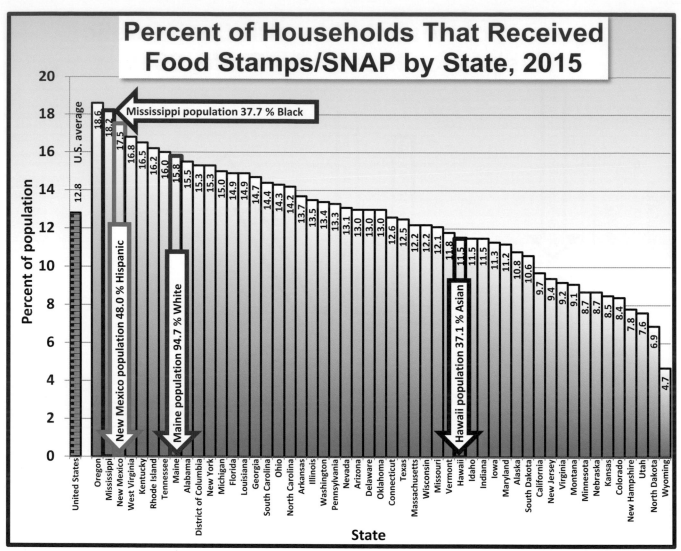

Percent of Households That Received Food Stamps/SNAP by State, 2015

In 2015, almost one-of-five households in Oregon received Supplemental Nutrition Assistance (SNAP, formerly called food stamps). This was the highest participation level of any state.

Supplemental Nutrition Assistance Program (SNAP) was formerly called the Food Stamp Program.

Although the American Community Survey (ACS) produces population, demographic and housing unit estimates, it is the Census Bureau's Population Estimates Program that produces and disseminates the official estimates of the population for the nation, states, counties, cities, and towns as well as estimates of housing units for states and counties.

Source: U.S. Census Bureau, 2015 American Community Survey 1-Year Estimates Table R2201, http://www.census.gov/programs-surveys/acs/data/summary-file.html

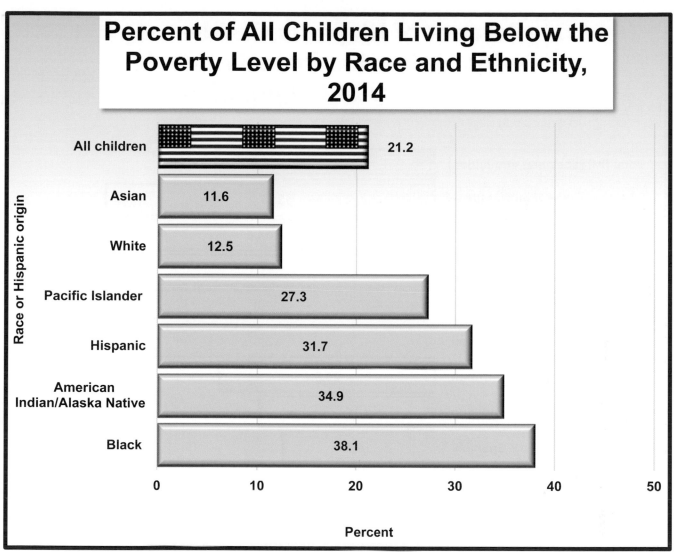

Percent of All Children Living Below the Poverty Level by Race and Ethnicity, 2014

Race or Hispanic origin	Percent
All children	21.2
Asian	11.6
White	12.5
Pacific Islander	27.3
Hispanic	31.7
American Indian/Alaska Native	34.9
Black	38.1

In 2014, one-of-five children under the age of 18 was living below the poverty level. Black or African American children had the highest poverty rate at 38.1 percent while Asian children had the lowest rate at 11.6 percent.

Includes all children under age 18 and totaled 15.28 million children in 2014.

Children are classified by their parents' marital status or, if no parents are present in the household, by the marital status of the householder who is related to the children. Living arrangements with only a "female parent" or "male parent" are those in which the parent or the householder who is related to the child does not have a spouse living in the household. The householder is the person (or one of the people) who owns or rents (maintains) the housing unit.

Includes foster children, children in unrelated subfamilies, children living in group quarters, and children who were reported as the householder or spouse of the householder.

Source: U.S. Department of Commerce, Census Bureau, American Community Survey (ACS), 2009 and 2014. (This table was prepared January 2016.), Digest 2015, Table 102.60, https://nces.ed.gov/programs/digest/2015menu_tables.asp

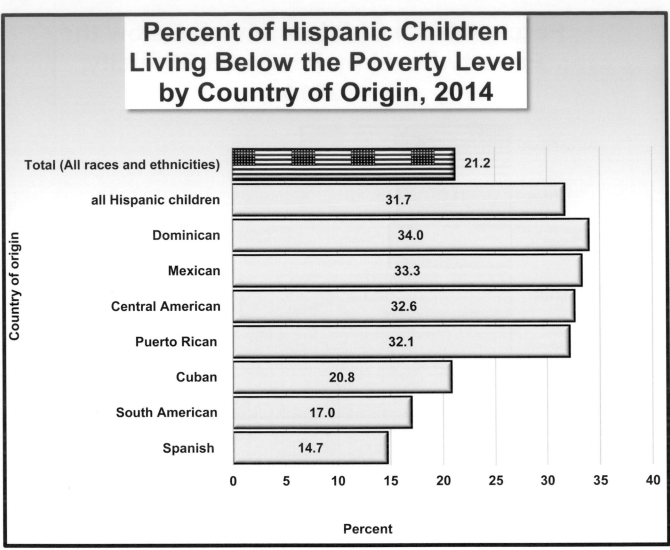

Percent of Hispanic Children Living Below the Poverty Level by Country of Origin, 2014

Country of origin:

Country of origin	Percent
Total (All races and ethnicities)	21.2
all Hispanic children	31.7
Dominican	34.0
Mexican	33.3
Central American	32.6
Puerto Rican	32.1
Cuban	20.8
South American	17.0
Spanish	14.7

Percent (0, 5, 10, 15, 20, 25, 30, 35, 40)

In 2014, almost one-of-three Hispanic children under the age of 18 was living below the poverty level compared with one-of-five children of the total population.

Includes all children under age 18 and totaled 15.28 million children in 2014 of which 5.6 million are Hispanic.

Children are classified by their parents' marital status or, if no parents are present in the household, by the marital status of the householder who is related to the children. Living arrangements with only a "female parent" or "male parent" are those in which the parent or the householder who is related to the child does not have a spouse living in the household. The householder is the person (or one of the people) who owns or rents (maintains) the housing unit.

Includes foster children, children in unrelated subfamilies, children living in group quarters, and children who were reported as the householder or spouse of the householder.

Source: U.S. Department of Commerce, Census Bureau, American Community Survey (ACS), 2009 and 2014. (This table was prepared January 2016.), Digest 2015, Table 102.60, https://nces.ed.gov/programs/digest/2015menu_tables.asp

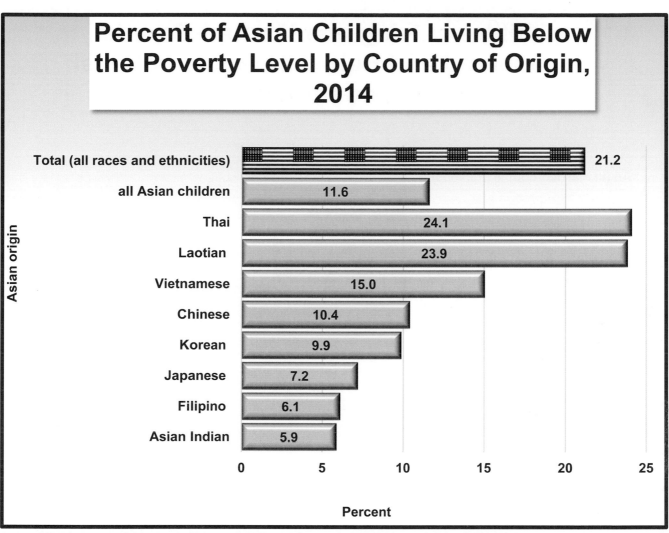

Percent of Asian Children Living Below the Poverty Level by Country of Origin, 2014

Asian origin

	Percent
Total (all races and ethnicities)	21.2
all Asian children	11.6
Thai	24.1
Laotian	23.9
Vietnamese	15.0
Chinese	10.4
Korean	9.9
Japanese	7.2
Filipino	6.1
Asian Indian	5.9

Percent

In 2014, approximately six percent of Asian Indian and Filipino children under the age of 18 were living below the poverty level—the lowest level of all persons of Asian origin.

Includes all children under age 18 and totaled 15.28 million children in 2014 of which 384,500 are Asian.

Children are classified by their parents' marital status or, if no parents are present in the household, by the marital status of the householder who is related to the children. Living arrangements with only a "female parent" or "male parent" are those in which the parent or the householder who is related to the child does not have a spouse living in the household. The householder is the person (or one of the people) who owns or rents (maintains) the housing unit.

Includes foster children, children in unrelated subfamilies, children living in group quarters, and children who were reported as the householder or spouse of the householder.

Source: U.S. Department of Commerce, Census Bureau, American Community Survey (ACS), 2009 and 2014. (This table was prepared January 2016.), Digest 2015, Table 102.60, https://nces.ed.gov/programs/digest/2015menu_tables.asp

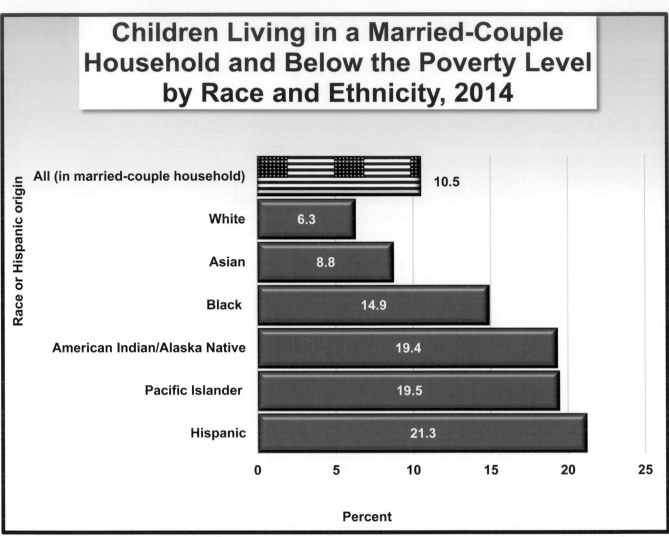

Children Living in a Married-Couple Household and Below the Poverty Level by Race and Ethnicity, 2014

Race or Hispanic origin

Category	Percent
All (in married-couple household)	10.5
White	6.3
Asian	8.8
Black	14.9
American Indian/Alaska Native	19.4
Pacific Islander	19.5
Hispanic	21.3

Percent

In 2014, approximately 10 percent of children under the age of 18 were living below the poverty level while living in a married-couple household.

Includes all children under age 18 who live either with their parent(s) or with a householder to whom they are related by birth, marriage, or adoption (except a child who is the spouse of the householder).

Children are classified by their parents' marital status or, if no parents are present in the household, by the marital status of the householder who is related to the children. Living arrangements with only a "female parent" or "male parent" are those in which the parent or the householder who is related to the child does not have a spouse living in the household. The householder is the person (or one of the people) who owns or rents (maintains) the housing unit.

Includes foster children, children in unrelated subfamilies, children living in group quarters, and children who were reported as the householder or spouse of the householder.

Source: U.S. Department of Commerce, Census Bureau, American Community Survey (ACS), 2009 and 2014. (This table was prepared January 2016.), Digest 2015, Table 102.60, https://nces.ed.gov/programs/digest/2015menu_tables.asp

Chapter 9: Income, Poverty, and Wealth

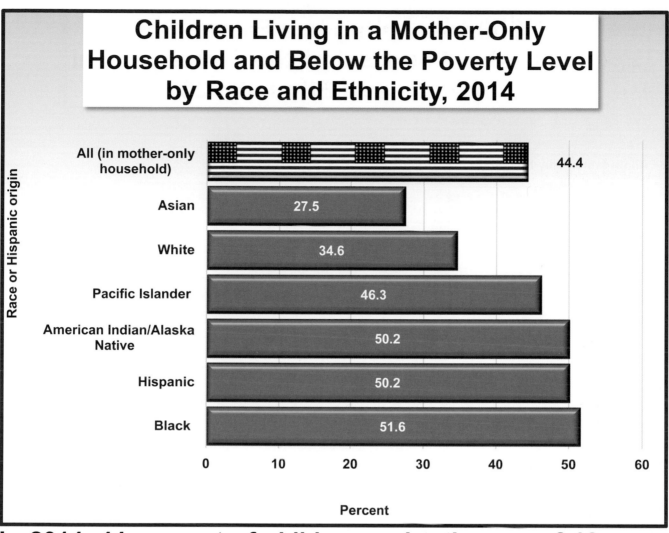

Children Living in a Mother-Only Household and Below the Poverty Level by Race and Ethnicity, 2014

All (in mother-only household): 44.4
Asian: 27.5
White: 34.6
Pacific Islander: 46.3
American Indian/Alaska Native: 50.2
Hispanic: 50.2
Black: 51.6

Race or Hispanic origin

Percent

In 2014, 44 percent of children under the age of 18 were living below the poverty level while living in a mother-only household.

Includes all children under age 18 who live either with their parent(s) or with a householder to whom they are related by birth, marriage, or adoption (except a child who is the spouse of the householder).

Children are classified by their parents' marital status or, if no parents are present in the household, by the marital status of the householder who is related to the children. Living arrangements with only a "female parent" or "male parent" are those in which the parent or the householder who is related to the child does not have a spouse living in the household. The householder is the person (or one of the people) who owns or rents (maintains) the housing unit.

Includes foster children, children in unrelated subfamilies, children living in group quarters, and children who were reported as the householder or spouse of the householder.

Source: U.S. Department of Commerce, Census Bureau, American Community Survey (ACS), 2009 and 2014. (This table was prepared January 2016.), Digest 2015, Table 102.60, https://nces.ed.gov/programs/digest/2015menu_tables.asp

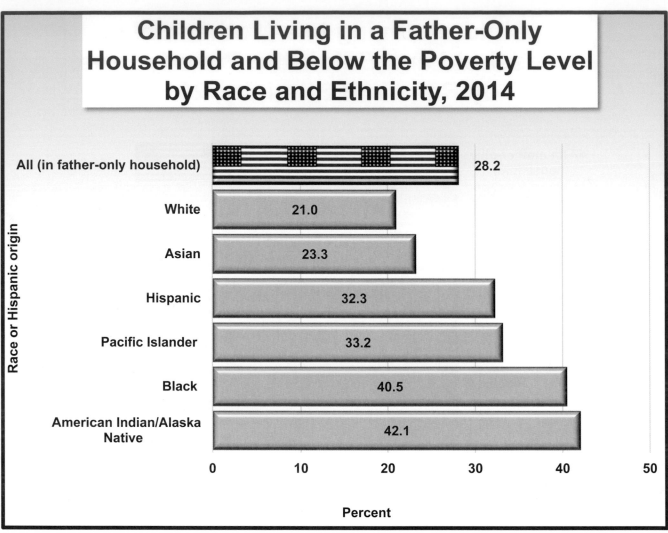

Children Living in a Father-Only Household and Below the Poverty Level by Race and Ethnicity, 2014

Race or Hispanic origin

	Percent
All (in father-only household)	28.2
White	21.0
Asian	23.3
Hispanic	32.3
Pacific Islander	33.2
Black	40.5
American Indian/Alaska Native	42.1

Percent: 0, 10, 20, 30, 40, 50

In 2014, 42 percent of American Indian and Alaska Native children under the age of 18 were living below the poverty level while living in a father-only household.

Includes all children under age 18 who live either with their parent(s) or with a householder to whom they are related by birth, marriage, or adoption (except a child who is the spouse of the householder).

Children are classified by their parents' marital status or, if no parents are present in the household, by the marital status of the householder who is related to the children. Living arrangements with only a "female parent" or "male parent" are those in which the parent or the householder who is related to the child does not have a spouse living in the household. The householder is the person (or one of the people) who owns or rents (maintains) the housing unit.

Includes foster children, children in unrelated subfamilies, children living in group quarters, and children who were reported as the householder or spouse of the householder.

Source: U.S. Department of Commerce, Census Bureau, American Community Survey (ACS), 2009 and 2014. (This table was prepared January 2016.), Digest 2015, Table 102.60, https://nces.ed.gov/programs/digest/2015menu_tables.asp

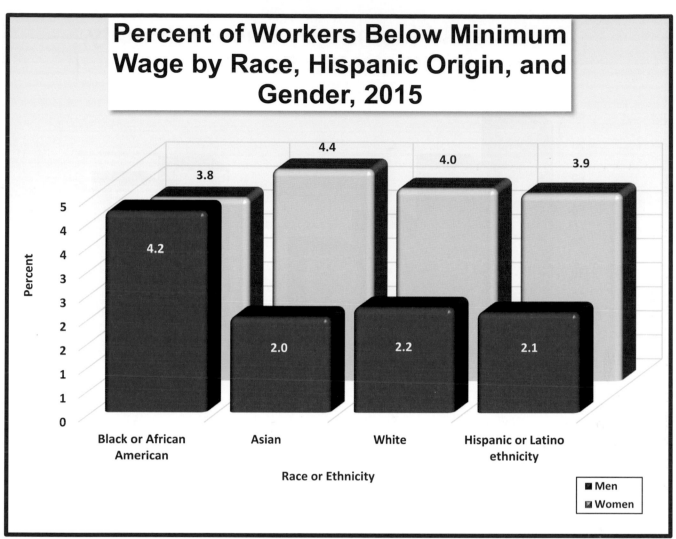

Percent of Workers Below Minimum Wage by Race, Hispanic Origin, and Gender, 2015

Black or African American — Men: 4.2, Women: 3.8
Asian — Men: 2.0, Women: 4.4
White — Men: 2.2, Women: 4.0
Hispanic or Latino ethnicity — Men: 2.1, Women: 3.9

Race or Ethnicity

■ Men
▨ Women

In 2015, between 2.0 and 4.4 percent of full-time workers across all races and ethnicities received wages that were at or below minimum wage.

Data are for full-time workers in 2015. Full-time is 35 hours or more per week.

The prevailing federal minimum wage was $7.25 per hour in 2015. Data are for wage and salary workers; all self-employed workers are excluded, both those with incorporated businesses and those with unincorporated businesses. The data refer to a person's earnings on the sole or principal job, and pertain only to workers who are paid hourly rates. Salaried workers and other non-hourly workers are not included. Hourly earnings for hourly-paid workers do not include overtime pay, commissions, or tips received. The presence of workers with hourly earnings below the minimum wage does not necessarily indicate violation of the Fair Labor Standards Act, as there are exceptions to the minimum wage provisions of the law. Estimates for the above race groups (White, Black or African American, and Asian) do not sum to totals because data are not presented for all races. Persons whose ethnicity is identified as Hispanic or Latino may be of any race. Updated population controls are introduced annually with the release of January data.

Source: U.S. Department of Labor, Bureau of Labor Statistics, Table CPSAA I44, http://www.bls.gov/cps/tables.htm,http://www.bls.gov/cps/tables.htm

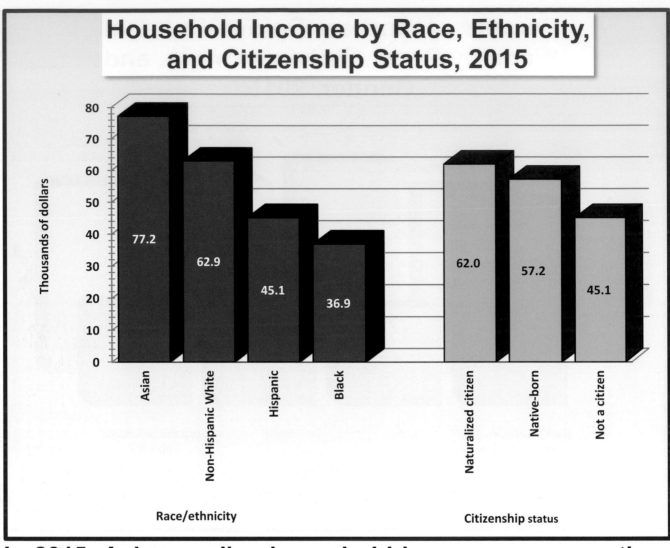

Household Income by Race, Ethnicity, and Citizenship Status, 2015

Thousands of dollars

Asian: 77.2
Non-Hispanic White: 62.9
Hispanic: 45.1
Black: 36.9
Naturalized citizen: 62.0
Native-born: 57.2
Not a citizen: 45.1

Race/ethnicity

Citizenship status

In 2015, Asian median household income was more than double that of Black or African American households. Also, citizens earned approximately one-third more than non-citizens.

Income in 2015 dollars.

Source: U.S. Census Bureau, Source: U.S. Census Bureau, Current Population Survey, 2015 and 2016 Annual Social and Economic Supplements, Table I, http://www.census.gov/data/tables/2016/demo/income-poverty/p60-256.html

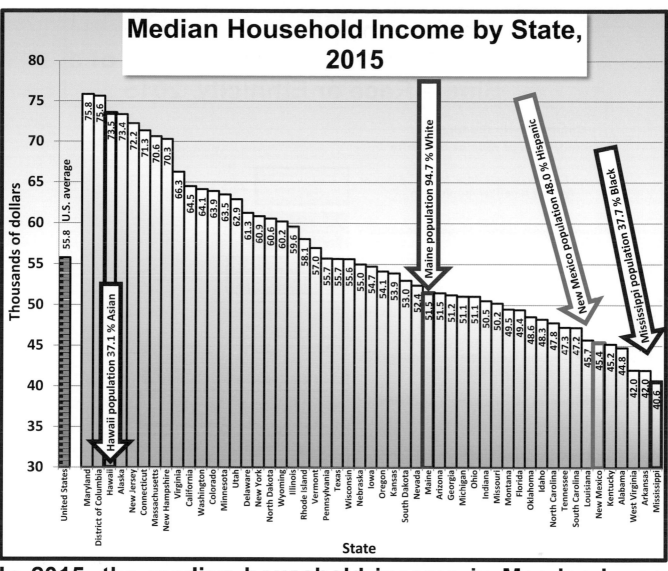

Median Household Income by State, 2015

In 2015, the median household income in Maryland was almost double that in Mississippi.

Although the American Community Survey (ACS) produces population, demographic and housing unit estimates, it is the Census Bureau's Population Estimates Program that produces and disseminates the official estimates of the population for the nation, states, counties, cities, and towns as well as estimates of housing units for states and counties.

Source: U.S. Census Bureau, 2015 American Community Survey 1-Year Estimates Table R1901, http://www.census.gov/programs-surveys/acs/data/summary-file.html

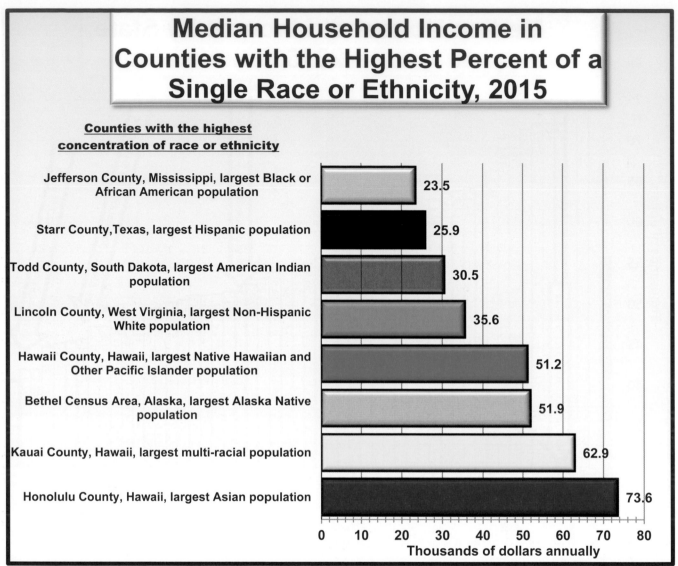

Median Household Income in Counties with the Highest Percent of a Single Race or Ethnicity, 2015

Counties with the highest concentration of race or ethnicity

County	Thousands of dollars annually
Jefferson County, Mississippi, largest Black or African American population	23.5
Starr County, Texas, largest Hispanic population	25.9
Todd County, South Dakota, largest American Indian population	30.5
Lincoln County, West Virginia, largest Non-Hispanic White population	35.6
Hawaii County, Hawaii, largest Native Hawaiian and Other Pacific Islander population	51.2
Bethel Census Area, Alaska, largest Alaska Native population	51.9
Kauai County, Hawaii, largest multi-racial population	62.9
Honolulu County, Hawaii, largest Asian population	73.6

Thousands of dollars annually

In 2015, the median household income for residents of Honolulu County, Hawaii—the county with the highest percent of Asians in the United States—was approximately triple that of Jefferson County, Mississippi—the county with the highest percent of Black or African American residents in the United States.

The United States is comprised of 3,142 counties. A county is a political and geographic subdivision of a state. The Census Bureau considers the parishes of Louisiana and the boroughs of Alaska and the District of Columbia to be equivalent to counties for statistical purposes. Hispanic origin is considered an ethnicity, not a race. Hispanics may be of any race.

Source: U.S. Census Bureau, American Fact Finder, Community Facts, 2015 Population Estimates Program, accessed 10/17/16, http://factfinder.census.gov/faces/nav/jsf/pages/community_facts.xhtml#

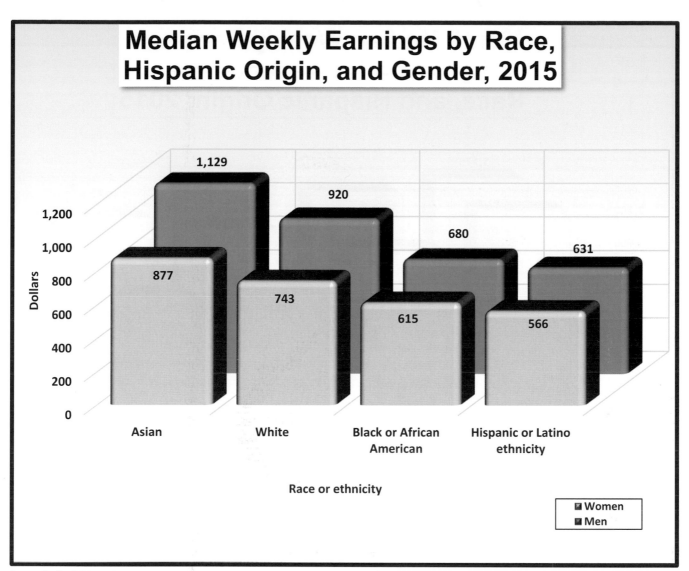

Median Weekly Earnings by Race, Hispanic Origin, and Gender, 2015

In 2015, Asian men were the highest paid workers among all races and ethnicities of either gender.

Estimates for the above race groups (White, Black or African American, and Asian) do not sum to totals because data are not presented for all races. Persons whose ethnicity is identified as Hispanic or Latino may be of any race.

Source: U.S. Department of Labor, Bureau of Labor Statistics, Table CPSAAT37, http://www.bls.gov/cps/tables.htm, http://www.bls.gov/cps/tables.htm

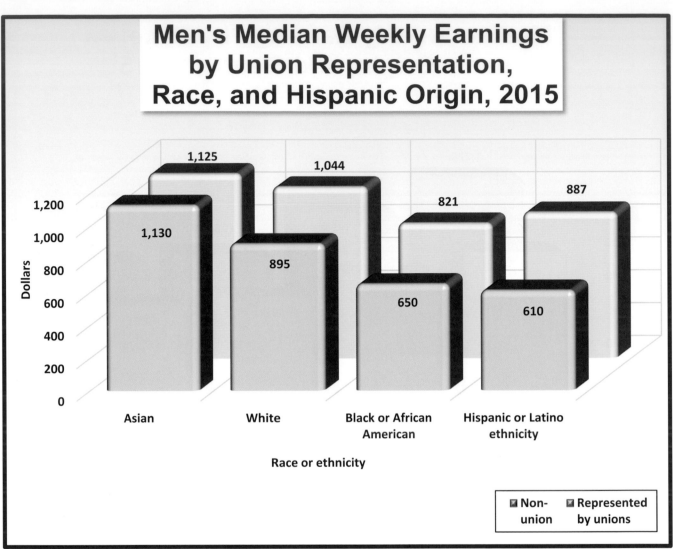

Men's Median Weekly Earnings by Union Representation, Race, and Hispanic Origin, 2015

Dollars

Asian: 1,130 | 1,125
White: 895 | 1,044
Black or African American: 650 | 821
Hispanic or Latino ethnicity: 610 | 887

Race or ethnicity

Non-union | Represented by unions

In 2015, representation by a union was not associated with higher earnings for Asian men but was associated with 45 percent higher earnings for Hispanic or Latino men.

Union representation refers to members of a labor union or an employee association similar to a union and also workers who report no union affiliation but whose jobs are covered by a union or an employee association contract.

Non-union refers to workers who are neither members of a union nor represented by a union on their job.

Estimates for the above race groups (White, Black or African American, and Asian) do not sum to totals because data are not presented for all races. Persons whose ethnicity is identified as Hispanic or Latino may be of any race.

Source: U.S. Department of Labor, Bureau of Labor Statistics, Table CPSAAT41, http://www.bls.gov/cps/tables.htm, http://www.bls.gov/cps/tables.htm

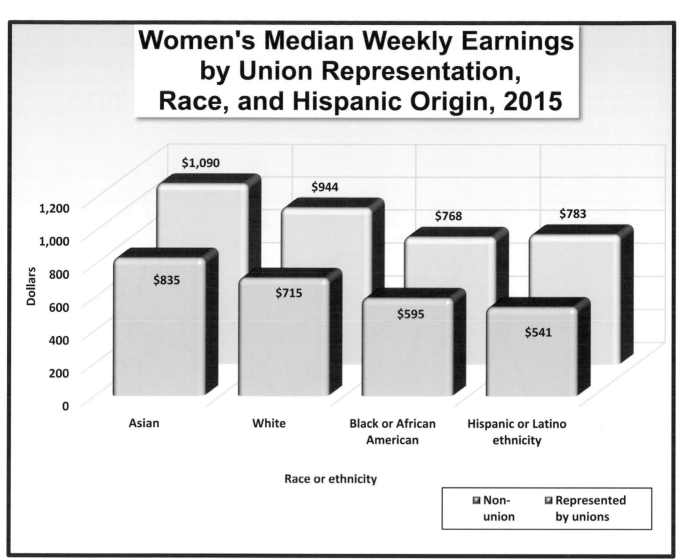

Women's Median Weekly Earnings by Union Representation, Race, and Hispanic Origin, 2015

Asian: $835, $1,090
White: $715, $944
Black or African American: $595, $768
Hispanic or Latino ethnicity: $541, $783

Dollars (y-axis): 0, 200, 400, 600, 800, 1,000, 1,200

Race or ethnicity (x-axis)

Legend: Non-union | Represented by unions

In 2015, representation by a union was associated with approximately 50 percent higher earnings for Hispanic women.

Union representation refers to members of a labor union or an employee association similar to a union and also workers who report no union affiliation but whose jobs are covered by a union or an employee association contract.

Non-union refers to workers who are neither members of a union nor represented by a union on their job.

Estimates for the above race groups (White, Black or African American, and Asian) do not sum to totals because data are not presented for all races. Persons whose ethnicity is identified as Hispanic or Latino may be of any race.

Source: U.S. Department of Labor, Bureau of Labor Statistics, Table CPSAAT41, http://www.bls.gov/cps/tables.htm, http://www.bls.gov/cps/tables.htm

Women's Earnings History as Percentage of Men's by Race and Hispanic Origin, 1988–2015

Legend: Non-Hispanic White • Black • Asian • Hispanic

In 2015, women earned between 75 and 90 percent of men's earnings.

Earnings in 2015 dollars. Based on median earnings of full-time, year-round workers 15 years old and over as of March, of the following year. Before 1989, earnings are for civilian workers only.

Prior to 2001, Asian race was reported to include Pacific Islanders.

Source: U.S. Census Bureau, Source: U.S. Census Bureau, Table P53, http://www.census.gov/data/tables/time-series/demo/income-poverty/historical-income-people.html

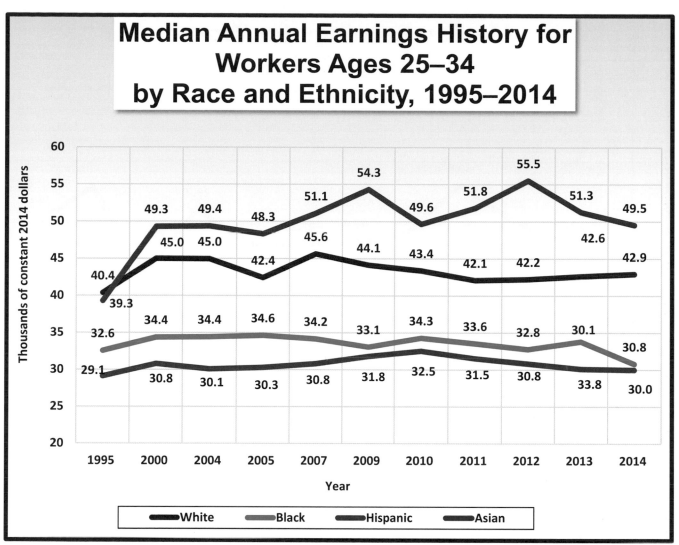

Median Annual Earnings History for Workers Ages 25–34 by Race and Ethnicity, 1995–2014

Median earnings for White, Black or African American, or Hispanic full-time, year-round workers has remained basically unchanged between 2000 and 2014—measured in constant 2014 dollars.

Median annual earnings of full-time year-round of workers aged 25 to 34 years old and full-time year-round workers by race and ethnicity, in constant 2014 dollars.

Note: Race categories exclude persons of Hispanic ethnicity.

For 1995 and 2000, data for Asians and Pacific Islanders were not reported separately; therefore, Pacific Islanders are included with Asians for 1995 and 2000.

Source: U.S. Department of Commerce, Census Bureau, Current Population Survey (CPS), Annual Social and Economic Supplement, 1996 through 2015. (This table was prepared November 2015.), https://nces.ed.gov/programs/digest/2015menu_tables.asp, Table 502.30

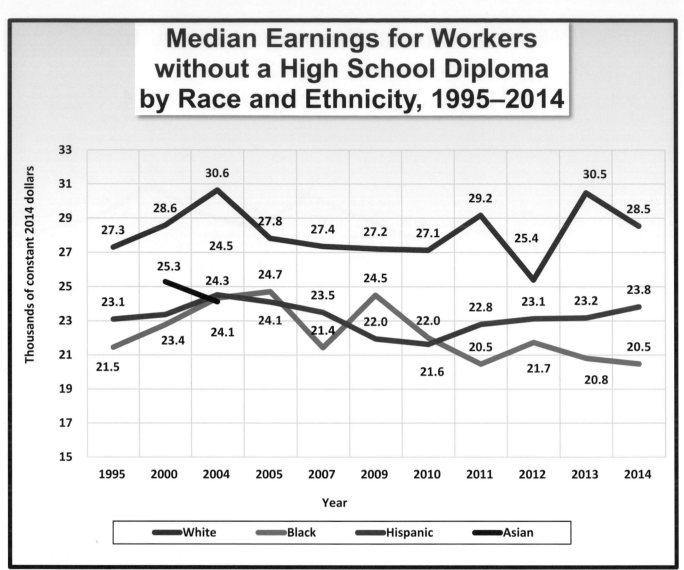

Median Earnings for Workers without a High School Diploma by Race and Ethnicity, 1995–2014

In 2014, White full-time workers aged 25–34 years old who did not finish high school earned almost 50 percent more than Black or African American workers with the same education level.

Median annual earnings of full-time year-round of workers aged 25 to 34 years old and full-time year-round workers with less than a completed high school education by race and ethnicity, in constant 2014 dollars. High school education includes GED completion.

Race categories exclude persons of Hispanic ethnicity.

For 1995 and 2000, data for Asians and Pacific Islanders were not reported separately; therefore, Pacific Islanders are included with Asians for 1995 and 2000.

Source: U.S. Department of Commerce, Census Bureau, Current Population Survey (CPS), Annual Social and Economic Supplement, 1996 through 2015. (This table was prepared November 2015.), https://nces.ed.gov/programs/digest/2015menu_tables.asp, Table 502.30

Chapter 9: Income, Poverty, and Wealth

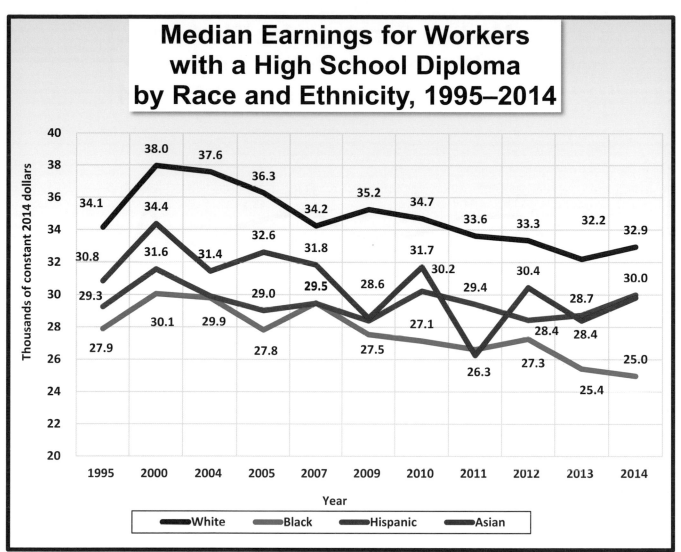

Median Earnings for Workers with a High School Diploma by Race and Ethnicity, 1995–2014

In 2014, Asian and Hispanic full-time workers aged 25–34 years old who completed high school earned approximately the same.

Median annual earnings of full-time year-round of workers aged 25 to 34 years old and full-time year-round workers with less than a completed high school education by race and ethnicity, in constant 2014 dollars. High school education includes GED completion.

Note: Race categories exclude persons of Hispanic ethnicity.

For 1995 and 2000, data for Asians and Pacific Islanders were not reported separately; therefore, Pacific Islanders are included with Asians for 1995 and 2000.

Source: U.S. Department of Commerce, Census Bureau, Current Population Survey (CPS), Annual Social and Economic Supplement, 1996 through 2015. (This table was prepared November 2015.), https://nces.ed.gov/programs/digest/2015menu_tables.asp, Table 502.30

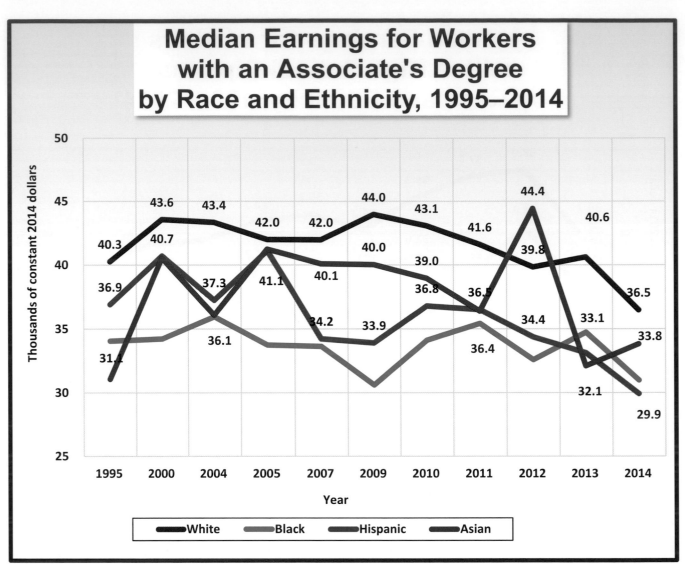

Median Earnings for Workers with an Associate's Degree by Race and Ethnicity, 1995–2014

In 2014, Asian full-time workers aged 25–34 years old with an associate's degree earned approximately the same as White workers.

Median annual earnings of full-time year-round of workers aged 25 to 34 years old and full-time year-round workers with less than a completed high school education by race and ethnicity, in constant 2014 dollars.

Note: Race categories exclude persons of Hispanic ethnicity.

For 1995 and 2000, data for Asians and Pacific Islanders were not reported separately; therefore, Pacific Islanders are included with Asians for 1995 and 2000.

Source: U.S. Department of Commerce, Census Bureau, Current Population Survey (CPS), Annual Social and Economic Supplement, 1996 through 2015. (This table was prepared November 2015.), https://nces.ed.gov/programs/digest/2015menu_tables.asp, Table 502.30

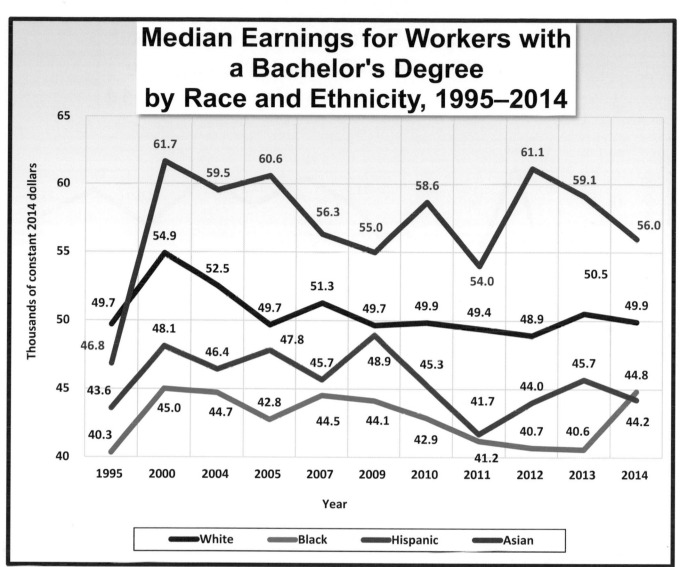

Median Earnings for Workers with a Bachelor's Degree by Race and Ethnicity, 1995–2014

Thousands of constant 2014 dollars

Year

Legend: White, Black, Hispanic, Asian

Asian full-time workers with a bachelor's degree aged 25–34 years old, earned 12 to 27 percent more than Black or African American, White, or Hispanic workers, between 2000 and 2014.

Median annual earnings of full-time year-round of workers aged 25 to 34 years old and full-time year-round workers with less than a completed high school education by race and ethnicity, in constant 2014 dollars.

Note: Race categories exclude persons of Hispanic ethnicity.

For 1995 and 2000, data for Asians and Pacific Islanders were not reported separately; therefore, Pacific Islanders are included with Asians for 1995 and 2000.

Source: U.S. Department of Commerce, Census Bureau, Current Population Survey (CPS), Annual Social and Economic Supplement, 1996 through 2015. (This table was prepared November 2015.), https://nces.ed.gov/programs/digest/2015menu_tables.asp, Table 502.30

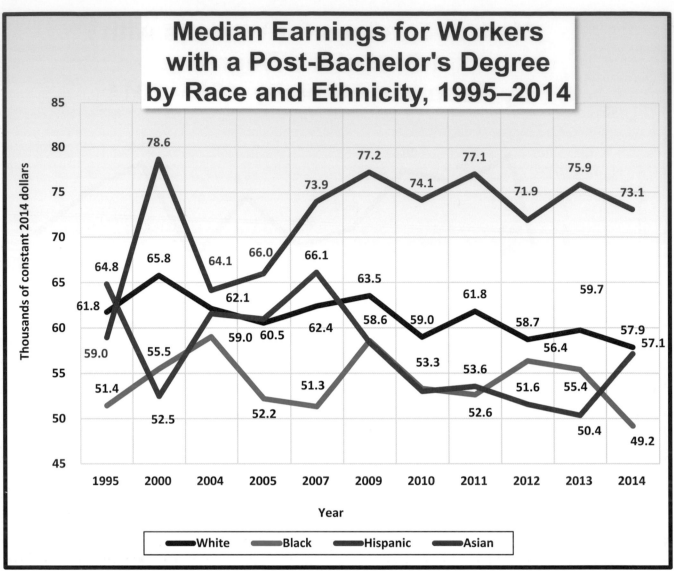

Median Earnings for Workers with a Post-Bachelor's Degree by Race and Ethnicity, 1995–2014

In 2014, Hispanic and White full-time workers with a master's degree or higher aged 25–34 years old earned the same.

Median annual earnings of full-time year-round of workers aged 25 to 34 years old and full-time year-round workers with less than a completed high school education by race and ethnicity, in constant 2014 dollars.

Note: Race categories exclude persons of Hispanic ethnicity.

For 1995 and 2000, data for Asians and Pacific Islanders were not reported separately; therefore, Pacific Islanders are included with Asians for 1995 and 2000.

Source: U.S. Department of Commerce, Census Bureau, Current Population Survey (CPS), Annual Social and Economic Supplement, 1996 through 2015. (This table was prepared November 2015.), https://nces.ed.gov/programs/digest/2015menu_tables.asp, Table 502.30

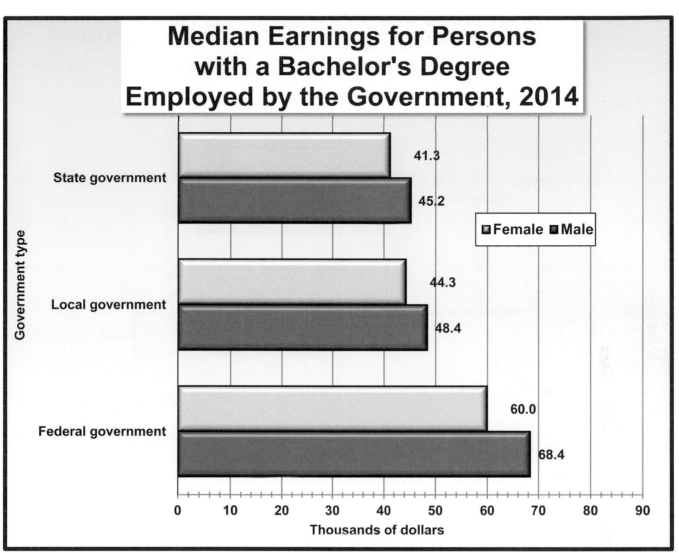

Median Earnings for Persons with a Bachelor's Degree Employed by the Government, 2014

Government type

State government
- Female: 41.3
- Male: 45.2

Local government
- Female: 44.3
- Male: 48.4

Federal government
- Female: 60.0
- Male: 68.4

Thousands of dollars

In 2014, men earned 14 percent more than women working for the federal government and 9 percent more working for state and local governments—all with bachelor's degrees and working full-time.

Median annual earnings of workers aged 25 to 34 years old with a bachelor's or higher degree.

Estimates by major occupation group and class of worker are restricted to individuals currently employed and estimates of median annual earnings are restricted to individuals working full time and year-round.

Estimates are for the entire population of civilian bachelor's degree holders, aged 25 to 34 years old, including persons living in households and persons living in group quarters (such as college residence halls, residential treatment centers, and correctional facilities). Race categories exclude persons of Hispanic ethnicity. Native Hawaiian or Other Pacific Islander is a person having origins in any of the original peoples of Hawaii, Guam, Samoa, or other Pacific Islands.

Source: U.S. Department of Commerce, Census Bureau, American Community Survey (ACS), 2014. (This table was prepared January 2016.), https://nces.ed.gov/programs/digest/2015menu_tables.asp, Table 505.15

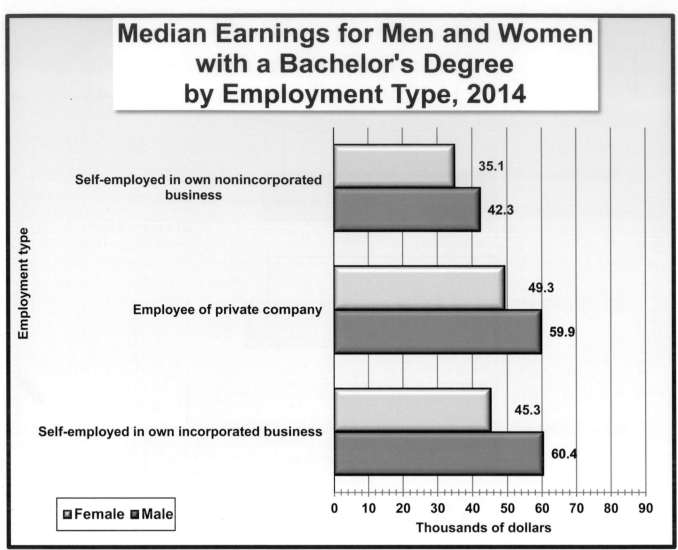

Median Earnings for Men and Women with a Bachelor's Degree by Employment Type, 2014

Employment type

Self-employed in own nonincorporated business
- Female: 35.1
- Male: 42.3

Employee of private company
- Female: 49.3
- Male: 59.9

Self-employed in own incorporated business
- Female: 45.3
- Male: 60.4

□ Female ■ Male

Thousands of dollars

In 2014, self-employed men earned 20 percent more than women when their business was incorporated and 33 percent more when not incorporated—all with bachelor's degrees and working full-time.

Median annual earnings of workers aged 25 to 34 years old with a bachelor's or higher degree.

Estimates by major occupation group and class of worker are restricted to individuals currently employed and estimates of median annual earnings are restricted to individuals working full time and year-round.

Estimates are for the entire population of civilian bachelor's degree holders, aged 25 to 34 years old, including persons living in households and persons living in group quarters (such as college residence halls, residential treatment centers, and correctional facilities). Race categories exclude persons of Hispanic ethnicity. Native Hawaiian or Other Pacific Islander is a person having origins in any of the original peoples of Hawaii, Guam, Samoa, or other Pacific Islands.

Source: U.S. Department of Commerce, Census Bureau, American Community Survey (ACS), 2014. (This table was prepared January 2016.), https://nces.ed.gov/programs/digest/2015menu_tables.asp, Table 505.15

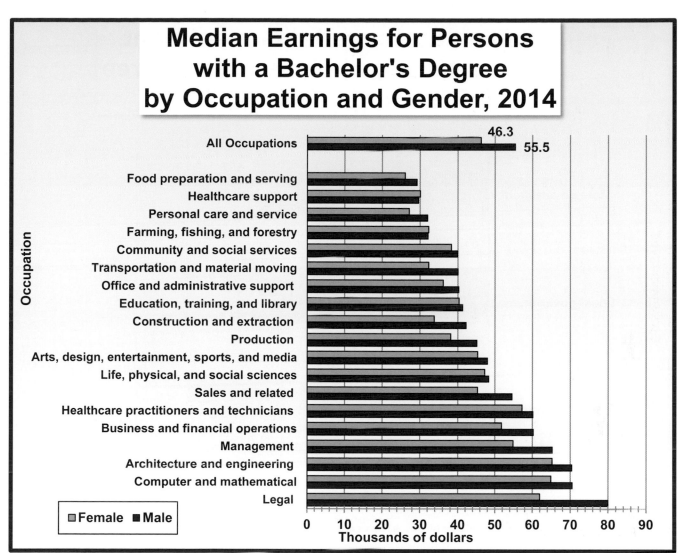

Median Earnings for Persons with a Bachelor's Degree by Occupation and Gender, 2014

Median annual earnings of workers aged 25 to 34 years old with a bachelor's or higher degree.

In 2014, men with a bachelor's degree and working full-time had median earnings approximately 20 percent higher than women across all occupations.

Median annual earnings of workers aged 25 to 34 years old with a bachelor's or higher degree.

Estimates by major occupation group and class of worker are restricted to individuals currently employed and estimates of median annual earnings are restricted to individuals working full time and year-round.

Estimates are for the entire population of civilian bachelor's degree holders, aged 25 to 34 years old, including persons living in households and persons living in group quarters (such as college residence halls, residential treatment centers, and correctional facilities). Race categories exclude persons of Hispanic ethnicity. Native Hawaiian or Other Pacific Islander is a person having origins in any of the original peoples of Hawaii, Guam, Samoa, or other Pacific Islands.

Source: U.S. Department of Commerce, Census Bureau, American Community Survey (ACS), 2014. (This table was prepared January 2016.), https://nces.ed.gov/programs/digest/2015menu_tables.asp, Table 505.15

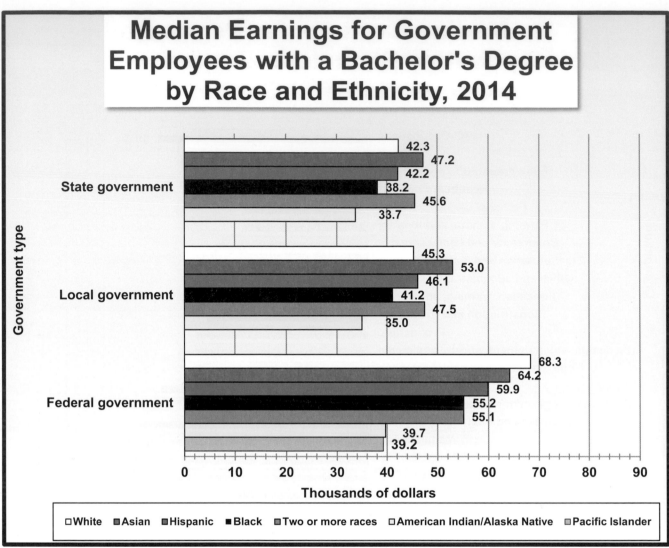

Median Earnings for Government Employees with a Bachelor's Degree by Race and Ethnicity, 2014

Government type

State government
- 42.3
- 47.2
- 42.2
- 38.2
- 45.6
- 33.7

Local government
- 45.3
- 53.0
- 46.1
- 41.2
- 47.5
- 35.0

Federal government
- 68.3
- 64.2
- 59.9
- 55.2
- 55.1
- 39.7
- 39.2

Thousands of dollars

□White ■Asian ■Hispanic ■Black ■Two or more races □American Indian/Alaska Native □Pacific Islander

In 2014, White federal government workers earned more than other races and ethnicities while Asian workers earned the most when employed by state and local governments.

Median annual earnings of workers aged 25 to 34 years old with a bachelor's or higher degree.

Estimates by major occupation group and class of worker are restricted to individuals currently employed and estimates of median annual earnings are restricted to individuals working full time and year-round.

Estimates are for the entire population of civilian bachelor's degree holders, aged 25 to 34 years old, including persons living in households and persons living in group quarters (such as college residence halls, residential treatment centers, and correctional facilities). Race categories exclude persons of Hispanic ethnicity. Native Hawaiian or Other Pacific Islander is a person having origins in any of the original peoples of Hawaii, Guam, Samoa, or other Pacific Islands.

Source: U.S. Department of Commerce, Census Bureau, American Community Survey (ACS), 2014. (This table was prepared January 2016.), https://nces.ed.gov/programs/digest/2015menu_tables.asp, Table 505.15

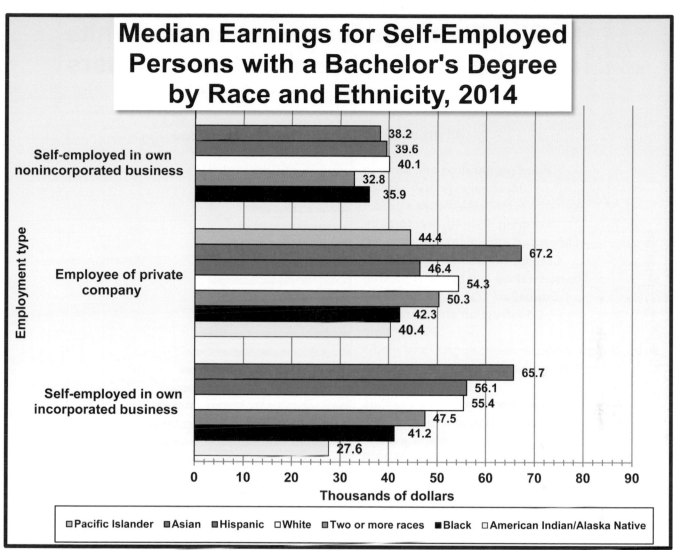

Median Earnings for Self-Employed Persons with a Bachelor's Degree by Race and Ethnicity, 2014

Self-employed in own nonincorporated business
- 38.2
- 39.6
- 40.1
- 32.8
- 35.9

Employee of private company
- 44.4
- 67.2
- 46.4
- 54.3
- 50.3
- 42.3
- 40.4

Self-employed in own incorporated business
- 65.7
- 56.1
- 55.4
- 47.5
- 41.2
- 27.6

Employment type

Thousands of dollars

□ Pacific Islander ■ Asian ■ Hispanic □ White ■ Two or more races ■ Black □ American Indian/Alaska Native

In 2014, Asians earned more than other race and ethnic groups when they were self-employed in their own incorporated business or when working for a private company.

Median annual earnings of workers aged 25 to 34 years old with a bachelor's or higher degree. Estimates by major occupation group and class of worker are restricted to individuals currently employed and estimates of median annual earnings are restricted to individuals working full time and year-round.

Estimates are for the entire population of civilian bachelor's degree holders, aged 25 to 34 years old, including persons living in households and persons living in group quarters (such as college residence halls, residential treatment centers, and correctional facilities). Race categories exclude persons of Hispanic ethnicity. Native Hawaiian or Other Pacific Islander is a person having origins in any of the original peoples of Hawaii, Guam, Samoa, or other Pacific Islands.

Source: U.S. Department of Commerce, Census Bureau, American Community Survey (ACS), 2014. (This table was prepared January 2016.), https://nces.ed.gov/programs/digest/2015menu_tables.asp, Table 505.15

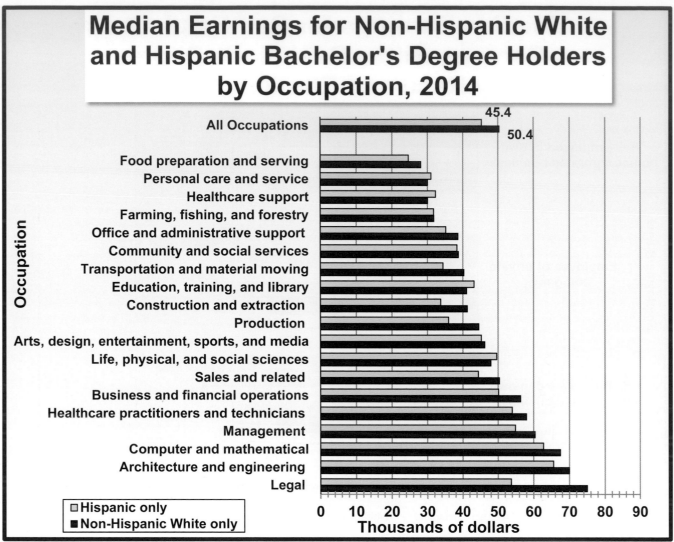

Median Earnings for Non-Hispanic White and Hispanic Bachelor's Degree Holders by Occupation, 2014

In 2014, non-Hispanic White workers with a bachelor's degree and working full-time, earned approximately 11 percent more than Hispanic workers across most occupations.

Median annual earnings of workers aged 25 to 34 years old with a bachelor's or higher degree.

Estimates by major occupation group and class of worker are restricted to individuals currently employed and estimates of median annual earnings are restricted to individuals working full time and year-round.

Estimates are for the entire population of civilian bachelor's degree holders, aged 25 to 34 years old, including persons living in households and persons living in group quarters (such as college residence halls, residential treatment centers, and correctional facilities). Race categories exclude persons of Hispanic ethnicity. Native Hawaiian or Other Pacific Islander is a person having origins in any of the original peoples of Hawaii, Guam, Samoa, or other Pacific Islands.

Source: U.S. Department of Commerce, Census Bureau, American Community Survey (ACS), 2014. (This table was prepared January 2016.), https://nces.ed.gov/programs/digest/2015menu_tables.asp, Table 505.15

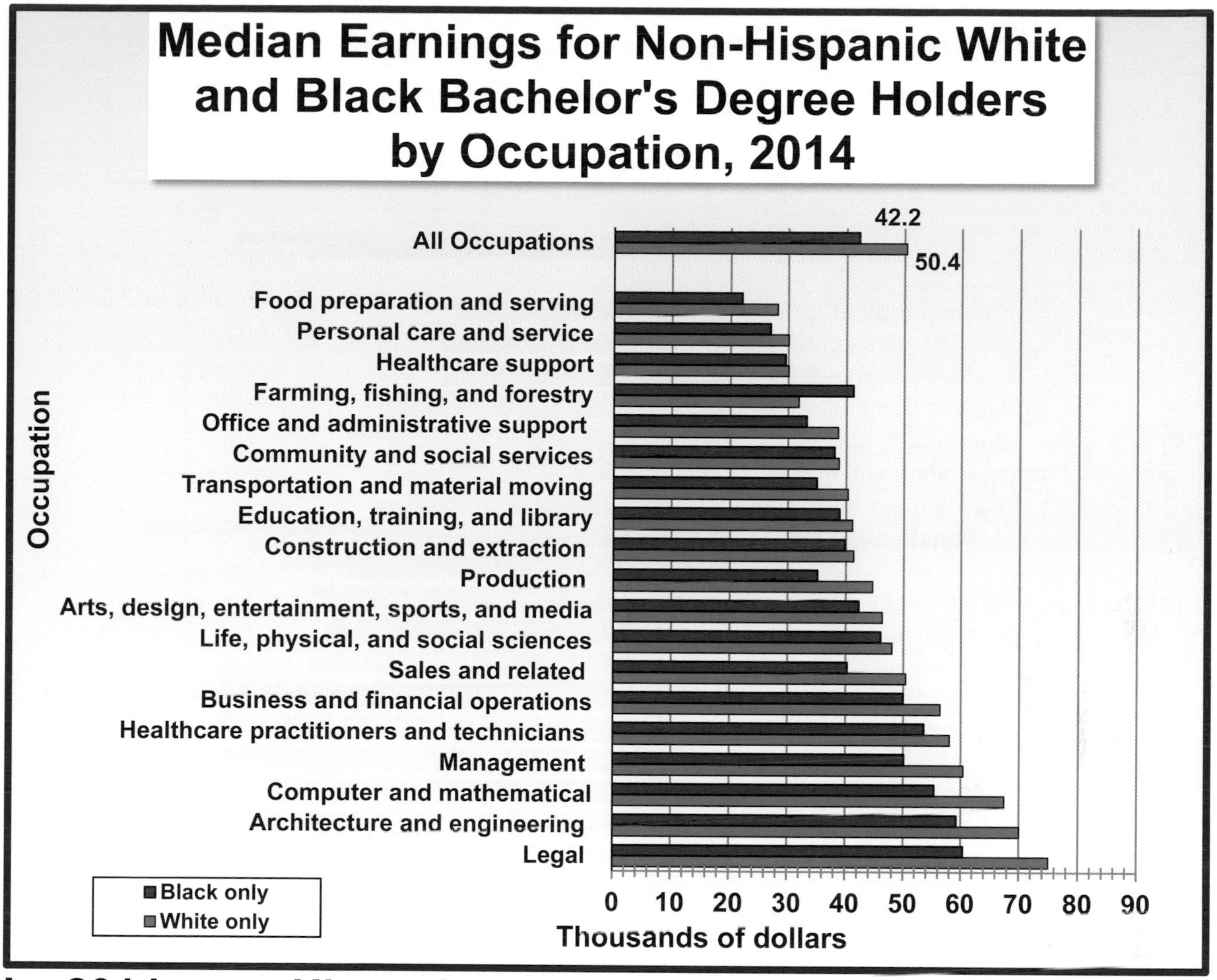
Median Earnings for Non-Hispanic White and Black Bachelor's Degree Holders by Occupation, 2014
42.2
All Occupations
50.4
Food preparation and serving
Personal care and service
Healthcare support
Farming, fishing, and forestry
Office and administrative support
Community and social services
Transportation and material moving
Education, training, and library
Construction and extraction
Production
Arts, design, entertainment, sports, and media
Life, physical, and social sciences
Sales and related
Business and financial operations
Healthcare practitioners and technicians
Management
Computer and mathematical
Architecture and engineering
Legal
Occupation
Black only
White only
0 10 20 30 40 50 60 70 80 90
Thousands of dollars

In 2014, non-Hispanic White workers with a bachelor's degree and working full-time, earned approximately 20 percent more than Black or African American workers across most occupations.

Median annual earnings of workers aged 25 to 34 years old with a bachelor's or higher degree.

Estimates by major occupation group and class of worker are restricted to individuals currently employed and estimates of median annual earnings are restricted to individuals working full time and year-round.

Estimates are for the entire population of civilian bachelor's degree holders, aged 25 to 34 years old, including persons living in households and persons living in group quarters (such as college residence halls, residential treatment centers, and correctional facilities). Race categories exclude persons of Hispanic ethnicity. Native Hawaiian or Other Pacific Islander is a person having origins in any of the original peoples of Hawaii, Guam, Samoa, or other Pacific Islands.

Source: U.S. Department of Commerce, Census Bureau, American Community Survey (ACS), 2014. (This table was prepared January 2016.), https://nces.ed.gov/programs/digest/2015menu_tables.asp, Table 505.15

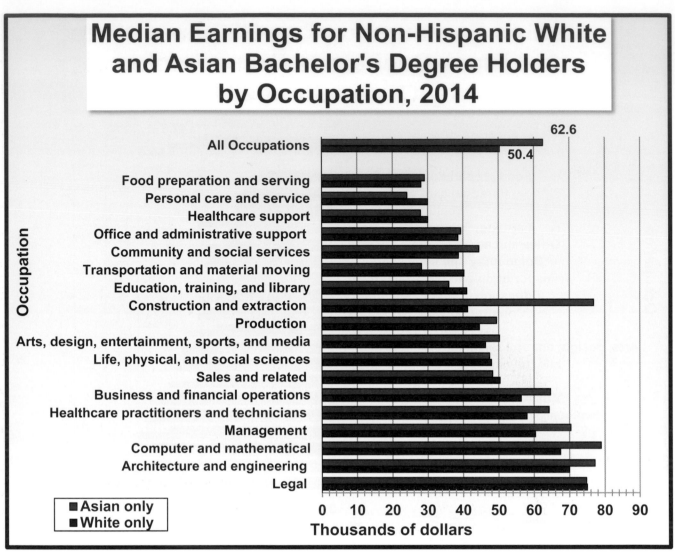

Median Earnings for Non-Hispanic White and Asian Bachelor's Degree Holders by Occupation, 2014

In 2014, full-time Asian workers with bachelor's degrees had median incomes generally higher than non-Hispanic White workers across most occupations.

Median annual earnings of workers aged 25 to 34 years old with a bachelor's or higher degree. Estimates by major occupation group and class of worker are restricted to individuals currently employed and estimates of median annual earnings are restricted to individuals working full time and year-round.

Estimates are for the entire population of civilian bachelor's degree holders, aged 25 to 34 years old, including persons living in households and persons living in group quarters (such as college residence halls, residential treatment centers, and correctional facilities). Race categories exclude persons of Hispanic ethnicity. Native Hawaiian or Other Pacific Islander is a person having origins in any of the original peoples of Hawaii, Guam, Samoa, or other Pacific Islands.

Source: U.S. Department of Commerce, Census Bureau, American Community Survey (ACS), 2014. (This table was prepared January 2016.), https://nces.ed.gov/programs/digest/2015menu_tables.asp, Table 505.15

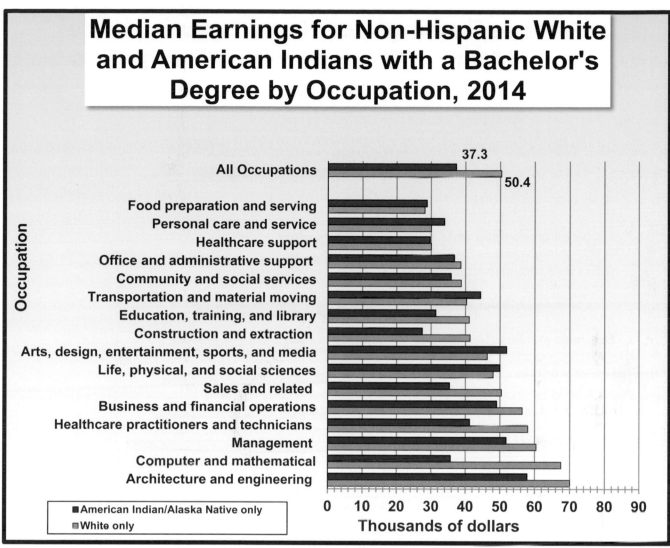

Median Earnings for Non-Hispanic White and American Indians with a Bachelor's Degree by Occupation, 2014

Occupation (y-axis):
- All Occupations — 37.3 / 50.4
- Food preparation and serving
- Personal care and service
- Healthcare support
- Office and administrative support
- Community and social services
- Transportation and material moving
- Education, training, and library
- Construction and extraction
- Arts, design, entertainment, sports, and media
- Life, physical, and social sciences
- Sales and related
- Business and financial operations
- Healthcare practitioners and technicians
- Management
- Computer and mathematical
- Architecture and engineering

Legend:
- ■ American Indian/Alaska Native only
- ▨ White only

x-axis: 0 10 20 30 40 50 60 70 80 90
Thousands of dollars

In 2014, full-time non-Hispanic White workers, with bachelor's degrees, had median incomes generally one-third higher than American Indian and Alaska Native workers across most occupations.

Median annual earnings of workers aged 25 to 34 years old with a bachelor's or higher degree. Estimates by major occupation group and class of worker are restricted to individuals currently employed and estimates of median annual earnings are restricted to individuals working full time and year-round.

Estimates are for the entire population of civilian bachelor's degree holders, aged 25 to 34 years old, including persons living in households and persons living in group quarters (such as college residence halls, residential treatment centers, and correctional facilities). Race categories exclude persons of Hispanic ethnicity. Native Hawaiian or Other Pacific Islander is a person having origins in any of the original peoples of Hawaii, Guam, Samoa, or other Pacific Islands.

Source: U.S. Department of Commerce, Census Bureau, American Community Survey (ACS), 2014. (This table was prepared January 2016.), https://nces.ed.gov/programs/digest/2015menu_tables.asp, Table 505.15

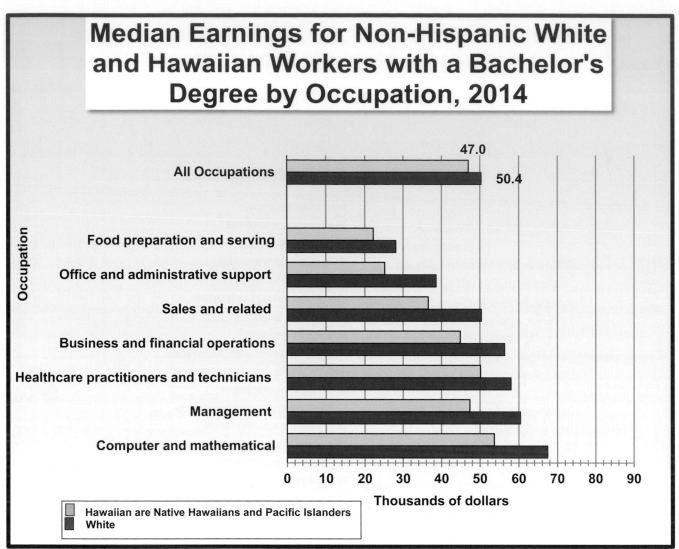

Median Earnings for Non-Hispanic White and Hawaiian Workers with a Bachelor's Degree by Occupation, 2014

Hawaiian are Native Hawaiians and Pacific Islanders
White

In 2014, full-time non-Hispanic White workers with bachelor's degrees had median incomes generally higher than Native Hawaiian and Pacific Island workers across most occupations.

Median annual earnings of workers aged 25 to 34 years old with a bachelor's or higher degree. Estimates by major occupation group and class of worker are restricted to individuals currently employed and estimates of median annual earnings are restricted to individuals working full time and year-round.

Estimates are for the entire population of civilian bachelor's degree holders, aged 25 to 34 years old, including persons living in households and persons living in group quarters (such as college residence halls, residential treatment centers, and correctional facilities). Race categories exclude persons of Hispanic ethnicity. Native Hawaiian or Other Pacific Islander is a person having origins in any of the original peoples of Hawaii, Guam, Samoa, or other Pacific Islands.

Source: U.S. Department of Commerce, Census Bureau, American Community Survey (ACS), 2014. (This table was prepared January 2016.), https://nces.ed.gov/programs/digest/2015menu_tables.asp, Table 505.15

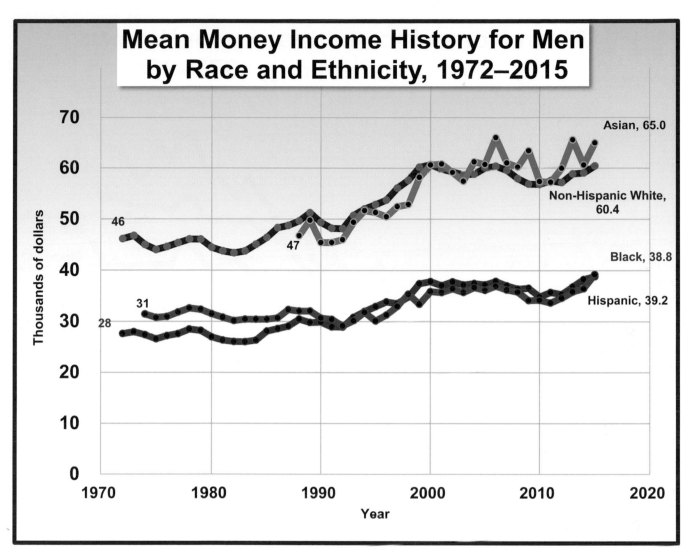

Mean Money Income History for Men by Race and Ethnicity, 1972–2015

Asian, 65.0

Non-Hispanic White, 60.4

Black, 38.8

Hispanic, 39.2

46

47

31

28

Thousands of dollars

Year

In 2015, Asian and non-Hispanic men's mean money income was approximately two-thirds higher than for Black or African American, or Hispanic men.

Money income in 2015 CPI-U-RS adjusted dollars. The CPI-U-RS is a price index of inflation that incorporates most of the improvements in methodology made to the current CPI-U since 1978 into a single, uniform series.

People 15 years and older beginning with March 1980, and people 14 years and older as of March, of the following year for previous years. After 2002 the data for Black and Asian races do not include people of more than one race.

Source: U.S. Census Bureau, Money Income of People, by Race, Hispanic Origin and Sex, Table P-54, http://www.census.gov/data/tables/2016/demo/income-poverty/p60-256.html

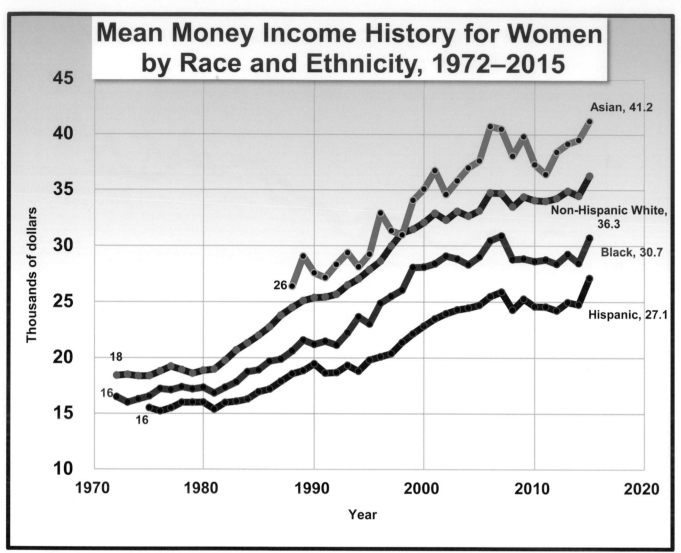

Mean Money Income History for Women by Race and Ethnicity, 1972–2015

In 2015, Asian women had the highest mean money income while Hispanic women had the lowest. The mean money income for Hispanic women was approximately one-third less than for Asian women.

Money income in 2015 CPI-U-RS adjusted dollars. The CPI-U-RS is a price index of inflation that incorporates most of the improvements in methodology made to the current CPI-U since 1978 into a single, uniform series.

People 15 years and older beginning with March 1980, and people 14 years and older as of March, of the following year for previous years. After 2002 the data for Black and Asian races do not include people of more than one race.

Source: U.S. Census Bureau, Money Income of People, by Race, Hispanic Origin and Sex, Table P-54, http://www.census.gov/data/tables/2016/demo/income-poverty/p60-256.html

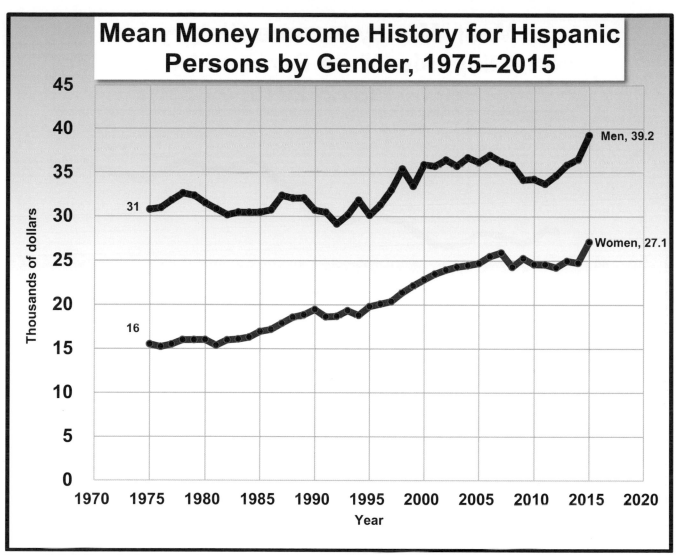

Mean Money Income History for Hispanic Persons by Gender, 1975–2015

Men, 39.2
Women, 27.1

31

16

Thousands of dollars

Year

In 2015, Hispanic men's mean money income was 44 percent more than for Hispanic women.

Money income in 2015 CPI-U-RS adjusted dollars. The CPI-U-RS is a price index of inflation that incorporates most of the improvements in methodology made to the current CPI-U since 1978 into a single, uniform series.

People 15 years and older beginning with March 1980, and people 14 years and older as of March, of the following year for previous years.

Source: U.S. Census Bureau, Money Income of People, by Race, Hispanic Origin and Sex, Table P-54,
http://www.census.gov/data/tables/2016/demo/income-poverty/p60-256.html

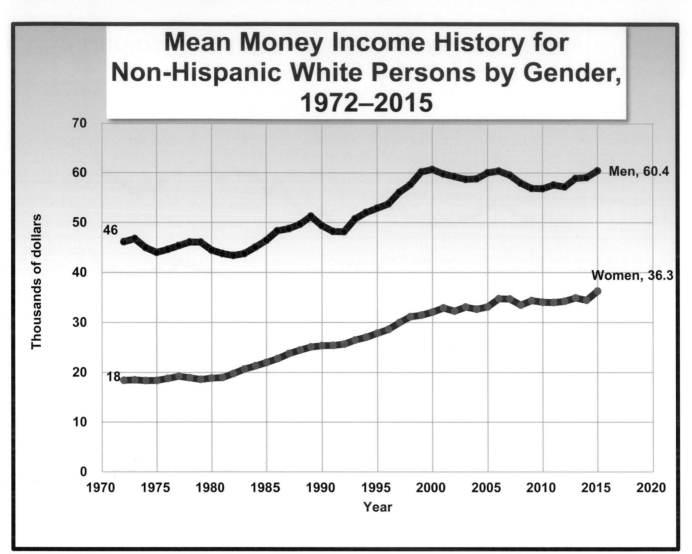

Mean Money Income History for Non-Hispanic White Persons by Gender, 1972–2015

Men, 60.4

Women, 36.3

Thousands of dollars

Year

In 2015, non-Hispanic White men's mean money income was approximately two-thirds higher than for non-Hispanic White women.

Money income in 2015 CPI-U-RS adjusted dollars. The CPI-U-RS is a price index of inflation that incorporates most of the improvements in methodology made to the current CPI-U since 1978 into a single, uniform series. People 15 years and older beginning with March 1980, and people 14 years and older as of March, of the following year for previous years.

Source: U.S. Census Bureau, Money Income of People, by Race, Hispanic Origin and Sex, Table P-54, http://www.census.gov/data/tables/2016/demo/income-poverty/p60-256.html

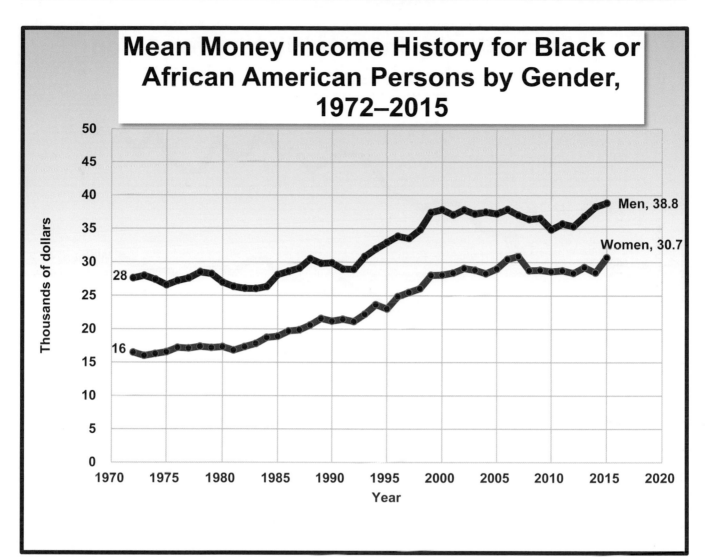

Mean Money Income History for Black or African American Persons by Gender, 1972–2015

Men, 38.8

Women, 30.7

Thousands of dollars

28

16

Year

In 2015, Black or African American men's mean money income was 26 percent more than for Black or African American women.

Money income in 2015 CPI-U-RS adjusted dollars. The CPI-U-RS is a price index of inflation that incorporates most of the improvements in methodology made to the current CPI-U since 1978 into a single, uniform series. People 15 years and older beginning with March 1980, and people 14 years and older as of March, of the following year for previous years. After 2002, the data for Black workers do not include people of more than one race.

Source: U.S. Census Bureau, Money Income of People, by Race, Hispanic Origin and Sex, Table P-54, http://www.census.gov/data/tables/2016/demo/income-poverty/p60-256.html

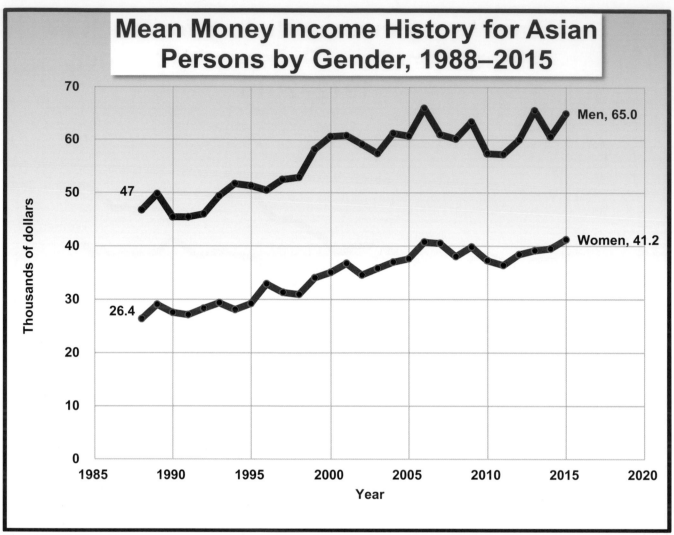

Mean Money Income History for Asian Persons by Gender, 1988–2015

Men, 65.0

Women, 41.2

47

26.4

Thousands of dollars

Year

In 2015, the mean money income for Asian men was 58 percent higher than for Asian women.

Money income in 2015 CPI-U-RS adjusted dollars. The CPI-U-RS is a price index of inflation that incorporates most of the improvements in methodology made to the current CPI-U since 1978 into a single, uniform series.

People 15 years and older beginning with March 1980, and people 14 years and older as of March, of the following year for previous years. After 2002, the data for Asian workers do not include people of more than one race.

Source: U.S. Census Bureau, Money Income of People, by Race, Hispanic Origin and Sex, Table P-54, http://www.census.gov/data/tables/2016/demo/income-poverty/p60-256.html

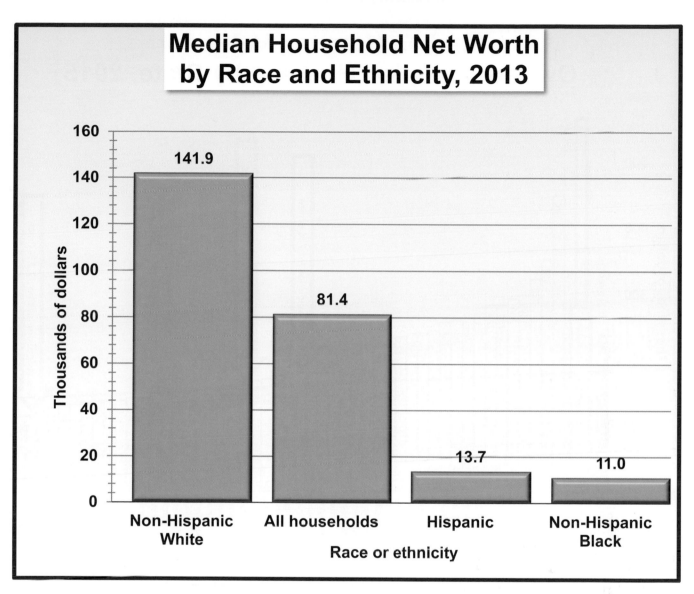

Median Household Net Worth by Race and Ethnicity, 2013

In 2013, the median net worth for non-Hispanic White households was 12.9 times greater than for non-Hispanic Black households.

The Federal Reserve published net worth for non-Hispanic White families at 7.8 times higher than for non-White or Hispanic groups, and that data were refined by PEW Research Center to isolate the data for Hispanic and non-Hispanic Black households.

Source: Federal Reserve Bulletin, September 2014, https://www.federalreserve.gov/pubs/bulletin/2014/pdf/scf14.pdf, and PEW Research Center, http://www.pewresearch.org/fact-tank/2014/12/12/racial-wealth-gaps-great-recession/

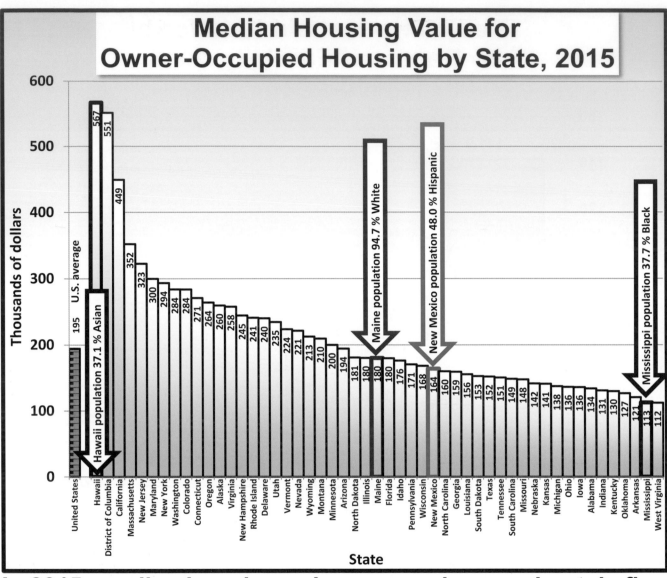

Median Housing Value for Owner-Occupied Housing by State, 2015

Thousands of dollars

- United States: 195 — U.S. average
- Hawaii: 567 — Hawaii population 37.1 % Asian
- District of Columbia: 551
- California: 449
- Massachusetts: 352
- New Jersey: 323
- Maryland: 300
- New York: 294
- Washington: 284
- Colorado: 284
- Connecticut: 271
- Oregon: 264
- Alaska: 260
- Virginia: 258
- New Hampshire: 245
- Rhode Island: 241
- Delaware: 240
- Utah: 235
- Vermont: 224
- Nevada: 221
- Wyoming: 213
- Montana: 210
- Minnesota: 200
- Arizona: 194
- North Dakota: 181
- Illinois: 180 — Maine population 94.7 % White
- Maine: 180
- Florida: 176
- Idaho: 171
- Pennsylvania: 168
- Wisconsin: 164 — New Mexico population 48.0 % Hispanic
- New Mexico: 160
- North Carolina: 159
- Georgia: 156
- Louisiana: 153
- South Dakota: 152
- Texas: 151
- Tennessee: 149
- South Carolina: 148
- Missouri: 142
- Nebraska: 141
- Kansas: 138
- Michigan: 136
- Ohio: 136
- Iowa: 134
- Alabama: 131
- Indiana: 130
- Kentucky: 127
- Oklahoma: 121
- Arkansas: 113 — Mississippi population 37.7 % Black
- Mississippi: 112
- West Virginia

State

In 2015, median housing values ranged approximately five to one, with the lowest values in West Virginia and Mississippi to the highest values in Hawaii.

Although the American Community Survey (ACS) produces population, demographic, and housing unit estimates, it is the Census Bureau's Population Estimates Program that produces and disseminates the official estimates of the population for the nation, states, counties, cities, and towns as well as estimates of housing units for states and counties.

Source: U.S. Census Bureau, 2015 American Community Survey 1-Year Estimates Table R2510, http://www.census.gov/programs-surveys/acs/data/summary-file.html

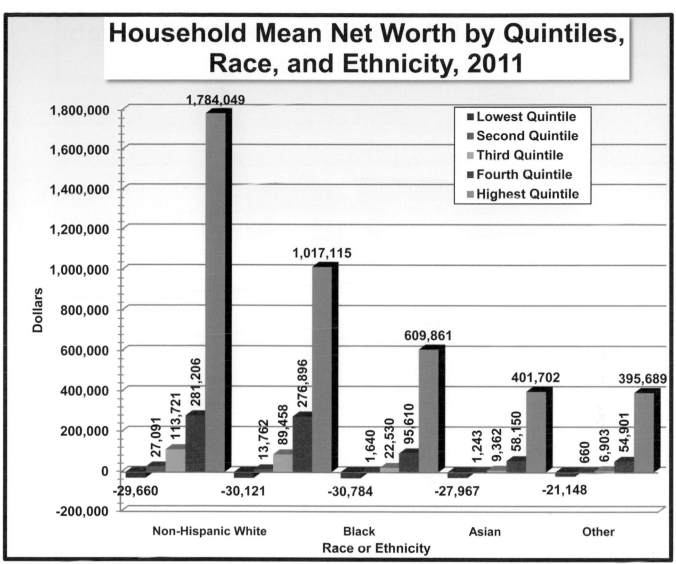

Household Mean Net Worth by Quintiles, Race, and Ethnicity, 2011

Legend:
- Lowest Quintile
- Second Quintile
- Third Quintile
- Fourth Quintile
- Highest Quintile

Non-Hispanic White: 27,091; 113,721; 281,206; 1,784,049; -29,660

Black: 13,762; 89,458; 276,896; 1,017,115; -30,121

Asian: 1,640; 22,530; 95,610; 609,861; -30,784

Other (column 4): 1,243; 9,362; 58,150; 401,702; -27,967

Other: 660; 6,903; 54,901; 395,689; -21,148

Y-axis: Dollars (−200,000 to 1,800,000)
X-axis: Race or Ethnicity (Non-Hispanic White, Black, Asian, Other)

In 2011, households in the bottom mean net worth quintile had a negative net worth—between $21,000–$31,000— across all races and ethnicities.

Net worth may be zero or negative when a household's gross wealth is zero or because the value of a household's liabilities exceeds the value of its assets. Total number of households in the United States represented by these data was 118.7 million.

Excludes race/ethnicity unknown and nonresident alien and race excludes Hispanic origin.

Source: U.S. Census Bureau, Survey of Income and Program Participation, 2008 Panel, Wave 10, Internet Release Date: 8/21/2014, accessed 10/17/16, http://www.census.gov/people/wealth/data/disttables.html

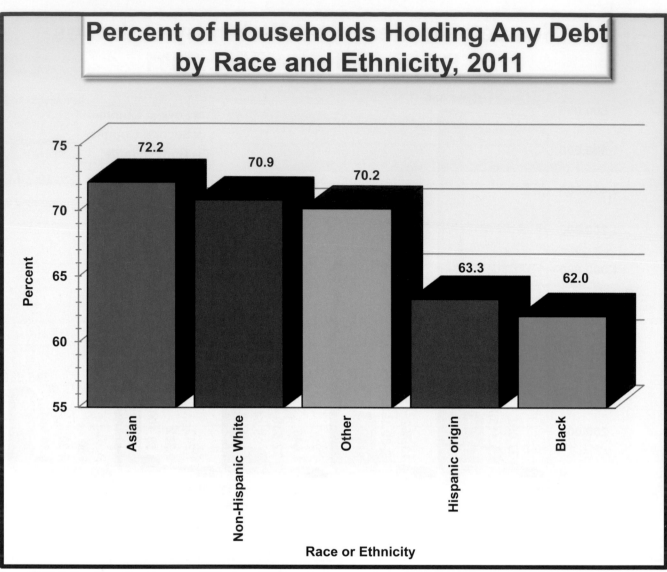

Percent of Households Holding Any Debt by Race and Ethnicity, 2011

Percent

- Asian: 72.2
- Non-Hispanic White: 70.9
- Other: 70.2
- Hispanic origin: 63.3
- Black: 62.0

Race or Ethnicity

In 2011, between 60 to 70 percent of households held debt across all races and ethnicities.

Households excludes group quarters. Total number of households in the United States represented by these data was 118.7 million.

Race excludes Hispanic origin.

Source: U.S. Census Bureau, Survey of Income and Program Participation, 2008 Panel, Wave 10, Updated: May 13, 2013, accessed 10/17/16, http://www.census.gov/people/wealth/data/disttables.html

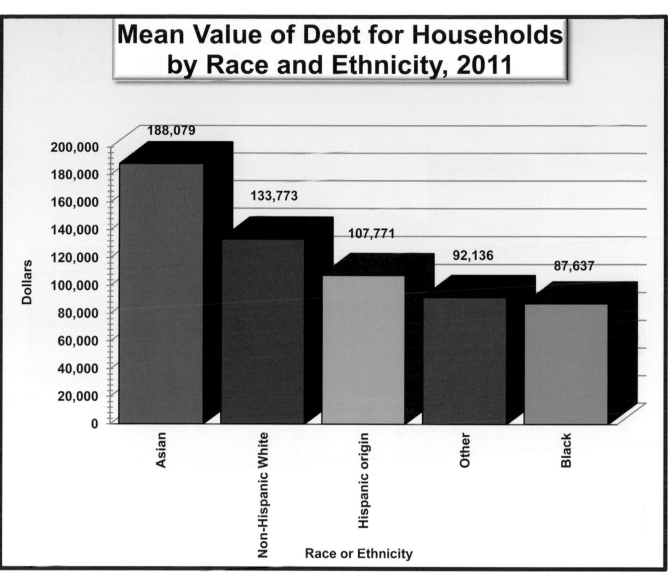

Mean Value of Debt for Households by Race and Ethnicity, 2011

Dollars vs Race or Ethnicity

- Asian: 188,079
- Non-Hispanic White: 133,773
- Hispanic origin: 107,771
- Other: 92,136
- Black: 87,637

In 2011, Asian households held the most debt of all leading races and ethnicities and twice as much debt as Black or African American households which held the least amount.

Hispanics may be any race.

Data for American Indians and Alaska Natives are not shown because of their small sample size. The race or Hispanic origin of the householder designates the race or Hispanic origin of the household. Total number of households in the United States represented by these data was 118.7 million.

Source: U.S. Census Bureau, Survey of Income and Program Participation, 2008 Panel, Wave 10, Updated: May 13, 2013, accessed 10/17/16, http://www.census.gov/people/wealth/data/disttables.html

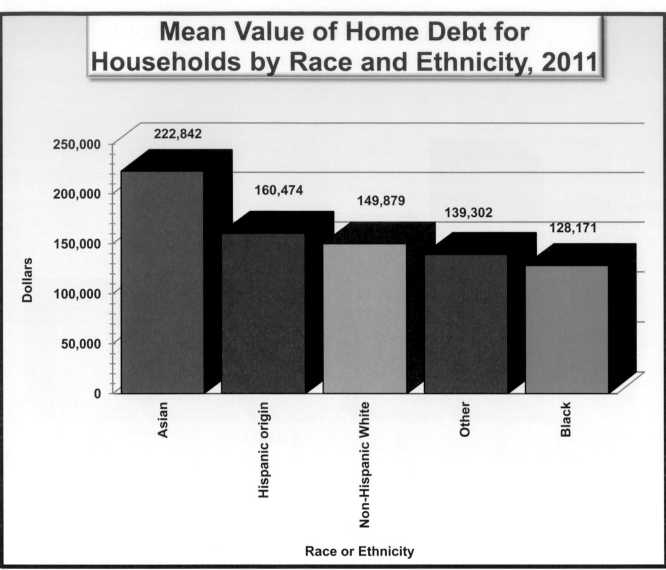

Mean Value of Home Debt for Households by Race and Ethnicity, 2011

Dollars

Asian	222,842
Hispanic origin	160,474
Non-Hispanic White	149,879
Other	139,302
Black	128,171

Race or Ethnicity

In 2011, mean household home debt was highest for Asian households compared with other races or ethnicities.

Because Hispanics may be any race, data in this table for Hispanics overlap slightly with data for the Black population. Data for American Indians and Alaska Natives are not shown because of their small sample size. The race or Hispanic origin of the householder designates the race or Hispanic origin of the household. Total number of households in the United States represented by these data was 118.7 million.

Source: U.S. Census Bureau, Survey of Income and Program Participation, 2008 Panel, Wave 10, Updated: May 13, 2013, accessed 10/17/16, http://www.census.gov/people/wealth/data/disttables.html

Chapter 9: Income, Poverty, and Wealth

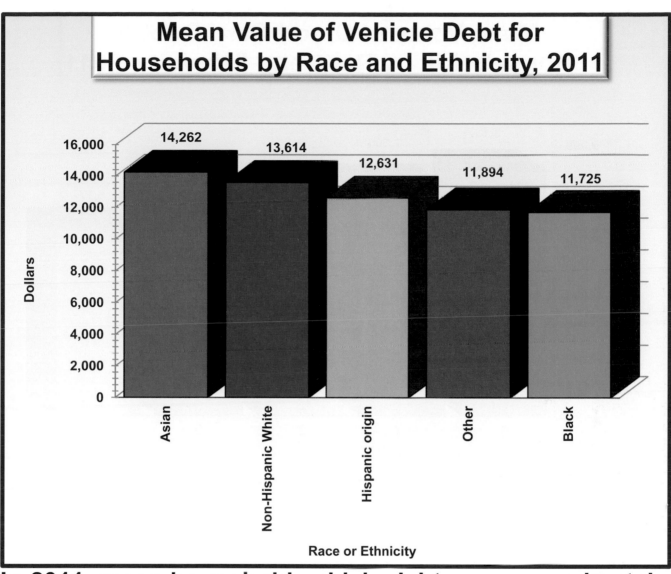

Mean Value of Vehicle Debt for Households by Race and Ethnicity, 2011

Dollars / Race or Ethnicity

Asian — 14,262
Non-Hispanic White — 13,614
Hispanic origin — 12,631
Other — 11,894
Black — 11,725

In 2011, mean household vehicle debt was approximately $13,000 across all races and ethnicities.

Because Hispanics may be any race, data in this table for Hispanics overlap slightly with data for the Black population. Data for American Indians and Alaska Natives are not shown because of their small sample size. The race or Hispanic origin of the householder designates the race or Hispanic origin of the household. Total number of households in the United States represented by these data was 118.7 million.

Source: U.S. Census Bureau, Survey of Income and Program Participation, 2008 Panel, Wave 10, Updated: May 13, 2013, accessed 10/17/16, http://www.census.gov/people/wealth/data/disttables.html

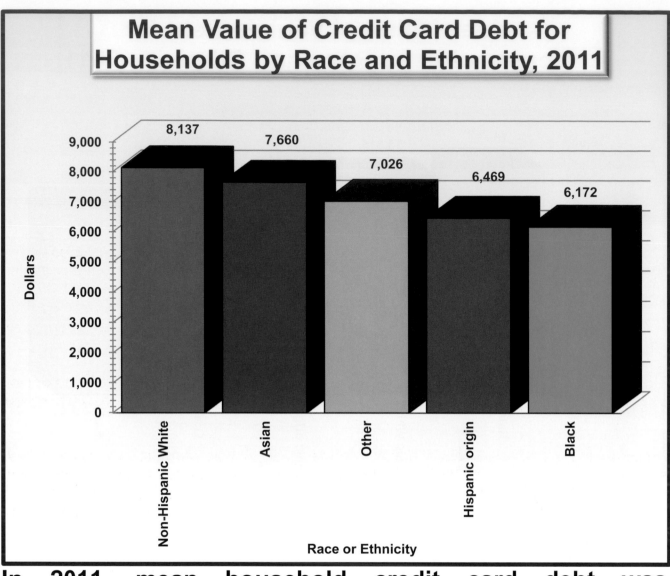

Mean Value of Credit Card Debt for Households by Race and Ethnicity, 2011

In 2011, mean household credit card debt was approximately $7,000 across all races and ethnicities.

Because Hispanics may be any race, data in this table for Hispanics overlap slightly with data for the Black population. Data for American Indians and Alaska Natives are not shown because of their small sample size. The race or Hispanic origin of the householder designates the race or Hispanic origin of the household. Total number of households in the United States represented by these data was 118.7 million.

Source: U.S. Census Bureau, Survey of Income and Program Participation, 2008 Panel, Wave 10, Updated: May 13, 2013, accessed 10/17/16, http://www.census.gov/people/wealth/data/disttables.html

Chapter 10: Education

The National Center for Education Statistics (NCES) is the primary federal entity for collecting and analyzing data related to education in the United States and other nations. NCES is located within the U.S. Department of Education and the Institute of Education Sciences. NCES fulfills a congressional mandate to collect, collate, analyze, and report complete statistics on the condition of American education. It conducts and publishes reports as well as reporting on education activities internationally.

The gap between Black and White high school completion rates has been continually closing over the past 95 years and in 2015, 93 percent of Black students completed high school compared with 95 percent of White students.

Nationally in 2015, 91.8 percent of adults over the age of 25 who were native-born had a high school degree or higher and 32.7 percent had a bachelor's degree or higher. In comparison, 61.6 percent of non-citizens had a high school degree or higher and 25.1 percent had a bachelor's degree or higher. Those foreign-born from India had the highest percent of bachelor's degree completion at 73 percent.

In 2013, the percent enrollment in public schools of non-Hispanic White children, grades K–8, fell below 50 percent for the first time, as did grades 9–12 in 2016. In the same time-frame, the percentage of Hispanic students in public schools had grown to one-in-four, nationally.

Comparing 2015 test scores across race and ethnicity groups, Asian or Pacific Islanders had the highest scores for 4th grade and 12th grade. Black or African American students performed the most poorly.

In 2014, 22 percent of non-citizens studied engineering for their bachelor's degree, in 2014, compared with six percent of U.S. born students, eight percent of Black students, and 28 percent of Asian students.

~

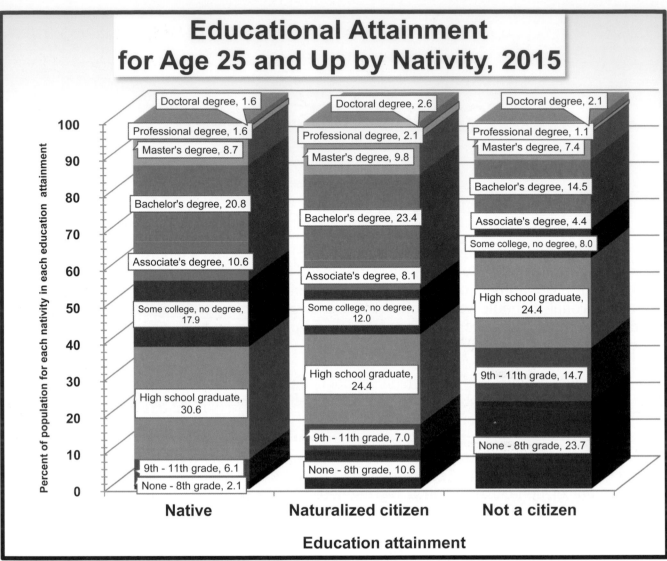

Educational Attainment for Age 25 and Up by Nativity, 2015

In 2015, 37.8 percent of persons who were non-citizens had an education below high school completion level compared with 8.3 percent of native citizens.

Native means both parents were born in the United States.

Source: U.S. Census Bureau, Current Population Survey, 2015 Annual Social and Economic Supplement,
https://www.census.gov/content/dam/Census/library/publications/2016/demo/p20-578.pdf

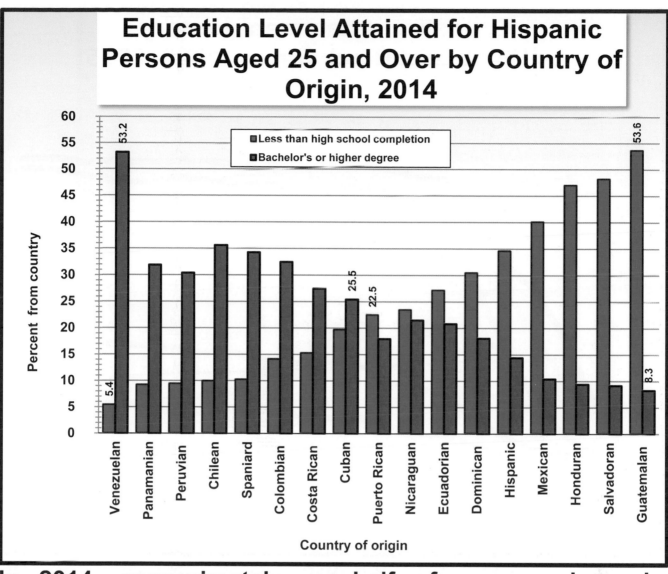

Education Level Attained for Hispanic Persons Aged 25 and Over by Country of Origin, 2014

In 2014, approximately one-half of persons born in Venezuela aged 25 and over had a bachelor's degree while one-half of those born in Guatemala had not completed high school.

High school completers include diploma recipients and those completing high school through alternative credentials, such as a GED.

Estimates are for the entire population in the 25 and over age range, including persons living in households and persons living in group quarters (such as college residence halls, residential treatment centers, military barracks, and correctional facilities).

Source: U.S. Department of Commerce, Census Bureau, American Community Survey (ACS), 2009 and 2014. (This table was prepared January 2016.), Digest 2015, Table 104.40, https://nces.ed.gov/programs/digest/2015menu_tables.asp

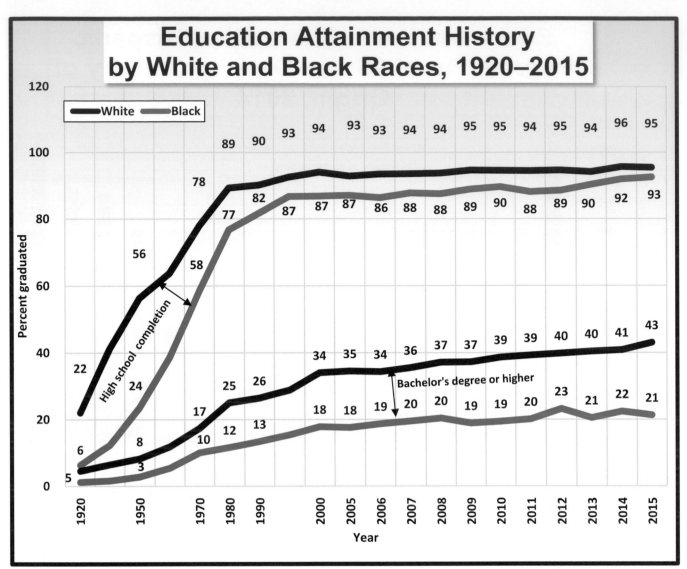

Education Attainment History by White and Black Races, 1920–2015

In 2015, approximately two-of-five White persons aged 25 to 29 years old had a bachelor's degree or higher compared with one-of-five Black or African Americans. High school graduation rates were nearly equal.

Percentage of persons of both sexes for aged 25 to 29 years old. Includes persons of Hispanic ethnicity for years prior to 1980. Data for years prior to 1993 are for persons with 4 or more years of high school or college. Data for later years are for high school completers—i.e., those persons who graduated from high school with a diploma as well as those who completed high school through equivalency programs, such as a GED program. Estimates are based on Census Bureau reverse projection of 1940 census data on education by age.

Source: U.S. Department of Commerce, Census Bureau, U.S. Census of Population: 1960, Vol. I, Part 1; J.K. Folger and C.B. Nam, Education of the American Population (1960 Census Monograph); Current Population Reports, Series P-20, various years; and Current Population Survey (CPS), Annual Social and Economic Supplement, 1970 through 2015. (This table was prepared October 2015.), Table 104.20, https://nces.ed.gov/fastfacts/display.asp?id=61

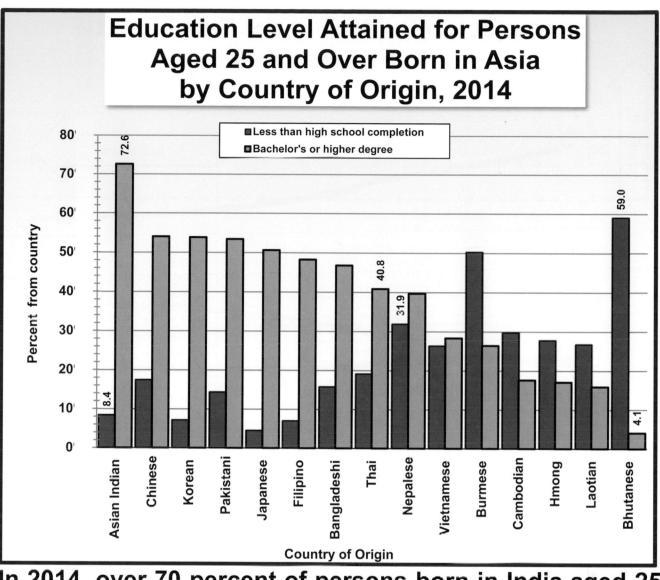

Education Level Attained for Persons Aged 25 and Over Born in Asia by Country of Origin, 2014

Legend:
- ■ Less than high school completion
- ▨ Bachelor's or higher degree

Y-axis: Percent from country
X-axis: Country of Origin

Data labels shown: Asian Indian 8.4 / 72.6; Thai 40.8; Nepalese 31.9; Bhutanese 59.0 / 4.1

In 2014, over 70 percent of persons born in India aged 25 and over had a bachelor's degree.

High school completers include diploma recipients and those completing high school through alternative credentials, such as a GED.

Estimates are for the entire population in the 25 and over age range, including persons living in households and persons living in group quarters (such as college residence halls, residential treatment centers, military barracks, and correctional facilities).

Source: U.S. Department of Commerce, Census Bureau, American Community Survey (ACS), 2009 and 2014. (This table was prepared January 2016.), https://nces.ed.gov/programs/digest/2015menu_tables.asp

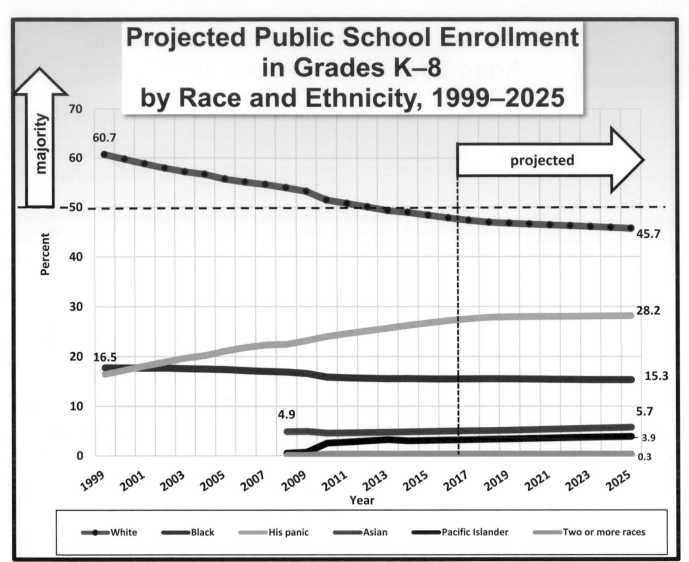

Projected Public School Enrollment in Grades K–8 by Race and Ethnicity, 1999–2025

In 2013, non-Hispanic White children in kindergarten through eighth grade no longer made up a majority of the students.

Enrollment and percentage distribution of enrollment in public elementary schools, kindergarten to eight grade, by race/ethnicity: Fall 1999 through fall 2025.

Race categories exclude persons of Hispanic ethnicity.

Enrollment data for students not reported by race/ethnicity were prorated by state and grade to match state totals. Prior to 2008, data on students of two or more races were not collected separately. Total counts of ungraded students were prorated to prekindergarten through grade 8 and grades 9 through 12 based on prior reports.

Source: U.S. Department of Education, National Center for Education Statistics, Common Core of Data (CCD), "State Non-fiscal Survey of Public Elementary and Secondary Education," 1998-99 through 2013-14; and National Elementary and Secondary Enrollment by Race/Ethnicity Projection Model, 1972 through 2025. (This table was prepared January 2016), https://nces.ed.gov/programs/digest/2015menu_tables.asp, https://nces.ed.gov/programs/digest/2015menu_tables.asp, Table 203.60

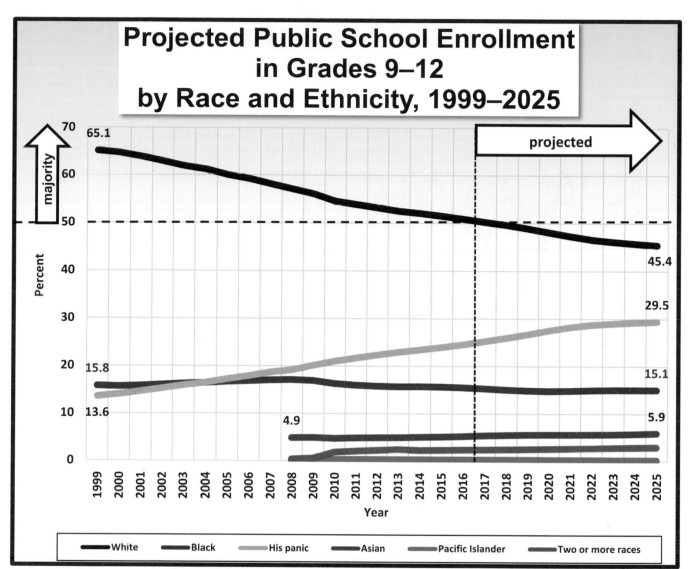

Projected Public School Enrollment in Grades 9–12 by Race and Ethnicity, 1999–2025

In 2016, non-Hispanic White children in grades nine to twelve were no longer a majority of students.

Enrollment and percentage distribution of enrollment in public elementary schools, kindergarten to eight grade, by race/ethnicity: Fall 1999 through fall 2025.

Race categories exclude persons of Hispanic ethnicity.

Enrollment data for students not reported by race/ethnicity were prorated by state and grade to match state totals. Prior to 2008, data on students of two or more races were not collected separately. Total counts of ungraded students were prorated to prekindergarten through grade 8 and grades 9 through 12 based on prior reports.

Source: U.S. Department of Education, National Center for Education Statistics, Common Core of Data (CCD), "State Non-fiscal Survey of Public Elementary and Secondary Education," 1998-99 through 2013-14; and National Elementary and Secondary Enrollment by Race/Ethnicity Projection Model, 1972 through 2025. (This table was prepared January 2016), https://nces.ed.gov/programs/digest/2015menu_tables.asp, https://nces.ed.gov/programs/digest/2015menu_tables.asp, Table 203.60

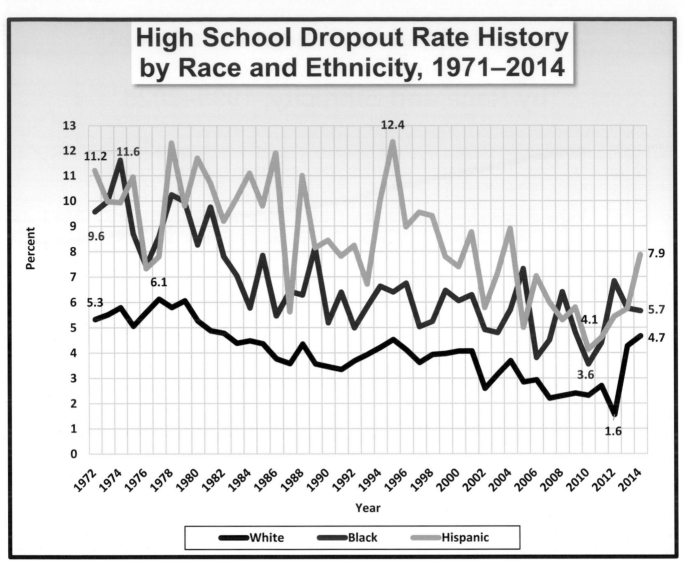

High School Dropout Rate History by Race and Ethnicity, 1971–2014

High school dropout rates declined for Black and Hispanic students by approximately a factor of three between 1972 and 2012, and then almost doubled between 2012 and 2014.

Among students aged 15 to 24 years old enrolled in grades 10 through 12. Percentage are those who dropped out by race/ethnicity: 1972 through 2014.

Data are based on sample surveys of the civilian noninstitutionalized population, which excludes persons in prisons, persons in the military, and other persons not living in households. Because of changes in data collection procedures, data for 1992 and later years may not be comparable with figures for prior years.

Race categories exclude persons of Hispanic ethnicity.

Source: U.S. Department of Commerce, Census Bureau, Current Population Survey (CPS), October, 1972 through 2014. (This table was prepared March 2016.), Table 219.55, https://nces.ed.gov/programs/digest/2015menu_tables.asp

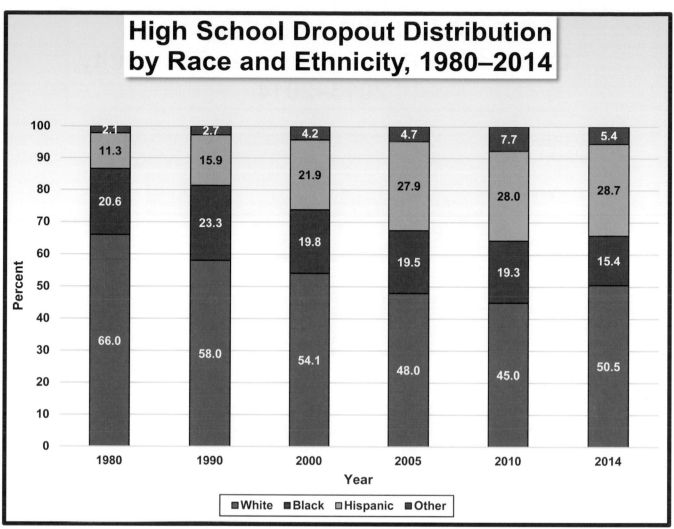

High School Dropout Distribution by Race and Ethnicity, 1980–2014

	1980	1990	2000	2005	2010	2014
Other	2.1	2.7	4.2	4.7	7.7	5.4
Hispanic	11.3	15.9	21.9	27.9	28.0	28.7
Black	20.6	23.3	19.8	19.5	19.3	15.4
White	66.0	58.0	54.1	48.0	45.0	50.5

■White ■Black □Hispanic ■Other

In 2014, approximately 29 percent of high school dropouts were Hispanic students, nearly double their percentage in 1990.

Data are for October of a given year. Dropouts are considered persons 16 to 24 years old who dropped out of school in the 12-month period ending in October of years shown. Includes dropouts from any grade, including a small number from elementary and middle schools. Percentages are only shown when the base is 75,000 or greater. Totals include race categories not separately shown. Race categories exclude persons of Hispanic ethnicity.

Source: U.S. Department of Commerce, Census Bureau, Current Population Survey (CPS), selected years, October 1979 through 2014. (This table was prepared May 2016.), https://nces.ed.gov/programs/digest/2015menu_tables.asp, Table 504.20, https://nces.ed.gov/fastfacts/display.asp?id=61

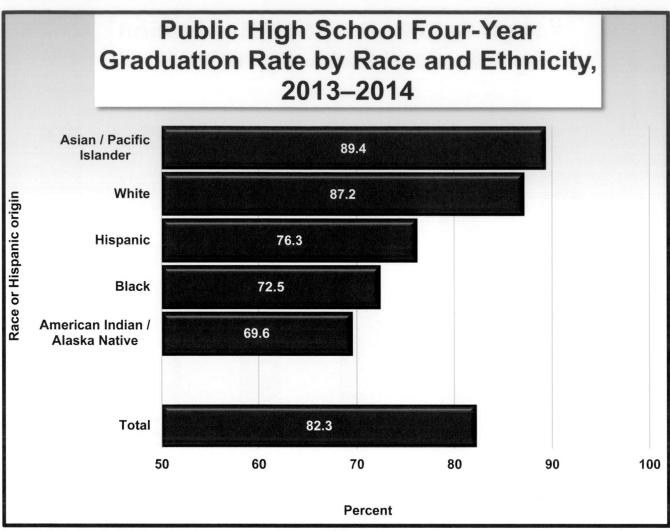

Public High School Four-Year Graduation Rate by Race and Ethnicity, 2013–2014

In 2013–2014, Asian and Pacific Islanders had the highest four-year graduation rate from public high schools among all races and ethnicities at 89.4 percent.

The four-year Adjusted Cohort Graduation Rate (ACGR) is the number of students who graduate in four years with a regular high school diploma divided by the number of students who form the adjusted cohort for the graduating class. From the beginning of 9th grade (or the earliest high school grade), students who are entering that grade for the first time form a cohort that is "adjusted" by adding any students who subsequently transfer into the cohort and subtracting any students who subsequently transfer out, emigrate to another country, or die.

To protect the confidentiality of individual student data, ACGRs are shown at varying levels of precision depending on the size of the cohort population for each category cell. Black includes African American, Hispanic includes Latino, Asian/Pacific Islander includes Native Hawaiian or Other Pacific Islander, and American Indian includes Alaska Native. Race categories exclude Hispanic origin unless specified.

Source: Public high school 4-year adjusted cohort graduation rate (ACGR), by race/ethnicity and selected demographics for the United States, the 50 states, and the District of Columbia: School year 2013–14, Table 1, Data Groups 695 and 696, School year 2013–14; September 4, 2015., https://nces.ed.gov/ccd/tables/ACGR_RE_and_characteristics_2013-14.asp

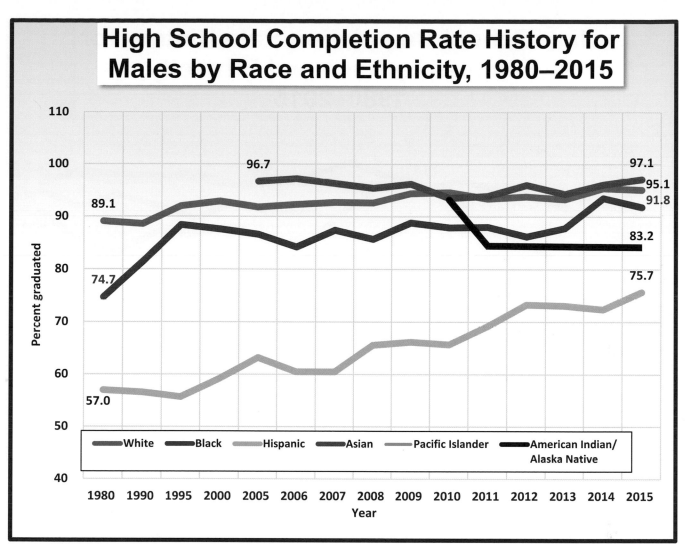

High School Completion Rate History for Males by Race and Ethnicity, 1980–2015

In 2015, Asian students had the highest high school graduation rate for males of all races and ethnicities at 97 percent.

Percentage of males aged 25 to 29 years old.

Includes persons of Hispanic ethnicity for years prior to 1980. Data for years prior to 1993 are for persons with four or more years of high school. Data for later years are for high school completers—i.e., those persons who graduated from high school with a diploma as well as those who completed high school through equivalency programs, such as a GED program.

Source: U.S. Department of Commerce, Census Bureau, U.S. Census of Population: 1960, Vol. I, Part 1; J.K. Folger and C.B. Nam, Education of the American Population (1960 Census Monograph); Current Population Reports, Series P-20, various years; and Current Population Survey (CPS), Annual Social and Economic Supplement, 1970 through 2015. (This table was prepared October 2015.), Table 104.20, https://nces.ed.gov/fastfacts/display.asp?id=61

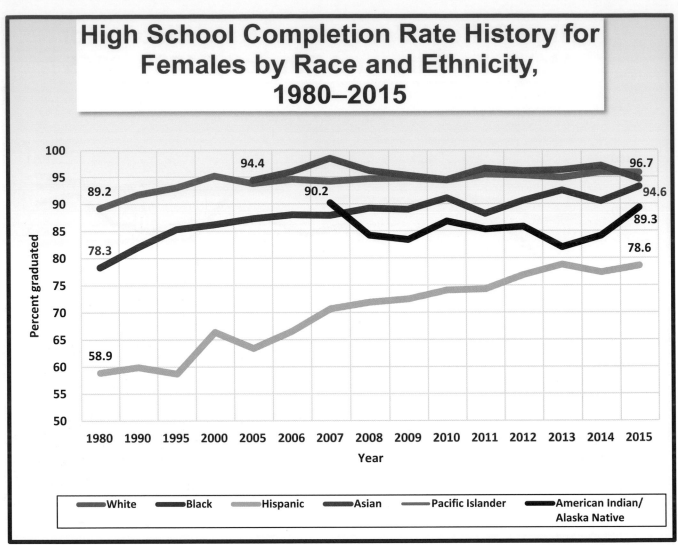

High School Completion Rate History for Females by Race and Ethnicity, 1980–2015

In 2014, Asian and White females had the highest high school completion rate of over 95 percent. Females of Hispanic origin had the lowest rate at 79 percent.

Percentage of females aged 25 to 29 years old.

Source: U.S. Department of Commerce, Census Bureau, U.S. Census of Population: 1960, Vol. I, Part 1; J.K. Folger and C.B. Nam, Education of the American Population (1960 Census Monograph); Current Population Reports, Series P-20, various years; and Current Population Survey (CPS), Annual Social and Economic Supplement, 1970 through 2015. (This table was prepared October 2015.), Table 104.20,

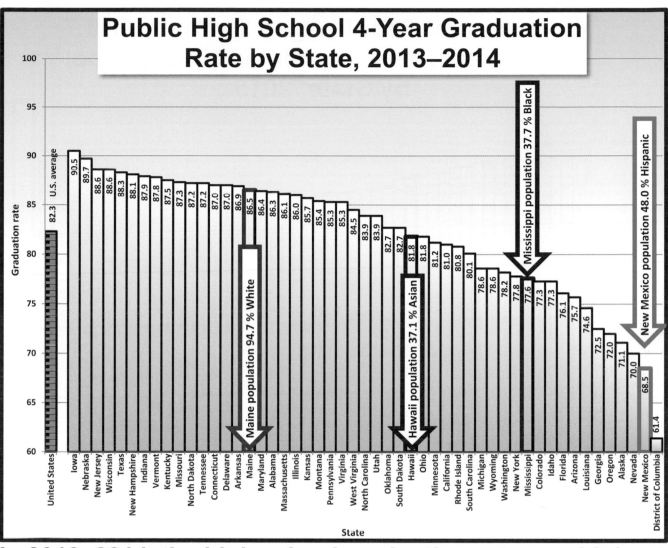

Public High School 4-Year Graduation Rate by State, 2013–2014

Graduation rate (y-axis): 100, 95, 90, 85, 80, 75, 70, 65, 60

United States (U.S. average): 82.3
Iowa: 90.5
Nebraska: 89.7
New Jersey: 88.6
Wisconsin: 88.6
Texas: 88.3
New Hampshire: 88.1
Indiana: 87.9
Vermont: 87.8
Kentucky: 87.5
Missouri: 87.3
North Dakota: 87.2
Tennessee: 87.2
Connecticut: 87.0
Delaware: 87.0
Arkansas: 86.9
Maine: 86.5 — Maine population 94.7 % White
Maryland: 86.4
Alabama: 86.3
Massachusetts: 86.1
Illinois: 86.0
Kansas: 85.7
Montana: 85.4
Pennsylvania: 85.3
Virginia: 85.3
West Virginia: 84.5
North Carolina: 83.9
Utah: 83.9
Oklahoma: 82.7
South Dakota: 82.7
Hawaii: 81.8 — Hawaii population 37.1 % Asian
Ohio: 81.8
Minnesota: 81.2
California: 81.0
Rhode Island: 80.8
South Carolina: 80.1
Michigan: 78.6
Wyoming: 78.6
Washington: 78.2
New York: 77.8
Mississippi: 77.6 — Mississippi population 37.7 % Black
Colorado: 77.3
Idaho: 77.3
Florida: 76.1
Arizona: 75.7
Louisiana: 74.6
Georgia: 72.5
Oregon: 72.0
Alaska: 71.1
Nevada: 70.0
New Mexico: 68.5 — New Mexico population 48.0 % Hispanic
District of Columbia: 61.4

State (x-axis)

In 2013–2014, the high school graduation rate was highest for students in Iowa at 90.5 percent while they were the lowest for students in New Mexico and the District of Columbia at below 70 percent.

The graduation rate is the number of students who graduate in four years with a regular high school diploma divided by the number of students who form the adjusted cohort for the graduating class. From the beginning of 9th grade (or the earliest high school grade), students who are entering that grade for the first time form a cohort that is "adjusted" by adding any students who subsequently transfer into the cohort and subtracting any students who subsequently transfer out, emigrate to another country, or die. Black includes African American, Hispanic includes Latino, Asian/Pacific Islander includes Native Hawaiian or Other Pacific Islander, and American Indian includes Alaska Native. Race categories exclude Hispanic origin unless specified.

Source: Public high school 4-year adjusted cohort graduation rate (ACGR), by race/ethnicity and selected demographics for the United States, the 50 states, and the District of Columbia: School year 2013–14, Table 1, Data Groups 695 and 696, School year 2013–14; September 4, 2015., https://nces.ed.gov/ccd/tables/ACGR_RE_and_characteristics_2013-14.asp

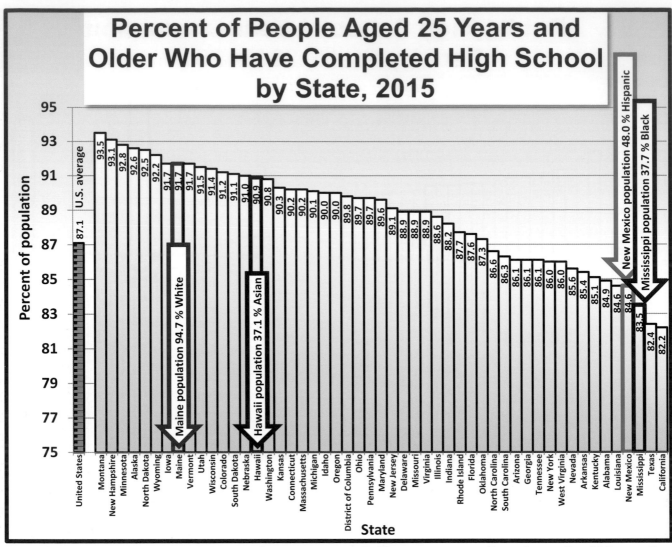

Percent of People Aged 25 Years and Older Who Have Completed High School by State, 2015

In 2015, approximately one-of-five people in California aged 25 years and older had not completed high school.

Although the American Community Survey (ACS) produces population, demographic, and housing unit estimates, it is the Census Bureau's Population Estimates Program that produces and disseminates the official estimates of the population for the nation, states, counties, cities, and towns as well as estimates of housing units for states and counties.

Source: U.S. Census Bureau, 2015 American Community Survey 1-Year Estimates Table R1501, http://www.census.gov/programs-surveys/acs/data/summary-file.html

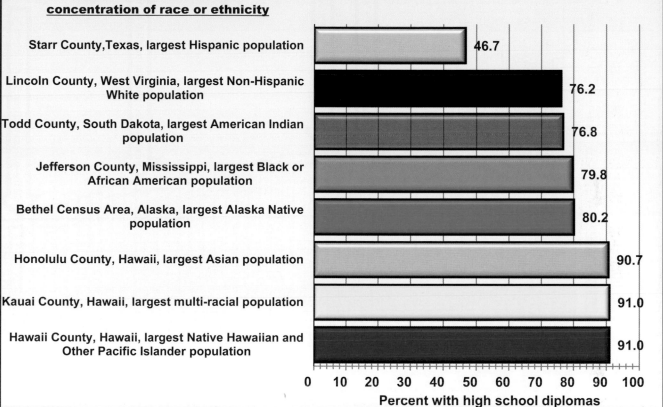

High School Diploma Rate in Counties with the Highest Percent of a Single Race or Ethnicity, 2015

Counties with the highest concentration of race or ethnicity

County	Percent with high school diplomas
Starr County, Texas, largest Hispanic population	46.7
Lincoln County, West Virginia, largest Non-Hispanic White population	76.2
Todd County, South Dakota, largest American Indian population	76.8
Jefferson County, Mississippi, largest Black or African American population	79.8
Bethel Census Area, Alaska, largest Alaska Native population	80.2
Honolulu County, Hawaii, largest Asian population	90.7
Kauai County, Hawaii, largest multi-racial population	91.0
Hawaii County, Hawaii, largest Native Hawaiian and Other Pacific Islander population	91.0

Percent with high school diplomas (scale 0 to 100)

In 2015, approximately one-half of Hispanic or Latino residents aged 25 years and older in Starr County, Texas— the county with the highest percent of Hispanic or Latino population—did not have a high school diploma.

The United States is comprised of 3,142 counties. A county is a political and geographic subdivision of a state. The Census Bureau considers the parishes of Louisiana and the boroughs of Alaska and the District of Columbia to be equivalent to counties for statistical purposes.

Hispanic origin is considered an ethnicity, not a race. Hispanics may be of any race.

Source: U.S. Census Bureau, American Fact Finder, Community Facts, 2015 Population Estimates Program, accessed 10/17/16, http://factfinder.census.gov/faces/nav/jsf/pages/community_facts.xhtml#

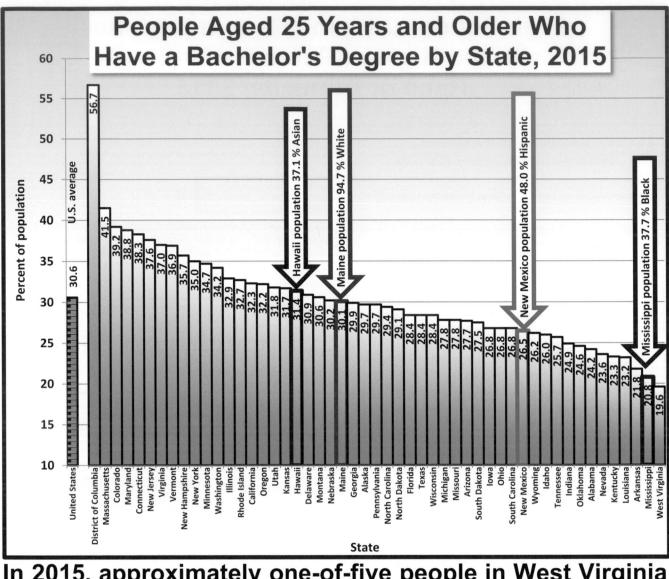

People Aged 25 Years and Older Who Have a Bachelor's Degree by State, 2015

Percent of population / State

United States: 30.6 (U.S. average)
District of Columbia: 56.7
Massachusetts: 41.5
Colorado: 39.2
Maryland: 38.8
Connecticut: 38.3
New Jersey: 37.6
Virginia: 37.0
Vermont: 36.9
New Hampshire: 35.7
New York: 35.0
Minnesota: 34.7
Washington: 34.2
Illinois: 32.9
Rhode Island: 32.7
California: 32.3
Oregon: 32.2
Utah: 31.8
Kansas: 31.7
Hawaii: 31.4 (Hawaii population 37.1 % Asian)
Delaware: 30.9
Montana: 30.6
Nebraska: 30.2
Maine: 30.1 (Maine population 94.7 % White)
Georgia: 29.9
Alaska: 29.7
Pennsylvania: 29.7
North Carolina: 29.4
North Dakota: 29.1
Florida: 28.4
Texas: 28.4
Wisconsin: 28.4
Michigan: 27.8
Missouri: 27.8
Arizona: 27.7
South Dakota: 27.5
Iowa: 26.8
Ohio: 26.8
South Carolina: 26.8
New Mexico: 26.5 (New Mexico population 48.0 % Hispanic)
Wyoming: 26.2
Idaho: 26.0
Tennessee: 25.7
Indiana: 24.9
Oklahoma: 24.6
Alabama: 24.2
Nevada: 23.6
Kentucky: 23.3
Louisiana: 23.2
Arkansas: 21.8
Mississippi: 20.8 (Mississippi population 37.7 % Black)
West Virginia: 19.6

In 2015, approximately one-of-five people in West Virginia aged 25 years and older had completed a bachelor's degree, compared with approximately two-of-five in Massachusetts.

Although the American Community Survey (ACS) produces population, demographic, and housing unit estimates, it is the Census Bureau's Population Estimates Program that produces and disseminates the official estimates of the population for the nation, states, counties, cities, and towns as well as estimates of housing units for states and counties.

Source: U.S. Census Bureau, 2015 American Community Survey 1-Year Estimates Table R1502, http://www.census.gov/programs-surveys/acs/data/summary-file.html

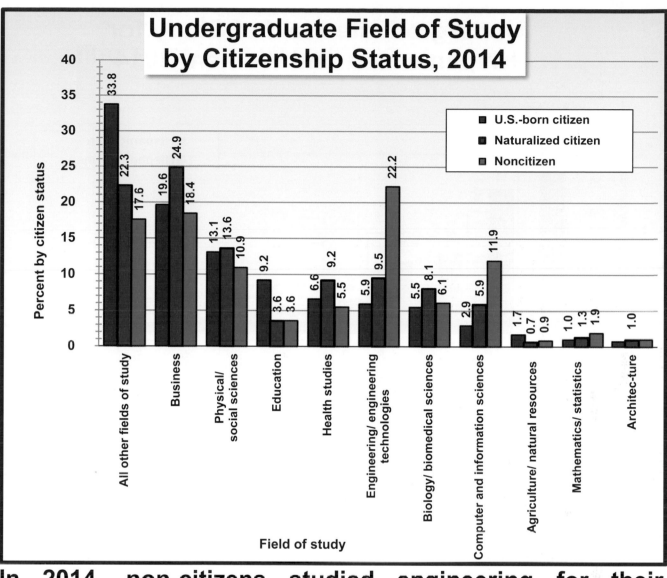

Undergraduate Field of Study by Citizenship Status, 2014

Legend:
- U.S.-born citizen
- Naturalized citizen
- Noncitizen

Percent by citizen status (y-axis: 0 to 40)

Field of study (x-axis):

Field of study	U.S.-born citizen	Naturalized citizen	Noncitizen
All other fields of study	33.8	22.3	17.6
Business	19.6	24.9	18.4
Physical/ social sciences	13.1	13.6	10.9
Education	9.2	3.6	3.6
Health studies	6.6	9.2	5.5
Engineering/ engineering technologies	5.9	9.5	22.2
Biology/ biomedical sciences	5.5	8.1	6.1
Computer and information sciences	2.9	5.9	11.9
Agriculture/ natural resources	1.7	0.7	0.9
Mathematics/ statistics	1.0	1.3	1.9
Architec-ture		1.0	

In 2014, non-citizens studied engineering for their bachelor's degree at a rate four times higher than citizens born in the United States.

Data are for persons aged 25 to 34 years old and percentage with a bachelor's or higher degree by undergraduate field of study.

Estimates are for the entire population in the 24–35 age range, including persons living in households and persons living in group quarters (such as college residence halls, residential treatment centers, military barracks, and correctional facilities). The first bachelor's degree major reported by respondents was used to classify their field of study, even though they were able to report a second bachelor's degree major and may possess advanced degrees in other fields.

Source: U.S. Department of Commerce, Census Bureau, American Community Survey (ACS), 2014. (This table was prepared December 2015.), Table 104.60 https://nces.ed.gov/programs/digest/2015menu_tables.asp

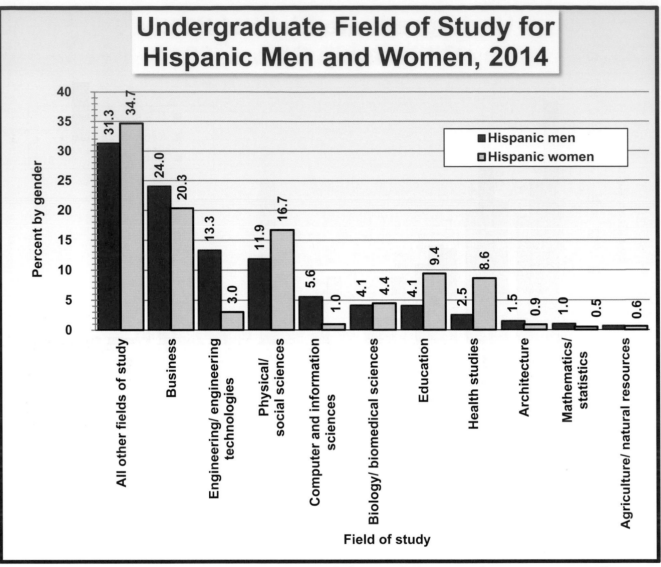

Undergraduate Field of Study for Hispanic Men and Women, 2014

Percent by gender

Legend:
- ■ Hispanic men
- □ Hispanic women

Field of study	Hispanic men	Hispanic women
All other fields of study	31.3	34.7
Business	24.0	20.3
Engineering/ engineering technologies	13.3	3.0
Physical/ social sciences	11.9	16.7
Computer and information sciences	5.6	1.0
Biology/ biomedical sciences	4.1	4.4
Education	4.1	9.4
Health studies	2.5	8.6
Architecture	1.5	0.9
Mathematics/ statistics	1.0	0.5
Agriculture/ natural resources		0.6

Field of study

In 2014, approximately one-of-four Hispanic men and one-of-five Hispanic women studied business for their bachelor's degree.

Persons aged 25 to 34 years old and percentage with a bachelor's or higher degree, by undergraduate field of study.

Estimates are for the entire population in the 24–35 age range, including persons living in households and persons living in group quarters (such as college residence halls, residential treatment centers, military barracks, and correctional facilities). The first bachelor's degree major reported by respondents was used to classify their field of study, even though they were able to report a second bachelor's degree major and may possess advanced degrees in other fields. Race categories exclude persons of Hispanic ethnicity.

Source: U.S. Department of Commerce, Census Bureau, American Community Survey (ACS), 2014. (This table was prepared December 2015.), Table 104.60 https://nces.ed.gov/programs/digest/2015menu_tables.asp

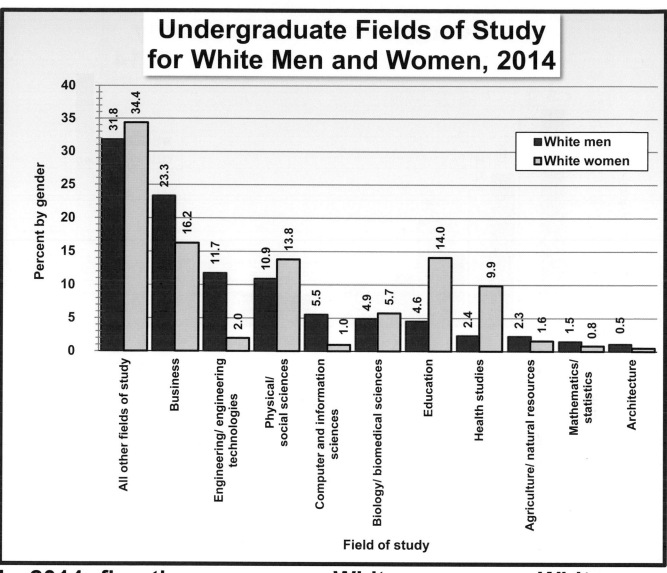

Undergraduate Fields of Study for White Men and Women, 2014

Percent by gender — Field of study

- White men
- White women

All other fields of study: White men 31.8, White women 34.4
Business: White men 23.3, White women 16.2
Engineering/ engineering technologies: White men 11.7, White women 2.0
Physical/ social sciences: White men 10.9, White women 13.8
Computer and information sciences: White men 5.5, White women 1.0
Biology/ biomedical sciences: White men 4.9, White women 5.7
Education: White men 4.6, White women 14.0
Health studies: White men 2.4, White women 9.9
Agriculture/ natural resources: White men 2.3, White women 1.6
Mathematics/ statistics: White men 1.5, White women 0.8
Architecture: White men 0.5

In 2014, five times as many White women as White men studied engineering for their bachelor's degree.

Persons aged 25 to 34 years old and percentage with a bachelor's or higher degree, by undergraduate field of study.

Estimates are for the entire population in the 24–35 age range, including persons living in households and persons living in group quarters (such as college residence halls, residential treatment centers, military barracks, and correctional facilities). The first bachelor's degree major reported by respondents was used to classify their field of study, even though they were able to report a second bachelor's degree major and may possess advanced degrees in other fields. Race categories exclude persons of Hispanic ethnicity.

Source: U.S. Department of Commerce, Census Bureau, American Community Survey (ACS), 2014. (This table was prepared December 2015.), Table 104.60 https://nces.ed.gov/programs/digest/2015menu_tables.asp

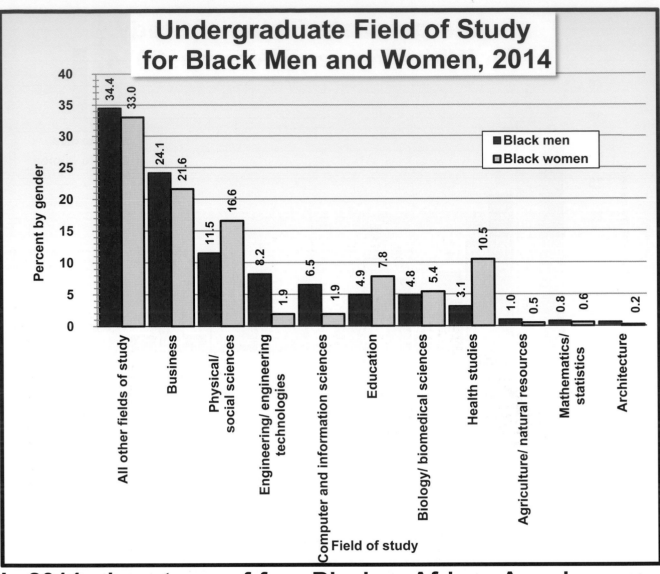

Undergraduate Field of Study for Black Men and Women, 2014

Black men
Black women

Percent by gender

Field of study	Black men	Black women
All other fields of study	34.4	33.0
Business	24.1	21.6
Physical/ social sciences	11.5	16.6
Engineering/ engineering technologies	8.2	1.9
Computer and information sciences	6.5	1.9
Education	4.9	7.8
Biology/ biomedical sciences	4.8	5.4
Health studies	3.1	10.5
Agriculture/ natural resources	1.0	0.5
Mathematics/ statistics	0.8	0.6
Architecture	0.2	

In 2014, almost one-of-four Black or African American men and over one-of-five women studied business for their bachelor's degree.

Persons aged 25 to 34 years old and percentage with a bachelor's or higher degree, by undergraduate field of study.

Estimates are for the entire population in the 24–35 age range, including persons living in households and persons living in group quarters (such as college residence halls, residential treatment centers, military barracks, and correctional facilities). The first bachelor's degree major reported by respondents was used to classify their field of study, even though they were able to report a second bachelor's degree major and may possess advanced degrees in other fields. Race categories exclude persons of Hispanic ethnicity.

Source: U.S. Department of Commerce, Census Bureau, American Community Survey (ACS), 2014. (This table was prepared December 2015.), Table 104.60 https://nces.ed.gov/programs/digest/2015menu_tables.asp

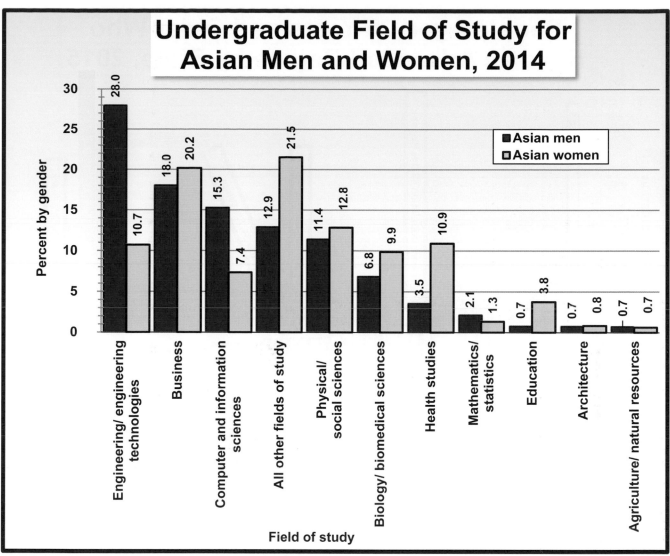

Undergraduate Field of Study for Asian Men and Women, 2014

Legend: ■ Asian men □ Asian women

Y-axis: Percent by gender (0 to 30)
X-axis: Field of study

Engineering/ engineering technologies: 28.0 (men), 10.7 (women)
Business: 18.0 (men), 20.2 (women)
Computer and information sciences: 15.3 (men), 7.4 (women)
All other fields of study: 12.9 (men), 21.5 (women)
Physical/ social sciences: 11.4 (men), 12.8 (women)
Biology/ biomedical sciences: 6.8 (men), 9.9 (women)
Health studies: 3.5 (men), 10.9 (women)
Mathematics/ statistics: 2.1 (men), 1.3 (women)
Education: 0.7 (men), 3.8 (women)
Architecture: 0.7 (men), 0.8 (women)
Agriculture/ natural resources: 0.7 (men), 0.7 (women)

In 2014, Asian men studied engineering for their bachelor's degree at a rate approximately three times the rate of Asian women.

Persons aged 25 to 34 years old and percentage with a bachelor's or higher degree, by undergraduate field of study.

Estimates are for the entire population in the 24–35 age range, including persons living in households and persons living in group quarters (such as college residence halls, residential treatment centers, military barracks, and correctional facilities). The first bachelor's degree major reported by respondents was used to classify their field of study, even though they were able to report a second bachelor's degree major and may possess advanced degrees in other fields. Race categories exclude persons of Hispanic ethnicity.

Source: U.S. Department of Commerce, Census Bureau, American Community Survey (ACS), 2014. (This table was prepared December 2015.), Table 104.60 https://nces.ed.gov/programs/digest/2015menu_tables.asp

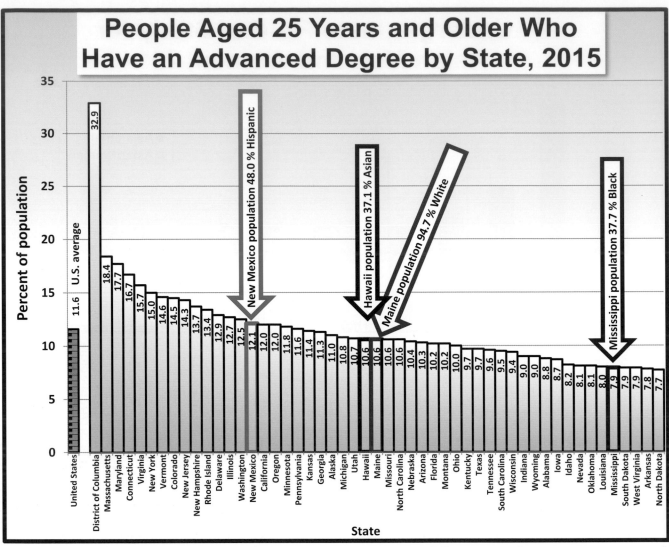

People Aged 25 Years and Older Who Have an Advanced Degree by State, 2015

In 2015, almost one-of-five people in Massachusetts aged 25 years and older had completed an advanced degree.

Although the American Community Survey (ACS) produces population, demographic, and housing unit estimates, it is the Census Bureau's Population Estimates Program that produces and disseminates the official estimates of the population for the nation, states, counties, cities, and towns as well as estimates of housing units for states and counties.

Source: U.S. Census Bureau, 2015 American Community Survey 1-Year Estimates Table R1503, http://www.census.gov/programs-surveys/acs/data/summary-file.html

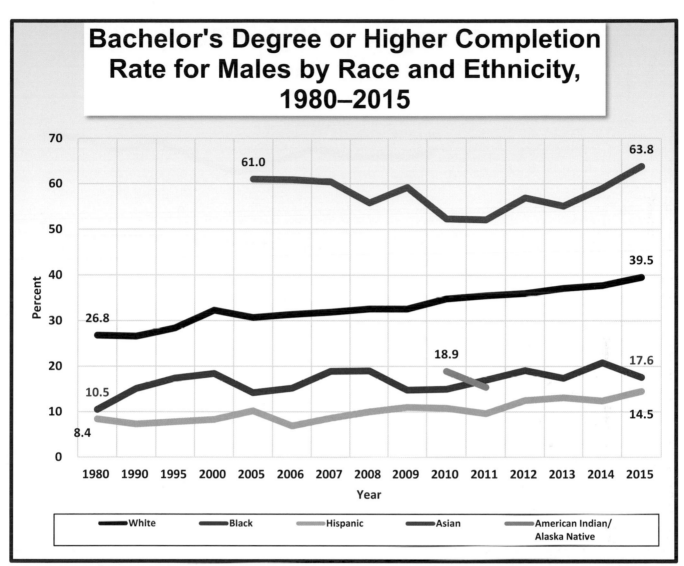

Bachelor's Degree or Higher Completion Rate for Males by Race and Ethnicity, 1980–2015

The bachelor's degree completion rate for Black or African American males aged 25 to 29 years old doubled between 1980–2015. However, at 14.5 percent in 2015, it was still the lowest completion rate among all races and ethnicities. Asians had the highest completion rate at 63.8 percent.

Percentage of females for aged 25 to 29 years old.

Source: U.S. Department of Commerce, Census Bureau, U.S. Census of Population: 1960, Vol. I, Part 1; J.K. Folger and C.B. Nam, Education of the American Population (1960 Census Monograph); Current Population Reports, Series P-20, various years; and Current Population Survey (CPS), Annual Social and Economic Supplement, 1970 through 2015. (This table was prepared October 2015.), Table 104.20, https://nces.ed.gov/fastfacts/display.asp?id=61

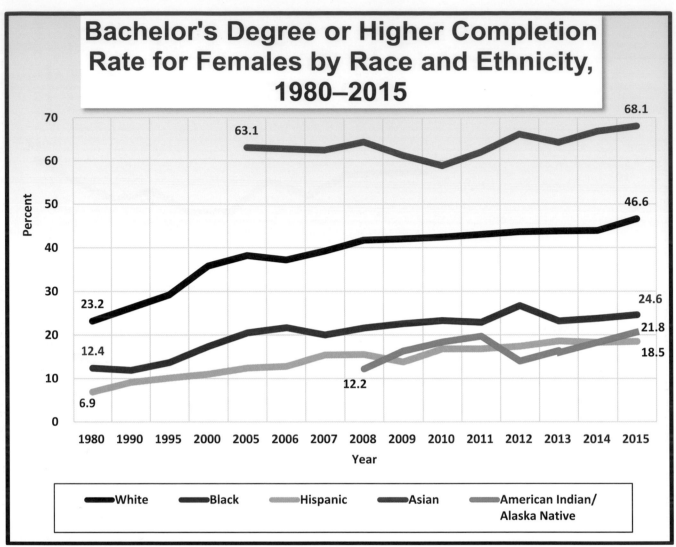

Bachelor's Degree or Higher Completion Rate for Females by Race and Ethnicity, 1980–2015

Percent (y-axis)

Year (x-axis)

White · Black · Hispanic · Asian · American Indian/Alaska Native

Data labels: 70, 60, 50, 40, 30, 20, 10, 0

63.1, 68.1, 46.6, 23.2, 24.6, 21.8, 18.5, 12.4, 12.2, 6.9

Years: 1980, 1990, 1995, 2000, 2005, 2006, 2007, 2008, 2009, 2010, 2011, 2012, 2013, 2014, 2015

In 2015, two-thirds of Asian females aged 25 to 29 years old had a bachelor's degree or higher, the highest rate of any female group.

Percentage of females aged 25 to 29 years old.

Source: U.S. Department of Commerce, Census Bureau, U.S. Census of Population: 1960, Vol. I, Part 1; J.K. Folger and C.B. Nam, Education of the American Population (1960 Census Monograph); Current Population Reports, Series P-20, various years; and Current Population Survey (CPS), Annual Social and Economic Supplement, 1970 through 2015. (This table was prepared October 2015.), Table 104.20, https://nces.ed.gov/fastfacts/display.asp?id=61

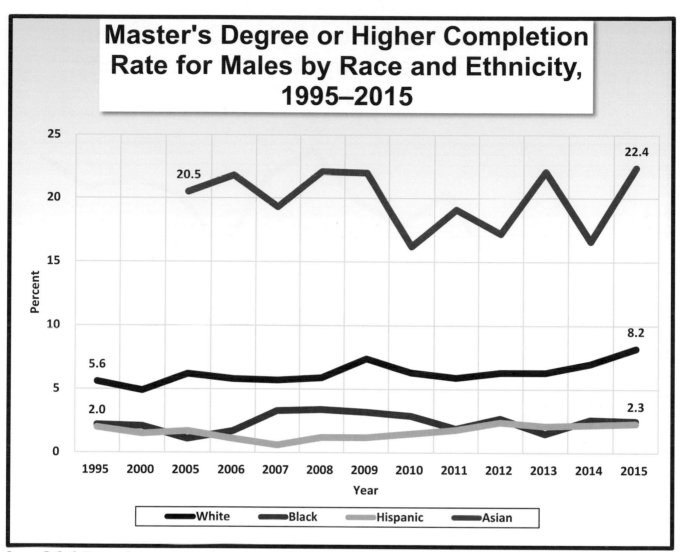

Master's Degree or Higher Completion Rate for Males by Race and Ethnicity, 1995–2015

In 2015, almost one-of-four Asian males aged 25 to 29 years old had a master's degree or higher compared with one-of-twelve White males.

Percentage of males for aged 25 to 29 years old.

Source: U.S. Department of Commerce, Census Bureau, U.S. Census of Population: 1960, Vol. I, Part 1; J.K. Folger and C.B. Nam, Education of the American Population (1960 Census Monograph); Current Population Reports, Series P-20, various years; and Current Population Survey (CPS), Annual Social and Economic Supplement, 1970 through 2015. (This table was prepared October 2015.), Table 104.20, https://nces.ed.gov/fastfacts/display.asp?id=61

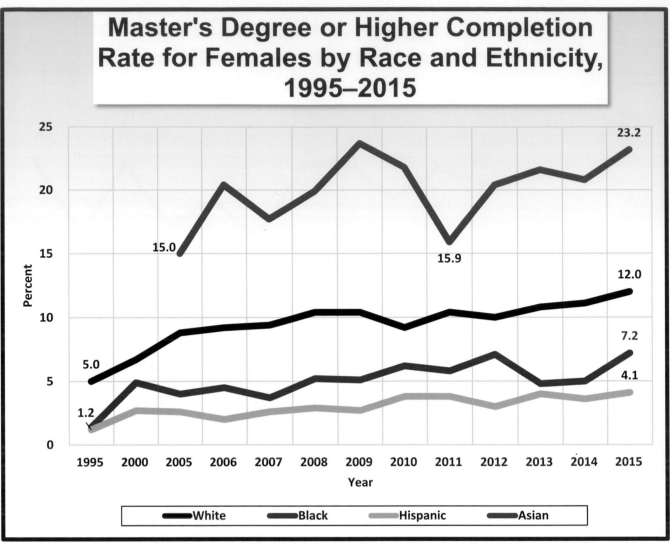

Master's Degree or Higher Completion Rate for Females by Race and Ethnicity, 1995–2015

In 2015, almost one-of-four Asian females aged 25 to 29 years old had a master's degree, the highest rate of any race or ethnicity.

Percentage of females for aged 25 to 29 years old.

Source: U.S. Department of Commerce, Census Bureau, U.S. Census of Population: 1960, Vol. I, Part 1; J.K. Folger and C.B. Nam, Education of the American Population (1960 Census Monograph); Current Population Reports, Series P-20, various years; and Current Population Survey (CPS), Annual Social and Economic Supplement, 1970 through 2015. (This table was prepared October 2015.), Table 104.20, https://nces.ed.gov/fastfacts/display.asp?id=61

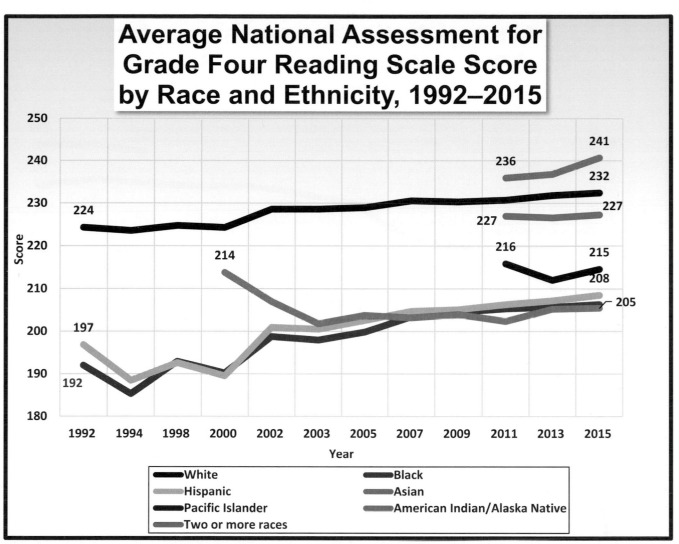

Average National Assessment for Grade Four Reading Scale Score by Race and Ethnicity, 1992–2015

Legend:
- White
- Black
- Hispanic
- Asian
- Pacific Islander
- American Indian/Alaska Native
- Two or more races

The average national assessment of grade four reading scale scores for White students remained almost unchanged between 2005–2015.

Scale ranges from 0 to 500. Includes public and private schools. For 1998 and later years, includes students tested with accommodations (1 to 13 percent of all students, depending on grade level and year); excludes only those students with disabilities and English language learners who were unable to be tested even with accommodations (2 to 6 percent of all students). Data on race/ethnicity are based on school reports. Race categories exclude persons of Hispanic ethnicity.

Prior to 2011, separate data for Asian students, Pacific Islander students were not collected.

Race categories exclude persons of Hispanic ethnicity.

Source: U.S. Department of Education, National Center for Education Statistics, National Assessment of Educational Progress (NAEP), 1992, 1994, 1998, 2000, 2002, 2003, 2005, 2007, 2009, 2011, 2013, and 2015 Reading Assessments, retrieved June 10, 2016, from the Main NAEP Data Explorer (http://nces.ed.gov/nationsreportcard/naepdata/). (This table was prepared June 2016.), Table 221.10, https://nces.ed.gov/programs/digest/2015menu_tables.asp

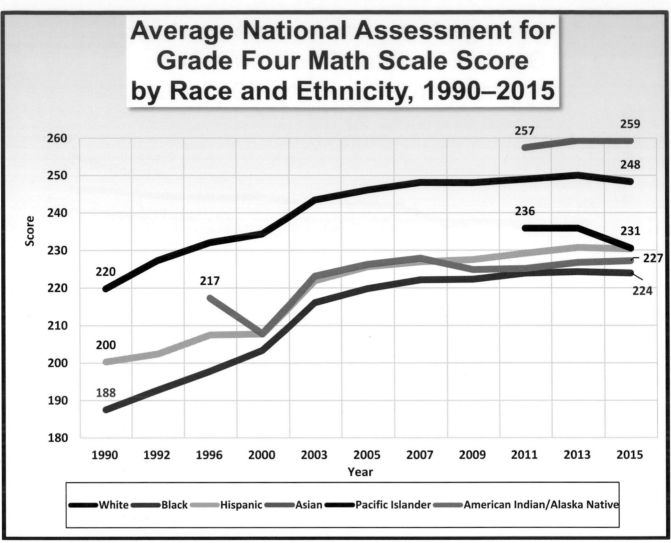

Average National Assessment for Grade Four Math Scale Score by Race and Ethnicity, 1990–2015

The average national assessment of grade four math scale score for Black or African American students improved 19 percent between 1990–2015.

For the grade four assessment the scale ranges from 0 to 500. Includes public and private schools. For 1996 and later years, includes students tested with accommodations (1 to 14 percent of all students, depending on grade level and year); excludes only those students with disabilities and English language learners who were unable to be tested even with accommodations (1 to 4 percent of all students).

Race categories exclude persons of Hispanic ethnicity.

Prior to 2011, separate data for Asian students, Pacific Islander students were not collected.

Source: U.S. Department of Education, National Center for Education Statistics, National Assessment of Educational Progress (NAEP), 1992, 1994, 1998, 2000, 2002, 2003, 2005, 2007, 2009, 2011, 2013, and 2015 Reading Assessments, retrieved June 10, 2016, from the Main NAEP Data Explorer (http://nces.ed.gov/nationsreportcard/naepdata/). (This table was prepared June 2016.), Table 222.10, https://nces.ed.gov/programs/digest/2015menu_tables.asp

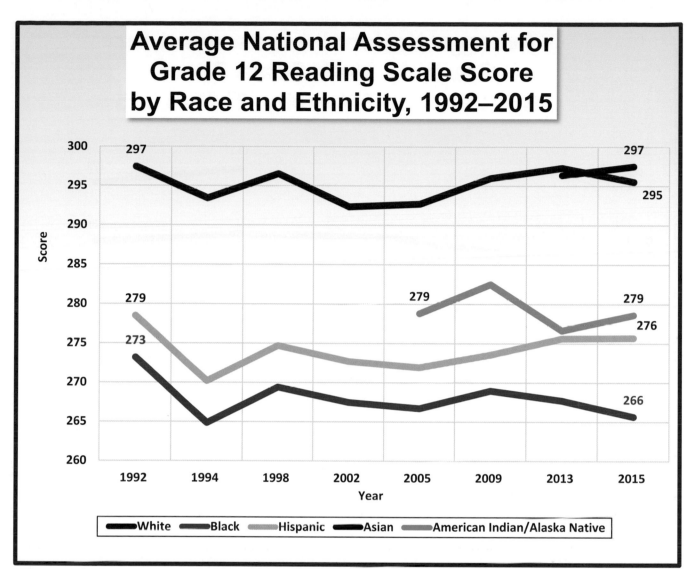

Average National Assessment for Grade 12 Reading Scale Score by Race and Ethnicity, 1992–2015

The average national assessment of grade 12 reading scale score for White students remained almost unchanged between 1992–2015.

Scale ranges from 0 to 500. Includes public and private schools. For 1998 and later years, includes students tested with accommodations (1 to 13 percent of all students, depending on grade level and year); excludes only those students with disabilities and English language learners who were unable to be tested even with accommodations (2 to 6 percent of all students). Data on race/ethnicity are based on school reports. Race categories exclude persons of Hispanic ethnicity.

Prior to 2011, separate data for Asian students, Pacific Islander students were not collected. Race categories exclude persons of Hispanic ethnicity.

Source: U.S. Department of Education, National Center for Education Statistics, National Assessment of Educational Progress (NAEP), 1992, 1994, 1998, 2000, 2002, 2003, 2005, 2007, 2009, 2011, 2013, and 2015 Reading Assessments, retrieved June 10, 2016, from the Main NAEP Data Explorer (http://nces.ed.gov/nationsreportcard/naepdata/). (This table was prepared June 2016.), Table 221.10, https://nces.ed.gov/programs/digest/2015menu_tables.asp

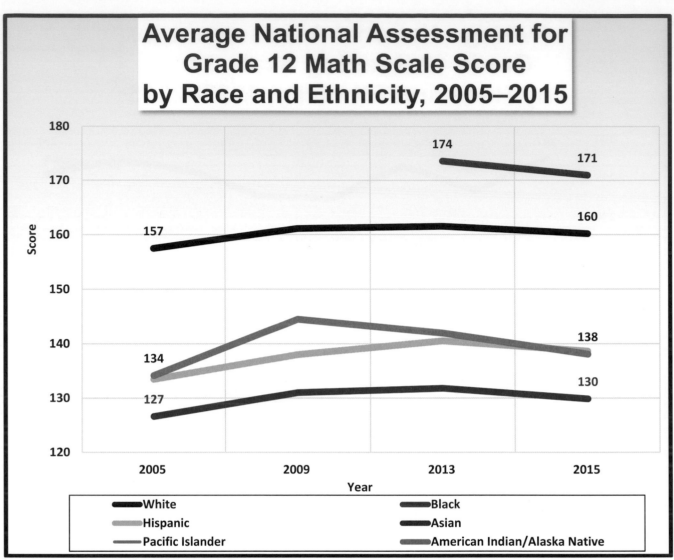

Average National Assessment for Grade 12 Math Scale Score by Race and Ethnicity, 2005–2015

The average national assessment of grade 12 math scale score remained almost unchanged between 2005–2015 for all races and ethnicities.

For the grade 12 assessment the scale ranges from 0 to 300. Includes public and private schools. For 1996 and later years, includes students tested with accommodations (1 to 14 percent of all students, depending on grade level and year); excludes only those students with disabilities and English language learners who were unable to be tested even with accommodations (1 to 4 percent of all students).

Race categories exclude persons of Hispanic ethnicity.

Prior to 2011, separate data for Asian students, Pacific Islander students were not collected.

Source: U.S. Department of Education, National Center for Education Statistics, National Assessment of Educational Progress (NAEP), 1992, 1994, 1998, 2000, 2002, 2003, 2005, 2007, 2009, 2011, 2013, and 2015 Reading Assessments, retrieved June 10, 2016, from the Main NAEP Data Explorer (http://nces.ed.gov/nationsreportcard/naepdata/). (This table was prepared June 2016.), Table 222.10, https://nces.ed.gov/programs/digest/2015menu_tables.asp

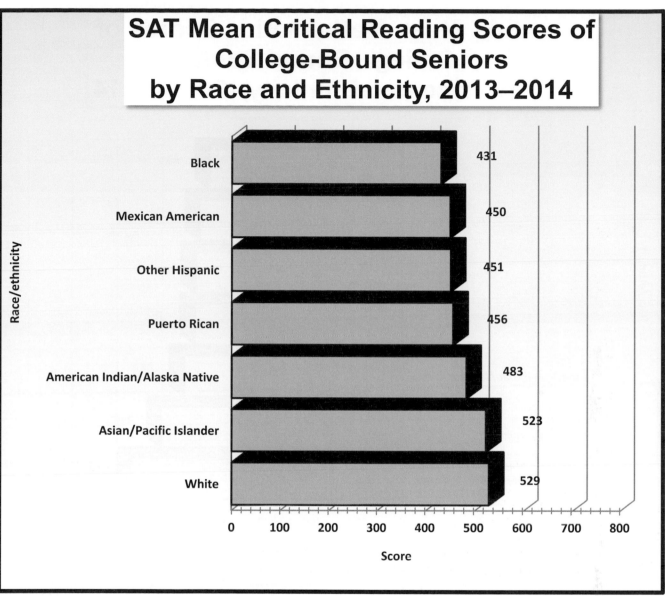

SAT Mean Critical Reading Scores of College-Bound Seniors by Race and Ethnicity, 2013–2014

Race/ethnicity (y-axis)

Black	431
Mexican American	450
Other Hispanic	451
Puerto Rican	456
American Indian/Alaska Native	483
Asian/Pacific Islander	523
White	529

Score (x-axis: 0, 100, 200, 300, 400, 500, 600, 700, 800)

The SAT mean critical reading scores for college-bound White seniors was the highest among all race groups and ethnicities in 2013–2014.

Data are for seniors who took the Scholastic Aptitude Test (SAT) any time during their high school years through March of their senior year. If a student took a test more than once, the most recent score was used. The SAT was formerly known as the Scholastic Assessment Test and the Scholastic Aptitude Test. Possible scores on each part of the SAT range from 200 to 800. The critical reading section was formerly known as the verbal section.

Race categories exclude persons of Hispanic ethnicity.

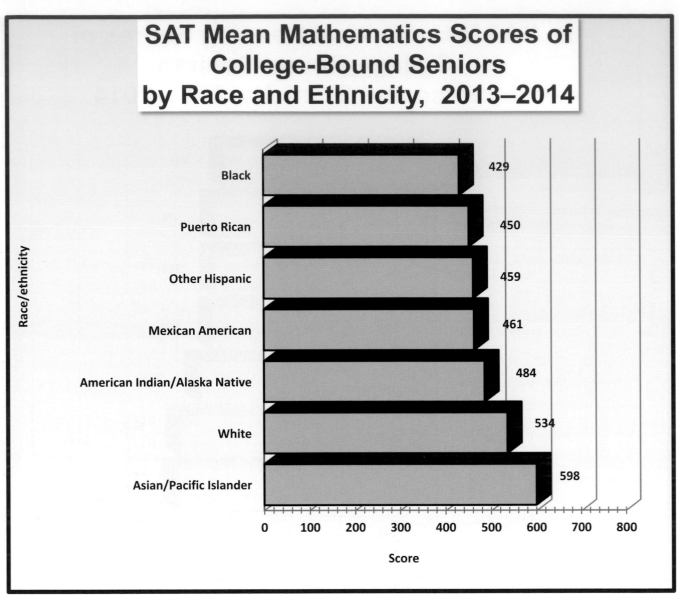

SAT Mean Mathematics Scores of College-Bound Seniors by Race and Ethnicity, 2013–2014

Race/ethnicity (y-axis)

Score (x-axis)

- Black: 429
- Puerto Rican: 450
- Other Hispanic: 459
- Mexican American: 461
- American Indian/Alaska Native: 484
- White: 534
- Asian/Pacific Islander: 598

The SAT mean critical mathematics scores for college-bound Asian seniors was the highest among all race groups and Hispanics in 2013–2014.

Note: Data are for seniors who took the Scholastic Aptitude Test (SAT) any time during their high school years through March of their senior year. If a student took a test more than once, the most recent score was used. The SAT was formerly known as the Scholastic Assessment Test and the Scholastic Aptitude Test. Possible scores on each part of the SAT range from 200 to 800. The critical reading section was formerly known as the verbal section.

Race categories exclude persons of Hispanic ethnicity.

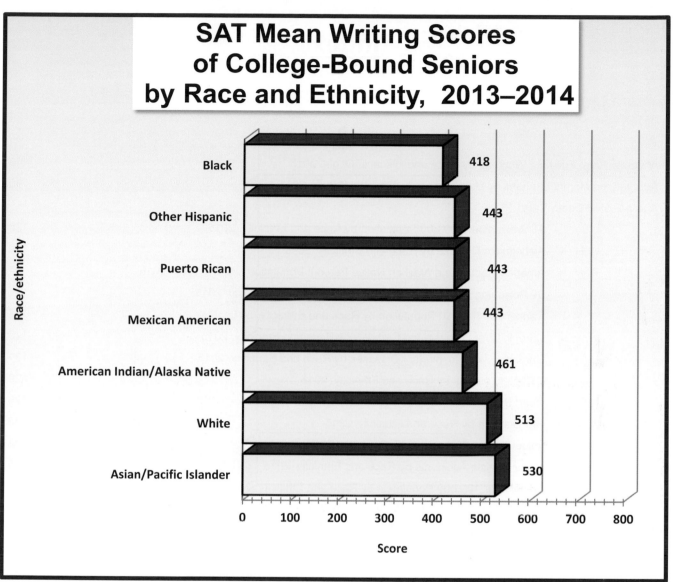

SAT Mean Writing Scores of College-Bound Seniors by Race and Ethnicity, 2013–2014

The SAT mean critical writing scores for college-bound Asian seniors was the highest among all races and ethnicities in 2013–2014.

Data are for seniors who took the Scholastic Aptitude Test (SAT) any time during their high school years through March of their senior year. If a student took a test more than once, the most recent score was used. The SAT was formerly known as the Scholastic Assessment Test and the Scholastic Aptitude Test. Possible scores on each part of the SAT range from 200 to 800. The critical reading section was formerly known as the verbal section.

Race categories exclude persons of Hispanic ethnicity.

Index

A

B

C

Causes of Death:

D

E

F

G

H

I

J, K

L

M

N

O

P, Q

T

U

V

W, X

Y, Z

~